Your Personal HOROSCOPE

—2003—

Your Personal HOROSCOPE

— 2003 —

The only one-volume horoscope you'll ever need

Joseph Polansky

Thorsons

The author is grateful to the people of STAR ★ DATA, who truly fathered this book and without whom it could not have been written.

Thorsons
An Imprint of HarperCollins*Publishers*
77–85 Fulham Palace Road,
Hammersmith, London W6 8JB

The Thorsons website address is:
www.thorsons.com

and *Thorsons*
are trademarks of
HarperCollins*Publishers* Limited

Published by Thorsons 2002

1 3 5 7 9 10 8 6 4 2

A catalogue record for this book is
available from the British Library

ISBN 0 00 713403 7

Printed in Great Britain by
Clays Ltd, St Ives plc

Contents

Introduction

Welcome to the fascinating and intricate world of astrology!

For thousands of years the movements of the planets and other heavenly bodies have intrigued the best minds of every generation. Life holds no greater challenge or joy than this: knowledge of ourselves and the universe we live in. Astrology is one of the keys to this knowledge.

Your Personal Horoscope 2003 gives you the fruits of astrological wisdom. In addition to general guidance on your character and the basic trends of your life, it shows you how to take advantage of planetary influences so you can make the most of the year ahead.

The section on each Sign includes a Personality Profile, a look at general trends for 2003 and in-depth month-by-month forecasts. The Glossary (*page 3*) explains some of the astrological terms you may be unfamiliar with.

One of the many helpful features of this book is the 'Best' and 'Most Stressful' days listed at the beginning of each monthly forecast. Read these sections to learn which days in each month will be good overall, good for money and good for love. Mark them on your calendar – these will be your best days. Similarly, make a note of the days that will be most stressful for you. It is best to avoid taking important meetings or major decisions on these days, as well as on those days when important planets in your Horoscope are retrograde (moving backwards through the Zodiac).

The Major Trends section for your Sign lists those days when your vitality is strong or weak, or when relationships with your co-workers or loved ones may need a bit more effort on your part. If you are going through a difficult time, take a look at the colour, metal, gem and scent listed in the 'At a Glance' section of your Personality Profile. Wearing a piece of jewellery that contains your metal and/or gem will strengthen your vitality; just as wearing clothes or decorating your room or office in the colour ruled by your Sign, drinking teas made from the herbs ruled by your Sign or wearing the scents associated with your Sign will sustain you.

Another important virtue of this book is that it will help you to know not only yourself but those around you: your friends, co-workers, partners and/or children. Reading the Personality Profile and forecasts for their Signs will provide you with an insight into their behaviour that you won't get anywhere else. You will know when to be more tolerant of them and when they are liable to be difficult or irritable.

I consider you – the reader – my personal client. By studying your Solar Horoscope I gain an awareness of what is going on in your life – what you are feeling and striving for and the challenges you face. I then do my best to address these concerns. Consider this book the next best thing to having your own personal astrologer!

It is my sincere hope that *Your Personal Horoscope 2003* will enhance the quality of your life, make things easier, illuminate the way forward, banish obscurities and make you more aware of your personal connection to the universe. Understood properly and used wisely, astrology is a great guide to knowing yourself, the people around you and the events in your life – but remember that what you do with these insights – the final result – is up to you.

Glossary of Astrological Terms

Ascendant

We experience day and night because the Earth rotates on its axis once every 24 hours. It is because of this rotation that the Sun, Moon and planets seem to rise and set. The Zodiac is a fixed belt (imaginary, but very real in spiritual terms) around the Earth. As the Earth rotates, the different Signs of the Zodiac seem to the observer to rise on the horizon. During a 24-hour period every Sign of the Zodiac will pass this horizon point at some time or another. The Sign that is at the horizon point at any given time is called the Ascendant or Rising Sign. The Ascendant is the Sign denoting a person's self-image, body and self-concept – the personal ego, as opposed to the spiritual ego indicated by a person's Sun Sign.

Aspects

Aspects are the angular relationships between planets, the way in which one planet stimulates or influences another. If a planet makes a harmonious aspect (connection) to another, it tends to stimulate that planet in a positive and helpful way. If it makes a stressful aspect to another planet, this disrupts the planet's normal influence.

Astrological Qualities

There are three astrological qualities: *cardinal, fixed* and *mutable*. Each of the 12 Signs of the Zodiac falls into one of these three categories.

Cardinal Signs	Aries, Cancer, Libra and Capricorn The cardinal quality is the active, initiating principle. Those born under these four Signs are good at starting new projects.
Fixed Signs	Taurus, Leo, Scorpio and Aquarius Fixed qualities include stability, persistence, endurance and perfectionism. People born under these four Signs are good at seeing things through.
Mutable Signs	Gemini, Virgo, Sagittarius and Pisces Mutable qualities are adaptability, changeability and balance. Those born under these four Signs are creative, if not always practical.

Direct Motion

When the planets move forwards through the Zodiac – as they normally do – they are said to be going 'direct'.

Grand Trine

A Grand Trine differs from a normal Trine (where two planets are 120 degrees apart) in that three or more planets are involved. When you look at this pattern in a chart, it takes the form of a complete triangle – a Grand Trine. Usually (but not always) it occurs in one of the four elements: Fire, Earth, Air or Water. Thus the particular element in which it occurs will be highlighted. A Grand Trine in Water is not the same as a Grand Trine in Air or Fire, etc. This is a very fortunate and happy aspect, and quite rare.

Grand Square

A Grand Square differs from a normal Square (usually two planets separated by 90 degrees) in that four or more planets are involved. When you look at the pattern in a chart you will see a whole and complete square. This, though stressful, usually denotes a new manifestation in the life. There is much work and balancing involved in the manifestation.

Houses

There are 12 Signs of the Zodiac and 12 Houses of experience. The 12 Signs are personality types and ways in which a given planet expresses itself; the 12 Houses show 'where' in your life this expression takes place. Each House has a different area of interest. A House can become potent and important – a House of Power – in different ways: if it contains the Sun, the Moon or the Ruler of your chart, if it contains more than one planet, or if the Ruler of that House is receiving unusual stimulation from other planets.

1st House	Personal Image and Sensual Delights
2nd House	Money/Finance
3rd House	Communication and Intellectual Interests
4th House	Home and Family
5th House	Children, Fun, Games, Creativity, Speculations and Love Affairs
6th House	Health and Work
7th House	Love, Marriage and Social Activities
8th House	Transformation and Regeneration
9th House	Religion, Foreign Travel, Higher Education and Philosophy
10th House	Career
11th House	Friends, Group Activities and Fondest Wishes
12th House	Spirituality

Karma

Karma is the law of cause and effect which governs all phenomena. We are all where we find ourselves because of karma – because of actions we have performed in the past. The universe is such a balanced instrument that any act immediately sets corrective forces into motion – karma.

Long-term Planets

The planets that take a long time to move through a Sign show the long-term trends in a given area of life. They are important for forecasting the prolonged view of things. Because these planets stay in one Sign for so long, there are periods in the year when the faster-moving (short-term) planets will join them, further activating and enhancing the importance of a given House.

Jupiter	stays in a Sign for about 1 year
Saturn	2½ years
Uranus	7 years
Neptune	14 years
Pluto	15 to 30 years

Lunar

Relating to the Moon.
See also 'Phases of the Moon', below.

Natal

Literally means 'relating to birth'. In astrology this term is used to distinguish between planetary positions that occurred at the time of a person's birth (natal) and those that are current (transiting). For example, Natal Sun refers to where the Sun was when you were born; transiting Sun refers to where the Sun's position is currently at any given moment – which usually doesn't coincide with your birth, or Natal, Sun.

Out of Bounds

The planets move through the Zodiac at various angles relative to the celestial equator (if you were to draw an imaginary extension of the Earth's equator out into the universe, you would have an illustration of this celestial equator). The Sun – being the most dominant and powerful influence in the Solar system – is the measure astrologers use as a standard. The Sun never goes more than approximately 23 degrees north or south of the celestial equator. At the winter solstice the Sun reaches its maximum southern angle of orbit (declination); at the summer solstice it reaches its maximum northern angle. Any time a planet exceeds this Solar boundary – and occasionally planets do – it is said to be 'out of bounds'. This means that the planet exceeds or trespasses into strange territory – beyond the limits allowed by the Sun, the Ruler of the Solar system. The planet in this condition becomes more emphasized and exceeds its authority, becoming an important influence in the forecast.

Phases of the Moon

After the full Moon, the Moon seems to shrink in size (as perceived from the Earth), gradually growing smaller until it is virtually invisible to the naked eye – at the time of the next new Moon. This is called the waning Moon phase, or the waning Moon.

After the new Moon, the Moon gradually gets bigger in size (as perceived from the Earth) until it reaches its maximum size at the time of the full Moon. This period is called the waxing Moon phase, or waxing Moon.

Retrogrades

The planets move around the Sun at different speeds. Mercury and Venus move much faster than the Earth, while Mars, Jupiter, Saturn, Uranus, Neptune and Pluto move more slowly. Thus there are times when, relative to the Earth, the planets appear to be going backwards. In reality they are always going forward, but relative to our vantage point on Earth they seem to go backwards through the Zodiac for a period of time. This is called 'retrograde' motion and tends to weaken the normal influence of a given planet.

Short-term Planets

The fast-moving planets move so quickly through a Sign that their effects are generally of a short-term nature. They reflect the immediate, day-to-day trends in a Horoscope.

Moon	stays in a Sign for only 2½ days
Mercury	20 to 30 days
Sun	30 days
Venus	approximately 1 month
Mars	approximately 2 months

T-square

A T-square differs from a Grand Square in that it is not a complete square. If you look at the pattern in a chart it appears as 'half a complete square', resembling the T-square tools used by architects and designers. If you cut a complete square in half, diagonally, you have a T-square. Many astrologers consider this more stressful than a Grand Square, as it creates tension that is difficult to resolve. T-squares bring learning experiences.

Transits

This refers to the movements or motions of the planets at any given time. Astrologers use the word 'transit' to make the distinction between a birth or Natal planet (see 'Natal', above) and the planet's current movement in the heavens. For example, if at your birth Saturn was in the Sign of Cancer in your 8th House, but is now moving through your 3rd House, it is said to be 'transiting' your 3rd House. Transits are one of the main tools with which astrologers forecast trends.

Aries

♈

THE RAM

Birthdays from

21st March to

20th April

Personality Profile

ARIES AT A GLANCE

Element – Fire

Ruling Planet – Mars
Career Planet – Saturn
Love Planet – Venus
Money Planet – Venus
Planet of Fun, Entertainment, Creativity and Speculations – Sun
Planet of Health and Work – Mercury
Planet of Home and Family Life – Moon
Planet of Spirituality – Neptune
Planet of Travel, Education, Religion and Philosophy – Jupiter

Colours – carmine, red, scarlet

Colours that promote love, romance and social harmony – green, jade green

Colour that promotes earning power – green

Gem – amethyst

Metals – iron, steel

Scent – honeysuckle

Quality – cardinal (= activity)

Quality most needed for balance – caution

Strongest virtues – abundant physical energy, courage, honesty, independence, self-reliance

Deepest need – action

Characteristics to avoid – haste, impetuousness, over-aggression, rashness

Signs of greatest overall compatibility – Leo, Sagittarius

Signs of greatest overall incompatibility – Cancer, Libra, Capricorn

Sign most helpful to career – Capricorn

Sign most helpful for emotional support – Cancer

Sign most helpful financially – Taurus

Sign best for marriage and/or partnerships – Libra

Sign most helpful for creative projects – Leo

Best Sign to have fun with – Leo

Signs most helpful in spiritual matters – Sagittarius, Pisces

Best day of the week – Tuesday

Understanding an Aries

Aries is the activist *par excellence* of the Zodiac. The Arien need for action is almost an addiction and those who do not really understand the Arien personality would probably use this hard word to describe it. In reality 'action' is the essence of the Arien psychology – the more direct, blunt and to-the-point the action, the better. When you think about it, this is the ideal psychological make-up for the warrior, the pioneer, the athlete or the manager.

Ariens like to get things done and in their passion and zeal often lose sight of the consequences for themselves and others. Yes, they often try to be diplomatic and tactful, but it is hard for them. When they do so they feel that they are being dishonest and phony. It is hard for them even to understand the mind-set of the diplomat, the consensus builder, the front office executive. These people are involved in endless meetings, discussions, talks and negotiations – all of which seem a great waste of time when there is so much work to be done, so many real achievements to be gained. An Aries can understand, once it is explained, that talks and negotiations – the social graces – lead ultimately to better, more effective actions. The interesting thing is that an Aries is rarely malicious or spiteful – even when waging war. Aries people fight without hate for their opponents. To them it is all good-natured fun, a grand adventure, a game.

When confronted with a problem many people will say, 'Well, let's think about it, let's analyze the situation.' But not an Aries. An Aries will think, 'Something must be done. Let's get on with it.' Of course neither response is the total answer. Sometimes action is called for, sometimes cool thought. But an Aries tends to err on the side of action.

Action and thought are radically different principles. Physical activity is the use of brute force. Thinking and deliberating require one not to use force – to be still. It is not good for the athlete to be deliberating the next move; this will only slow down his or her reaction time. The athlete must act instinctively and instantly. This is how Aries people tend to behave in life. They are quick, instinctive decision-makers and their decisions tend to be translated into action almost immediately. When their intuition is sharp and well tuned, their actions are powerful and successful. When their intuition is off, their actions can be disastrous.

Do not think this will scare an Aries. Just as a good warrior knows that in the course of combat he or she might acquire a few wounds, so too does an Aries realize – somewhere deep down – that in the course of being true to yourself you might get embroiled in a disaster or two. It is all part of the game. An Aries feels strong enough to weather any storm.

There are many Aries people who are intellectual: Ariens make powerful and creative thinkers. But even in this realm they tend to be pioneers – outspoken and blunt. These types of Ariens tend to elevate (or sublimate) their desire for physical combat in favour of intellectual, mental combat. And they are indeed powerful.

In general, Aries people have a faith in themselves that others could learn from. This basic, rock-bottom faith carries them through the most tumultuous situations of life. Their courage and self-confidence make them natural leaders. Their leadership is more by way of example than by actually controlling others.

Finance

Arien people often excel as builders or estate agents. Money in and of itself is not as important as are other things – action, adventure, sport, etc. They are motivated by the need to support and be well-thought-of by their partners. Money as a way of attaining pleasure is another important motivation. Ariens function best in their own businesses or as managers of their own departments within a large business or corporation. The fewer orders they have to take from higher up, the better. They also function better out in the field rather than behind a desk.

Ariens are hard workers with a lot of endurance; they can earn large sums of money due to the strength of their sheer physical energy.

Venus is their Money Planet, which means that Ariens need to develop more of the social graces in order to realize their full earning potential. Just getting the job done – which is what an Aries excels at – is not enough to create financial success. The co-operation of others needs to be attained. Customers, clients and co-workers need to be made to feel comfortable; many people need to be treated properly in order for success to happen. When Aries people develop these abilities – or hire someone to do this for them – their financial potential is unlimited.

Career and Public Image

One would think that a pioneering type would want to break with the social and political conventions of society. But this is not so with the Aries-born. They are pioneers within conventional limits, in the sense that they like to start their own businesses within an established industry.

Capricorn is on the 10th House (Career) cusp of Aries' Solar Horoscope. Saturn is the planet that rules their life's work and professional aspirations. This tells us some interesting things about the Arien character. First off, it shows that in order for Aries people to reach their full career potential they need to develop some qualities that are a bit alien to their basic nature: they need to become better administrators and organizers; they need to be able to handle details better and to take a long-range view of their projects and their careers in general. No one can beat an Aries when it comes to achieving short-range objectives, but a career is long-term, built over time. You cannot take a 'quickie' approach to it.

Some Aries people find it difficult to stick with a project until the end. Since they get bored quickly and are in constant pursuit of new adventures, they prefer to pass an old project or task on to somebody else in order to start something new. Those Ariens who learn how to put off the search for something new until the old is completed will achieve great success in their careers and professional lives.

In general, Aries people like society to judge them on their own merits, on their real and actual achievements. A reputation acquired by 'hype' feels false to them.

Love and Relationships

In marriage and partnerships Ariens like those who are more passive, gentle, tactful and diplomatic – people who have the social grace and skills they sometimes lack. Our partners always represent a hidden part of ourselves – a self that we cannot express personally.

An Aries tends to go after what he or she likes aggressively. The tendency is to jump into relationships and marriages. This is especially true if Venus is in Aries as well as the Sun. If an Aries likes you, he or she will have a hard time taking no for an answer; many attempts will be made to sweep you off your feet.

Though Ariens can be exasperating in relationships – especially if they are not understood by their partners – they are never consciously or wilfully cruel or malicious. It is just that they are so independent and sure of themselves that they find it almost impossible to see somebody else's viewpoint or position. This is why an Aries needs as a partner someone with lots of social grace.

On the plus side, an Aries is honest, someone you can lean on, someone with whom you will always know where you stand. What he or she lacks in diplomacy is made up for in integrity.

Home and Domestic Life

An Aries is of course the ruler at home – the Boss. The male will tend to delegate domestic matters to the female. The female Aries will want to rule the roost. Both tend to be handy round the house. Both like large families and both believe in the sanctity and importance of the family. An Aries is a good family person, although he or she does not especially like being at home a lot, preferring instead to be roaming about.

Considering that they are by nature are so combative and wilful, Aries people can be surprisingly soft, gentle and even vulnerable with their children and partners. The Sign of Cancer, ruled by the Moon, is on the cusp of their Solar 4th House (Home and Family). When the Moon is well aspected – under favourable influences – in the birth chart, an Aries will be tender towards the family and want a family life that is nurturing and supportive. Ariens like to come home after a hard day on the battlefield of life to the understanding arms of their partner and the unconditional love and support of their family. An Aries feels that there is enough 'war' out in the world – and he or she enjoys participating in that. But when Aries comes home, comfort and nurturing are what's needed.

Horoscope for 2003

Major Trends

The past few years have been good, Aries, and most of you pretty much had your own way. Almost all the long-term planets were supporting you. This trend continues for the first half of the year. But then stern Saturn, the Cosmic

Tester, moves into the Sign of Cancer. Basically he is urging you to 'get serious' and to correct whatever excesses you've got into the past year or so. Perhaps you ignored spiritual issues and spiritual values. Perhaps you ignored family and emotional issues. Let's face it, it's hard to think about these things when life is a big party. But Saturn knows how to get you on track. Your boundless physical energy will have to be used better. You'll have to pace yourself. You won't be able to get away with burning the candle at both ends. Family responsibilities come to you that can't be ignored. In the meantime, enjoy the party for the first half of the year.

Work is also going to become a priority in the year ahead. You will be shown how to become more productive. Many of you will land your dream job. You are also going to take a greater interest in health.

Spirituality, charity and good works are becoming ever-more important in your life. This year Uranus makes a major move from Aquarius (where he's been for about seven years) into Pisces. Now this is not the full-blown transit – but a flirtation with the Sign of Pisces and your 12th House. In effect, it is an announcement – a wake-up call – a harbinger of a new long-term trend. Spiritual changes are taking place on very deep levels. Your spiritual well-being will become as important to you as your other forms of well-being. More on this later.

Like last year, friendships, groups, organizations and group activities will continue to be important.

Personal creativity and having fun are also prominent interests – but as we mentioned, this will change in the latter part of the year.

Your paths to greatest fulfilment in the year ahead are: personal creativity, children, entertainment and the cultivation of the joy of life; communication and intellectual pursuits; finance (after April 14).

Health

Health has been good of late and it should continue to be good – especially for the first half of the year. But then Saturn moves into the Sign of Cancer for the next two years and makes a stressful aspect to you. Now this doesn't mean sickness *per se,* only that you have to watch your physical energy more. You will have to pace yourself better and eliminate frivolous activities or responsibilities. Your energy is like your capital. You cannot waste it with impunity, but should rather use it to good effect. It should be invested for maximum return both personally and for your world. So, come June of this year, you will get lessons on this.

The good news is that, though you probably have to slow down, Jupiter moving into your 6th House is going to make health regimes more enjoyable to you and also teach you much about health. Jupiter in the House of Health is *NOT* an announcement of sickness, but rather the reverse – good news on the health front.

You will probably spend more on health – health products, equipment and courses and perhaps even earn from this field. You will probably be more conscious of good nutrition, too.

Jupiter is the planet that rules religion and metaphysics. Thus, many of you are going to learn the power of metaphysical techniques – such as prayer and meditation – as it is applied to health. Also, there is power in holding a true conception – a true philosophy – on health and disease. All of this plays right into the spiritual changes that are starting to happen in your life.

The health of your spouse or partner could benefit from new and unorthodox techniques. Recommended surgery requires a second opinion.

The health of a parent is more delicate these days. He or she should avoid depression and depressed states. Jupiter's move into Virgo in August should be a help here. The same is true for children.

Try to rest and relax more from January 1 to January 20th, June 21 to July 22 and September 23 to October 23.

Mercury, your Health Planet, will be retrograde four times this year – an unusual event. Usually he retrogrades only three times a year. During these periods try to avoid making important changes to your diet or health regime. Study things more. Things are not what they seem. We will cover these periods in the monthly reports.

Mercury as your Health Planet shows that in general you need to give more attention to the brain, nervous system, arms and shoulders, lungs and intestines. Keeping these organs fit is powerful preventive medicine.

Mercury as your health ruler also shows the importance of good mental health in your life. The mind should be fed with the nutrients it needs – great thoughts by inspired writers, wisdom, truth, right ideas. Good communication is also important – and many a health problem has its origin in blocked communication. If you have good friends with whom you can communicate on an intellectual level, that is wonderful. If not, keep a diary and express your ideas in that way.

Home, Domestic and Family Issues

Home and family issues have not been that important for a number of years. That is about to change on June 4 when Saturn moves into your 4th House for the next two years.

Generally this transit shows a need to get your emotional and domestic life in order. To re-order the home. To make the best use of space. (Many of you have had children in the past year or are having them this year – this could be one of the reasons.) Saturn is saying, 'Though you feel cramped, a move is not necessarily the answer' – use what you have more efficiently.

Sometimes this need to get one's emotional life in order happens through taking on more family responsibilities –

either children or grown-up family members need your help. Through these kinds of events one learns about the true priorities in life.

Many an Aries will leave the corporate world for the domestic scene in the coming years. Many will want to (and some will *have* to) spend more time with their families. Many will want to make their family their career.

Saturn in the Sign of Cancer (and in the 4th House) shows a tendency to repress emotions. One feels it is 'not safe' to express the true feelings and so they stay hidden. This would be a mistake as this often leads to depression – one of the dangers of this transit. If it's not safe to express your feelings to the person involved, try writing them out, or talking them out on a tape – in privacy. You'll feel much better.

Basically, there is a need for discipline and order in the home. How you do this will be very important. If you over-discipline or under-discipline there is a price to pay. You've got to find that delicate balance. One of the best ways to handle this is to set 'reasonable limits'. Allow freedom within these limits, but not beyond them.

A healthy domestic routine will be instituted in the next two years. Many people rebel when 'corporate management' techniques are applied in the home. Though this is understandable, there is much to be said for it. Everyone knows their job, everyone has their responsibility and things get done on time. Though you shouldn't go 'totally corporate', a little of this seems called for.

For those of you involved in psychotherapy, the next two years will be full of progress and growth.

Aries of child-bearing age are unusually fertile this year.

If you're beautifying, redecorating or buying objects of beauty for the home, the period between June 21 and July 9 is best. This period is also good for entertaining from home. The aspects for heavy renovations are good from April 21 onwards.

Love and Social Life

Since your 7th House is not a House of Power this year, I expect that the status quo will prevail for most of you. Marrieds will tend to stay married. Singles will tend to stay single. The Cosmos is not pushing you one way or the other. Thus there is great freedom and latitude to make your social life what you want it to be. The problem is really lack of interest. Other areas of life, such as friendship, family, travel and creativity, are much more alluring to you.

Though marriage doesn't seem on the cards this year, there is much romantic opportunity of the non-serious type. Love affairs. This trend began last year and continues for most of this year. With so much non-committed love around – and so much joy from this – it is understandable that marriage wouldn't be interesting to you.

There are love opportunities with foreigners or in foreign lands; with people of a different cultural or ethnic backgrounds; with people who are educated, cultured and refined; with people you can look up to and respect. Perhaps with a teacher or mentor. Love affairs are not only fun, but educational as well. Romantic trips for two are also indicated.

But the main headline this year is *friendship*. This has been the trend for some years now and is continuing. There is much networking, joining of groups and meeting people of like minds. You've been learning how to be a good friend and are thus attracting good friends. This is a very happy and satisfying area in the year ahead. Like last year, you are meeting creative and spiritually-orientated people. Your intuition, when it comes to friends, is sharp and true. You can feel it immediately you meet someone. You know whom to cultivate and whom to avoid. There is something comforting about having a real friend. There are no commitments, no obligations, nothing to prove, etc. You are friends whether you are together or apart. You both hold the other's highest and best interest in your heart and rejoice in each other's good. It is love but without commitment or onerous demands.

The marriage of a parent or parental figure gets tested in the year ahead. A separation or divorce would not be a surprise.

Children of marriageable age have good opportunities for marriage in the year ahead. They seem prosperous and bring joy to you. The love life of grandchildren of marriageable age is vastly improved in the year ahead. They might not marry, but there is more social happiness. The marriage of siblings is still being tested – things are highly unstable there.

Some of your best (and most active) romantic periods will be from April 21 to May 16; July 29 to August 23; September 23 to October 23.

Venus is your Love Planet – the best possible one to have. But she is a fast-moving planet and will move through all the Signs and Houses of your Horoscope in the year ahead. Thus romantic opportunity can come from many places and in many ways. Your needs and attitudes to love also change rapidly. These short-term trends will be covered in the month-by-month forecasts.

Those in a second marriage, or working towards a second marriage, have an easier time this year. Those already married will have greater harmony in the marriage. And those looking will have more opportunities. Those in a third marriage will maintain the status quo this year. Those looking to marry for a third time still have wonderful aspects – through joining clubs, organizations or spiritual groups.

Finance and Career

Neither your 10th House of Career nor your 2nd House of Money are Houses of Power this year, Aries. Thus they are not big priorities in the year ahead. Presumably most of you are where you want to be careerwise and financially, and there is no need to make much change or focus too much on these things. In financial matters, I expect the status quo to prevail.

As you already know, Venus is your Financial Planet. She is a fast-moving planet. In the course of a year she will move through all the Signs and Houses of your Horoscope. Thus financial opportunity and earnings will come from a variety of sources and in a variety of ways. We will cover these short-term trends in the month-by-month forecasts.

With benevolent Jupiter in your 5th House, there is luck in speculations – especially until August 27. Of course, always speculate under intuition and never with more than you can afford to lose. After August 27, there is luck for job-seekers and those who employ others. A dream job is likely to manifest in the latter part of the year. Employers will be expanding the work force – and attracting good workers to boot.

Investors should look at utilities, resorts, gaming companies, toy companies and the entertainment industry. Don't rush out and blindly buy these stocks, but do your homework and follow the prices. Opportunities will come and you will have an instinct for it. After August 27, the healthcare industry seems profitable. (Your individual Horoscope, cast for your exact time and place of birth, could modify this.)

Speculative success could come from telecommunications, journalism, media companies (print) and transport. Again, keep in mind what we said above about being prudent.

As we mentioned, career changes are brewing. But these changes are not coming from failure, but rather from a new perspective on your part. You like outward success and achievement but you want to feel good as you go about it. You have much less of an appetite to sacrifice emotional or domestic comfort than you had in the past. So, this changed perspective will inevitably change your career – in some cases your entire career path. For those of you who must work, a family-type business or working from home looks good. Many will opt to work from home and with all the new technology available, it becomes ever more feasible. You make your own hours, you can tend to family matters and feel more at ease in your own environment. In many cases, Aries will want to make the family and the home his or her career. Family values are becoming more important than business values.

Finally, for those still pursuing an 'outward' career, there will be greater focus on the psychological underpinnings of career success. These Ariens will study the psychology of successful people – learn to think how they think and feel how they feel. It's as if the psychological aspects are more important than actual achievement. Even those in outward career mode will want to spend more time with their families and take more home leave.

You're not always going to feel this way, but for now – the next two years or so – this is how it is.

Your strongest (and most active) financial periods in the year ahead are from March 21 to May 17 (very prosperous), July 23 to August 23 (speculative success) and November 2 to December 22.

Your spouse, parent or parental figures prosper this year. The aspects for selling a home are unusually good until August 27. Children grow prosperous after August 27.

Debt-repayment or re-financing, tax issues and access to outside capital are well aspected this year – but especially from June 4 to August 27.

Self-improvement

As we mentioned, it is the inner spiritual life which is under the most ferment in the year ahead. You are only just beginning to feel this, but as the years go by the trend will get stronger and stronger. Two important developments are taking place. One, Uranus, which has been in Aquarius for the past seven years, starts to move into Pisces. Mars, your

Ruling Planet, rarely spends more than two months in any one Sign. This year (because of his retrograde), he will spend six months in the Sign of Pisces and your 12th House of Spirituality. This shows a search for the deeper things in life – a search for meaning. It would be normal to feel a need for seclusion and to be alone in one's own space and with one's own thoughts. Sometimes we get so caught up in the world (and Aries is most prone to this) that we forget who we are and why we are here. We forget the sanctity of our own aura.

Now, when the worldly-minded see this kind of behaviour they label it depression. But this is not so. This kind of seclusion is as necessary to a soul (at certain times) as a good diet, love and sexual expression. The soul must have it. So when these feelings hit you, don't run off and start popping pills. Co-operate with it. Get into a prayer and meditation regime. The Higher Power which sent you into expression is calling you – has revelation and knowledge for you. It doesn't want to take anything from you, only to replace the mediocre with something infinitely better. In general you're going to have a need to live intuitively and not by rote or some artificial mechanistic routine.

Those of you already on a spiritual path will make many changes to it in the year ahead and in coming years. Spirituality gets deepened and widened as Mars stays in Pisces from June 17 to December 12. It will be a period for coming to terms not only with your personal past, but with the past of the entire species. Many problems that you thought were personal were not personal at all, but merely a product of human evolution. These things lie in the depths of every person's subconscious. The solutions to them are also evolutionary.

Month-by-month Forecasts

January

Best Days Overall: 1st, 9th, 10th, 19th, 20th, 27th, 28th

Most Stressful Days Overall: 2nd, 3rd, 16th, 17th, 23rd, 24th, 29th, 30th

Best Days for Love: 9th, 10th, 19th, 20th, 23rd, 24th, 27th, 28th

Best Days for Money: 1st, 9th, 10th, 11th, 12th, 13th, 19th, 20th, 27th, 28th

70% to 80% of the planets are above the horizon. Your 10th House of Career is very powerful, while your 4th House of Home and Family is mostly empty (only the Moon will visit there, for two days out of the month). The message is clear – this is a strong career month and you can safely de-emphasize home, family and domestic responsibilities.

Of course you can't ignore them completely, but you can safely shift your priorities now. Though you will make good career progress this month (70% to 80% of the planets are moving forward), the progress is not glitch-free. There are bumps on the road. Your Career Planet, Saturn, is retrograde and Mercury is retrograde in the 10th House of Career. Thus good communication with bosses, elders or those involved in your career is essential. You will have to take extra precautions to make sure that people are really hearing what you say or write as you intend it. Take nothing for granted. When in doubt, repeat yourself. Spell everything out. The same goes for you: if you are not sure of a directive from a superior or a message from an employee, get clarification. Simple precautions can prevent a lot of needless stress this month.

Those of you into marketing and selling – whether it be on a professional or temporary basis (i.e. you are selling a personal item) – should try to schedule mailings and ads after Mercury moves forward on the 22nd.

The planetary power is more or less evenly balanced between the Eastern and Western sectors of the Horoscope. Thus, you are neither as independent as you would like nor as dependent as you think. You need the good graces of others, but there are many instances where you can go it alone. This month is about balancing personal desires with those of others.

Health is good this month and two Grand Trines – one in Air and one in Fire – are both harmonious to you. Still, it won't hurt to rest and relax more until the 20th. Also try to avoid making important changes to your diet or health regime until Mercury moves forward on the 22nd. You are as much concerned about the health of a parent and the health of your public image as you are about personal health.

Finances grow powerful after the 7th. Until then use spare cash to pay off debt and eliminate needless expense. This will make your financial expansion (after the 7th) much healthier. Speculations are favourable and all kinds of lucky financial opportunities are on their way. Overspending is probably the main financial danger.

Though there are plenty of romantic opportunities, love will be volatile this month – especially towards the end of the month when Venus conjuncts Pluto and then opposes Saturn. These will test relationships. The good news is that the volatility is short term.

February

Best Days Overall: 5th, 6th, 15th, 16th, 23rd, 24th

Most Stressful Days Overall: 13th, 14th, 19th, 20th, 25th, 26th

Best Days for Love: 8th, 9th, 17th, 18th, 19th, 20th, 25th, 26th

Best Days for Money: 5th, 6th, 8th, 9th, 15th, 16th, 17th, 18th, 23rd, 24th, 25th, 26th

Like last month, the overwhelming majority of planets are above the horizon of your Horoscope. Mercury is now moving forward in your Career House and Saturn, your Career Planet, will move forward after the 22nd. Continue to focus on your career and watch the obstructions and glitches just melt away. There are pay rises and promotions in store for many of you – there are favours from those on high. Communication with them is much improved. The Career House is still strong and the 4th House of Home and Family is still practically empty (again, only the Moon will visit there for two days out of the month). Let family issues slide and focus on your outer life.

On the 4th, the planetary power makes a decisive shift into the Eastern sector. Thus you are growing ever more independent – which is your natural style. Of course you can't ignore others completely, but you can basically go your own way if they don't co-operate. The Cosmos will support your independence. You are now in a period where you have greater ability to create your life as you want it to be. No need to adapt to discomfort. Create comfort on your own terms.

Both love and money are high on the agenda in the month ahead, as Venus crosses your Solar Midheaven on the 4th and spends the rest of the month as the most elevated planet in the chart.

Financial expansion comes from those on high. It can come as a pay rise, a government contract, a favour from a boss or a parent. Your good reputation and professional status also bring financial opportunity to you. Venus in the practical Sign of Capricorn shows that you will be a savvy investor and spender – getting value for your money and with a solid, long-term perspective on wealth.

This month you socialize with people of power and prominence. Singles find love opportunities as they pursue career goals or with people involved in their career – perhaps a boss. You are more cautious in love this month – which is probably a good thing. You need to look before you leap. Will this opportunity that seems so great look as great a month from now?

Friends, organizations, networking and group activities are also highlighted this month. All seem very happy. Job-seekers find opportunity through friends.

A happy travel or educational opportunity comes around the 5th. Athletic excellence is enhanced as well. A sudden love opportunity comes around the 17th.

Health is fabulous.

March

Best Days Overall: 5th, 6th, 14th, 15th, 23rd

Most Stressful Days Overall: 12th, 13th, 19th, 25th, 26th

Best Days for Love: 10th, 11th, 19th, 20th, 21st, 29th, 30th

Best Days for Money: 5th, 6th, 7th, 8th, 10th, 11th, 14th, 15th, 19th, 20th, 21st, 23rd, 29th, 30th

The overall forward motion of the planets is much stronger this month. 80% to 90% of them will be moving forward. The power in the Eastern sector of your chart increases even more on the 4th. So, your independence is getting stronger and there is rapid progress towards your goals. You manifest your desires very quickly this month. Now is the time (especially after the 21st) to go for the gold and reach for your dreams.

The upper hemisphere of the chart still dominates the lower hemisphere, though the percentage weakens after the 21st. Your 4th House is still empty (except for the Moon for two days out of the month) and your 10th House of Career is strong (Mars, your Ruling Planet, enters there on the 4th). So, this is still very much a career month. Ambitions take priority over emotional and family issues.

When the Ruler of a person's Horoscope crosses the Midheaven (which happens for you beginning the 4th), it is a sign that the person is reaching the pinnacles of success and attainment or is working towards them. Much depends on the stage of life you are in. There are honours coming to you. More recognition. You create your own luck through hard work and real achievement. This is a wonderful aspect for someone running for public office. Many of you will go off on your own careerwise too – perhaps start your own business or practice. The point is that you're letting the world know that you're there – you're around. Job-seekers have great opportunities all month, but especially after the 21st.

Two Grand Trines in Fire and much power in your own Sign show that you have the energy of 10 people. You simply run your competitors into the ground.

Your 12th House of Spirituality is also very powerful this month – especially until the 21st. The March Lunation (the New Moon) occurs there as well. Thus, though you are ambitious, try not to ignore your spiritual values. See if you can succeed in the outer world without sacrificing your principles. Volunteer-type activity, charities and ministerial activities are emphasized in the month ahead. Also a little seclusion wouldn't hurt either. Time by yourself, to think clearly and plan your next steps – to get in closer contact with your real self – will be time well spent. Yes, you are strong this month and things are going your way, but even the strongest need the grace of a Higher Power.

Finances will soar after the 21st (they are merely good before then). Speculations are favourable. Money comes in easy and happy ways. It won't hurt to use extra earnings to pay off debt. Those of you in the creative arts or athletics should do exceptionally well.

Love is tender and romantic after the 21st. The main danger to love is hypersensitivity. Your spouse or partner is too easily hurt. Be very gentle.

April

Best Days Overall: 1st, 2nd, 11th, 12th, 19th, 20th, 28th, 29th

Most Stressful Days Overall: 8th, 9th, 10th, 15th, 16th, 21st, 22nd

Best Days for Love: 8th, 9th, 15th, 16th, 17th, 18th, 28th, 29th

Best Days for Money: 1st, 2nd, 3rd, 4th, 5th, 8th, 9th, 10th, 11th, 12th, 17th, 18th, 19th, 20th, 28th, 29th

Rejoice in the testings of love on the 13th and 17th, for right behind them lies increased bliss – either with the same or a new person. Love pursues you ardently this month – all you have to do is show up. You probably won't be able to avoid romance now.

The planetary power is now 70% to 80% in the East. Even if you weren't an Aries there would be more independence, self-will and an ability to have life on your terms. With you, this could make you insufferable. Happily, Venus moves into your Sign, enhancing your social grace and making you more considerate of others.

Like last month, push confidently towards your dreams. Build your paradise on earth. Look for what makes you happy and which doesn't hurt others. Watch how everyone conforms and adapts to you.

Though career is still important until the 21st (Mars, the Lord of the Horoscope, is in your Career House) – the planetary power has now shifted to the bottom half of your Horoscope. Family and emotional issues are becoming ever more important. Presumably, by now, career objectives have been attained or are on the way to attainment. Now you can focus on your home and family. Find your emotional comfort zone now, Aries, and then function from there.

The two most important interests this month involve personal pleasure: bodily and sensual fulfilment/the image/personal appearance, and finance. Both are going well. Seldom have you looked or felt so good. The Sun in your own Sign gives you energy and joy in life. Venus in your own Sign gives you personal glamour and social magnetism. Happy financial surprises are on their way. Also you are getting new clothing or personal accessories – objects of beauty. All of these are expensive – of good quality. Speculations are still favourable. Personal appearance plays an unusually important role in earnings this month and you are dressing for success. Job-seekers find that employers are seeking them rather than vice versa. Your lover or spouse is bending over backwards to please you and this is a month where you get your way in love as well as in life. Like last month, watch for hypersensitivity in your spouse or lover until the 21st. Actually, the hypersensitivity is making them better lovers – only it has to be channelled in the right way.

Health is fabulous and you seem more open to health regimes and diets. Good health this month is about 'looking good' – not just the absence of disease. Give more attention to your head – massage it regularly.

May

Best Days Overall: 8th, 9th, 16th, 17th, 25th, 26th, 27th

Most Stressful Days Overall: 6th, 7th, 12th, 13th, 18th, 19th

Best Days for Love: 8th, 9th, 12th, 13th, 18th, 28th, 29th

Best Days for Money: 1st, 2nd, 8th, 9th, 16th, 17th, 18th, 25th, 26th, 27th, 28th, 29th

Important changes are happening to the world and to the people in your environment. You can feel it. Things are not the same anymore. Last month, the planet Uranus changed Signs. This month we have two eclipses – always signals for long-term change. Next month Saturn will change Signs. Changes of the status quo generally produce feedings of insecurity, but rest assured all will be well.

70% to 80% of the planets are still in the East, so your sense of independence is still strong. You can and will have things your way. Your way is the best way – for you.

60% to 70% of the planets are now below the horizon. Your 4th House is set to become very powerful (next month), while your 10th House of Career is empty. So, it's time to find your sense of emotional and family harmony. It's time to be less ambitious and to start 'feeling good'. It's time for building the psychological foundation for future career success and time for enjoying the simple pleasures of home and hearth.

The two eclipses this month are benign to you (though your individual Horoscope, cast for your date and time of birth, could modify this). The Lunar eclipse of May 16 occurs in your 8th House, which shows changes in the finances of your spouse or partner – changes in financial strategy, investments, etc. Often people change financial advisors, brokers or consultants under this kind of aspect. An insurance or estate issue comes to a head – a decisive turning-point. Perhaps this eclipse announces the breaking of an addiction or emotional attachment to something unhealthy. An eclipse in the 8th House doesn't necessarily mean a death, but often forces you to confront your fears of death or your attitudes towards it.

The Solar eclipse of May 31 occurs in your 3rd House, showing a long-term change in your educational status or educational plans. (Often these are normal things, albeit major – e.g. graduation from school, a change of what you want to study, etc.) Important and long-term changes happen in your neighbourhood or with neighbours – perhaps new construction is going on or new neighbours move in. Relations with a sibling could be stormy. It would be a good idea to have your car, computer or phone lines checked out, too.

Happily, these eclipses are creating changes in the world that open up opportunities for you. Obstructions to your good are coming down. Old patterns are changing, leaving you free to walk on through.

Still, it won't hurt to take a reduced schedule during these eclipses – two days before and a day after. You're OK but others might not be – no need to expose yourself to unnecessary risk.

Love still blooms this month, though singles find love as they pursue their financial goals after the 16th. Material gifts are romantic turn-ons.

June

Best Days Overall: 4th, 5th, 13th, 14th, 22nd, 23rd

Most Stressful Days Overall: 2nd, 3rd, 9th, 10th, 15th, 16th, 30th

Best Days for Love: 7th, 8th, 9th, 10th, 17th, 18th, 27th, 28th

Best Days for Money: 4th, 5th, 7th, 8th, 13th, 14th, 17th, 18th, 22nd, 23rd, 24th, 25th, 27th, 28th

Two very important planetary shifts happen this month. Mars, your Ruling Planet, makes a move into Pisces on the 17th and will stay there (pretty much) for the rest of the year. Saturn makes a once-in-two-and-a-half-years' move from Gemini into Cancer, your 4th House. Mars represents you on a personal level. Saturn represents your career. So these shifts involve major issues. For the next six months your interests are going to become more spiritual. Many of you will seek out teachers, begin a prayer-meditation regime or spend more time with an existing one. Family, emotional and psychological issues are now taking on deep importance as well – and they all work together. It's as if you don't care about career success or 'outer achievement', but really want to get at the root of who you are and why you are here. You want to find out what makes you tick, what life is all about. You are looking for 'meaning'. As you search, rest assured you will find. Many of you are making long-term changes in your career path.

60% to 70% of the planets are below the horizon. Your 4th House becomes the strongest in the Horoscope after the 21st, thus reinforcing all that we said above. Right now you need a career that allows you to function from your 'comfort zone'. You need a career that gives you 'inner space'. Some of you might make the finding of your 'emotional comfort zone' your number one priority in coming years.

The Eastern sector of the chart is now much less powerful than it has been the past few months. The Eastern and Western sectors are now balanced. Thus, you are neither completely independent nor completely dependent. You're somewhere in between. At times you can have your way and go your way, at other times you are forced to seek consensus. As the months go by, however, the power is shifting to the West. You will soon have to live with what you created in the past few months – good, bad or indifferent. This is called karma. There is a time for making karma (the past few months, when the Eastern sector was strong) and a time for paying it (when the Western sector gets strong).

Finances are strong but becoming ever less important to you. I read this as a good thing – you have enough and you don't need to worry about it. Singles find love (like last month) as they pursue financial goals or with people involved in their financial life. After the 10th, romantic opportunity comes into the neighbourhood, at school or school functions, or at seminars.

Health is reasonable. Definitely rest and relax more after the 21st. Overall, you are now in a period where you have to pace yourself better. Your throat, lungs, arms, shoulders and intestines could use more attention.

July

Best Days Overall: 2nd, 3rd, 10th, 11th, 19th, 20th, 29th, 30th

Most Stressful Days Overall: 6th, 7th, 12th, 13th, 26th, 27th, 28th

Best Days for Love: 6th, 7th, 8th, 9th, 17th, 18th, 28th, 29th

Best Days for Money: 2nd, 3rd, 8th, 9th, 10th, 11th, 17th, 18th, 19th, 20th, 21st, 22nd, 23rd, 28th, 29th, 30th

Rest and relax more this month, Aries – especially until the 23rd. With the planetary power now mostly in the West, there's not much you can do personally to change things. Good is coming from others and not so much from personal effort. Listen to your body. When it is tired, rest. Avoid burning the candle at both ends. Organize yourself so that more gets done with less effort. Work with a rhythm and take frequent breaks. Try to alternate activities. This month, health is enhanced by taking better care of your stomach, breasts and heart and watching your diet. Moods play an unusually dramatic role on physical well-being this period. So avoid depression and cultivate positive states of mind.

This month you will see how joy itself is the great healer. For after the 23rd, when you start enjoying life more, health problems, aches and pains just disappear.

Home, family and domestic (and psychological) issues dominate until the 23rd. Your 4th House of Home and Family is the most powerful House. This is a time for getting your house in order, for beautifying or redecorating and for entertaining from home. There are more family gatherings these days, too. Family relationships are bitter-sweet.

Venus serves double duty in your Horoscope. She is both your Love and your Money Planet. This month, she is moving unusually fast, covering three different Signs and Houses in your chart. This shows social and financial confidence and progress. Singles are dating more and meeting more people. Financial goals are attained rapidly. Love needs and attitudes change quickly – perhaps mystifying yourself and those you are involved with. Until the 4th, you want a confidante, someone you can talk to – someone who is like your brother or sister. After the 4th, you want nurturing and emotional support. After the 29th, you want fun – a good time. Love is close to home this month – in the neighbourhood. An old flame could make a re-appearance.

Sales, marketing and media activities bolster your bottom line until the 4th. Family connections and family support enhance earnings after the 4th. Speculations and creative projects are very favourable after the 23rd.

After the 23rd you are in a well-deserved party period.

August

Best Days Overall: 7th, 15th, 16th, 17th, 25th, 26th

Most Stressful Days Overall: 2nd, 3rd, 9th, 10th, 23rd, 24th, 30th

Best Days for Love: 2nd, 3rd, 7th, 8th, 16th, 17th, 27th, 28th, 30th

Best Days for Money: 7th, 8th, 16th, 17th, 18th, 19th, 26th, 27th, 28th

The planetary power is now firmly in the Western sector of your chart – 60% to 70% of the planets are there. Your normal desire for independence must be tempered this month. This is a time for seeking consensus in all that you do and for learning the art of adaptability. Your way is probably not the best way, as there are factors that you're not aware of. A time to develop charm and grace. Adding to this is the retrograde of Mars, your Ruling Planet, and an increase (in general) of retrograde activity. Do what is possible and let the rest go. Not a time for forcing situations.

Though family life is less hectic than last month, it is still an important area of life and should be given more priority than your career. Finding your emotional comfort zone is still very important.

Health is much improved this month over last month. But still, you need to pace yourself and recognize your physical limits. Health is being enhanced by the fact that you show more interest in this area – especially after the 22nd. Jupiter, which has spent the past year in your 5th House, will move into your 6th House of Health on the 27th. And your 6th House will be the most powerful in your chart this month. Thus, you are more interested in health regimes, are more likely to be on top of problems before they get out of hand and are probably getting more educated in health matters. All of this is to the good.

Most of the month is a party month. But by the 23rd you get more serious and work-orientated. Job-seekers have beautiful aspects for landing a dream job towards the end of the month. Employers will be adding to their staff.

Earnings come easily and happily until the 22nd; after that they come the old-fashioned way – through work. Until the 22nd, money and financial opportunity can come as you pursue leisure or creative activities – you meet someone who has an offer, you overhear a tip on the golf course, you get an inspired creative idea while you are at the seaside enjoying yourself. Money comes easily but you spend it easily too. The danger here is over-spending.

Love seems happy this month – especially until the 22nd. Singles have ample romantic opportunities. A significant meeting can happen from the 20th to the 22nd. Marrieds are enjoying their marriage more as well. After the 22nd, Venus moves into Virgo, which is not her happiest position. Be careful of a tendency to be destructively critical or nit-picky with your beloved. Romance and criticism (though you mean well) just don't mix.

September

Best Days Overall: 3rd, 4th, 12th, 13th, 22nd, 23rd, 30th

Most Stressful Days Overall: 5th, 6th, 19th, 20th, 26th, 27th

Best Days for Love: 5th, 6th, 16th, 17th, 26th, 27th

Best Days for Money: 5th, 6th, 14th, 15th, 16th, 26th, 27th

A month-long T-square affects Mars, your Ruling Planet – so give more attention to health issues and remember our previous discussions. This is a month for pacing yourself and resting more – especially after the 23rd.

Mars has been retrograde for the past few months, forcing you to re-think and re-evaluate your personal desires (and your image). Job offers are coming, but you are not sure whether these things are what you really want to do – or whether you can feel spiritually and emotionally comfortable with these things. Happily, Mars will start going direct on the 27th and with this forward motion come clarity and confidence.

Mercury's retrograde until the 20th also complicates the job situation – these things definitely need more study and analysis. Terms and conditions are not what they seem. Don't just rush into a job without being clear. There are many, many opportunities in the coming months.

Major changes to your health regime should be avoided until the 20th as well. Use Mercury's retrograde to do more study and research and then make changes after the 20th (perhaps after you study the matter, change won't be necessary).

60% to 70% of the planets are in the Western sector this month and your 7th House of Love and Social Activities becomes very powerful after the 23rd. Continue to develop your social skills and attain your goals through charm, grace and consensus. High-handed independent tactics won't work this month.

This is a powerful social month, Aries, perhaps the most powerful of 2003. (Next month will also be strong.) Definitely accept social invitations and put yourself 'out there'. Singles have good opportunities for serious, lasting relationships now. The main challenges to love can come from feeling down because of family issues or the need to balance your social life with family duties. Family members could feel slighted by your attention to romance and your romantic partner could feel slighted because of your devotion to family. Family members could have difficulty accepting a current love and vice versa.

Romantic opportunities come at the work place or as you pursue your health goals until the 15th. After that they come in the normal ways – at parties, gatherings, museums, art galleries or places of beauty.

Your financial judgement is particularly astute until the 15th. You will get value for your money then and have greater ability to control expenses and waste. A debt issue or sudden expense early in the month is short-term and doesn't affect long-term wealth. Social connections bolster your bottom line after the 15th.

October

Best Days Overall: 1st, 9th, 10th, 19th, 20th, 27th, 28th

Most Stressful Days Overall: 2nd, 3rd, 16th, 17th, 18th, 23rd, 24th, 29th, 30th

Best Days for Love: 4th, 5th, 16th, 17th, 23rd, 24th, 25th, 26th

Best Days for Money: 2nd, 3rd, 4th, 5th, 11th, 12th, 13th, 16th, 17th, 21st, 22nd, 25th, 26th, 29th, 30th

Continue your health vigilance this month, especially until the 23rd. Take a reduced schedule on the 14th and 15th, as a Grand Square stresses out Mars, your Ruling Planet. Health can be enhanced through better care of your intestines and kidneys, good diet and harmony with friends and your spouse. After the 24th, de-tox regimes seem effective. Surgical procedures need more thought and perhaps a second opinion.

Your 7th House of Love, Romance and Social Activities, continues to be powerful this month. Most of the planets are still in the West. Thus, like last month, this is a period for cultivating the social graces and modifying your tendencies towards independence and trying to have your way. Continue to seek consensus and allow your good to come to you through others (don't force it).

Romance is in the air this month, but you need to let it grow and develop as it will. Take everything slow and easy. If love is real, there is no rush. If love is unreal, then there is certainly no rush. Getting your lover and family to get along with each other is still a challenge – but it will get easier after the 9th.

Finances will be much improved after the 9th as well. Until then you just have to work a little harder for earnings, and be patient with various obstructions and delays. (Dealing with delay in a positive way is one of the great life lessons for an Aries – once you master this, the rest is a snap.)

When your Money Planet enters Scorpio on the 9th, it will be an excellent time for paying off debt, cutting costs and expenses and setting up tax strategies. Those of you who have good ideas might find it a good time to approach outside investors right now. Spare funds should go to pay off debt. Opportunities for profit will come at junk shops, or with troubled and bankrupt companies, properties or people. You have a good ability to spot value where others see 'junk'.

Your spouse or lover prospers in this period and is generous towards you.

A Grand Trine in Water grows in power from the 9th onwards and brings career, financial and social opportunities. Health will start improving after the 23rd. The problem with career is that you're still not sure where you want to go. Study all the opportunities very carefully. Don't violate your sense of emotional harmony, no matter how lucrative the offer.

From the 23rd onwards you are in a period where addictions – whether they be food, substance or emotional addictions – are more easily dealt with and broken. It is also a wonderful period for personal transformation and reinvention.

November

Best Days Overall: 5th, 6th, 15th, 16th, 24th, 25th

Most Stressful Days Overall: 13th, 14th, 20th, 21st, 26th, 27th

Best Days for Love: 5th, 6th, 15th, 16th, 20th, 21st, 25th, 26th, 27th

Best Days for Money: 5th, 6th, 8th, 9th, 15th, 16th, 18th, 19th, 25th, 26th, 27th

Career is starting to take on more importance again. The planetary power has shifted to the top of the Horoscope, and your 10th House of Career is starting to get strong again. With Saturn in your 4th House of Family for the long term, you won't be able to let go of family responsibilities completely, but you can safely de-emphasize them and focus on your career and outer aspirations. Like last month, the problem with career is one of confusion and indecision – Saturn is retrograde. Though this won't stop career progress, it does slow it down a bit. Your career options and plans need more study than usual. The challenge is to combine emotional comfort with outer success – a delicate balancing act.

The planets are still mostly in the West (though this will soon change), so continue to adapt to conditions and avoid power struggles and excessive self-will. Put other people ahead of yourself and your good will come easily and effortlessly.

Health is vastly improved over last month. By the 22nd, you feel like your normal self. Health can be enhanced by de-tox regimes and by taking better care of your sexual organs, liver and thighs. Many new and positive health insights – philosophical and metaphysical insights – are happening this month.

Two eclipses this month shake things up in the world and in your environment, but they are benign to you. The Lunar eclipse of the 9th occurs in your Money House, showing a re-shuffling – a re-organization of your finances, financial strategy and perhaps your investments. Avoid speculations in that period. The Solar eclipse of the 23rd occurs in your 9th House, showing a re-vamping of your religious and metaphysical beliefs and your world view. Perhaps you suffer a crisis of faith. Students make important changes in their education – perhaps they change schools or areas of study. Upheavals in their present school (not even pertaining to them) could also prompt change.

Venus, your Love and Money Planet, moves unusually quickly this month and covers three Signs and Houses of your Horoscope. Thus there is greater social and financial confidence. You cover more territory in these areas, and progress towards your goals is swift. (Keep in mind that 90% of the planets are forward after the 8th – also showing rapid progress in most areas of life.)

Be careful of over-spending from the 2nd to the 27th. Sure you can afford it, but don't lose your head. Keep a sense of proportion.

Speculations are mixed. Financial opportunities come in foreign lands or with foreigners. Your financial horizons are definitely expanding. You're a better shopper after the 27th.

Love, too, can happen in foreign lands or with foreigners. This month singles are attracted to people who can teach them things – mentor types. Those working towards a second marriage have wonderful opportunities now.

December

Best Days Overall: 2nd, 3rd, 4th, 12th, 13th, 14th, 21st, 22nd, 30th, 31st

Most Stressful Days Overall: 10th, 11th, 17th, 18th, 23rd, 24th

Best Days for Love: 5th, 6th, 15th, 16th, 17th, 18th, 25th, 26th

Best Days for Money: 5th, 6th, 15th, 16th, 23rd, 24th, 25th, 26th

The past six months have been a very spiritual and introverted period. Much spiritual progress and growth has taken place. You have a new clarity about yourself and life in general and now you are ready to apply these new insights to your life. (Spiritual growth is meaningless unless it leads to changes in behaviour and the way you live your life.) On the 16th, Mars, your Ruling Planet, leaves your 12th House and enters your own Sign of Aries. Healthwise, this brings new energy and vitality. Mars' shift is also accompanied by a shift of the overall planetary power – to the East. Thus, your need to adapt and seek consensus is about over. You are your normal independent and self-willed self. You know what's good for you and you have the power to go after it. You can have life on your terms and create new conditions if the present ones don't suit you. It's like being born again.

With Mars in your own Sign and 90% of the planets in forward motion, you live life in the fast lane. Progress towards your goals is breathtakingly swift – just the way you like it. The important thing now is to mind your temper and avoid haste and impatience. True, you are now fully in charge of your life, but there's no need to be arrogant with others. Be nice to them, but follow your own path.

Career is unusually important this month. Your 10th House is probably the strongest in the chart. Most of the planets are still above the horizon. Thus, de-emphasize home and family issues and pursue your career. Even Saturn's retrograde will not stop your success now.

This month we have a similar situation to the one we had in January. Your Career Planet is retrograde and Mercury is retrograde in your House of Career (from the 17th onwards). Again, communication with people involved in your career – with bosses especially – needs more care. Take nothing for granted. Dot the 'i's' and cross the 't's'. Make sure that others are hearing what you intend and that you hear what they intend. A little forethought will save much trouble later on.

With your Money Planet in your 10th House of Career until the 21st, there are pay rises and bonuses in store. There are favours from those in authority. Your professional reputation brings earnings opportunities. Parents or elders seem unusually generous.

Socially, you are mixing with the high and mighty, the prestigious and the powerful. Romantic opportunities could happen with these people or through these people – e.g. a parent or boss tries to play Cupid. You find romance as you pursue your career goals. Once again, getting your family to like your lover and vice versa seems a challenge.

Health needs to be watched after the 22nd. Definitely rest and relax more. Avoid making drastic changes to your health regime after the 17th. Study the issue more in the meantime. Health is enhanced through more attention to your spine, knees and teeth. Chiropractic and osteopathy seem unusually powerful therapies this period.

Taurus

♉

THE BULL

Birthdays from

21st April to

20th May

Personality Profile

TAURUS AT A GLANCE

Element – Earth

Ruling Planet – Venus
Career Planet – Uranus
Love Planet – Pluto
Money Planet – Mercury
Planet of Health and Work – Venus
Planet of Home and Family Life – Sun
Planet of Spirituality – Mars
Planet of Travel, Education, Religion and Philosophy – Saturn

Colours – earth tones, green, orange, yellow

Colours that promote love, romance and social harmony – red-violet, violet

Colours that promote earning power – yellow, yellow-orange

Gems – coral, emerald

Metal – copper

Scents – bitter almond, rose, vanilla, violet

Quality – fixed (= stability)

Quality most needed for balance – flexibility

Strongest virtues – endurance, loyalty, patience, stability, a harmonious disposition

Deepest needs – comfort, material ease, wealth

Characteristics to avoid – rigidity, stubbornness, tendency to be overly possessive and materialistic

Signs of greatest overall compatibility – Virgo, Capricorn

Signs of greatest overall incompatibility – Leo, Scorpio, Aquarius

Sign most helpful to career – Aquarius

Sign most helpful for emotional support – Leo

Sign most helpful financially – Gemini

Sign best for marriage and/or partnerships – Scorpio

Sign most helpful for creative projects – Virgo

Best Sign to have fun with – Virgo

Signs most helpful in spiritual matters – Aries, Capricorn

Best day of the week – Friday

Understanding a Taurus

Taurus is the most earthy of all the Earth Signs. If you understand that Earth is more than just a physical element, that it is a psychological attitude as well, you will get a better understanding of the Taurus personality.

A Taurus has all the power of action that an Aries has. But Taureans are not satisfied with action for its own sake. Their actions must be productive, practical and wealth-producing. If Taureans cannot see a practical value in an action they will not bother taking it.

Taureans' forte lies in their power to make real their own or other people's ideas. They are generally not very inventive but they can take another's invention and perfect it, making it more practical and useful. The same is true for all projects. Taureans are not especially keen on starting new projects, but once they get involved they bring things to completion. A Taurus carries everything through. They are finishers and will go the distance so long as no unavoidable calamity intervenes.

Many people find Taureans too stubborn, conservative, fixed and immovable. This is understandable, because Taureans dislike change – in their environment or in their routine. Taureans even dislike changing their minds! On the other hand, this is their virtue. It is not good for a wheel's axle to waver. The axle must be fixed, stable and unmovable. Taureans are the axle of society and the heavens. Without their stability and so-called stubbornness, the wheels of the world (and especially the wheels of commerce) would not turn.

Taureans love routine. A routine, if it is good, has many virtues. It is a fixed – and, ideally, perfect – way of taking care of things. Mistakes can happen when spontaneity comes into the equation, and mistakes cause discomfort and uneasiness – something almost unacceptable to a Taurus. Meddling with Taureans' comfort and security is a sure way to irritate and anger them.

While an Aries loves speed, a Taurus likes things slow. They are slow thinkers – but do not make the mistake of assuming they lack intelligence. On the contrary, Taureans are very intelligent. It is just that they like to chew on ideas, to deliberate and weigh them up. Only after due deliberation is an idea accepted or a decision taken. Taureans are slow to anger – but once aroused, take care!

Finance

Taureans are very money-conscious. Wealth is more important to them than to many other Signs. Wealth to a Taurus means comfort and security. Wealth means stability. Where some Zodiac Signs feel that they are spiritually rich if they have ideas, talents or skills, Taureans only feel their wealth when they can see and touch it. Taurus' way of thinking is 'What good is a talent if it has not been translated into a home, furniture, car and holidays?'

These are all reasons why Taureans excel in estate agency and agricultural industries. Usually a Taurus will end up owning land. They love to feel their connection to the Earth. Material wealth began with agriculture, the tilling of the soil. Owning a piece of land was humanity's earliest form of wealth: Taureans still feel that primeval connection.

It is in the pursuit of wealth that Taureans develop their intellectual and communication abilities. Also, in this pursuit Taureans are forced to develop some flexibility. It is in the quest for wealth that they learn the practical value of the intellect and come to admire it. If it were not for the search for wealth and material things, Taureans might not try to reach a higher intellect.

Some Taureans are 'born-lucky' – the type of people who win any gamble or speculation. This luck is due to other factors in their Horoscope; it is not part of their essential nature. By nature they are not gamblers. They are hard workers and like to earn what they get. Taureans' innate conservatism makes them abhor unnecessary risks in finance and in other areas of their lives.

Career and Public Image

Being essentially down-to-earth people, simple and uncomplicated, Taureans tend to look up to those who are original, unconventional and inventive. Taureans like their bosses to be creative and original – since they themselves are content to perfect their superiors' brain-waves. They admire people who have a wider social or political consciousness and they feel that someday (when they have all the comfort and security they need) they too would like to be involved in these big issues.

In business affairs, Taureans can be very shrewd – and that makes them valuable to their employers. They are never lazy; they enjoy working and getting good results. Taureans do not like taking unnecessary risks and do well in positions of authority, which makes them good managers and supervisors. Their managerial skills are reinforced by their natural talents for organization and handling details, their patience and thoroughness. As mentioned, through their connection with the Earth, Taureans also do well in farming and agriculture.

In general, a Taurus will choose money and earning power over public esteem and prestige. A position that pays more – though it has less prestige – is preferred to a position with a lot of prestige but fewer earnings. Many other Signs do not feel this way, but a Taurus does, especially if there is nothing in his or her personal birth chart that modifies this. Taureans will pursue glory and prestige only if it can be shown that these things have a direct and immediate impact on their wallet.

Love and Relationships

In love, the Taurus likes to have and to hold. They are the marrying kind. They like commitment and they like the terms of a relationship to be clearly defined. More importantly, Taureans like to be faithful to one lover and they expect that lover to reciprocate this fidelity. When this does not happen their whole world comes crashing down. When they are in love, Taureans are loyal, but they are also very possessive. They are capable of great fits of jealousy if they are hurt in love.

Taureans are satisfied with the simple things in a relationship. If you are involved romantically with a Taurus there is no need for lavish entertainments and constant courtship. Give them enough love, food and comfortable shelter and they will be quite content to stay home and enjoy your company. They will be loyal to you for life. Make a Taurus feel comfortable and – above all – secure in the relationship, and you will rarely have a problem.

In love, Taureans can sometimes make the mistake of trying to control their partners, which can cause great pain on both sides. The reasoning behind their actions is basically simple: Taureans feel a sense of ownership over their partners and will want to make changes that will increase their own general comfort and security. This attitude is OK when it comes to inanimate, material things – but is dangerous when applied to people. Taureans need to be careful and attentive to this possible trait within themselves.

Home and Domestic Life

Home and family are vitally important to Taureans. They like children. They also like a comfortable and perhaps glamorous home – something they can show off. They tend to buy heavy, ponderous furniture – usually of the best quality. This is because Taureans like a feeling of substance in their environment. Their house is not only their home, but their place of creativity and entertainment. The Taureans' home tends to be truly their castle. If they could choose, Taureans would prefer living in the countryside to being city-dwellers.

If they cannot do so during their working lives, many Taureans like to holiday in or even retire to the country, away from the city and closer to the land.

At home, a Taurus is like a country squire – lord (or lady) of the manor. They love to entertain lavishly, to make others feel secure in their home and to encourage others to derive the same sense of satisfaction as they do from it. If you are invited for dinner at the home of a Taurus you can expect the best food and best entertainment. Be prepared for a tour of the house and expect to see your Taurus friend exhibit a lot of pride and satisfaction in his or her possessions.

Taureans like children, but they are usually strict with them. The reason for this is they tend to treat their children – as they do most things in life – as their possessions. The positive side to this is that their children will be well cared for and well supervised. They will get every material thing they need to grow up properly. On the down side, Taureans can get too repressive with their children. If a child dares to upset the daily routine – which Taureans love to follow – he or she will have a problem with a Taurus parent.

Horoscope for 2003

Major Trends

2002 was easier than 2001; 2001 was easier than 2000. 2003 is going to be even easier than 2002. Uranus, which has been in a stressful aspect to you for seven years or so, is now getting ready to make nice aspects. Come June of this year Saturn starts making nice aspects to you and, in August, Jupiter joins the party. This means vast improvements in health and well-being. It means that most of the disruptive and uncomfortable changes are about over and that new prosperity and joy can enter your life. The year starts off slow but will end up very successful.

Career is becoming gradually and subtly less important. Presumably because you are where you want to be. Finances are improving this year and the lessons you learned in money management over the past two years will stand you in good stead. You should be financially healthier than ever before. With finances in order, it's now time to cultivate the mind and pursue intellectual interests. True, you might have to work harder at these things than you are used to, but it's well worth the effort. You know that physical muscles get stronger when you make them work – the same is true for intellectual muscles.

You've worked hard these past few years and, come August 27, the Cosmos gives you a party period. You will have both the means and the opportunity to explore the rapture side of life. It will be like becoming a child again – looking at the world with fresh eyes, with total faith – finding joy in little things or for no reason at all. They call this 'finding the child within' and this will be a good period for that.

Your areas of greatest interest in the year ahead are: finance (until June 4); communication and intellectual interests (after June 4); home and family (until August 27); children, creativity and leisure activities (after August 27); debt and the repayment of debt; sex; personal transformation; prospering other people; the deeper things of life; career; friendships, groups and group activities, organizations and clubs.

Your paths of greatest fulfilment in the year ahead are: finance; home and family life; children; creativity and sensual delights.

Health

Health is vastly improved this year and, come August, will get even better. Your 6th House is not a House of Power, but

I read this as a good sign. You have no interest in these things because you have no need to be interested.

In general, since Venus is your Health Planet, the neck, throat, kidneys and hips need more attention. Giving them the extra attention they need (e.g. neck, throat and hips can be regularly massaged) will act as a powerful preventive to disease. Although your individual horoscope (created according to your precise time and place of birth) could modify this, most health problems will tend to originate in these areas.

Venus is a fast-moving planet and will move through every Sign and House in the course of a year. Thus, feelings of health will tend to fluctuate and different kinds of therapies will work at different times. We will cover these short-term trends in the month-by-month forecasts.

Though health is good, there will be periods where your energy is not up to par. These are times to take it easy, rest and relax more, and try to work smarter, not harder. This year these periods will be from January 20 to February 19, July 23 to August 23 and October 23 to November 22. You are more vulnerable to problems during these periods than at other times.

Pluto has been in your 8th House for some years now. This shows that most of you have been undergoing very deep psychological cleansings. Now, these cleansings reach deeper than the areas that orthodox psychology deals with – these involve your past incarnations and the patterns and traumas that were installed then. So this is really deep. You should co-operate with this process and let it happen. Pluto in your 8th House also shows that you benefit from physical and herbal de-tox regimes as well.

Emotional health looks wonderful this year. True, you could benefit from more emotional equilibrium, but basically moods are upbeat and positive.

The health of a parent or parental figure is improving day by day. The health of your spouse looks good. Health of children could benefit from new and experimental treatments and therapies. The health of siblings will improve after August 27 – if health is good now it will get even better then.

Venus is your Health Planet. Thus, in general, the kidneys and hips need more attention. Keeping these organs in good shape is powerful preventive medicine. But this also shows the importance of healthy and harmonious relationships to good health and that good health for you means more than just physical wellness, but social wellness too. Good health also means looking good. Health problems often have their origins in dis-harmony with your spouse or friends of the heart. For real healing to take place, you must clear these dis-harmonies as well as deal with the physical symptoms.

Venus moves through all sectors of your Horoscope in any given year. Thus, your health needs and health attitudes are always changing. Do not be mystified if a therapy that worked last month doesn't work this month. Venus has merely changed position and something else will work better.

Home, Domestic and Family Issues

Like last year, your 4th House is a House of Power in the year ahead. Benevolent Jupiter is there until August 27. This is showing many happy things on the domestic front. First off, there is great happiness from the family. In general, good things are happening for family members and this rebounds on you. There is increased emotional and material support from the family. The family circle expands through birth or marriage. You are also meeting people who are 'like family' to you. Your home or residence suddenly becomes worth more. You are in a fortunate period for buying or selling a home. In many cases this transit shows a move – a happy one – to larger and more magnificent quarters. In other cases it shows the acquisition of a second or third home. In still other cases it shows the enlargement –

through renovation – of the present home. Almost always it shows big-ticket items for the home coming to you.

There are other good things about this transit. For many years now you have been career-orientated. It has been hectic and demanding. There probably wasn't much time for the simple pleasures of home and hearth. Now you get to enjoy these things. The main challenge this year is balancing this domestic happiness with your career. Career demands have eased up, but they are not over with.

Perhaps the greatest boon of this transit is the emotional optimism it brings – almost for no reason. You just feel more optimistic though nothing has 'caused' it on material plane. Armed with this optimism you can more readily succeed in other areas of life.

A parent or parental figure is prospering this year and leading the 'good life'. They should mind their weight. Excess of the good life is the main danger to their health. This parent or parental figure could also move. He or she is more generous with you. Grandparents are more generous this year, too.

Children begin prospering after August. Taureans of childbearing age are more fertile. Many are thinking of having children or even adopting them.

Siblings are having a more difficult time. There is a need to pull in the horns, take on responsibility and re-structure their lives. They need to take a low profile, keep their ego in check and work hard for the next two years.

Redecorating projects will go well almost any time until August 27. But May 16 to June 10 and July 29 to August 22 seem especially good. Your aesthetic sense is very strong during these periods.

Love and Social Life

Your 7th House is not a House of Power this year, Taurus, so I expect that the status quo will prevail. Singles will tend to remain single and marrieds, married. You have more freedom and latitude in this area, but also less interest.

With Saturn opposing your Love Planet (Pluto) for the past two years, many of you have had your relationships tested. Many of these relationships fell by the wayside. Those that survived got better than before. Happily, much of this testing is over. Saturn moves away from his stressful aspect in June. In the meantime, benevolent Jupiter is making nice aspects to your Love Planet. For singles, this means romantic opportunity. For marrieds, it means more happiness within the relationship and more socializing in general.

The main disagreements with your beloved over the past two years seem to have been financial ones. But new prosperity (especially on your partner's part) seems to have alleviated things. Your need to be on top of every expense – to micro-manage finance – is also lessening.

Singles have much romantic opportunity in the coming year – whether it will lead to marriage is another story. Very doubtful. Until August, romantic opportunity comes through your family or through people who are like family. They either provide introductions or support an existing relationship. An old flame from the past can come back into the picture – this might conjure up images of marital bliss, but as we mentioned, marriage is doubtful this year. Later in the year, marriage is denied because of other reasons – happy reasons. There is just so much romantic opportunity – so much fun without commitment – that marriage would seem boring in comparison. You're headed for a very exciting social life this year (and in the coming years), Taurus, so don't be in a rush to decide anything.

Singles find love in various places in the year ahead. Early in the year it is through family or family connections. Later on (after August 27) love comes at parties, sporting events, entertainment venues, resorts and at your job.

Those of you working towards a second marriage have reasonable aspects. Marriage opportunity comes as you pursue financial goals or perhaps with someone involved in your finances. Love is in the neighbourhood, close to home. The person could be a foreigner or someone of a different cultural or ethnic background. Very conservative.

Those of you working towards a third marriage also have some good opportunities coming up. These come at groups, organizations and perhaps on-line. You're looking more for friendship these days. The lover has to be your friend as well as lover.

Your best and most active social periods in the year ahead are from April 21 to June 10, July 29 to August 22 and October 9 to November 27.

The marriage of your parent(s) or parental figure seems happier this year. If he or she is single, there is good opportunity for a marriage or serious relationship. In general his or her social activity will increase and be happier.

Children of marriageable age are starting to feel instability in their love lives. Things are going well for them overall, but love is unstable. If they are married, the marriage could get tested. If single, there seem to be serial love affairs – they begin and end suddenly. Grandchildren of marriageable age need more patience this year. They are going to learn that love carries burdens and responsibilities. They seem (and perhaps rightly so) unusually cautious in love – not in a hurry to rush to the altar.

Single siblings could meet someone older and more established. They are being pursued and there's nothing much they need to do except show up. But they too seem cautious in love.

Perhaps the biggest social headline this year is in the realm of friendship. This area of life gets highly activated by two powerful planets: Uranus will move into your 11th House from March 10 to September 15 and Mars will spend six months there (this is highly unusual) from June 17 to December 16. This is showing change and upheavals with friends. Friendships that weren't right or that were based on false motivations now get purified and cleansed. Old friends go and new ones come into the picture. Many of you will start re-thinking what friendship means to you. Your relationship with groups and organizations also seems unstable in the year ahead. A good idea to examine your motives for being there and the true motives of the group. But all of this change is good. In the coming years, friendship is going to become ever more important and you will be doing much experimenting in this area. There needs to be a good housecleaning for the new to manifest.

Finance and Career

Both your 2nd and 8th Houses have been strong in recent years. The trend continues this year. The 2nd House rules personal earnings and portable possessions. The 8th House rules other people's money, your ability to access outside capital and your ability to help other people to prosper. So finances are a big priority this year.

Saturn has been in your Money House for the past two years. He will be there until June 4 of this year. Thus, the major lesson has been about the management of resources and not so much about money-making. There was a need to invest wisely, to make realistic budgets and stick by them, to become a better shopper, to cut waste and to make the most of the resources available to you. By now you have seen that you never really lacked much, you just didn't use what you had in the most efficient way. There was a need to get your financial life in order – to give it some structure, to set intelligent limits. In so doing, many difficult choices had to be made. Perhaps you sacrificed one night out a month in order to reduce debt or to invest. Perhaps you bought a less flashy car and used the excess money to better yourself financially. You had to discriminate sharply between essential and non-essential spending.

The interesting thing is that those who followed these prescriptions prospered greatly these past two years. Those who didn't faced one glitch after another. Saturn is stern, but he is not punitive. The fact is, his purpose is to enable you to have long-term, enduring wealth. But a person who doesn't understand money or can't manage it can never have enduring wealth. No matter how much you give to such a person, it is like throwing it in a black hole. They will always be lacking. So, Saturn comes along and creates some crises in order to change behaviour and thinking. Once this happens, you find that you are financially blessed. You will look back on these past two years someday and say 'those were the best things that ever happened to me.'

Happily, you Taureans are natural money-managers anyway and these lessons were probably easily learned. You can now apply these lessons to the acquisition of long-term wealth.

Generically, Saturn rules property. You Taureans are naturally good at property anyway. So this industry should have been profitable in the past two years (though your individual horoscope could modify this) and should continue to be profitable this year. Jupiter in your 4th House until August is reinforcing this.

Mercury, your Financial Planet, does unusual things this year. Usually he retrogrades three times a year. This year he does it four times. These retrogrades have financial significance. It means that there are more days when your financial judgement might not be up to par – more days when glitches are likely to occur – and more days where more homework needs to be done. We will keep you abreast of these periods in the month-by-month forecasts.

Pluto has been in your 8th House for many years now. This shows a need, an urge and the ability to pay off debt and to access other people's money. With Saturn in your Money House for the past two years, most of you have pared down your debt. Channelling spare cash to pay off debt is still a good idea in the coming year.

After June 4, the need to micro-manage finances is reduced. Earnings should be stable and finance in general will become less important and less of a burden. I presume it is because you have attained what you wanted to attain and now there's no need to pay too much attention to these things.

Your spouse or partner also increases prosperity this year. There is also less conflict and tension between you regarding finances. Children and grandchildren prosper as well.

Career, too, is becoming less important. Many of you will make important career changes this year as your Career Planet (Uranus) changes Signs for a time. In many cases you won't make the actual change, but you will start planning it. There is still a need to feel that you are doing something meaningful for yourself and for the world. Just money-making and outer success is not enough.

Self-improvement

We've already discussed the need to structure and order your financial life. Now you will be called on to do the same with your mental and intellectual life. In general, students will have to work harder to earn their grades. Those who are not students will find a need to discipline their speech and their thought. There is a need to learn to communicate accurately and with economy. Quality talk – talk that is uplifting and accurate – is better than hours of idle chatter that achieves nothing. You will find it a good practice to do your homework before making an opinion or judgement. Intellectual pretence will be ruthlessly exposed. There is no shame in saying 'I can't comment because I haven't studied the subject.' Intelligent people will respect you for that. On a deeper level, it is a good period to learn to discipline the mind. Weed out non-constructive and idle thinking. Learn to turn your mind on when you need it and turn it off when not in use. Meditative practices and awareness exercises will help you do this.

Mental energy is energy. It is life-force. The more it is wasted, the less you have for the things that are important to you. Idle speech and non-constructive thought keep people from reaching their goals. You have a beautiful two-year period ahead to work on this.

Month-by-month Forecasts

January

Best Days Overall: 2nd, 3rd, 11th, 12th, 13th, 21st, 22nd, 29th, 30th

Most Stressful Days Overall: 4th, 5th, 19th, 20th, 25th, 26th

Best Days for Love: 1st, 9th, 10th, 19th, 20th, 25th, 26th, 27th, 28th

Best Days for Money: 1st, 2nd, 3rd, 9th, 10th, 11th, 12th, 13th, 14th, 15th, 19th, 20th, 21st, 22nd, 27th, 28th, 29th, 30th

70% to 80% of the planets are above the horizon of your chart, Taurus, and your 10th House of Career is very powerful – so this is a good career month. With Jupiter in your 4th House you still enjoy your domestic life, but it's a good idea to shift attention to the career – seize the moment. The good news is that family seems supportive of your career aspirations so long as you don't lose your balance. Family members are also making good career progress.

Most of the planets are in the Western (social) sector of your chart – though this will soon change. Your 7th House is strong until the 17th. Not a good idea to go off on your own just yet. Cultivate the social graces, put other people first, and adapt as best you can to situations. Very soon the time will come when you can have your own way.

Health needs to be watched more after the 20th. Rest, relax and pace yourself. Focus on what is truly important and let lesser things go. Invest your energy for maximum return. Health can be enhanced by de-tox regimes, giving more attention to the kidneys, sexual organs, liver and thighs. Sexual expression needs to be balanced – neither too much nor too little. Dietary regimes and weight-loss programmes go exceptionally well during this period.

Finances are more complicated this month and more caution is necessary – especially when making big purchases or investments. Mercury (your Financial Planet) is retrograde from the 2nd to the 22nd and Saturn is retrograde in your House of Money. Best to research these things and act after the 22nd. If you exercise more caution, earnings should be very good – Mercury and Saturn are in mutual reception (each occupies the House of the other) showing good co-operation between them. Thus there could be financial opportunities in foreign lands or with foreigners. Your ability to cut costs enhances earnings and brings other financial opportunities – such as an ability to sell a business or property. Let patience do his perfect work.

As mentioned, this is a strong social month. You are reaching out to others, going after what you want. The main danger in love is a tendency to a power-struggle with the beloved – you should avoid this as much as possible. Singles are meeting more spiritually-orientated people.

After the 20th there is almost no power in your native element of Earth. Thus people will tend to be impractical and disorganized. They confuse words and ideas with actions and physical reality. Your steady, down-to-earth virtues seem out of style. But stick to being who you are, you are needed more now than ever.

February

Best Days Overall: 8th, 9th, 17th, 18th, 25th, 26th

Most Stressful Days Overall: 1st, 2nd, 15th, 16th, 21st, 22nd, 28th

Best Days for Love: 5th, 6th, 8th, 9th, 15th, 16th, 17th, 18th, 21st, 22nd, 23rd, 24th, 25th, 26th

Best Days for Money: 5th, 6th, 8th, 9th, 10th, 11th, 15th, 16th, 19th, 20th, 23rd, 24th, 28th

Continue to give more attention to your health until the 19th. Overwork is perhaps the main health danger, as your career seems hectic (but also successful). Health can be enhanced by paying more attention to your spine, knees and teeth. You respond unusually well to chiropractice and osteopathy. Therapies that align the skeletal system – such as Alexander Technique or Rolfing – are also good.

Like last month, 70% to 80% of the planets are above the horizon. Your 10th House of Career is even stronger than last month. With Jupiter retrograde in your House of Home and Family, family issues can't be immediately resolved – you may as well turn your attention to your career. Much progress is being made now. Career changes are brewing, but have no fear, they will be good. Some of the recent career volatility is about to ease up. This is a period where doing right will lead to feeling right. With all the changes about to happen career issues can be confusing, but the New Moon of the 1st is going to clarify these issues as the month progresses. All the information you need will come.

Mercury (your Financial Planet) crosses the Midheaven, suggesting a pay rise or a job offer for more money. It suggests that bosses, parents and authority figures are co-operating with your financial goals and providing you with lots of opportunities. Finance is high on your list of priorities.

Mercury's conjunction with Neptune on the 21st suggests a strong financial intuition and help from friends and organizations to which you belong. It would be a good idea to visualize your highest and best financial goals on that day.

Professional investors should look at property, oil, natural gas and high-technology companies for profit ideas.

The planetary power is beginning to shift to the East. It is not there yet (only 50% to 60% this month), but that's where the trend is heading. Thus you are, little by little, becoming more independent and free – becoming your own person, with power to go your own way and create your own life. The grace of others (though you shouldn't be rude) is becoming less and less necessary. Right now you are in a cusp situation – you are partly dependent and partly independent.

Mars, travelling near Pluto, your Love Planet, is testing a current relationship. On the other hand it also brings more physical passion to love. You are socially more aggressive and fearless – going after what you really want. If you love someone this month, that person is going to know it.

Looks like many of you are travelling (abroad) or receiving travel opportunities. Happy educational opportunities are also coming your way.

Your financial judgement is improved over last month now that Mercury is moving forward and will get even better come the 22nd when Saturn starts moving forward in your Money House.

Like last month there is almost no Earth element in the Horoscope. So you will have to be the 'practical' one for everyone else. Don't force issues, but give others sound, down-to-earth guidance – they surely do need it.

March

Best Days Overall: 7th, 8th, 17th, 25th, 26th

Most Stressful Days Overall: 1st, 14th, 15th, 21st, 27th, 28th

Best Days for Love: 5th, 6th, 10th, 11th, 14th, 15th, 19th, 20th, 21st, 23rd, 29th, 30th

Best Days for Money: 1st, 5th, 6th, 10th, 11th, 12th, 13th, 14th, 15th, 22nd, 23rd

By the 4th, the planetary power will be firmly in the East. 70% to 80% of the planets will be there – a strong percentage. Thus it is time to build your personal paradise on the Earth. You no longer need to put up with undesirable conditions or situations. You can build the new according to your specifications. The universe assents to your independence now and you'll be surprised to find you won't lose popularity either.

Career issues are still important – in certain respects even more important than in the past few months. Uranus, your Career Planet, makes a major move into Pisces on the 10th. This signals a career change, but even more – a change in career attitude and direction. You have been idealistic about your career for many years now. Now your idealism will increase. Whereas in previous years you were willing to make compromises, now you aren't. Friends and social connections are supporting these career changes, too. Perhaps these are the actual mechanisms by which the change happens.

Your three most important interests this month are career, friendships and spirituality.

Mercury, your Financial Planet, moves unusually fast this month, showing that your financial confidence is strong and that financial goals are achieved quickly. Earnings and earning opportunities will come in various ways. Until the 5th, they come from bosses, elders and your good reputation.

After the 5th, they come through friends, organizations and social connections. After the 21st, they come through intuition, dreams and spiritual guidance. You are unusually generous this month – giving to charities, ministries and good causes.

Venus, your Ruling Planet, also moves very fast this month. She will move through three Signs and Houses of your Horoscope. This shows that you are making rapid personal progress and shows great personal confidence and creativity. You are moving towards your goals rapidly. (90% of the planets are in forward motion until the 23rd, reinforcing the sense of progress and achievement.)

From the 2nd to the 21st, you are ambitious, career-orientated and maintaining an image of someone upwardly mobile. After the 21st, you are more glamorous and sensitive. You can take on any image you desire.

Health is vastly improved over the past two months. You can enhance it further by paying more attention to your ankles and feet. You respond particularly well to foot reflexology.

Love is complicated and delicate this month. Pluto, your Love Planet, starts to retrograde on the 23rd, showing a need for space in a current relationship. Financial and domestic disagreements seem a problem as well. Getting family and your beloved to get along is a challenge. True love will prevail through all these things.

April

Best Days Overall: 3rd, 4th, 5th, 13th, 14th, 21st, 22nd

Most Stressful Days Overall: 11th, 12th, 17th, 18th, 23rd, 24th

Best Days for Love: 1st, 2nd, 8th, 9th, 11th, 12th, 17th, 18th, 19th, 20th, 28th, 29th

Best Days for Money: 1st, 2nd, 6th, 7th, 11th, 12th, 13th, 14th, 19th, 20th, 21st, 22nd, 28th, 29th

Like last month, most of the planets are above the horizon of your chart. Your 10th House of Career is still very powerful (though not as strong as last month). Continue to de-emphasize home and family issues and focus on the career.

Two very spiritual planets are in your 10th House of Career this month. Neptune has been there for many years. But Mars (the Lord of your 12th House) will move in there on the 21st. This reinforces the career idealism that we wrote of last month. (Your Career Planet in the spiritual Sign of Pisces reinforces all this even more.) Mere name and fame and money-making are not enough for you. You want meaningful work – work that makes a difference for the world. Many Taureans are artists and musicians and these should have a very successful month – creativity is exceptionally strong. Those of you who are not artists will be more involved in charity work or volunteering for causes you believe in. Though you are altruistic, you will find that these activities have practical side-benefits – they enhance your career. This spirituality also suggests that, for many of you, intuition and higher guidance are the only solutions to a current problem. You must be ready to listen to your intuition and, more importantly, be ready to follow it. Many of you have under-rated your career prospects – intuition is going to straighten that out. Also we get a sense that you many of you will get more career guidance than you bargained for – many of you will get revelation about your mission in life for this incarnation. This is important knowledge.

The Eastern sector of the Horoscope is even stronger than last month. By the 21st, 80% of the planets will be there. Thus, continue to create your life the way you desire it to be. Don't compromise, don't consult unnecessarily with others. Determine what makes you happy and focus on it. With

80% to 90% of the planets moving forwards, you should make rapid progress towards your goals.

Mercury, your Financial Planet, goes retrograde on the 26th. Try to wrap up all financial dealings – contracts, important purchases, investments, etc. – before then.

There are a few financial bumps on the road this month, but none of these things is a long-term trend. A sudden expense (looks like in the home) could create some discomfort around the 10th and your financial judgement could be better on the 13th. Try to avoid snap decisions on the 13th.

Your love and social life are much improved over last month. There is more harmony with your spouse or lover – disagreements can be patched up. Singles will have many love opportunities after the 21st – especially as they get involved in charities, ministries, good causes and spiritual activities. But with Pluto still retrograde major love decisions one way or another should be delayed. Enjoy your relationships for what they are now without projecting too much into the future.

May

Best Days Overall: 1st, 2nd, 10th, 11th, 18th, 19th, 28th, 29th

Most Stressful Days Overall: 8th, 9th, 14th, 15th, 21st, 22nd

Best Days for Love: 8th, 9th, 14th, 15th, 16th, 17th, 18th, 25th, 26th, 27th, 29th

Best Days for Money: 1st, 2nd, 3rd, 4th, 8th, 9th, 10th, 11th, 16th, 17th, 18th, 19th, 25th, 26th, 27th, 28th, 29th, 30th, 31st

By the 16th, the dominance of planetary power will have shifted to the bottom half of the Horoscope. Until then the power is more or less evenly balanced. The message is clear: balance emotional and family concerns with your drives for outer success. Don't give too much weight to one or the other. Probably this will manifest as a pendulum effect, as first you swing one way and then another. But gradually the need to 'feel right' will be more important than the need for success. What good is success if you don't feel right, don't feel in harmony?

Most of the planets are forward and most of them are still in your Eastern sector. Thus, like last month, you are in a period where you can have things your way – have life on your terms. Others will adapt to you. As you build you should see rapid progress.

Mercury, your Financial Planet, is still retrograde until the 20th. So caution in financial matters is in order. You can research major purchases, investments, deals during the retrograde and act on them after the 20th.

We have two eclipses this month and one of them impacts strongly on you. Do take a reduced schedule a few days before and a day after the eclipse (especially the Lunar eclipse of the 16th). An eclipse, aside from being a signal of long-term change, is like a cosmic 'brown-out'. The energy that we should get from the two great lights, the Sun and the Moon, is interrupted. And just as a machine or computer will get up to all kinds of antics when there is less voltage, so too do people under the influence of an eclipse.

The Lunar eclipse of May 16 occurs in your 7th House and will probably test a relationship. If it is found wanting, the relationship will dissolve. If the relationship is strong, the eclipse will clear the air and you can take it to the next level. Those involved in non-committed relationships will probably be forced to make choices one way or another – either take the next step in the relationship or dissolve it. Friendships can also get tested.

The Solar eclipse of May 31 is less strong on you, but still take a reduced schedule. It occurs in your 2nd House of Finance, and signals long-term changes in financial strategy, investments and plans. Weaknesses in your finances will be glaringly revealed by the eclipse and you will be able to take corrective action.

Health is wonderful this period and can be enhanced by taking better care of your throat, neck and head. Self-esteem, self-confidence and personal appearance have seldom been better. The opposite sex takes notice, but are you interested?

June

Best Days Overall: 7th, 8th, 15th, 16th, 24th, 25th

Most Stressful Days Overall: 4th, 5th, 11th, 12th, 17th, 18th

Best Days for Love: 4th, 5th, 7th, 8th, 11th, 12th, 13th, 14th, 17th, 18th, 22nd, 23rd, 27th, 28th

Best Days for Money: 1st, 4th, 5th, 7th, 8th, 13th, 14th, 17th, 18th, 22nd, 23rd, 27th, 28th, 29th

Last month's Solar eclipse seems to have helped you. Financial burdens, cares and worries are lifted off your shoulders. You are more of a free spirit in finance. There is much less of a need to micro-manage and squeeze every penny. Looks like big-ticket items for the home are coming your way. Perhaps you are even buying a home. With Mercury now moving forward (and very fast), your financial confidence and judgement are good. There is rapid progress towards your goals. Until the 13th, your personal appearance and image are unusually important to earnings (you are also spending more on these things); after the 13th communication, marketing, sales and good public relations become important.

50% to 60% of the planets are below the horizon and your Career Planet, Uranus, starts retrograding on the 7th. You can safely de-emphasize the career and focus on your home base. The spiritual connection with your career is still very much in evidence – perhaps it is even stronger this month. You Taureans are thinking far beyond mere career. You are thinking about your spiritual mission in life. As you think and seek and pray, it will be revealed to you in very wonderful and subtle ways. Interesting spiritual experiences – very much out of the ordinary – await you this month. Rest assured, you will know that there is more to you than what is beneath your hat.

Finances and intellectual interests are the two most important areas of interest in the coming month. Finances are strong and getting stronger. You are now in a position where you can read those books you always wanted to get to or study those subjects that have always interested you.

With Pluto, your Love Planet, still retrograde, love is not exactly on hold, but moving slowly. Your social confidence and judgement could be better. You look great and your health is wonderful, but it's a matter of picking the right person.

Good health can be enhanced even further by paying more attention to your neck, throat, lungs, arms, shoulders and intestines. Make sure you always say positive things about your body and organs.

Mars enters your 11th House on the 17th and will stay there an unusually long time – six months. You can expect a shake-up among your friends and perhaps in organizations to which you belong. A purification will take place. The air will get cleared, hidden motives and grievances will come to the surface. Those friendships that are good will get even better, but some will fall by the wayside. This is a time for applying spiritual values to your friendships – and choosing them based on spiritual values.

July

Best Days Overall: 4th, 5th, 12th, 13th, 21st, 22nd, 23rd, 31st

Most Stressful Days Overall: 2nd, 3rd, 8th, 9th, 14th, 15th, 29th, 30th

Best Days for Love: 2nd, 3rd, 8th, 9th, 10th, 11th, 17th, 18th, 19th, 20th, 28th, 29th, 30th

Best Days for Money: 2nd, 3rd, 8th, 9th, 10th, 11th, 19th, 20th, 24th, 25th, 29th, 30th

Most of the planets are still below the horizon and your 4th House really gets powerful this month. Finding your emotional comfort zone seems easy, but the trick is staying there and governing your life from that place. If you make that your priority, it will be easier to do. The right 'inner state' takes priority over the right 'outer state'. Family relations and home life seem unusually happy right now – and active. A move or sale of the home (or expansion of the home) seems imminent.

The planetary power is about to make an important shift from the East, where it has been for a few months, to the West. Right now you are in a 'twilight zone' – what astrologers call a 'cusp situation'. You are not completely dependent, nor are you completely independent. You're somewhere in between. Sometimes you can have your way and sometimes you must bow to others. Sometimes your way is the right way and sometimes not. Sometimes you create your good by your personal effort and sometimes it will come by the good graces of others. Sometimes you can create new conditions and sometimes you will have to adapt to things. But the trend is westward and thus you should get ready to develop more of your social graces and skills. This is a month of preparation.

Mercury's speedy motion this month shows that your financial confidence and judgement are excellent. Rapid financial progress takes place. Money comes from many sources (and is probably spent in many different ways, too). Financial attitudes and needs shift rapidly. Until the 13th you are financially conservative but also very intuitive. Financial ideas can come in a dream or vision. After the 13th you are more risk-taking – but also much luckier. Money comes as you're having fun or indulging in leisure activities. Creative projects go well. A nice windfall comes around the 26th. Family and family connections play a major role most of the month.

Intellectual activities are still important this month and many of you are discovering the joys of learning and of solving intellectual problems. Your idea of fun could be solving a difficult crossword puzzle or logic problem. Indeed, there is great joy in these things.

Health is good, but rest and relax more after the 23rd. Good health can be enhanced by paying more attention to your arms, shoulders, intestines, lungs, stomach, breasts and heart. Emotional states have an unusual impact on your health from the 4th onwards. Cultivate happy and constructive states of mind.

August

Best Days Overall: 1st, 9th, 10th, 18th, 19th, 27th

Most Stressful Days Overall: 4th, 5th, 11th, 12th, 25th, 26th

Best Days for Love: 4th, 5th, 7th, 8th, 15th, 16th, 17th, 25th, 26th, 27th, 28th

Best Days for Money: 1st, 7th, 8th, 9th, 10th, 16th, 17th, 18th, 19th, 20th, 21st, 22nd, 26th, 27th, 28th

For over two years you've worked hard and diligently on your career and finances, Taurus. Whatever you achieved was on your own merits. The Cosmos didn't just hand you lucky breaks. You created your own luck, and now comes the payoff. Saturn is now out of your Money House (since June), giving you considerable financial liberation, and now Jupiter will move into your 5th House and start making fabulous aspects to you. For two years you earned by 'the sweat of the brow', now things happen 'by grace' – a completely different state of affairs. The thinking, planning, strategizing, worrying drop away – no longer needed – and the appropriating and enjoying of life, begin. You are in the Garden partaking of the fruits of the Tree of Life freely. You are entering one of the happiest periods of your year (and perhaps your life).

This is a month for the enjoyment of life. And, when the Cosmos grants this, it also grants all the funds (and everything else) necessary for this to happen. A holiday in a foreign land wouldn't surprise me. There will be more going to the cinema, theatre, concerts and other places of entertainment. Those of you who are involved in the creative arts will have unusual success. Those not involved in art professionally will still have enhanced creativity. It's as if you have found the 'child within' – that innocent state that looks at the world with new eyes, that expresses itself freely, and that has total faith that its needs will be supplied.

Watch how this joy impacts on your health. Joy itself is the healing agent this month (your Health Planet is joining the party of planets in your 5th House).

Many a Taurean will get pregnant or give birth this period (and in the year ahead). Most will be more involved with children in other ways, too. Now you have a special knack for getting on with them, as you are as much as child as they are – and thus relate well.

Perhaps the main challenge in the month ahead is getting used to all this freedom. When one is used to one thing for a long time, adjustment is difficult. Yes, it takes some time to adjust to paradise, but it's worth it. Eventually it will become normal.

Health is wonderful this month, but rest and relax more until the 22nd.

Singles have ample romantic opportunities, but of the non-serious kind. Singles don't want to be tied down right now. The abundance of love affair opportunities could test a current relationship.

September

Best Days Overall: 5th, 6th, 14th, 15th, 24th, 25th

Most Stressful Days Overall: 1st, 2nd, 7th, 8th, 22nd, 23rd, 28th, 29th

Best Days for Love: 1st, 2nd, 3rd, 4th, 5th, 6th, 12th, 13th, 16th, 17th, 22nd, 23rd, 26th, 27th, 28th, 29th, 30th

Best Days for Money: 5th, 6th, 14th, 15th, 24th, 25th, 26th, 27th

The party period continues. And with the planetary power in the West, personal effort doesn't really bring success – it comes through the graces of others and from on high. Let go and allow good to come to you. No need for power struggles or self-will. Seek consensus in all that you do. No need to figure things out – you don't have the whole picture, so your thinking won't do much and is probably not accurate. Your good will come in ways that you can't yet conceive. At best, we can only give you some hints here.

Financially, things are still super. There are honours and recognition coming. These can translate to cash as well. Speculations were favourable last month and are still favourable now – especially until the 20th. Mercury, your Financial Planet, is retrograde until the 20th (it began retrograding on August 28), so delay important purchases, investments or financial commitments until after the 20th. In the mean time do your homework and resolve all doubts.

Your earning power is so strong that even Mercury's retrograde will not stop it – only slow it down somewhat, or introduce a few kinks and glitches. You can minimize these by taking more care in how you communicate about money matters and with those involved in your finances – and also (as we mentioned) by postponing important decisions and purchases.

Your Love Planet, Pluto, has been retrograding for many months now, slowing down your social life (but not stopping it) and putting serious romance on hold. At the end of last month, Pluto started moving forward, so a current relationship moves forward. Singles have more options these days. They can choose either serious or non-serious relationships. Both seem plentiful. Choosing one or the other seems the difficult part. There is great allure in both.

Marrieds have to balance their devotion to their children with their obligation to their mates. There is some tension here. The welfare of children is, of course, important. But your relationship is equally important. A harmonious marital relationship is also in the children's best interest.

Health is wonderful and can be enhanced further by paying attention to your kidneys and intestines.

Though this is a month for enjoying life, job-seekers should meet with good success after the 15th. Very important that you find work that you can enjoy for its own sake.

October

Best Days Overall: 2nd, 3rd, 11th, 12th, 13th, 21st, 22nd, 29th, 30th

Most Stressful Days Overall: 4th, 5th, 19th, 20th, 25th, 26th

Best Days for Love: 1st, 4th, 5th, 9th, 10th, 16th, 17th, 19th, 20th, 25th, 26th, 27th, 28th

Best Days for Money: 2nd, 3rd, 11th, 12th, 13th, 14th, 15th, 21st, 22nd, 24th, 25th, 29th, 30th

Though the rest of the year is pretty much a party period, this month you are more interested in work and health issues. You are interested in work not because you have to be, but because you want to be – this makes all the difference in the world. Someone who works by choice is a free person exercising freedom. Someone who works because of necessity is still in bondage.

The planetary power is mostly in the West. Your 1st House of Self is empty, while your 7th House of Others becomes very powerful. So, as in the past few months, this is a period for developing social skills and graces and for attaining your ends through consensus and consulting the desires of others. It is difficult to change conditions by personal effort; adapting to situations is the best strategy right now.

The planetary power (especially of the fast-moving, short-term planets) is beginning to shift from the lower half of the Horoscope to the upper half. It doesn't happen straight away, but by the 24th the shift will be complete. Thus you are gradually shifting attention from family and emotional concerns to outer, career concerns. Inner happiness is not enough, you want that to be translated into outer achievement. Your Career Planet, Uranus, is still retrograde, so make haste slowly and carefully.

Job-seekers and those who employ others meet with good success this period. Speculations are favourable all month, but especially until the 7th – of course, always follow your intuition. After the 7th, money comes through work and through opportunities from co-workers or employees. After the 24th, it comes through social connections and the generosity of your spouse or partner. Mercury moves speedily this month, so financial progress is rapid. Your financial judgement and confidence are good – especially until the 7th. A business partnership or joint venture is in the works.

Students – especially pre-university – need to study harder in the next two years, but this month is one of the easier periods. Studies go relatively well.

You are entering one of the strongest and most active social periods of your year. Singles encounter both marriage-orientated relationships and fun-and-games type relationships. You seem unusually popular after the 9th as you go out of your way for others and reach out to people. You are on a charm offensive. From the 9th onwards, there is a Grand Trine in Water which makes fabulous aspects to your Ruling Planet, Venus. This brings spiritual and religious revelation, opportunities to travel (both in a physical sense and in a mental sense) and new friends. Health is good, but it won't hurt to rest and relax more after the 23rd.

November

Best Days Overall: 8th, 9th, 18th, 19th, 26th, 27th

Most Stressful Days Overall: 1st, 2nd, 15th, 16th, 22nd, 23rd, 28th, 29th

Best Days for Love: 5th, 6th, 15th, 16th, 22nd, 24th, 25th, 26th, 27th

Best Days for Money: 3rd, 4th, 8th, 9th, 10th, 11th, 12th, 15th, 16th, 18th, 19th, 24th, 25th, 26th, 27th

The planetary power is now firmly established above the horizon (in the upper half) of your Horoscope. Uranus, your Career Planet, starts moving forwards on the 8th. Thus, your focus on career will start showing results. Bottlenecks and delays, confusion and indecision melt away and your forward path lies open for you. You can safely de-emphasize family and domestic duties and focus on your career now.

The beautiful Grand Trine in Water is still in effect most of this month – until the 22nd. Like last month, this brings new friends, social popularity and much spiritual progress.

Socially, this is a powerful month. Many, many love opportunities for singles. Marrieds are enjoying their relationship more. Your spouse or partner prospers (thanks in large part to your efforts and support) and seems generous. There is more attending of parties and social gatherings.

Venus, your Ruling Planet, moves unusually quickly this month, showing that you have great personal confidence, that you cover a lot of territory and that you make fast progress towards your goals (90% of the planets moving forwards also shows fast progress).

There are two eclipses this month, which shake things up in the world and in your environment. Only one of them is strong on you – the Lunar eclipse of the 9th. The Solar eclipse of the 23rd doesn't affect you directly, but it won't hurt to take a reduced schedule anyway.

The Lunar eclipse of the 9th occurs in your 1st House of Self. This shows important (and long-term) changes to your image, the way you dress and your concept of yourself. You are going to re-define your personality – upgrade it, clarify it to yourself and to others. Events produced by the eclipse could force you to do this – and a good thing too. You get a chance to improve yourself.

The Solar eclipse of the 23rd occurs in your 8th House, which affects the income of your spouse or partner. Thus he or she is making important financial changes now and over the next few months. Flawed investments, plans or strategies are revealed and corrective actions will be taken. Every Solar eclipse affects your home and family situation, as the Sun is your Family Planet. Thus, if there are flaws in the home, they will come up for correction. Long-brewing issues with family members can surface and force a clearing of the air and positive action.

Finances are wonderful this month, though beware of over-spending after the 12th. Keep a sense of proportion.

December

Best Days Overall: 5th, 6th, 15th, 16th, 23rd, 24th

Most Stressful Days Overall: 12th, 13th, 14th, 19th, 20th, 25th, 26th

Best Days for Love: 2nd, 3rd, 4th, 5th, 6th, 12th, 13th, 14th, 15th, 16th, 19th, 20th, 21st, 22nd, 25th, 26th, 30th, 31st

Best Days for Money: 5th, 6th, 7th, 8th, 9th, 15th, 16th, 23rd, 24th

The planetary power (like last month) is above the horizon. Your 10th House of Career grows more powerful day by day, while your 4th House of Home and Family is practically empty – only the Moon will visit there for three days out of the month. Venus, your Ruling Planet, will move into your Career House on the 21st. The message is clear: your ambitions are unusually strong. Family and home issues are less important. Push forwards towards your career goals. It is your very interest in career that attracts the attention of bosses and elders and helps produce the success that you crave. They note your interest and act on it.

Your 8th and 9th Houses are also very strong this month. Thus, it is a good month for paying off debt, for personal transformation and reinvention, and for helping other people prosper. Also a good month to break addictions and change character traits – if you feel moved to do so.

Power in your 9th House shows an interest in foreign travel, foreign lands and cultures. Higher education, in general, is more interesting to you and opportunities will come to indulge this interest. Many of you will be having mystical experiences after the 16th and these will challenge long-held philosophical beliefs and perhaps your current world view. A good thing. You will be forced to square your experience with your belief systems, thus modifying them. You are in a situation where everyone around says there is no sun. Yet you go outside and you experience the sun and you know it exists. The deniers say you are hallucinating and not well – perhaps suffering from some mental disorder. Yet your experience is real to you and can't be denied. Uncomfortable? Perhaps. But welcome to the club. There are more people in this situation than you can imagine.

Prosperity is unusually strong this month. It is a prosperous month in a prosperous year. But Mercury's retrograde on the 17th could complicate matters. Definitely do your Christmas shopping before the 17th. As always, when your Financial Planet is retrograde it's best not to commit to major purchases or investments. The retrograde is for studying, researching and negotiating, not for buying.

Pluto, your Love Planet, is moving forward and receiving strong stimulation. So this is a socially active (and happy) month. Singles find love close to home and through family connections. Family gatherings go well. A move or fortunate purchase or sale of a home is likely after the 22nd. In many cases there will be big-ticket items coming for the home.

Gemini

♊

THE TWINS

Birthdays from

21st May

to 20th June

Personality Profile

GEMINI AT A GLANCE

Element – Air

Ruling Planet – Mercury
Career Planet – Neptune
Love Planet – Jupiter
Money Planet – Moon
Planet of Health and Work – Pluto
Planet of Home and Family Life – Mercury

Colours – blue, yellow, yellow-orange

Colour that promotes love, romance and social harmony – sky blue

Colours that promote earning power – grey, silver

Gems – agate, aquamarine

Metal – quicksilver

Scents – lavender, lilac, lily of the valley, storax

Quality – mutable (= flexibility)

Quality most needed for balance – thought that is deep rather than superficial

Strongest virtues – great communication skills, quickness and agility of thought, ability to learn quickly

Deepest need – communication

Characteristics to avoid – gossiping, hurting others with harsh speech, superficiality, using words to mislead or misinform

Signs of greatest overall compatibility – Libra, Aquarius

Signs of greatest overall incompatibility – Virgo, Sagittarius, Pisces

Sign most helpful to career – Pisces

Sign most helpful for emotional support – Virgo

Sign most helpful financially – Cancer

Sign best for marriage and/or partnerships – Sagittarius

Sign most helpful for creative projects – Libra

Best Sign to have fun with – Libra

Signs most helpful in spiritual matters – Taurus, Aquarius

Best day of the week – Wednesday

Understanding a Gemini

Gemini is to society what the nervous system is to the body. It does not introduce any new information but is a vital transmitter of impulses from the senses to the brain and vice versa. The nervous system does not judge or weigh these impulses – it only conveys information. And does so perfectly.

This analogy should give you an indication of a Gemini's role in society. Geminis are the communicators and conveyors of information. To Geminis the truth or falsehood of information is irrelevant, they only transmit what they see, hear or read about. Thus they are capable of spreading the most outrageous rumours as well as conveying truth and light. Geminis sometimes tend to be unscrupulous in their communications and can do great good or great evil with their power. This is why the Sign of Gemini is called the Sign of the Twins: Geminis have a dual nature.

Their ability to convey a message – to communicate with such ease – makes Geminis ideal teachers, writers and media and marketing people. This is helped by the fact that Mercury, the Ruling Planet of Gemini, also rules these activities.

Geminis have the gift of the gab. And what a gift this is! They can make conversation about anything, anywhere, at any time. There is almost nothing that is more fun to Geminis than a good conversation – especially if they can learn something new as well. They love to learn and they love to teach. To deprive a Gemini of conversation or of books and magazines, is cruel and unusual punishment.

Geminis are almost always excellent students and take well to education. Their minds are generally stocked with all kinds of information, trivia, anecdotes, stories, news items, rarities, facts and statistics. Thus they can support any intellectual position that they care to take. They are awesome debaters and, if involved in politics, make good orators.

Geminis are so verbally smooth that even if they do not know what they are talking about, they can make you think that they do. They will always dazzle you with their brilliance.

Finance

Geminis tend to be more concerned with the wealth of learning and ideas than with actual material wealth. As mentioned, they excel in professions that involve writing, teaching, sales and journalism – and not all of these professions pay very well. But to sacrifice intellectual needs merely for money is unthinkable to a Gemini. Geminis strive to combine the two.

Cancer is on Gemini's Solar 2nd House (of Money) cusp, which indicates that Geminis can earn extra income (in a harmonious and natural way) from investments in residential property, restaurants and hotels. Given their verbal skills, Geminis love to bargain and negotiate in any situation, but especially when it has to do with money.

The Moon rules Gemini's 2nd Solar House. The Moon is not only the fastest-moving planet in the Zodiac but actually moves through every Sign and House every 28 days. No other heavenly body matches the Moon for swiftness or the ability to change quickly. An analysis of the Moon – and lunar phenomena in general – describes Gemini's financial attitudes very well. Geminis are financially versatile and flexible. They can earn money in many different ways. Their financial attitudes and needs seem to change daily. Their feelings about money change also: sometimes they are very enthusiastic about it, at other times they could not care less.

For a Gemini, financial goals and money are often seen only as means of supporting a family; these things have little meaning otherwise.

The Moon, as Gemini's Money Planet, has another important message for Gemini financially: in order for Geminis to realize their financial potential they need to develop more of an understanding of the emotional side of life. They need to combine their awesome powers of logic with an understanding of human psychology. Feelings have their own logic; Geminis need to learn this and apply it to financial matters.

Career and Public Image

Geminis know that they have been given the gift of communication for a reason, that it is a power that can achieve great good or cause unthinkable distress. They long to put this power at the service of the highest and most transcendental truths. This is their primary goal, to communicate the eternal verities and prove them logically. They look up to people who can transcend the intellect – to poets, artists, musicians and mystics. They may be awed by stories of religious saints and martyrs. A Gemini's highest achievement is to teach the truth, whether it is scientific, inspirational or historical. Those who can transcend the intellect are a Gemini's natural superiors – and a Gemini realizes this.

The Sign of Pisces is in Gemini's Solar 10th House of Career. Neptune, the Planet of Spirituality and Altruism, is Gemini's Career Planet. If Geminis are to realize their highest career potential they need to develop their transcendental – their spiritual and altruistic – side. They need to understand the larger cosmic picture, the vast flow of human evolution – where it came from and where it is heading. Only then can a Gemini's intellectual powers take their true position and he or she can become the 'messenger of the gods'. Geminis need to cultivate a facility for 'inspiration', which is something that does not originate in the intellect, but which comes through the intellect. This will further enrich and empower a Gemini's mind.

Love and Relationships

Geminis bring their natural garrulousness and brilliance into their love life and social life as well. A good talk or a verbal joust is an interesting prelude to romance. Their only problem in love is that their intellect is too cool and passionless to incite ardour in others. Emotions sometimes disturb them and their partners tend to complain about this. If you are in love with a Gemini you must understand why this is so. Geminis avoid deep passions because these would interfere with their ability to think and communicate. If they are cool towards you, understand that this is their nature.

Nevertheless, Geminis must understand that it is one thing to talk about love and another actually to love – to feel it and radiate it. Talking about love glibly will get them nowhere. They need to feel it and act on it. Love is not of the intellect but of the heart. If you want to know how a Gemini feels about love you should not listen to what he or she says, but rather observe what he or she does. Geminis can be quite generous to those they love.

Geminis like their partners to be refined, well educated and well travelled. If their partners are more wealthy than they, that is all the better. If you are in love with a Gemini you had better be a good listener as well.

The ideal relationship for the Gemini is a relationship of the mind. They enjoy the physical and emotional aspects, of course, but if the intellectual communion is not there they will suffer.

Home and Domestic Life

At home, the Gemini can be uncharacteristically neat and meticulous. They tend to want their children and partner to live up to their idealistic standards. When these standards are not met they moan and criticize. However, Geminis are good family people and like to serve their families in practical and useful ways.

The Gemini home is comfortable and pleasant. They like to invite people over and they make great hosts. Geminis are also good at repairs and improvements around the house – all fuelled by their need to stay active and occupied with something they like to do. Geminis have many hobbies and interests that keep them busy when they are home alone.

Geminis understand and get along well with their children, mainly because they are very youthful people themselves. As great communicators, Geminis know how to explain things to children; in this way they gain their children's love and respect. Geminis also encourage children to be creative and talkative, just like they are.

Horoscope for 2003

Major Trends

Though many good things happened for you in the past year and a half, it was not what we would call a fun period. Some periods in life are for joy, lazing around and doing what you want to do. This wasn't it. The past year and half has been about work, taking on responsibility, facing some of life's seemingly unpleasant realities. It was a kind of Cosmic Boot Camp. It was about learning lessons, about doing your duty in spite of what you felt like. Most of this is about over, though you've got another five months to go. But by now, the lessons and learning experiences should be a lot easier. By now (and over the next five months), you should be a better, stronger person. The lessons you've learned this past year and half will stand you in good stead this year and for many years to come.

This year, the planet Uranus is making a major move from Aquarius to Pisces. It will only be in Pisces for about six months, but it will send unmistakable signals about your life. It's about to become much more exciting – especially careerwise. Whereas this past year or so you stuck by a routine and did what you had to do, now you will start tasting some career freedom – many changes – many opportunities – much experimentation going on there.

Your love life has been going through a testing and transformative period for some years now. And though this trend continues, things will get much easier. The power struggles in your love life, though not over, will abate considerably.

Saturn will make a major move out of your Sign on June 4 and move into your Solar 2nd House of Money. There he will stay for the next two years or so. The lessons to be learned will be financial ones and, when Saturn is finished with you, you will be able both to earn and handle big wealth. He's going to make you financially healthy.

Jupiter also makes a major move this year, moving from Leo, your 3rd House, to Virgo, your 4th House. Thus, many of you are moving in the year ahead. More on this later.

Your important areas of interest in the coming year will be: communication and intellectual interests (especially until August 27); home, family and domestic issues (after August 27); love, romance and social activities; higher education, foreign travel and religious and philosophical studies; career (after March 15).

Your paths of greatest fulfilment in the coming year will be: the body, the image, personal appearance and personal pleasure (until April 14); spirituality (after April 14); communication and intellectual pursuits (until August 27); home, family and domestic interests (after August 27).

Health

Health will be pretty much as it was last year. Though Saturn moves off you this year (and this will feel like a great weight lifting off you), other long-term planets come in to keep the pressure on.

Like last year, you will need to pace yourself, rest when tired, work smarter and not harder and focus on priorities. You will have plenty of energy to handle your true responsibilities, but not enough for frittering away on non-essentials.

Now Gemini, in general, has a tendency to disperse energy. You are so curious about everything, you want to be everywhere at once, so your focus and concentration is often lacking. The lessons in the past year and in coming years are about focus. Focus is not as difficult as it seems. It is really about 'letting go'. You persistently let go of trivia until only what is important remains. And what is important? Your goals, your dreams, the things that make you happy.

Saturn will still be in your 1st House until June 4. Though this tends to make you feel old and serious and to limit your energy, it has got some good points. It gives you the urge to watch your diet, to lose weight, to take on a disciplined health regime and to get your body and image in order. By now most of you are on a steady health regime. This should be continued. (It will be harder when Saturn leaves Gemini in June.)

Pluto, your Health Planet, is a very slow-moving planet. He stays in a Sign or House anywhere between 20 and 35 years. His position in your 7th House of Love, Marriage and Social Life suggests (like last year) that good health for you is not just the absence of disease, but a healthy love life, a healthy marriage, healthy social relationships. And this is as it should be. It also shows that health problems tend to originate with dis-harmonies with your spouse, lover or friends. If you feel under the weather, check out your relationships. Try to clear the dis-harmony out there before running to a health professional. Chances are, the condition will clear up on its own. And, even if the services of a health professional are needed, the healing will go much more quickly and easily if you look to your relationships as well.

Pluto rules the sexual organs. Thus you should give extra attention to these organs through natural, drugless therapies.

A balanced sex life – neither too much nor too little – is important for health.

Pluto in the Sign of Sagittarius suggests that more attention be given to the liver and thighs. The thighs can be massaged regularly. The liver, like the sexual organs, can be strengthened through foot and hand reflexology, chiropractice, kinesiology, acupressure, acupuncture, reiki and many other natural methods.

Pluto, the natural ruler of elimination, suggests that you would get wonderful results with de-tox therapies – therapies that don't 'add things' to the body but which cleanse it of impurities.

If you take these simple precautions you should come through the coming year with flying colours.

Home, Domestic and Family Issues

Home and domestic issues haven't been that important (as compared to other things) for some years now. But this year, come August 27, they become important – as Jupiter moves into your 4th House. Jupiter will spend about a year in that House and it is a very happy transit.

Generally this brings a move to larger and more sumptuous quarters. It brings good fortune from property and from buying and selling a home. You might find that your existing home is suddenly worth more. Some people won't move house, but will enlarge their residence. Others may find that big-ticket items for the home come to them. Others acquire second and third homes. Family life and your family situation becomes much happier. There is more financial and emotional support from family members. The simple pleasures of home and hearth are revealed. The family expands through birth or marriage. You meet people who are like family to you and who give you unconditional love and support. In many cases where a person has no biological family or where there was estrangement from them, the

Jupiter transit brings them into contact with their 'spiritual family'.

When Jupiter moves into your 4th House (and you are of childbearing age), you become more fertile. Pregnancies are more likely under this transit than under other transits.

Perhaps the most important effect of the transit is the emotional optimism and ebullience that it brings. This optimism helps you to deal with any and all of life's challenges. Geminis will become more nurturing in the coming year – both to their own families and to people in general. They will be kinder, more generous and more compassionate.

Now, this move that we talked about seems related to your career. It could be that you change career or jobs and are forced to move. Or it could be the other way around – you move and now you are searching for a new job or career. The thing to keep in mind is that all of this is happy. You will enjoy it.

Jupiter also happens to be your Love Planet. Thus, his move into the 4th House suggests either a marriage, a live-in relationship or much socializing and entertaining from home. It often shows a redecoration or beautification of the home. Any of these scenarios wouldn't surprise me.

Redecorating projects will go well any time after August 27. But I especially like August 27 to September 15.

Love and Social Life

Your love and social life have been important for many years. These areas are undergoing long-term and very deep transformation. Your interest in social affairs (not just marriage) and other people is one-pointed. You want to get at the depths of love and relationships – get to the core of things – solve all the mysteries. Eventually you will, but enjoy the process – it's a long road. Many a Gemini has been divorced in recent years and many have re-married. Many have faced trials and tests in their marriages and, though they did not divorce, the marriage is so changed that it is as if it were new. This is all part of the plan and programme.

The trials and tests of love get easier this year. Singles have wonderful marriage opportunities until August 27. But then, the relationship gets tested. I think that it is good that it gets tested so that flaws can be discovered early on and dealt with. The Cosmos is trying to protect you from yourself. The Solar eclipse of November 23 (in your 7th House of Love) will probably be the trigger for this testing.

Pluto in your 7th House of Love and Marriage intensifies the love feelings – almost to superhuman levels. The intensity of feeling is so great that the highs of love are stratospheric. But if the feeling is allowed to get negative – if jealousy, possessiveness, mistrust or power plays come into the picture – the lows can be ultra-low. Pluto never does anything halfway. 'All or nothing' is his motto. But it is only as you go through these extremes in love that you can gain the wisdom you desire. How would you know the bliss if you didn't taste the hell? How would you know what real love is if you never experienced the counterfeits? How would you know the beauty of relationship if you were never alone? So many things masquerade as love these days that it takes a very perceptive person to discern the difference.

Pluto is going to purify your love and social life so that only the 'real thing' is left. And this is what you want. You don't just want a relationship, you want something pure and healthy.

For singles, love is close to home, in the neighbourhood. Family, family connections and family gatherings are also paths to love. Family members enjoy playing Cupid.

Your needs in love are different this year. Of course you want good communication and a good time. You want to have fun with your beloved. But you also want nurturing and emotional support. This is how Gemini feels loved and how Gemini will show love in the year ahead. You want to feel that you and your beloved are 'family' – and thus a marriage could be on the cards for singles. It's the family feeling that is pushing you.

Two things are obstructing love this year – they aren't major problems but they are issues to deal with. Work and career are definitely interfering with your social life and with a special relationship. You will have to balance and juggle, never going too far one way or another. Religious and philosophical differences could also be a problem, but not an insurmountable one.

Finance and Career

Finances are status quo early in the year as your 2nd House is not a House of Power. But come June 4, when Saturn moves into that House, finances do become more important – and for the next two years.

Good luck comes to people in many ways. Most people think of good luck as when something wonderful happens – you win the lottery, your stock goes through the roof, you land that dream job, someone gives you an unexpected gift, etc. But good luck often comes to us deeply disguised. And not many of us recognize it at the time. Only years later do we realize that, yes, getting jilted by the man/woman we loved at the time was great luck. Because later on it enabled us to meet Mr/Ms Really Right. Not landing that job you lusted for turned out to be a good thing in hindsight – not just good, but great. For right behind that was an even better job. The man who got ill and couldn't take his dream cruise on the *Titanic* thought he was unlucky at the time.

The luck that Jupiter brings is the former kind. An overt, undisguised, wonderful thing. But the good luck that Saturn brings is usually the latter kind. Who says Saturn doesn't have a sense of humour?

Your ability to penetrate these disguises will be an important factor in your overall happiness and financial well-being in the coming year.

Everyone desires wealth. Some desire it more, some less. Some have greater needs for wealth than others. But everyone desires it. It is built into the psyche. Part of our soul structure. But how many of us understand the laws behind it? How many of us know how to manage and use our resources properly? How many of us could handle great wealth if it came upon us suddenly? Not many. So, Saturn, the teacher and trainer, has to come into the picture and prepare and teach us. This is what is happening this year.

You will find that you cannot be the free-spender that you have always been. Perhaps you are faced with a big expense. Perhaps creditors stop being patient with you and want their cash. Many of you will buy homes and take on mortgages in the coming year. Perhaps there are extra mouths to feed. Suddenly you are forced to make long-term financial decisions. You need to think, prioritize, budget, research.

The path to financial success this year is not so much about increasing earnings – though it would help. It's about using what you have effectively. Saturn is going to teach you all these things and, when he's finished (if you co-operate), you will be financially healthier than you've ever been.

Saturn will teach you to be neither a big spender nor a little spender – but a proportional spender. He will teach you the *arcana* of finance – about long-term planning and gauging long-term values. He will show you how to have 'stable' wealth – not 'flash in the pan' or 'here today, gone tomorrow' wealth.

Important changes are happening in your career, as we have mentioned elsewhere. Uranus is flirting with your 10th House of Career this year. He will enter in for six months and then retreat back to your 9th House. But this is an announcement of things to come. You are not only changing jobs but also career paths. Career is going to be very exciting in coming years, but also much more unstable. Many of you will opt for more freedom in this area – going freelance or starting your own business. This is all the more reason to learn how to manage money.

Self-improvement

For the first half of the year the trend to self-improvement will be what it has been for the past two years – the improvement of the body and the image. Things like diet, exercise, dressing in proper ways and re-defining your concept of yourself are all-important. In reality you are much more than your highest vision of yourself. In truth you are a direct projection of the Divine. So, on this level, there is nothing to attain and nothing to improve. But on your 'mortal-personality' level, there is much to improve to get in line with your ideal. On the 'mortal-personality' level you are neither as great as you think you are nor as small or worthless as you think. The past two years (and the first half of this year) are about developing a realistic sense of self-esteem.

The second half of the year, as we mentioned, is about learning how to handle money – its right use. Money has to be put in its right context. It should be neither worshiped nor feared. It is tool that you use. A good craftsman understands his tools and uses them – the tools don't use him.

A good idea in the coming years would be to take classes in personal finance, investing, budgeting and the like. Sometimes financial problems come from ignorance – we imagine scenarios that couldn't happen if we had the necessary knowledge. It's also good to learn the difference between constructive and destructive debt. Destructive debt is when you borrow for ephemeral pleasures or for things that will decrease in value. Constructive debt is when you borrow to invest in power and in things that will go up in value. Sometimes it is a smart thing to take on debt, sometimes it is poison. The discernment of these issues is one of your major lessons coming up this year.

Month-by-month Forecasts

January

Best Days Overall: 4th, 5th, 14th, 15th, 23rd, 24th

Most Stressful Days Overall: 1st, 6th, 7th, 8th, 21st, 22nd, 27th, 28th

Best Days for Love: 1st, 9th, 10th, 19th, 20th, 27th, 28th

Best Days for Money: 1st, 2nd, 3rd, 9th, 10th, 11th, 12th, 13th, 16th, 17th, 19th, 20th, 23rd, 24th, 27th, 28th

The Cosmos helps you during this period, not by eliminating or taking away your burdens, but rather by helping you to carry them. Air, your native element, dominates the period. 40% to 50% of the planets are there. A Grand Trine in Air on the 23rd and 24th improves health, helps you pay off debt and enhances your already fine mind. A Grand Trine in the Fire element on the 9th and 10th is also benevolent to you – it brings financial windfalls, earnings opportunities and romance.

Yes, the burdens you carry seem lawful and legitimate, but they will not overcome you.

This month the planets are shifting from the lower half (below the horizon) to the upper half. By the 17th, 70% to 80% of the planets will be above the horizon. Your 4th House of Home and Family is empty this month – except for a visit by the Moon on the 21st and 22nd. Your Career Planet, Neptune, receives strong stimulation. Thus you should be focusing on your 'outer' life and outer objectives. Family and domestic duties can be downplayed as you focus on career.

70% to 80% of the planets are in the Western sector, making this a social month. This is not a month for self-will, power struggles or trying to have things your way. This is a time for adjusting to the various circumstances around you and for developing your social skills and eliciting the co-operation of others. Put other people first, seek consensus, and compromise whenever necessary. Your good will come to you effortlessly.

Health is good this month and will get even better after the 20th. Pluto, your Health Planet, is in Sagittarius for the long term, so good health can be enhanced by paying more attention to your thighs and liver. Work to smooth out love dis-harmonies as well – as these can unduly impact your health.

This is a socially active month. Venus in your 7th House of Love and Marriage (from the 7th onwards) brings romantic opportunity. But Mars entering this House on the 17th will test it. Power struggles are the main threat to love this period. With dynamic Mars and Pluto in your 7th House, it will be difficult to resist temptation. On the positive side, these two planets increase romantic passion. When romance goes well, the intensity of it is incredible. But if the passions are negative – well, that too can be incredible. Your job will be to keep the passions constructive. There are many who like tempestuous love relationships. Too much peace and harmony bores them. This is their kind of month.

Finances are mixed this month. In general, earning power will be stronger when the Moon waxes (from the 2nd to the 18th) than when he wanes. The Full Moon of the 18th occurs in your Money House, bringing financial opportunity and also more energy for achieving your financial goals.

February

Best Days Overall: 1st, 2nd, 10th, 11th, 19th, 20th, 28th

Most Stressful Days Overall: 3rd, 4th, 17th, 18th, 23rd, 24th

Best Days for Love: 5th, 6th, 8th, 9th, 15th, 16th, 17th, 18th, 23rd, 24th, 25th, 26th

Best Days for Money: 1st, 2nd, 5th, 6th, 10th, 11th, 13th, 14th, 15th, 16th, 21st, 23rd, 24th

Career urges and interests are even stronger this month than last. Not only are 70% to 80% of the planets above the horizon, but now your 10th House becomes powerful on the 19th. Neptune, your Career Planet, continues to be strongly stimulated. By contrast, your 4th House of Home and Family is still empty (except for a visit by the Moon on the 17th and 18th). So, like last month, this is a time for pushing forward with your ambitions and reaching for the sky. Your chances for success are unusually good now. If your goals are modest, they will be attained. If they are great, you will see progress towards them.

Like last month, the planetary power is mostly in the West. So, continue to avoid power struggles (it won't be easy), practise your social skills and adapt, adapt, adapt. Others are seeing more of the big picture than you are, so your way might not be the best way. Reach for the stars, but silently and with a low profile.

Air is the still the dominant element this month – a positive signal for you both healthwise and intellectually. Many Geminis are writers, teachers and journalists and these should have a banner month. Still, you should take a reduced schedule after the 19th and focus only on what is important to you. Health is enhanced by maximizing energy now.

Mars and Pluto are still in your 7th House of Love, so, like last month, love is tempestuous. Passions run high, both positively and negatively. Sexual expression is unusually intense. Mars and Pluto in your 7th House show social aggressiveness – going after what you want in a direct and forceful way. Of course you should avoid caveman tactics, but the overcoming of social fear and inhibition is the main lesson here. When you are the social aggressor, you run a greater risk of rejection, but Mars and Pluto will teach you how to go on in spite of this. Conquering your fear of rejection will ultimately lead to acceptance and getting what you want. As any good marketing person knows – rejection is not the end of a project, but only the beginning.

Finances are status quo. Money can come to you in a variety of ways and means. The Moon waxes from the 1st to the 16th; this should be your strongest earning period (overall). The Full Moon of the 16th seems a particularly good financial day as the Moon conjuncts beneficial Jupiter. Expect a windfall or opportunity that day.

Your 9th House is by far the strongest house this month. Thus happy educational and travel opportunities are coming your way. Students learn more quickly and easily. There is much religious and philosophical revelation happening.

March

Best Days Overall: 1st, 10th, 11th, 19th, 27th, 28th

Most Stressful Days Overall: 2nd, 3rd, 17th, 23rd, 29th, 30th, 31st

Best Days for Love: 5th, 6th, 10th, 11th, 14th, 15th, 19th, 20th, 21st, 23rd, 29th, 30th

Best Days for Money: 2nd, 3rd, 5th, 6th, 12th, 13th, 14th, 15th, 22nd, 23rd

Rest and relax more, pace yourself and focus as much as possible on your career. You have amazing opportunities now, but if you deplete yourself you won't be able to take them.

Many of the trends we wrote of last month are still in effect now. The planetary power is still above the horizon. Your 4th House of Home and Family is still empty (except for a brief visit by the Moon). But your 10th House of Career! Wow! There's a convention going on there. 40% to

50% of the planets will be there or move through there. Uranus, which stays in a Sign for seven years, will move into your 10th House on the 10th and stay there for the next six months. The New Moon of the 3rd occurs there. This is where the action is and this should be your focus. Emotional harmony will come after you get your career straightened out.

Career is now exciting and perhaps unstable. You could have multiple job offers or multiple career moves. As soon as you think you've got the dream career, something else even better offers itself. For those who are young and just starting out, these aspects are showing experimentation and trial-and-error career moves. You try one thing for a while, then another and so on, until you find something you like. This process could go on for many years.

For those who are older and more settled we see 'sudden career advancement' – boom! Barriers break and you are in your promised land. There is great turmoil in your corporate hierarchy these days, too – the clerk can become president, the president can become the clerk. The dominant company can become the underdog and the underdog can become dominant. Revolutionary and surprising events are going on. Don't be surprised if you get assigned to a foreign country. If you can manage your health and energy, this is an exciting period.

Mars is leaving your 7th House on the 4th; this will cool down your love life a bit. I would say most of you welcome this change. Love is more sedate now. Important relationship decisions – such as marriage or divorce (or even a business partnership) – shouldn't be taken now as Jupiter, your Love Planet, is retrograde. Patience was the one thing lacking in your love life these past few months, but now it is called for. Let love develop as it will without trying to force things.

Finances are still status quo, though career success is certainly a help. You don't seem that interested in money *per se*

– status is more important than money. Earnings and earning power will be stronger from the 3rd to the 18th as the Moon waxes.

April

Best Days Overall: 6th, 7th, 15th, 16th, 23rd, 24th

Most Stressful Days Overall: 13th, 14th, 19th, 20th, 26th, 27th

Best Days for Love: 1st, 2nd, 8th, 9th, 11th, 12th, 17th, 18th, 19th, 20th, 28th, 29th

Best Days for Money: 1st, 2nd, 8th, 9th, 10th, 11th, 12th, 19th, 20th, 21st, 28th, 29th

Health is improving but still needs attention. Keep in mind our previous discussions. The retrograde of your Health Planet suggests much caution when it comes to changing health regimes, treatments or diets. This month and the next few months are times for researching these things. You can act on them later on, after you have resolved all doubts.

Career is still important, but a little less so than last month. 70% to 80% of the planets are still above the horizon, but the 10th House becomes less active. Your 4th House, as in the past few months, is still empty. It's still wise to focus on your career and let emotional and family issues be downplayed. Like last month, career is still very exciting. Change, surprise, sudden twists and turns are still the rule. Any good thing can happen at any time.

The planetary power has now shifted (decisively) to the Eastern sector of the chart. This means that there is less need to adapt to unpleasant situations. You have more independence and can change situations or create new ones if need be. Personal will and power are stronger. This is going to be a trend for the next few months. You'd be very wise now to get clear as to what you want to create and what will make you happy. (Mercury's retrograde from the 26th onwards might be a good time to indulge in these explorations.) Once you are clear your creations will happen faster and more easily. The world is starting to adapt to you rather than vice versa. Foreign assignments or involvement with foreigners are still very prominent careerwise.

Romance is definitely on the upswing for singles. Jupiter, your Love Planet, starts moving forward on the 4th and receives beautiful aspects from many planets. A current relationship starts moving forward again. Love opportunities come into your neighbourhood, in school or at meetings seminars or clubs and organizations to which you belong. Friends like to play Cupid this month. A Grand Trine in Fire all month is definitely helping – bringing optimism, confidence and energy to your love life. It sparkles. Your social magnetism is much stronger. You are like a magnet for love. It can come at the supermarket, the car dealership or car repair shop, the library or as you go about your daily chores. Love is everywhere.

Finances are still status quo, though like last month your career success can't help but boost your bottom line. But overall earnings should be stronger from the 1st to the 16th, as the Moon waxes, than at other times. I think you like the fact that money can come from anywhere and that it has no 'fixed' tendency. It's a liberating attitude.

May

Best Days Overall: 3rd, 4th, 12th, 13th, 21st, 22nd, 30th, 31st

Most Stressful Days Overall: 10th, 11th, 16th, 17th, 23rd, 24th

Best Days for Love: 8th, 9th, 16th, 17th, 18th, 25th, 26th, 27th, 28th, 29th

Best Days for Money: 1st, 2nd, 6th, 7th, 8th, 9th, 10th, 11th, 16th, 17th, 19th, 20th, 21st, 25th, 26th, 27th, 30th, 31st

Two eclipses and a dynamic T-square ensure that the month ahead will be volatile and full of change. Volatility is neither good nor evil. It's just something to be handled. Its virtue is that it breaks attachments to the wrong things and sets us free. Its challenge is that if we resist too much it can be unpleasant. Sit loose to change. Embrace it. Make it your friend. See it as your liberator and all will go well. Fasten your seat belt and keep your 'eyes on the prize'.

Health is reasonable this month and will improve after the 21st. Still, you needn't and shouldn't burn the candle at both ends, but focus on your priorities.

Most of the planets are still above the horizon, but a gradual shift is taking place towards the lower half of the Horoscope. By next month the shift will be complete. In the meantime, continue to focus on your career.

60% to 70% of the planets are in the East and your own Sign of Gemini is becoming more powerful beginning on the 21st. Thus, you can and should have your way this month. Set your own course and let the world adapt to you.

The Lunar eclipse of the 16th occurs in your 6th House of Health and Work. This shows job changes (which could happen as a delayed reaction and not exactly on the 16th) or important changes in the conditions of the work place. Health changes are also brewing – though, as mentioned, you should be cautious here until you have all the facts. Every Lunar eclipse affects you financially, since the Moon is your Financial Planet. Thus, you will have opportunities to see fallacies in your financial thinking, strategies or investments and thus be able to correct and fine-tune them.

The Solar eclipse of May 31 is much stronger on you, so take a reduced schedule a few days before and a day after. This eclipse occurs in your own Sign and suggests important and long-term changes to your image, appearance and self-concept. Basically this is a healthy thing, but an eclipse tends to 'force it'. It's nice to be able to take the time to re-define one's personality and fine-tune one's image – when it's forced we feel some discomfort. Impurities in the body could come up for cleansing as well – best to co-operate with the process.

Love is more complicated this month as your need for seclusion, spiritual urges or your charitable and philanthropic interests clash with your beloved. These clashes are short term and will resolve themselves by next month.

June

Best Days Overall: 1st, 9th, 10th, 17th, 18th, 27th, 28th

Most Stressful Days Overall: 9th, 10th, 17th, 18th

Best Days for Love: 4th, 5th, 7th, 8th, 13th, 14th, 17th, 18th, 22nd, 23rd, 27th, 28th

Best Days for Money: 1st, 2nd, 3rd, 4th, 5th, 9th, 10th, 13th, 14th, 17th, 18th, 22nd, 23rd, 29th, 30th

Mercury, your Ruling Planet, is now forward and moving very fast. The dominance of power is in the Eastern sector. Your own Sign of Gemini is very strong and your 1st House of Self, likewise. Now is the time to build your life as you desire it to be. To create new conditions. To create your Eden. Your way is the best way – at least for you. You know more about your needs than others do and you are best qualified to make these kinds of decisions. While you should never be rude or disdainful, let the world adapt to you. True, you might face much resistance on this path; it's not a smooth ride – but it's a very worthwhile one.

Health is mixed this month. Saturn leaving your Sign is a wonderful factor long-term, but no sooner does Saturn leave than Mars moves into stressful alignment with you on the 16th. Yes, you've turned a corner healthwise, but you still have to give it attention. The main health danger now is 'over-ambition' – or over-work. Your career is important, but work towards it in a balanced way. Mars will be conjunct with Uranus in your 10th House of Career for a good part of the month (the aspect is exact on the 23rd), showing volatility and change. Perhaps the job you took was not what you bargained for. This aspect will trigger the 'urge to experiment' that we've written about in past months.

By the 10th, the planetary power will be weighted below the horizon. Thus you need to start paying attention to your emotional needs and to how you feel. Family and domestic issues also start becoming more important. You won't be able to ignore career, as your 10th House is very strong, but you can shift some emphasis.

Finances are much stronger and more important than they've been all this year. Your 2nd House of Finance is now a House of Power and 30% to 40% of the planets will either be there or pass through there in the month ahead. Prosperity is increased to be sure, but you need to manage your wealth and earnings properly. With Saturn's advent into your Money House (he will be there for two more years), consider yourself a 'wealth trainee' – getting an internship in the art of getting rich. Those of you who are already rich will learn how to get even richer.

Love and romance are much improved since last month. Increased self-esteem and self-confidence are major factors. You look better and you are more attractive. A current relationship is much more harmonious. Singles still find love in the neighbourhood, with neighbours, at school, the library or at seminars.

From June 10 onwards, your sense of style is very strong – a good time to buy the wardrobe or accessories you need.

July

Best Days Overall: 6th, 7th, 14th, 15th, 24th, 25th

Most Stressful Days Overall: 4th, 5th, 10th, 11th, 17th, 18th, 31st

Best Days for Love: 2nd, 3rd, 8th, 9th, 10th, 11th, 17th, 18th, 19th, 20th, 28th, 29th, 30th

Best Days for Money: 2nd, 3rd, 8th, 9th, 10th, 11th, 17th, 18th, 19th, 20th, 26th, 27th, 28th, 29th, 30th

Retrograde activity increases this month and, by the 29th, 40% of the planets are retrograde. Things are slowing down in the world, but you are making good personal progress. Mercury, your Ruler, is moving unusually fast. Likewise Jupiter, your Love Ruler.

60% to 70% of the planets are below the horizon this month. And though your 10th House of Career is still powerful, the planets involved with it are *ALL* retrograde. Thus, you can safely let go of career issues for a while and focus on your domestic and family life – most importantly on your inner state: your moods and emotional comfort zone. Though you have strong urges for more career changes (and some of you might be forced to make these kinds of decisions), if you have options, delay. Think things through more. Things are not the way they seem at the moment.

Most of the planets are still in the East, so continue to build your life as you desire it to be. You can have your way and the world will adapt to you – eventually.

Finances are still strong. Media activities, public relations, sales and marketing are all paths to increased wealth. Spare cash should be used to pay off debt. Yet, good debt – leverage – if used properly can also bring more prosperity. Look for opportunities in things that other people might consider 'junk'. There are wealth opportunities right in the neighbourhood. You have a good instinct for this kind of thing these days. The Lord of your 5th House's move into your Money House suggests earnings from speculations or creative projects – of course, speculations should be well hedged. Don't speculate with more than you can afford to lose. Saturn abhors speculation, but rewards a calculated, well-hedged risk. Looks like Geminis are buying new toys this month – children's or adult toys – entertainment equipment, CDs, DVDs, camcorders and the like. You are also spending on yourself – investing in yourself – this is always the best investment.

From the 23rd onwards, you enter one of the best social periods of your year. Enjoy. Singles meet significant others. Current relationships are taken to the next level. Marrieds have more romance in the marriage. The neighbourhood is still the scene of the action.

Geminis are always taking classes in one thing or another, but now they are indulging this even more. There is more domestic travel this month, too.

August

Best Days Overall: 2nd, 3rd, 11th, 12th, 20th, 21st, 22nd, 30th

Most Stressful Days Overall: 1st, 7th, 13th, 14th, 27th, 28th

Best Days for Love: 7th, 8th, 16th, 17th, 26th, 27th, 28th

Best Days for Money: 6th, 7th, 8th, 16th, 17th, 23rd, 24th, 26th, 27th, 28th

This is not a month to be playing games with your health, Gemini. Health needs to be watched all year, but especially so in the coming month – from the 22nd onwards. 70% to 80% of the planets are in stressful alignment with you – so be serious now. Success, this month, is not measured in cash, deals or romantic conquests. Just getting through with your health and sanity intact is a major victory. You can do it. The most important thing is to keep your energy levels high. If you can take a holiday now (without losing your job), definitely do so. Reduce activities as much as possible. Take naps when you feel tired. If you must work, work to a rhythm and take frequent breaks. Try to alternate activities. Do mental work for a while and then switch to something physical, then switch to something social. Give the different brain centres time to recharge themselves. When you work, try to avoid build-ups of stress. Check the back of your neck and your shoulders. If they are tense, massage them or stretch. If you can afford it, schedule extra visits with a masseuse, reflexologist, acupuncturist or other natural practitioner. If this is too expensive, try to massage your own feet, hands and head regularly. The idea is to energize the whole system.

Avoid power struggles (though this will be difficult), 'agree with thine adversary quickly', avoid unnecessary thinking or talking.

Learn the art of relaxation – physical and mental. Go to sleep early and get up late (or whenever you feel you really want to be out of bed). Of course, if you work for others this will be difficult. If you work for yourself it is easier.

If you follow these simple rules, you should get through with flying colours.

Your 4th House of Home and Family becomes very powerful this month. You are called now to find your emotional comfort zone and to function from there. By the way, this will help your overall health too. The problem isn't *finding* it, but being able to *stay* there – there are so many distractions and pulls on you – social demands, career demands, etc. Many of you are moving or planning on moving now. Try to organize this in the least stressful way – even if you have to spend more money.

The three planets involved in your career are still retrograde, so although you are sorely tempted, try to avoid important career decisions this month.

Be patient in love issues this month.

September

Best Days Overall: 7th, 8th, 17th, 18th, 26th, 27th

Most Stressful Days Overall: 3rd, 4th, 9th, 10th, 24th, 25th, 30th

Best Days for Love: 3rd, 4th, 5th, 6th, 14th, 15th, 16th, 17th, 24th, 25th, 26th, 27th, 30th

Best Days for Money: 5th, 6th, 14th, 15th, 19th, 20th, 26th, 27th

Refer to our health discussion last month. The unusual stressful alignment is in effect until the 23rd. After that things get much easier – but not so easy that you can take your health for granted.

Career focus is easing up this month as Uranus leaves your 10th House of Career and moves back into your 9th House. You are still in a period where emotional and domestic harmony are most important. Moves, big-ticket items for the home, pregnancies, births, the fortunate buying or selling of a home are all likely this month.

Having gone through some unusual stress for a month, the Cosmos will give you a holiday – a play period – after the 23rd. There will be more leisure activities and more interest in exploring the joy of life.

Your Love Planet made a major move into Virgo from Leo late last month. This has changed your whole attitude to love. When Jupiter was in Leo, love was about a 'good time' – another source of fun and amusement. Now you seem more careful about love. You want perfection. You want purity in the relationship. A healthy love life is just as important to you as a healthy body. The danger here is that your pursuit of perfection can make you hyper-critical and judgemental of your partner, lover or spouse. This will not help romance. Look for constructive ways to make improvements, but avoid judgement and condemnation. Also realize that purity in love will happen as a process and not overnight. Patience and understanding will go a long way in solving romantic tangles. Rejoice when progress is made, even though the goal seems far off. Singles will now find love close to home or through family members. Old flames can come back into the picture. Emotional support is the way you show love and what you expect in love. Many of you want to marry now, so that you can raise a family.

Finances are reasonable this month. Earnings come much more easily before the 23rd than afterwards. Earning power will be strongest from the 1st to the 10th as the Moon waxes. The Full Moon of the 10th brings a windfall or opportunity through your career or by way of parents, bosses or elders. Take a reduced schedule that day. The need to manage your wealth better is still prominent.

At the end of the month, throw yourself a nice party and congratulate yourself for getting through a difficult period unscathed.

October

Best Days Overall: 4th, 5th, 14th, 15th, 23rd, 24th

Most Stressful Days Overall: 1st, 7th, 8th, 21st, 22nd, 27th, 28th

Best Days for Love: 1st, 2nd, 3rd, 4th, 5th, 11th, 12th, 13th, 16th, 17th, 21st, 22nd, 25th, 26th, 27th, 28th, 29th, 30th

Best Days for Money: 2nd, 3rd, 4th, 5th, 11th, 12th, 13th, 14th, 15th, 16th, 17th, 18th, 21st, 22nd, 25th, 26th, 29th, 30th

Health is getting better and better. But a dynamic T-square in mutable Signs all month still suggests caution. However, if you got through August and September, October will be a breeze by comparison. Your 6th House of Health becomes powerful after the 23rd and this shows that you are on top of things and giving priority to health issues.

The planetary power is now mostly in the Western sector of the chart – the social sector. Thus, independence and self-will must give way to consensus and co-operation. It is difficult now to change conditions by your own efforts or to attain goals on your own. Adapt and cultivate the graces of others. Others probably see more of the overall picture than you do, and thus your way might not be best.

Most of the planets are still below the horizon of your chart and your 4th House of Home and Family is much stronger than your 10th House of Career. Thus, continue to focus on emotional issues, the right inner state, and setting up a stable home base. Career is important, to be sure, but you can shift your emphasis.

The cosmic holiday that began last month is still in effect for most of this month. It is playtime – and you deserve it. Leisure and creative activities are called for. This is a great period for taking up a creative hobby. By the 23rd, the emphasis will shift to work – you get more serious.

The T-square we discussed earlier involves your Love Planet, so a current relationship is being challenged. Part of the problem is work and career, which perhaps distract you from your lover or spouse. Your lover might also be in conflict with dear friends and this is complicating things. Your need to focus on health could also cause complications. Somehow you've got to get these unruly children to co-operate with each other and not pull you in all directions. It is unlikely that you will earn acclaim from everyone. But if you give each their due, you will at least have the acclaim of yourself.

Finances get much easier after the 23rd. Your ability to cut costs, reduce debt and raise outside capital is greatly increased. In general, earning power will be strongest from the 1st to the 7th and from the 25th to the 31st – the times when the Moon will wax.

Job-seekers have wonderful aspects now. Pluto, your Work Planet, is moving forward and your 6th House of Work is powerful after the 23rd. Social connections seem the short-cut for getting work.

November

Best Days Overall: 1st, 2nd, 10th, 11th, 12th, 20th, 21st, 28th, 29th

Most Stressful Days Overall: 3rd, 4th, 18th, 19th, 24th, 25th, 30th

Best Days for Love: 5th, 6th, 8th, 9th, 15th, 16th, 18th, 19th, 24th, 25th, 26th, 27th

Best Days for Money: 3rd, 4th, 8th, 9th, 13th, 14th, 18th, 19th, 23rd, 24th, 26th, 27th

Once again this is another delicate health period. Not quite as difficult as August and September, but close. By the 23rd, 60% to 70% of the planets are arrayed in stressful alignment. Further, a Solar eclipse on the 23rd impacts strongly on you. Definitely reduce activities this month. Just getting through the month with your health and sanity intact will be a major victory.

Understand, when the Cosmos sends crisis your way, it is never punitive, but cathartic and redemptive. Crisis is beautiful when we understand it correctly. It is, as the sages say, 'the short-cut to heaven'. It builds character, teaches fortitude, reveals what your true priorities are and should be, uncovers the hidden obstacles that were blocking you so that you can do something about them and, perhaps most importantly, shows you who your true friends are. Quite a beautiful thing, this crisis. Often crisis is the answer to your prayers, though you don't see it at the time. For it is precisely through this crisis that your good will come to you. Right behind it is something very wonderful – your heart's true desire.

So, the important thing this month is to maintain both your energy and your wits. Refuse to let yourself get overtired, though you will be sorely tempted. When there is no petrol in the tank it is foolish to keep your foot on the pedal. Above all, keep your poise. If there are practical things you can do, do them. If not, let go and relax. Observe events non-judgementally. 'Agree with thine adversary quickly.' Avoid power struggles and needless confrontation. Keep fit to fight another day.

The Solar eclipse of the 23rd occurs in your 7th House of Love and Marriage. So either your marriage or your current relationship will get tested. Impurities, hidden grievances, etc. will come up. If love is real, the relationship will not only endure but emerge stronger. If love is not real, then it is good that the relationship dissolves. Singles might decide to marry during this period. The eclipse will either push a relationship to the next level or dissolve it. No more sitting on the fence; this is a time for action.

The Lunar eclipse of the 9th is much less stressful on you – still, it won't hurt to take a reduced schedule and avoid stressful, risky activities around that period. This eclipse occurs in your 12th House of Spirituality, announcing long-term changes in that department. Some of you might start on a spiritual path. Others might change their path or change their teachers, or change their techniques. There could be upheavals in your church or in charities that you are involved with.

Socially you are in one of the most active periods of the entire year – but also one of the most volatile.

December

Best Days Overall: 7th, 8th, 9th, 17th, 18th, 25th, 26th

Most Stressful Days Overall: 1st, 15th, 16th, 21st, 22nd, 27th, 28th

Best Days for Love: 5th, 6th, 15th, 16th, 21st, 22nd, 23rd, 24th, 25th, 26th

Best Days for Money: 2nd, 3rd, 4th, 5th, 6th, 10th, 11th, 12th, 13th, 14th, 15th, 16th, 23rd, 24th

Happily, your health is starting to improve day by day. Day by day, one planet after another leaves its stressful alignment with you – Mercury on the 2nd, Mars on the 16th and the Sun on the 22nd. The volatile T-square that's been hounding you dissipates by the 16th.

Your social life should be a lot calmer and happier too. You seem more in alignment with your beloved. There is harmony there. Singles still have great opportunities to meet someone new, for this is still a socially active month. Love is close to home. Love is passionate. Libido is unusually high. Hormones are flowing in torrents.

Most of the planets (as in the past few months) are still in the West and Mercury, your Ruling Planet, goes retrograde on the 17th. This reinforces the symbolism even further. Take a low profile; avoid power struggles or excessive self-will. Put other people first, cultivate the social graces and adapt yourself to situations. Do what is possible to do and then coast. Your good will come through others.

By the 22nd, the planets make a major shift to the upper half of the Horoscope, so you are becoming ever-more ambitious and concerned with outer success. Career is becoming ever-more exciting and any good thing can happen at any time. There is almost a breathless anticipation when it comes to your career.

Saturn in your Money House, urging conservatism and fiscal responsibility, is strongly out-powered this month. He is having a hard time keeping you in line. 'Watch out for over-spending,' he says. 'Keep Christmas in proportion, you've got nothing to prove to anyone.' It is doubtful whether you will listen. The good news is that money comes from your spouse or partner and your line of credit is increased. You also have a good eye for value where others see only 'junk' – and this perception can lead to nice profits. I know someone who hangs around local golf-courses collecting balls that no one wants. She sells many of them, the old ones for over $1,000 each – apparently they are collectors' items. Even the golfers don't realize it. This illustrates what we mean here. I don't know her chart, but for sure she has a strong 8th House.

Your power in the 8th House this month also makes it a good period for personal transformation, reinvention and deep psychological and domestic house-cleaning. Get rid of possessions, character traits or emotional patterns that are no longer useful to you. Make room for the new good that is constantly pouring in on you.

Cancer

♋

THE CRAB

Birthdays from

21st June

to 20th July

Personality Profile

CANCER AT A GLANCE

Element – Water

Ruling Planet – Moon

Career Planet – Mars
Love Planet – Saturn
Money Planet – Sun
Planet of Fun and Games – Pluto
Planet of Good Fortune – Neptune
Planet of Health and Work – Jupiter
Planet of Home and Family Life – Venus
Planet of Spirituality – Mercury

Colours – blue, puce, silver

Colours that promote love, romance and social harmony – black, indigo

Colours that promote earning power – gold, orange

Gems – moonstone, pearl

Metal – silver

Scents – jasmine, sandalwood

Quality – cardinal (= activity)

Quality most needed for balance – mood control

Strongest virtues – emotional sensitivity, tenacity, the urge to nurture

Deepest need – a harmonious home and family life

Characteristics to avoid – over-sensitivity, negative moods

Signs of greatest overall compatibility – Scorpio, Pisces

Signs of greatest overall incompatibility – Aries, Libra, Capricorn

Sign most helpful to career – Aries

Sign most helpful for emotional support – Libra

Sign most helpful financially – Leo

Sign best for marriage and/or partnerships – Capricorn

Sign most helpful for creative projects – Scorpio

Best Sign to have fun with – Scorpio

Signs most helpful in spiritual matters – Gemini, Pisces

Best day of the week – Monday

Understanding a Cancer

In the Sign of Cancer the heavens are developing the feeling side of things. This is what a true Cancerian is all about – feelings. Where Aries will tend to err on the side of action, Taurus on the side of inaction and Gemini on the side of thought, Cancer will tend to err on the side of feeling.

Cancerians tend to mistrust logic. Perhaps rightfully so. For them it is not enough for an argument or a project to be logical – it must feel right as well. If it does not feel right a Cancerian will reject it or chafe against it. The phrase 'follow your heart' could have been coined by a Cancerian, because it describes exactly the Cancerian attitude to life.

The power to feel is a more direct – more immediate – method of knowing than thinking is. Thinking is indirect. Thinking about a thing never touches the thing itself. Feeling is a faculty that touches directly the thing or issue in question. We actually experience it. Emotional feeling is almost like another sense which humans possess – a psychic sense. Since the realities that we come in contact with during our lifetime are often painful and even destructive, it is not surprising that the Cancerian chooses to erect barriers – a shell – to protect his or her vulnerable, sensitive nature. To a Cancerian this is only common sense.

If Cancerians are in the presence of people they do not know or find themselves in a hostile environment, up goes the shell and they feel protected. Other people often complain about this, but one must question these other people's motives. Why does this shell disturb them? Is it perhaps because they would like to sting and feel frustrated that they cannot? If your intentions are honourable and you are patient, have no fear. The shell will open up and you will be accepted as part of the Cancerian's circle of family and friends.

Thought-processes are generally analytic and dissociating. In order to think clearly we must make distinctions, comparisons and the like. But feeling is unifying and integrative.

To think clearly about something you have to distance yourself from it. To feel something you must get close to it. Once a Cancerian has accepted you as a friend he or she will hang on. You have to be really bad to lose the friendship of a Cancerian. If you are related to Cancerians they will never let you go no matter what you do. They will always try to maintain some kind of connection even in the most extreme circumstances.

Finance

The Cancerian has a deep sense of what other people feel about things and why they feel as they do. This faculty is a great asset in the workplace and in the business world. Of course it is also indispensable in raising a family and building a home, but it also has its uses in business. Cancerians often attain great wealth in a family type of business. Even if the business is not a family operation, they will treat it as one. If the Cancerian works for somebody else, then the boss is the parental figure and the co-workers are brothers and sisters. If a Cancerian is the boss, then all the workers are his or her children. Cancerians like the feeling of being providers for others. They enjoy knowing that others derive their sustenance because of what they do. It is another form of nurturing.

With Leo on their Solar 2nd House (of Money) cusp, Cancerians are often lucky speculators, especially with residential property or hotels and restaurants. Resort hotels and nightclubs are also profitable for the Cancerian. Waterside properties allure them. Though they are basically conventional people, they sometimes like to earn their livelihood in glamorous ways.

The Sun, Cancer's Money Planet, represents an important financial message: in financial matters Cancerians need to be less moody, more stable and fixed. They cannot allow their moods – which are here today and gone tomorrow – to get in the way of their business lives. They need to develop their self-esteem and feelings of self-worth if they are to realize their greatest financial potential.

Career and Public Image

Aries rules the 10th Solar House (of Career) cusp of Cancer, which indicates that Cancerians long to start their own business, to be more active publicly and politically and to be more independent. Family responsibilities and a fear of hurting other people's feelings – or getting hurt themselves – often inhibit them from attaining these goals. However, this is what they want and long to do.

Cancerians like their bosses and leaders to act freely and to be a bit self-willed. They can deal with that in a superior. Cancerians expect their leaders to be fierce on their behalf.

When the Cancerian is in the position of boss or superior he or she behaves very much like a 'warlord'. Of course the wars they wage are not egocentric but in defence of those under their care. If they lack some of this fighting instinct – independence and pioneering spirit – Cancerians will have extreme difficulty in attaining their highest career goals. They will be hampered in their attempts to lead others.

Since they are so parental, Cancerians like to work with children and make great educators and teachers.

Love and Relationships

Like Taurus, Cancer likes committed relationships. Cancerians function best when the relationship is clearly defined and everyone knows his or her role. When they marry it is usually for life. They are extremely loyal to their beloved. But there is a deep little secret that most Cancerians will never admit to: commitment or partnership is really a chore and a duty to them. They enter into it because they know of no other way to create the family that they desire.

Union is just a way – a means to an end – rather than an end in itself. The family is the ultimate end for them.

If you are in love with a Cancerian you must tread lightly on his or her feelings. It will take you a good deal of time to realize how deep and sensitive Cancerians can be. The smallest negativity upsets them. Your tone of voice, your irritation, a look in your eye or an expression on your face can cause great distress for the Cancerian. Your slightest gesture is registered by them and reacted to. This can be hard to get used to, but stick by your love – Cancerians make great partners once you learn how to deal with them. Your Cancerian lover will react not so much to what you say but to the way you are actually feeling at the moment.

Home and Domestic Life

This is where Cancerians really excel. The home environment and the family are their personal works of art. They strive to make things of beauty that will outlast them. Very often they succeed.

Cancerians feel very close to their family, their relatives and especially their mothers. These bonds last throughout their lives and mature as they grow older. They are very fond of those members of their family who become successful and they are also quite attached to family heirlooms and mementos. Cancerians also love children and like to provide them with all the things they need and want. With their nurturing, feeling nature, Cancerians make very good parents – especially the Cancerian woman, who is the mother par excellence of the Zodiac.

As a parent, the Cancerian's attitude is 'my children right or wrong.' Unconditional devotion is the order of the day. No matter what a family member does, the Cancerian will eventually forgive him or her, because 'you are, after all, family'. The preservation of the institution – the tradition – of the family is one of the Cancerian's main reasons for living. They have many lessons to teach others about this.

Being so family-orientated, the Cancerian's home is always clean, orderly and comfortable. They like old-fashioned furnishings but they also like to have all the modern comforts. Cancerians love to have family and friends over, to organize parties and to entertain at home – they make great hosts.

Horoscope for 2003

Major Trends

Last year was a year of great prosperity. Benevolent Jupiter was bringing financial opportunity and lots of good luck. This trend continues in 2003 – especially for the first half of the year.

In 2002, you were getting clear on love issues, formulating your ideals and your needs. This year love is coming into concrete manifestation. What was dreamed of in secret is now shouted from the rooftops.

Image and appearance issues were not a big deal last year, but this year they are becoming a big deal. Saturn will move into your own Sign on June 4 and stay there for the next two years or so. This will be a period where you get your body in order, lose weight, cut down on excesses and re-define your personality.

Religion, philosophy, higher education and your own view of the world have not been big issues for a long time. This year (and for many years to come) they do become important. Uranus begins a flirtation with your 9th House in the year ahead. Thus all these areas (and they have a far more lasting impact than you can imagine) are undergoing radical change. You will see how so much of your suffering and inability to accomplish had to do with your world view and personal metaphysics. Once these are changed, your world changes. The options available to you change. Sudden educational opportunities (and travel opportunities) will come, out of the blue – and you should take them. Education is a big interest in the year ahead.

Your paths to greatest fulfilment this year are: finance (until August 27); communication and intellectual interests (after August 27); spirituality (until April 14); friendships, groups and group activities (after April 14).

Health

Health aspects have been pretty reasonable the past few years. They are reasonable this year, but with an important difference: Saturn, as mentioned, moves into your Sign on June 4. The good news here is that you will feel more inclined to take up a steady, serious and disciplined health regime and lifestyle. The fact that your 6th House is a House of Power also reinforces this. Health is important to you – a priority – and you are likely to stay on top of things. You'll deal with problems promptly before they get out of hand.

Saturn in your own Sign produces many kinds of phenomena. People tend to feel older than they are – even young people feel old. People start thinking about old age – even if they are young. A feeling of seriousness, sobriety and sense of limits comes over a person. And while this is often good, if overdone it can lead to undue pessimism and depression. People start looking at worst-case scenarios in every situation.

Depression should be avoided like the plague. Where a Fire or Air Sign can get out of depression rather easily, not so with you – you feel it more deeply.

Depression is caused by various things – a wrong philosophy of life, negative thinking and, as mentioned, undue pessimism. But one of the leading causes of depression – which modern medicine doesn't yet acknowledge – is lack of energy and vitality. Perhaps we could argue that it is the *main* cause of depression (and also of physical illness). So you must guard against getting overly tired in the year ahead – against burning the candle at both ends. There is a need to pace yourself better and to get things done more efficiently with less waste of energy. By all means, rest when tired. Eliminate frivolous or wasteful activities. Focus on what is really important in your life. This is all Saturn wants from you.

Self-esteem could be better in the year ahead. Better to avoid ego games and ego conflicts and use the energy to further your goals. If self-esteem has been unrealistically high, Saturn will test it and bring it into balance. The same is true if self-esteem is unrealistically low. Saturn wants to give you a realistic – a functional – perspective on yourself and your abilities.

Pluto in your 6th House suggests that you benefit from de-tox regimes; on a psychological level the enjoyment of life – and overall happiness – is of itself a great health tonic. Many of you will benefit more from a night out on the town than from visits to health professionals.

Your heart and stomach should be given extra attention in the year ahead.

Home, Domestic and Family Issues

Though you are always interested in family issues, with your 4th House empty this year the interest is less intense. The Cosmos isn't pushing you one way or the other. You can make of this area what you will. I expect that in most major areas of the home and family life, the status quo will prevail.

Venus is your Home and Family Planet. As most steady readers know, she is a fast-moving planet, moving through all the Signs and Houses of the Horoscope in a given year.

Thus family relationships will tend to vary with the movements and aspects to Venus. Since these are short-term trends, we will cover them in the month-by-month forecasts.

Redecorating projects and entertaining from home will go better from February 5 to March 2, July 4 to July 29, September 15 to October 9 and November 27 to December 29.

In August, we can see the fortunate purchase or sale of a home (for those who are in the market). Others will probably acquire some big-ticket items for the home. Be careful of unrealistic spending during this period. Family members will be unusually supportive.

Love and Social Life

This is a very interesting area of life in the year ahead – especially for singles or those involved in their first marriage. For singles we can see marriage, as your Love Planet, Saturn, moves into your own Sign. The beautiful thing about this is that there's nothing much you need to do to attract this or find this. This love is pursuing you – and very methodically and calculatingly to boot. There is a long-term, patient campaign going on to win your heart and your hand. All you have to do is show up. Perhaps this person is older than you (not an old person, but only older than you) and more established than you are. He or she seems like a corporate or traditional type. It's unlikely that this person will show up with nose rings and tattoos all over the place. You might object in the beginning, as the person seems overly controlling. But he or she is going way out of his or her way to please you. You are number one in this person's life. A word of advice to this person – if you love this Cancerian, give him or her some breathing room.

In many cases, I can see a marriage or significant relationship with a boss or parent figure.

Those who are already married should have more romance within the marriage. Your spouse or partner makes you number one in his or her life. He or she is out to please you. You are getting your way in love this year.

For the past two years most of you craved a spiritually-orientated relationship. Spiritual comparability was perhaps most important. Now love is more physical – tangible. Love has to be expressed through the body.

Those of you working towards a second marriage have an exciting year ahead, too (and for many years to come). Your love life starts to get unusually exciting. New vistas open up. You are freer than you've been in a long time. You are meeting people suddenly and unexpectedly. Love can happen suddenly – and end suddenly. Uranus in your House of Marriage is not an especially good signal for marriage – because it destabilizes relationships. But it does show serial and exciting love affairs. There are numerous marriage opportunities.

Those working towards a third marriage need patience. There are no special trends in this area. Perhaps you lack interest or have a *laissez-faire* attitude. The Cosmos isn't pushing you one way or the other. I expect the status quo will prevail. Those married for the third time will stay married. Those who are single will stay single.

Your most active and happiest social periods this year will be from January 1 to March 27, May 21 to June 21, July 4 to July 29 and October 9 to November 22.

Children of marriageable age will have a status quo year. Grandchildren of marriageable age are likely to marry or be involved in a serious relationship (like a marriage) – love is blooming after August 27.

Finance and Career

Finances started becoming more important in the latter half of last year. This area is important (and happy) this year too.

When Jupiter moved into your Money House last summer, prosperity started to rain down on you. There was luck in speculations. You made fortunate business contacts. Some of you got involved in lucrative business partnerships. All of you received windfalls or financial opportunities in one form or another. This trend continues this year too. By the summer, most of your financial goals should be sated.

This is still a very good year for speculations, though of course never do this blindly – only under intuition and not with the mortgage or food money.

Money comes easily this year. The money that comes is 'happy money' – it comes as you're having fun, being creative, attending parties or engaging in sport. Perhaps you overhear something as you are playing football or leaving the theatre; perhaps you meet someone at a party who has good information for you. Creative projects are both fun and profitable.

Investors should look at the healthcare industry, utilities, banks, publishers and travel companies. Gold, too, looks like an interesting speculative investment. Of course, your individual horoscope, based on your precise time and place of birth, could modify what we say here.

This is an excellent year for getting out of debt. We see unusual co-operation between you and your lenders in the year ahead. Perhaps they enable you to refinance existing debt at more favourable rates, or stand ready to fund your creative projects. A good year, too, for attracting investors to your projects, if you have a good idea.

After the summer we see a new car and communication equipment coming to you – of good quality too.

The main financial danger in the year ahead is 'irrational exuberance'. Easy money can easily lead to hysteria or mania. This leads to mental mistakes – lack of judgement – rash and wild over-spending – and thus eventually to loss. But if you keep your ahead about you – enjoy your good fortune without losing perspective – it should be a great financial year.

You seem especially generous with children. Children old enough to be earning a living are prospering this year too.

(Often under this aspect, even young toddlers prosper as they come into windfalls from grandma or grandpa or some rich relation.)

Jupiter is your Health and Work Planet. His presence in your Money House is showing that much of your earnings will come in the normal way – through work. Probably there is a pay rise in store. Perhaps co-workers have an interesting money-making proposition. This transit is also showing that what you really crave is not 'riches' *per se*, but a feeling of financial health. Financial health is very different from vast sums in the bank. In fact it is not measured in quantitative terms. It is a feeling of financial freedom and comfort, a day-by-day living faith that your needs will be supplied abundantly, a sense of steady supply, the feeling of 'no lack' in your life, the state of 'taking no thought for the purse or what you shall eat or wear'. Many of you will aspire to this. And many of you will get 'closer' to it and will remember the feeling for the future.

Short-term financial trends are ruled by the Sun, your Financial Planet. Since the Sun moves through all the different Signs and Houses of your Horoscope in any given year, earnings and earnings opportunities tend to come to you in a variety of ways and through a variety of people. We will cover these trends in the month-by-month forecasts.

Every Solar eclipse tends to affect your finances and gives you the opportunity to correct flaws or misconceptions. So be aware of when these things happen. There are two Solar eclipses in the coming year; we will cover them in the month-by-month forecasts.

Though finances will be wonderful most of the year, I especially like July 29 to August 23.

Self-improvement

For the past two years, the main thrust of self-improvement has been in the spiritual life. Many of you have undertaken serious, scientific spiritual disciplines. You had a need to test 'inner, psychic' phenomena – to test the viability of the invisible. Many of you have undertaken disciplined spiritual regimes of the traditional sort. This was all part of the plan. Many fears and blocks were encountered and dealt with. More will be dealt with in the first half of 2003. Important lessons came on how the law of karma works – from your own personal experience. Perhaps the main lesson of the past two years was the development of unconditional love. In many cases, this didn't manifest as love the way people normally understand it, but more as a feeling of 'appreciation and understanding' – this is a higher form of love.

By June, the area of self-improvement will be about the ego, self-concept and self-esteem. Basically, the ego is getting a reality check this year. If it is all puffed up with no substance behind it, you'll find out right quick. On the other hand, if you've been underestimating yourself, you'll find that out, too.

The idea now is to put your ego into perspective. Your ego is not really you, but an instrument you use to achieve certain ends. It is good neither to over-estimate nor under-estimate the instrument. Good to avoid power struggles during the year ahead. Shine, but shine silently.

Month-by-month Forecasts

January

Best Days Overall: 6th, 7th, 8th, 16th, 17th, 25th, 26th

Most Stressful Days Overall: 2nd, 3rd, 9th, 10th, 23rd, 24th, 29th, 30th

Best Days for Love: 2nd, 3rd, 4th, 5th, 9th, 10th, 14th, 15th, 19th, 20th, 23rd, 24th, 27th, 28th, 29th, 30th

Best Days for Money: 1st, 2nd, 3rd, 9th, 10th, 11th, 12th, 13th, 19th, 20th, 23rd, 24th, 27th, 28th

Health is good right now, Cancer, and you are in a strong social and party period. Still, it won't hurt to rest and relax more until the 20th. After the 17th, there are no planets in your native element of Water (except for the Moon, on the 25th and 26th). Thus you will see more emotional insensitivity going on – don't take it personally. This is 'cosmic weather'. People are less in touch with their feelings. Don't be surprised at emotional eruptions over trifles either. The tendency will be to repress feelings, so when they do get expressed, they are way out of proportion.

70% to 80% of the planets are in your Western sector, and your 7th House of Love and Social Activities is very strong. Thus, this is a period for cultivating the social graces and for seeking consensus in your actions and plans. It is very difficult to attain goals now without the co-operation of others. Adapt to unpleasant situations as best you can, and avoid power struggles or too much self-will. Put other people first and your good will come to you naturally and normally. 'My strength is made perfect in your weakness.'

The upper and lower hemispheres of your chart are more or less in balance. Neither your 10th House of Career nor your 4th House of Family is powerful. So this is a month where you will focus on one area or the other (Home or Career) according to circumstances. You seem equally indifferent to, or equally interested in either.

You are in an unusually prosperous year and your long-term prospects are wonderful. But temporarily, with Jupiter retrograde in your Money House and with Mercury retrograde (from the 2nd to the 22nd), you could be experiencing delays and snafus. Probably big financial developments are happening, so more approvals and more people are involved. A business partnership seems in the works. Money (and financial opportunity) come from social connections or the generosity of your spouse or partner. There is a need to put the financial interests of others ahead of your own these days and to focus on helping other people prosper. This attitude naturally creates personal prosperity, by the karmic law.

After the 20th, channel spare cash towards debt repayment. It is a time for getting financially healthier, for reducing expenses and waste. Financial intuition is amazing this month – especially towards the end of the month. Your dreams have a strong financial import then. Many financial questions or confusions will be solved in dreams or through psychics and astrologers.

Though love and social activities are active, there is a need for caution as many planets involved in your love life are retrograde. Mercury is retrograde in your 7th House of Love from the 2nd to the 22nd. And Saturn, your actual Love planet, is retrograde all month. Don't try to rush love or judge it too much. Let love develop as it will. Your social judgement could be better too, so don't make any important decisions one way or another.

February

Best Days Overall: 3rd, 4th, 13th, 14th, 21st, 22nd

Most Stressful Days Overall: 5th, 6th, 19th, 20th, 25th, 26th

Best Days for Love: 1st, 2nd, 8th, 9th, 10th, 11th, 17th, 18th, 19th, 20th, 25th, 26th

Best Days for Money: 1st, 2nd, 5th, 6th, 10th, 11th, 15th, 16th, 21st, 23rd, 24th

Like last month, the planetary power is almost all in the West. Your 7th House of Social Activities (and other people in general) is very strong, while your 1st House of the Self is empty (except for the Moon on the 13th and 14th). Thus, like last month, this is a time for compromise and consensus. Difficult to go it alone or have your way. It has to be 'our' way. So again, adapt and take a low profile. Put other people first.

By the 4th, the dominance of planetary power will have shifted to the upper half of your Horoscope. You are getting more ambitious and it is a time to push them forward. Ambitions have not yet reached their peak – but their importance will now grow stronger every month.

Health is good this month and will get even better after the 19th. With your Health Planet still retrograde, this is not a time for making major changes to your diet or health regime. It is a time for studying and researching these things. Health is enhanced through de-tox type regimes and through strengthening the liver, thighs and heart.

Financially, the trends of last month continue. This is a good time to pay off debt and to help other people prosper – to put their financial interests ahead of your own. (This doesn't mean that you cheat yourself, but that you think of the prosperity of others – you prosper as you help others to do so.) Your spouse or partner is prospering and continues to be generous. Job-seekers should be more patient now and research job offers more carefully. Things are not what they seem. The 17th brings a sudden financial windfall or opportunity – out of the blue. After the 19th, financial opportunity can come from foreign lands or with foreigners. Keeping a positive attitude and understanding the metaphysical laws of wealth will also bring strong results.

Career is furthered in the old-fashioned way – through work.

Your love life is getting better day by day. Saturn, your Love Planet, will start moving forward on the 22nd, removing obstacles, restoring confidence and helping a current relationship move forward. Venus in your 7th House of Love from the 4th onwards shows romance, parties, going out, etc. You are socializing with the young and the beautiful. Love is very idealistic this period – it has been that way for a number of years, but especially so now. Spiritual compatibility is perhaps the most important of the compatibilities these days. There is high glamour in your social sphere these days.

March

Best Days Overall: 2nd, 3rd, 12th, 13th, 21st, 29th, 30th, 31st

Most Stressful Days Overall: 5th, 6th, 19th, 25th, 26th

Best Days for Love: 1st, 10th, 11th, 19th, 20th, 21st, 25th, 26th, 27th, 28th, 29th, 30th

Best Days for Money: 2nd, 3rd, 5th, 6th, 12th, 13th, 14th, 15th, 22nd, 23rd

Career urges are intensifying. By the 4th, 70% to 80% of the planets will be above the horizon. Your 10th House will become ultra-powerful after the 21st, while your 4th House of Home, Family and Emotional Issues will be empty (except for the Moon's visit on the 19th). 80% to 90% of the planets are moving forward this month. So, this is a time for pushing hard for career objectives. Success and rapid forward progress is likely. Let go of family issues for the time being and seize the 'outer' opportunities coming your way. Pay rises and promotions are likely this period. You catch the favourable eye of bosses and superiors. Your good professional reputation brings financial opportunity to you. You are recognized for your contributions. Career can be enhanced through networking and the right social connections.

The planets are still mostly in the West, like last month. Gradually, the percentage is changing. By the 21st, the Eastern sector is stronger than last month, but not yet dominant. So you are slightly more independent now, but still need to operate by consensus and through the exercise of social skills. Avoid self-will and too much independence. The time will soon come when you can have things your way. In the meantime, coast and prepare.

Love is a little less romantic this month. Practical issues dominate. You are allured by people who can help your career. Much of your social life revolves around business or career. There is romantic opportunity with a boss or with someone involved in your career. The main danger to romance is a power struggle. You seem more socially aggressive these days and are reaching out to others.

Finances are a high priority this month – much more important to you than they've been in a while. A happy financial opportunity (perhaps a job offer) comes around the 21st as the Sun crosses the Midheaven of your Horoscope. This could happen later for those of you born later in the Sign. Speculations turn favourable after the 21st. Money is earned easily and creatively. Be careful of over-spending. You will have more, so you can spend more, but keep things in proportion.

Health is wonderful for most of the month, but rest and relax more after the 21st. Pace yourself as you focus only on what's important to you.

Your 8th and 9th Houses are very powerful this month. Thus, it is still a time for helping others prosper, paying off debt, breaking addictions and changing undesirable habits, and for personal transformation.

Foreign lands call to many of you. There is foreign travel on the horizon – perhaps related to business. Educational opportunities will also come. Overall, a happy and optimistic month.

April

Best Days Overall: 8th, 9th, 10th, 17th, 18th, 26th, 27th

Most Stressful Days Overall: 1st, 2nd, 15th, 16th, 21st, 22nd, 28th, 29th

Best Days for Love: 6th, 7th, 8th, 9th, 15th, 16th, 17th, 18th, 21st, 22nd, 23rd, 24th, 28th, 29th

Best Days for Money: 1st, 2nd, 11th, 12th, 19th, 20th, 21st, 28th, 29th

The planetary power helping your career is peaking this month. Like last month, 70% to 80% of the planets are above the horizon. But your 10th House of Career is even stronger than last month. You are in a yearly career peak – go for it full-speed ahead. Bosses and elders are still supporting your financial goals and this is still a good month for getting a pay rise or promotion. Family seems very supportive of your career goals as well – so you are not really sacrificing your family life here. Family members also seem ambitious now and your success helps them. After the 21st, your career is helped by your inner vision. You have a dream and are working hard to execute it. Psychics and astrologers have important career guidance for you as well. Career guidance might come in dreams or as hunches. Job-seekers have beautiful aspects now and Jupiter's forward motion on the 4th shows clarity and good judgement.

Overall health is good, but more rest and relaxation are called for until the 20th. With Jupiter moving forward on the 4th, you can make those health regime or dietary changes that you've been researching.

The planetary shift to the Eastern sector of your Horoscope gets even stronger after the 21st. Now you have less need to compromise or adapt to unpleasant situations. You are more independent and can go it alone if necessary. This trend will continue over the next few months. Start thinking about how you want to design your life and then put your design into action, little by little.

Mercury's retrograde from the 26th onwards affects your dream life and ESP faculties. They need more verification. Probably what you dream is accurate, but your interpretation could be amiss.

Finances are amazingly strong until the 20th. After the 20th, you might have to work a little harder for your money. Jupiter's forward motion in your Money House shows that assets you own increase in value and indicates luck in speculations. Bumps on the road notwithstanding, wealth is on the increase.

Your love life is less active after the 21st, but also less turbulent. Like last month, you seem interested in people of high status and those who can help your career. You tend to see marriage as a career move. But this attitude changes after the 21st. The need for spiritual values in a relationship still prevails.

Friendships and group activities become important after the 14th. The North Node of the Moon moves into your 11th House of Friends and will stay there for the rest of the year. This shows that there is deep fulfilment from pursuing these interests. The Sun will move into this House on the 20th, showing that there are practical, bottom-line advantages to friendships and group activities as well. They support your financial goals and provide you with opportunities.

May

Best Days Overall: 6th, 7th, 14th, 15th, 23rd, 24th

Most Stressful Days Overall: 12th, 13th, 18th, 19th, 25th, 26th, 27th

Best Days for Love: 3rd, 4th, 8th, 9th, 12th, 13th, 18th, 19th, 21st, 22nd, 28th, 29th, 30th, 31st

Best Days for Money: 1st, 2nd, 8th, 9th, 10th, 11th, 16th, 17th, 19th, 20th, 21st, 25th, 26th, 27th, 30th, 31st

More than any other Sign, you are most affected by the Moon. Its position, aspects and phases have a direct and dramatic impact on you. 90% of what you feel on a given day has to do with the Moon. So, when we have two New Moons in a month, this is a headline for you. Throw in two eclipses (one of them Lunar) and we have a month of long-term change and adjustment. A good thing, too. The Cosmos needs to prepare you for Saturn coming into your Sign next month.

The two New Moons occur in your 11th and 12th Houses. This shows that you will be receiving information and clarity about friendship issues, organizations you belong to, technological know-how, and spiritual revelation. A New Moon for you is like a 'mini birthday' – it's a new cycle, a new incarnation. The old is over with and you start fresh. It's a happy time.

You should take a reduced schedule during every Lunar eclipse (there are usually about two a year). Since the Moon is your Ruling Planet, every Lunar eclipse brings an opportunity to improve your image and re-define your personality. The Lunar eclipse of the 16th occurs in your 5th House, showing long-term changes with children (these can be normal things like graduation, marriage, moving out, childbirth or pregnancy, depending on your stage of life) creative projects and a love affair (outside of marriage). Happily this eclipse is benign to you. Wouldn't hurt, though, to avoid speculations around this period. This eclipse makes aspects to Jupiter, the Lord of your 6th House, so job changes (and for the better) are in store. Likewise with health regimes, diets or doctors.

The Solar eclipse of the 31st is a more spiritual eclipse. It occurs in your 12th House of Spirituality. This eclipse is going to increase your dream life a hundred-fold, but don't take these things at face value – much of what you see is flotsam generated by the eclipse. But you can expect much spiritual revelation and understanding to come as the eclipse blasts away psychological and mental barriers. Many will change their prayer and meditation regimes or change teachers. Others will embark on a spiritual discipline for the first time.

Every Solar eclipse also brings financial changes. A good thing. You get many opportunities to fine-tune your investments and investment strategies. It's like your Cosmic Teacher grades you twice a year. If there are weaknesses, you get a chance to correct them before they get way out of hand. The financial changes of this eclipse are going to be good – much better than even you expect. Any upheaval is going to lead to greater profits and greater wealth. You just have to wait for the dust to settle and not judge.

June

Best Days Overall: 2nd, 3rd, 11th, 12th, 19th, 20th, 30th

Most Stressful Days Overall: 9th, 10th, 15th, 16th, 22nd, 23rd

Best Days for Love: 1st, 7th, 8th, 10th, 11th, 15th, 16th, 17th, 18th, 19th, 27th, 28th, 29th

Best Days for Money: 1st, 4th, 5th, 9th, 10th, 13th, 14th, 17th, 18th, 22nd, 23rd, 29th, 30th

Though on a long-term basis you need to watch your health more, this period you get a lot of help from other planets. Health will be good. You are more concerned with financial health at the moment and that too is very good. Saturn moving into your own Sign on the 4th represents a significant turning-point in your life. It is time to re-organize and re-structure; time to face realities which you have pushed under the rug; time to build a foundation for the future and make a frank assessment of yourself; time to take on more responsibility and stop looking for the 'easy way out' of situations; time to take a long-term perspective on things – especially your life.

60% of the planets are now in the East and your 1st House of Self is one of the strongest in the Horoscope. Thus you are independent and have both the power and the ability to create conditions as you like them. It is a time for having your way in life. Others will conform to you. And while it is never necessary to be rude, arrogant or high-handed, it is necessary for you to stick to your guns and go your own way. Only you know what is best for you.

When the 1st House is powerful, as it is this month, it is time for sensual pleasures and the fulfilment of sensual fantasies. It is a time to pamper yourself and treat yourself. (It's about giving the body its due.) Usually the danger is excess, but with Saturn in your own Sign this is not likely to happen.

This month, the planets make an important shift from the upper half to the lower half of your Horoscope. This shows a shift in attitude – a shift from ambition and career urges to your first love: home, family and emotional issues. The shift will be completed by the end of the month, but you are feeling the stirrings of this much earlier. Yet, important career changes are happening this month and this is all part of it. Mars, your Career Planet, begins an important six-month transit in the Sign of Pisces on the 17th. Thus many of you are finding that you need more education to advance your career and are seeking it. Mars will conjunct Uranus – the planet of sudden changes – from the 17th onwards (though the aspect will be exact on the 23rd). Thus there are sudden career changes happening. Some take a different career path, some change jobs, some are offered new jobs at other companies. Many are opting for more free time to be with their families and to cultivate emotional harmony.

Finances are truly wonderful this month. Speculations are favourable. Lady luck is with you. Intuition is powerful until the 21st and this is the shortcut to your financial goals. After the 21st, you are taking more personal control over this area. You adopt the image of success and invest in yourself.

Love is happy this month. You get your way and are being pursued. Lovers or spouses are bending over backwards to please you.

July

Best Days Overall: 8th, 9th, 17th, 18th, 26th, 27th, 28th

Most Stressful Days Overall: 6th, 7th, 12th, 13th, 19th, 20th

Best Days for Love: 7th, 8th, 9th, 12th, 13th, 16th, 17th, 18th, 26th, 28th, 29th

Best Days for Money: 2nd, 3rd, 8th, 9th, 10th, 11th, 17th, 18th, 19th, 20th, 29th, 30th

The past two years have been intensely spiritual. There was much inner growth and progress. Many of you tried to repress these experiences, but found that you could not and had to accept their reality (at least some of it). Now the time has come to apply what you have learned in the world and in your daily and personal life. This is the acid test.

Your independence and personal power are still very strong in the month ahead. Continue to build your life as you desire it to be, slowly, methodically, scientifically and thoroughly. Take a long-term perspective as you work to achieve the achievable each day. Though the journey is a thousand miles, each step forward brings you closer to the goal. Eventually the goal won't matter, only the daily progress. Life is an endless journey and we must enjoy the road.

Health continues to be good. You look great – glamorous and magnetic. Your aesthetic sense is very strong and it is good time to buy personal accessories. (Many of these things are coming to you on their own.) Image-wise, you need to strike a balance between glamour and tradition. Classic styles suit you now. Many of you will favour darker colours for the next two years.

Love is exceptionally good. Some of you will have to fight suitors off with a stick. It is still a good time for getting your way in love.

Finance is the main headline this month. It is perhaps the most prosperous month of your year. Money is earned easily and effortlessly. Your assets increase in value. You are more interested in finance and your interest creates opportunity. Job-seekers have great success, especially after the 23rd. Your career is active, but much less important than it has been. After the 4th, the percentage of planets below the horizon increases further. Thus, your main desire is to feel good and to pursue ambitions from this 'feel-good' state. Family relationships seem very harmonious now.

The New Moon of the 29th occurs in your 2nd House of Money, adding further power to this area of life. You can expect all kinds of new financial information to come, clearing up any confusion and helping you make right decisions.

Family members become more supportive after the 29th. Buying or selling a home becomes favourable then too. Good communication – marketing, PR and sales efforts – are important after the 13th.

August

Best Days Overall: 4th, 5th, 13th, 14th, 23rd, 24th

Most Stressful Days Overall: 2nd, 3rd, 9th, 10th, 15th, 16th, 17th, 30th

Best Days for Love: 4th, 5th, 7th, 8th, 9th, 10th, 13th, 14th, 16th, 17th, 23rd, 24th, 27th, 28th

Best Days for Money: 6th, 7th, 8th, 16th, 17th, 25th, 26th, 27th, 28th

Retrograde activity increases this month. 40% of the planets are moving backwards through the zodiac. Thus, it's a good time to take stock and perfect plans and projects. 60% to 70% of the planets are still below the horizon of your chart and your Career Planet, Mars, is retrograde. Thus you can safely de-emphasize the career and focus on family and emotional issues.

Though over the long term you still need to pace yourself, health looks good this period. Your Health Planet, Jupiter, makes a major move from Leo into Virgo late in the month. Thus you are taking a new (and much better) attitude to health. Virgo is the Sign of health and the presence of your Health Planet in this Sign is very positive. You will be on top of things and give more attention to this area. Your Health Planet in your 3rd House (late in the month) suggests that health can be enhanced through a better diet and more attention paid to your intestines, lungs, arms and shoulders.

Most of the planets are still in the East (like last month), so it is still a good time for creating your life as you desire it to be. But with 40% of the planets retrograde, you will have to proceed with caution and your progress might not be as rapid as in the past. Still, you are independent and less at the mercy of other people.

Finances are unusually powerful until the 27th. By then, beneficial Jupiter should have done his work on you and you will be ready to focus on other things – developing your mind, reading, studying and travelling. Speculations are still favourable and unexpected windfalls could happen – especially around the 22nd and 23rd. This is a wonderful period for job-seekers as well. The family prospers. Property deals seem lucrative. Family is still supportive of your financial goals.

After the 23rd, sales, marketing and good communication seem to be the path to profits. Good use of the media and getting the word out about your product, service or yourself is essential to the bottom line. But from here on in, finance is becoming less of an interest.

Love is still very much in the air and, as mentioned in the yearly report, go slow and steady. No need to rush anything. Your social magnetism is very strong and you express it in a subtle, understated way. You keep your charms well hidden – but this modesty might even add to it. Many of you are already in a love relationship by now. If not, have no fear – it is on the way.

September

Best Days Overall: 1st, 2nd, 9th, 10th, 19th, 20th, 28th, 29th

Most Stressful Days Overall: 5th, 6th, 12th, 13th, 26th, 27th

Best Days for Love: 1st, 2nd, 5th, 6th, 9th, 10th, 16th, 17th, 19th, 20th, 26th, 27th, 28th, 29th

Best Days for Money: 5th, 6th, 14th, 15th, 22nd, 23rd, 26th, 27th

Like last month, most of the planets are still below the horizon, your 10th House of Career is still empty and your Career Planet is still retrograde (until the 27th). But this month, your 4th House of Home and Family becomes very powerful. So, even more than last month, this is a time for getting your home and family relationships in right order, for cultivating positive inner states of mind and for getting your emotional life in harmony. Career opportunities – no matter how lucrative – should be judged from the perspective of emotional harmony. If they don't violate it, all well and good. If they do, pass them by.

Your home and family life seem very happy this month. We see more social gatherings at home and general harmony. And if there are some family disputes, this is a time when peace and harmony can be restored.

By the 23rd, the balance of power is shifting from the East, where it has been for some months. This month you are in a cusp situation – a borderline zone. 50% of the planets are in the East and 50% in the West. Thus, you are neither very independent nor very dependent. There are times when you can have your way and times when you must seek consensus. There are situations that you can change and others you will just have to adapt to.

Like last month, the bottom line is enhanced through sales, marketing, media projects and good PR. After the 23rd, financial increase and opportunity can come from family or through family connections. You are spending more on the home and perhaps earning money from the home – working from home, etc.

Educational interests are still strong all month. Students should do well – though they will do even better when Mercury goes forward on the 20th.

Mercury's retrograde (as the Lord of your 12th House of Spirituality) suggests a need for more verification of dream and intuitive phenomena. It's not the dream or hunch that should be questioned, but the interpretation of it. Also be cautious about abruptly changing teachers or meditation regimes until Mercury goes forward on the 20th.

Health is more delicate after the 23rd, so be sure to rest and relax more, avoid power struggles and cultivate positive states of mind.

Love is a bit stormier this month than last month, but mostly after the 23rd. Your family and your beloved seem at odds. Family responsibilities seem to conflict with social urges. Perhaps there is some financial disagreement with your beloved. But these are all short-term phenomena and not the end of the relationship.

October

Best Days Overall: 7th, 8th, 16th, 17th, 18th, 25th, 26th

Most Stressful Days Overall: 2nd, 3rd, 9th, 10th, 23rd, 24th, 29th, 30th

Best Days for Love: 2nd, 3rd, 4th, 5th, 7th, 8th, 16th, 17th, 25th, 26th, 29th, 30th

Best Days for Money: 2nd, 3rd, 4th, 5th, 11th, 12th, 13th, 14th, 15th, 19th, 20th, 21st, 22nd, 25th, 26th, 29th, 30th

80% of the planets are now moving forwards. Thus there is rapid progress towards your goals. But this month, the balance of planetary power has shifted decisively to the West (where last month you were in a borderline situation). Thus, personal effort and self-assertion don't bring progress – it comes through others and their good graces. This is a time for shifting your gears. Cultivate the social graces, seek consensus and adapt to uncomfortable situations as much as possible.

Like last month, your Career House is empty and your 4th House of Home and Family is very powerful. Like last month, most of the planets are still below the horizon. So, continue to devote yourself to your family and to your inner, emotional life. Family issues still seem very happy (though they conflict with your social life). Family is still a source of financial support or financial opportunity. New communication equipment (or perhaps new phone lines and/or roads) are being installed in your home or neighbourhood this month. Until the 9th, it is still an excellent period for decorating or beautifying the home. Family gatherings or more entertaining from home are also happening.

The conflicts between family and your beloved will ease up by the 23rd. But on the 25th, Saturn, your Love Planet, starts to retrograde, so love becomes even more cautious and careful than it has been. Your social confidence is not up to its usual standards and important decisions concerning marriage or divorce or moving in together, should be delayed. Part of the complications of love is that you are in a mood to play and not be so serious. Fun-and-games types of opportunities come your way – or for your lover as well. Both of you could use some space.

Health is delicate until the 23rd, so keep in mind what we wrote last month. After the 23rd, there is great improvement. Health of children seems a concern as well.

Your 5th House becomes powerful after the 23rd, so make sure you have some fun during this period. This is the time for more leisure-type activity – for creativity – and for becoming like a little child (not childish, but like a child – there's a difference). Speculations become favourable and your personal creativity could lead to profits. Over-spending is the main financial danger after the 23rd. On the other hand, you earn money very easily.

Happy career opportunities come after the 23rd and now you can see why you needn't have worried about your career over the past few months. These opportunities don't seem to violate your emotional comfort zone.

There is a wonderful Grand Trine in Water from the 9th onwards which enhances your psychic ability, your emotional sensitivity and your general popularity. It is a good health signal too – though you should still pace yourself. People in general will be more warm and compassionate.

November

Best Days Overall: 3rd, 4th, 13th, 14th, 22nd, 23rd, 30th

Most Stressful Days Overall: 5th, 6th, 20th, 21st, 26th, 27th

Best Days for Love: 3rd, 4th, 5th, 6th, 13th, 14th, 15th, 16th, 22nd, 23rd, 25th, 26th, 27th, 30th

Best Days for Money: 3rd, 4th, 8th, 9th, 13th, 14th, 15th, 16th, 18th, 19th, 23rd, 24th, 26th, 27th

Retrograde activity lessens during this period and by the 8th, 90% of the planets will be forward. Like last month, it is a period of rapid progress towards your goals. Again like last month, aims are attained through consensus and the ability to gain the co-operation of others – not through self-assertion, independence or self-will. This is still a period to practise adaptability and flexibility.

Neither your 4th House of Home and Family nor your 10th House of Career is strong this month, but most of the planets are still below the horizon – so family and emotional issues are more important than career. With your 5th House very strong until the 22nd, children, in particular (whether they be your own or others), are important. You get on well with them, as your child-like attitude gives you common ground and good understanding.

The Grand Trine in Water that began last month will be in effect until the 23rd. This enhances your health, brings career and financial opportunity and makes you incredibly intuitive and compassionate. Social popularity increases this period.

Two eclipses – both basically benign to you – happen this month. These will shake up your environment but leave you unscathed – perhaps they will even clear the obstructions to your good. Wait till the dust settles from these things and walk into your kingdom of heaven.

The Lunar eclipse of the 9th occurs in your 11th House of Friends, showing that a friendship gets tested and purified. The air will be cleared. Long-simmering issues will surface so that you can take positive steps. If the friendship is real, it will become better than before. Upheavals could happen in an organization or at a club you belong to – changing your relationship to it. Every Lunar eclipse affects your image and self-concept and gives you an opportunity to change, improve and re-define these things.

The Solar eclipse of the 23rd occurs in your 6th House of Health and Work. Thus there are job changes in the works, or upheavals and changes at the work place. (Sometimes people don't leave their jobs, but other employees leave or get reshuffled, so that the conditions of the work place are changed – a new environment.) This eclipse could also signal long-term changes in your health regime, with doctors or with your diet. Flaws in your present regime are clearly revealed so that you can take positive steps. Every Solar eclipse affects finances, so you should be an experienced hand at these sort of upheavals. These eclipses give you regular opportunities to fine-tune and improve your financial strategy and investments.

Finances are strong this month in spite of the changes. Speculations are favourable until the 23rd. Personal creativity enhances the bottom line as well. After that money comes the old-fashioned way – through work.

December

Best Days Overall: 1st, 10th, 11th, 19th, 20th, 27th, 28th

Most Stressful Days Overall: 2nd, 3rd, 4th, 17th, 18th, 23rd, 24th, 30th, 31st

Best Days for Love: 1st, 5th, 6th, 10th, 11th, 15th, 16th, 19th, 20th, 23rd, 24th, 25th, 26th, 27th, 28th

Best Days for Money: 2nd, 3rd, 4th, 5th, 6th, 12th, 13th, 14th, 15th, 16th, 23rd, 24th

You are in a cusp situation (a borderline condition) this month, Cancer. The planetary power is shifting from the lower half of your Horoscope to the upper half. The shift will be complete by the 22nd. Also, on the 16th, Mars (your Career Planet) moves into your 10th House of Career (his own Sign and House). The message is clear: ambitions and career are becoming ever more important and need your attention. Let go – de-emphasize – family and emotional issues and push forward towards your outer goals.

Mercury goes retrograde on the 17th, so try to do your Christmas shopping before then. Your judgement will be better. (I especially like the 5th and 6th for these kinds of things, as there will be a Grand Trine in Earth.)

The planetary power is even more in the West than it was last month. Your 7th House of Love, Romance and Social Activities is very strong. This is one of your strongest social months this year. Like last month, this is a time for attaining your ends through charm, diplomacy and consensus, not through independence or self-will. With 90% of the planets forward, progress towards your goals should happen quickly.

You are very active socially and in your career, so try to pace yourself and focus on essentials. Health is more delicate this month – especially after the 23rd. Don't let financial stresses or worries (there's no real reason for them) affect your health. Your financial life, like everything else in life, moves in cycles. Take the temporary ups and downs in your stride.

Try to be more selective in your social life, too. You can't attend every party or gathering, or go out with every prospect. Be picky.

There are romantic opportunities galore this month. But the retrograde of your Love Planet shows a need for caution. Try to enjoy every opportunity for what it is without worrying too much about what the future may bring. Love is complicated by the fact that your beloved wants to be with you while you want to be out partying.

Money comes from work most of this month, but a lucky speculation or windfall could happen around the 11th to 13th. There is some tension at work regarding pay. Perhaps you feel that your efforts are not being rewarded as they should. But stay calm; after the 23rd, this issue will get resolved. Looks like you receive a sizeable bonus. After the 23rd, social connections and networking play an important role in finances. Your spouse or beloved supports your financial goals and provides you with opportunities. Job-seekers meet with good success after the 23rd.

Leo

♌

THE LION

Birthdays from

21st July

to 21st August

Personality Profile

LEO AT A GLANCE

Element – Fire

Ruling Planet – Sun
Career Planet – Venus
Love Planet – Uranus
Money Planet – Mercury
Planet of Health and Work – Saturn
Planet of Home and Family Life – Pluto

Colours – gold, orange, red

Colours that promote love, romance and social harmony – black, indigo, ultramarine blue

Colours that promote earning power – yellow, yellow-orange

Gems – amber, chrysolite, yellow diamond

Metal – gold

Scents – bergamot, frankincense, musk, neroli

Quality – fixed (= stability)

Quality most needed for balance – humility

Strongest virtues – leadership ability, self-esteem and confidence, generosity, creativity, love of joy

Deepest needs – fun, elation, the need to shine

Characteristics to avoid – arrogance, vanity, bossiness

Signs of greatest overall compatibility – Aries, Sagittarius

Signs of greatest overall incompatibility – Taurus, Scorpio, Aquarius

Sign most helpful to career – Taurus

Sign most helpful for emotional support – Scorpio

Sign most helpful financially – Virgo

Sign best for marriage and/or partnerships – Aquarius

Sign most helpful for creative projects – Sagittarius

Best Sign to have fun with – Sagittarius

Signs most helpful in spiritual matters – Aries, Cancer

Best day of the week – Sunday

Understanding a Leo

When you think of Leo, think of royalty – then you'll get the idea of what the Leo character is all about and why Leos are the way they are. It is true that, for various reasons, some Leos do not always express this quality – but even if not, they should like to do so.

A monarch rules not by example (as does Aries) nor by consensus (as do Capricorn and Aquarius) but by personal will. Will is law. Personal taste becomes the style that is imitated by all subjects. A monarch is somehow larger than life. This is how a Leo desires to be.

When you dispute the personal will of a Leo, it is serious business. He or she takes it as a personal affront, an insult. Leos will let you know that their will carries authority and that to disobey is demeaning and disrespectful.

A Leo is king (or queen) of his or her personal domain. Subordinates, friends and family are the loyal and trusted subjects. Leos rule with benevolent grace and in the best interests of others. They have a powerful presence; indeed, they are powerful people. They seem to attract attention in any social gathering. They stand out because they are stars in their domain. Leos feel that, like the Sun, they are made to shine and rule. Leos feel that they were born to special privilege and royal prerogatives – and most of them attain this status, at least to some degree.

The Sun is the Ruler of this Sign and when you think of sunshine it is very difficult to feel unhealthy or depressed. Somehow the light of the Sun is the very antithesis of illness and apathy. Leos love life. They also love to have fun; they love drama, music, the theatre and amusements of all sorts. These are the things that give joy to life. If – even in their best interests – you try to deprive Leos of their pleasures, good food, drink and entertainment, you run the serious risk of depriving them of the will to live. To them life without joy is no life at all.

Leos epitomize humanity's will to power. But power in and of itself – regardless of what some people say – is neither good nor evil. Only when power is abused does it becomes evil. Without power, even good things cannot come to pass. Leos realize this and are uniquely qualified to wield power. Of all the Signs, they do it most naturally. Capricorn, the other power Sign of the Zodiac, is a better manager and administrator than Leo – much better. But Leo outshines Capricorn in personal grace and presence. Leo loves power, where Capricorn assumes power out of a sense of duty.

Finance

Leos are great leaders, but not necessarily good managers. They are better at handling the overall picture than the nitty-gritty details of business. If they have good managers working for them they can become exceptional executives. They have vision and a lot of creativity.

Leos love wealth for the pleasures it can bring. They love an opulent lifestyle, pomp and glamour. Even when they are not wealthy they live as if they are. This is why many fall into debt, from which it is sometimes difficult to emerge.

Leos, like Pisceans, are generous to a fault. Very often they want to acquire wealth solely so that they can help others economically. Wealth to Leos buys services and managerial ability. It creates jobs for others and improves the general well-being of those around them. Therefore – to a Leo – wealth is good. Wealth is to be enjoyed to the fullest. Money is not to be left to gather dust in a mouldy bank vault but to be enjoyed, spread around, used. So Leos can be quite reckless in their spending.

With the Sign of Virgo on Leo's 2nd House (of Money) cusp, Leo needs to develop some of Virgo's traits of analysis, discrimination and purity when it comes to money matters. They must learn to be more careful with the details of finance (or to hire people to do this for them). They have to be more cost-conscious in their spending habits. Generally, they need to manage their money better. Leos tend to chafe under financial constraints, yet these constraints can help Leos to reach their highest financial potential.

Leos like it when their friends and family know that they can depend on them for financial support. They do not mind – even enjoy – lending money, but they are careful that they are not taken advantage of. From their 'regal throne', Leos like to bestow gifts on their family and friends and then enjoy the good feelings these gifts bring to everybody. Leos love financial speculations and – when the celestial influences are right – are often lucky.

Career and Public Image

Leos like to be perceived as wealthy, for in today's world wealth often equals power. When they attain wealth they love having a large house with lots of land and animals.

At their jobs, Leos excel in positions of authority and power. They are good at making decisions – on a grand level – but they prefer to leave the details to others. Leos are well respected by their colleagues and subordinates, mainly because they have a knack for understanding and relating to those around them. Leos usually strive for the top positions even if they have to start at the bottom and work hard to get there. As might be expected of such a charismatic Sign, Leos are always trying to improve their work situation. They do so in order to have a better chance of advancing to the top.

On the other hand, Leos do not like to be bossed around or told what to do. Perhaps this is why they aspire so for the top – where they can be the decision-makers and need not take orders from others.

Leos never doubt their success and focus all their attention and efforts on achieving it. Another great Leo characteristic is that – just like good monarchs – they do not attempt to abuse the power or success they achieve. If they do so, this is not wilful or intentional. Usually they like to share their wealth and try to make everyone around them join in their success.

Leos are – and like to be perceived as – hard-working, well-established individuals. It is definitely true that they are capable of hard work and often manage great things. But do not forget that, deep down inside, Leos really are fun-lovers.

Love and Relationships

Generally, Leos are not the marrying kind. To them relationships are good so long as they are pleasurable. When the relationship ceases to be pleasurable a true Leo will want out. They always want to have the freedom to leave. That is why Leos excel at love affairs rather than commitment. Once married, however, Leo is faithful – even if some Leos have a tendency to marry more than once in their lifetime. If you are in love with a Leo, just show him or her a good time. Travel, go to casinos and clubs, the theatre and discos. Wine and dine your Leo love – it is expensive but worth it and you will have fun.

Leos generally have an active love life and are demonstrative in their affections. They love to be with other optimistic and fun-loving types like themselves, but wind up settling with someone more serious, intellectual and unconventional. The partner of a Leo tends to be more political and socially conscious than he or she is and more libertarian. When you marry a Leo, mastering the freedom-loving tendencies of your partner will definitely become a life-long challenge – and be careful that Leo does not master you.

Aquarius sits on Leo's 7th House (of Love) cusp. Thus, if Leos want to realize their highest love and social potential, they need to develop a more egalitarian, Aquarian perspective on others. This is not easy for Leo, for 'the king' finds his equals only among other 'kings'. But perhaps this is the solution to Leo's social challenge – to be 'a king among kings'. It is all right to be royal, but recognize the nobility in others.

Home and Domestic Life

Although Leos are great entertainers and love having people over, sometimes this is all show. Only very few close friends will get to see the real side of a Leo's day-to-day life. To a Leo, the home is a place of comfort, recreation and transformation; a secret, private retreat – a castle. Leos like to spend money, show off a bit, entertain and have fun. They enjoy the latest furnishings, clothes and gadgets – all things fit for kings.

Leos are fiercely loyal to their family and of course expect the same from them. They love their children almost to a fault; they have to be careful not to spoil them too much. They also must try to avoid attempting to make individual family members over in their own image. Leos should keep in mind that others also have the need to be their own people. That is why Leos have to be extra careful about being over-bossy or over-domineering in the home.

Horoscope for 2003

Major Trends

2002 started off slow but ended up ebullient and triumphant. This trend continues in 2003. Jupiter will be in your own Sign of Leo for the first nine months of this year, making that period one long party. But Jupiter is not finished with you – after he sates all your sensual desires, enhances your creativity and leads you to the good life, he's going to start enriching you – presumably so that you can afford to continue to live the high life you've become accustomed to.

Your social life has been one long soap opera for the past seven years. For sheer drama and excitement, no movie or play could match it. By now, many of you are craving some stability in your social life – some sense of permanence – and, little by little (not straight away), the Cosmos will provide this. Uranus is getting ready to leave your 7th House of Love and Marriage and enter the 8th House. He does actually leave it for about six months and then returns to your 7th House. But his leaving is a message for the future.

Saturn is going to make a major move from your 11th House into your 12th House. This happens beginning June 4. This initiates a more spiritual cycle in your life – for the next two to three years. More on this later.

In previous years, you were relentlessly bombed by one eclipse after another. This year, only two out of the four seem to affect you. They both show changes in the home and the career.

Your important areas of interest in the coming year will be: sensual pleasure, the body, the image and the appearance (until August 27); finance (after August 27); friendships, groups and group activities (until June 4); spirituality, especially spiritual healing (after June 4); love, romance and social relationships; sex, the deeper things of life; transformation; paying off debt and tax issues.

Your paths of greatest fulfilment this year are: friendships, groups and group activities (until April 14); career (after April 14); sensual pleasures and personal fulfilment.

Health

Since 1999–2000, your health has been getting better year by year. This year, Uranus' brief move (six months) out of Aquarius and into Pisces enhances your health even further. Your 6th House of Health is not a House of Power – showing that you don't need to focus much attention here. 'If it ain't broke, don't fix it.'

Your Health Planet (Saturn) moves from Gemini into Cancer – this is another positive health message, as Saturn leaves a stressful aspect to Pluto.

You can enhance your already good health by paying extra attention to your spine, knees, teeth, lungs, intestines (especially until June 4), stomach and breasts (after June 4). There are many natural, drugless ways to do this. Unless your individual horoscope (cast for your precise time and place of birth) says differently, health problems would seem to originate in these places.

On a psychological level, Saturn deals with order and control. When you feel out of control, it could have an impact on your health. When your life becomes too disorderly – likewise. You always have a need to establish reasonable limits in your life and not go beyond them. Whenever you are guilty of excess, the Cosmos brings you back through a health problem. Leos don't like to hear about limits. They are creative, spontaneous people. Yet, intelligent limits are the key to good health.

In the past year, health problems tended to have their origin in family and emotional dis-harmonies and in dis-harmonies with friends. This trend continues for the first half of 2003. If a health problem arises, first clear up any dis-harmony with friends or family before running to a health professional. If you do this, chances are that the condition will fall away on its own. Even if the symptoms persist, the health professional will have an easier time helping you if you also address the underlying dis-harmony.

Saturn's move into your 12th House of Spirituality in June shows a radical shift in your health attitudes. You're going to see the importance that your inner life has on your health. You're going to see how the best medicine is maintaining constant contact with the great life-power within. Many of you will now start reacting well to spiritual or meditative-type therapies – prayer, speaking the word, meditation, colour and sound, etc. For many of you, this will be a whole new world.

The 12th House rules the health of your spouse or partner – and friends in general. Thus you seem very much involved in their health issues in the coming year. You seem more concerned about their health than your own. All of them would benefit from a disciplined, daily health regime and an elimination of excess from their lives – excess eating, drinking, sex, etc.

Saturn is a long-term, slow-moving planet, so the trends we mention are in effect for a long time.

Though overall health is good, there will be periods where the energy is not up to its usual standards. These are times to rest and relax more and to pace yourself better. This year, these periods are January 20 to February 19, April 20 to May 21 and October 23 to November 22.

A reduced schedule is also called for during the period of the Lunar eclipses of May 16 and November 9. Activities should be reduced not only on the day of the eclipse but for a few days before and about a day afterwards.

The health of a parent or parent figure is improving later in the year. Health of children also improves. Siblings can enhance health by venturing out into the new and the untried. They seem to benefit from unorthodox therapies. Health of grandchildren seems wonderful.

Home, Domestic and Family Issues

Though your 4th House of Home and Family is not a House of Power, we still see a lot of activity here due to the aspects to Pluto – your Family Planet.

Last year, home and family issues were bittersweet. They improved during the latter half of the year. This year they improve even further – especially after June 4.

There were various challenges last year. Work and work demands conflicted with family duties. Friends and family were at odds, neither accepting the other. Many of you felt cramped in the present home. But things started to improve in the latter part of the year. And this improvement is still going on.

Jupiter in Leo is making fabulous aspects to your Family Planet and Saturn is moving away from a stressful aspect. Thus the above-mentioned conflicts are resolving themselves.

Moves, expansions of the present residence, fortunate buying and selling of a home, the acquisition of new homes and big-ticket items for the home are all likely this year. Family interests are happy. Your family circle expands through birth, marriage or through meeting people who are like family to you. Part of the reason for better family relations this year is that you are ebullient and feel better about yourself. The family responds well to that. Though you are always generous, this year you are even more so. Family is supporting your personal fulfilment and creativity – in fact, much of your creativity is family-inspired.

Your playful attitude this year – the fact that you are almost a child yourself – helps you get on better with kids. You understand them and they understand you. A great Master once said that no one gets into the Kingdom of Heaven except he becomes as a little child. Now you're beginning to see the truth and the logic behind this. (Even older Leos have a youthful look this year.)

Leos of childbearing age are more fertile this year. Leos want lots of children around them – and if not their own, they'll settle for other family members' children.

The whole period of January 1 to August 27 is good for redecorating and beautifying the home. But I like March 21 to May 16 and July 23 to August 23 best.

A parent or parent figure is likely to move or enlarge his or her residence this year. Children are prospering and bringing much joy to you. A sibling could move because of career changes.

Parent and parent figures seem very generous with you.

Love and Social Life

Your 7th House of Love and Marriage has been powerful for seven or so years now and this trend continues. Many of you have had serial relationships during this time. Some, even serial marriages. The whole romantic scene was fraught with much excitement but also much instability. Many of you were trying to attain impossibilities or at least experimenting in those ways – such as trying to have a committed relationship whilst also being absolutely free. In many cases you were learning about love and relationships through trial and error, with many an explosion along the way.

What we wrote of last year is still very much in effect this year. You don't know from moment to moment where you stand in a given relationship. Love can bloom for a week and then, in an instant, affections change. The highs of love are unusually high, but the lows are very low. Though you are meeting new and interesting people all the time, you find it difficult to make holiday or travel plans, as you don't know whether you will even be talking to your current love by the time you go away. Even a mere date is a matter of grave doubt.

As mentioned earlier, by now there is a craving for permanency and stability. This won't happen yet this year, but I can see it happening in coming years. Marriage is still not advisable this year. There is still too much of the playboy/playgirl in you.

Nevertheless, this is a year to enjoy what you have. Romantic opportunities are plentiful. There are parties and entertainments galore. You are in a playful mood and probably don't want to get too serious. Try to enjoy each relationship or each date in the NOW moment without worrying too much about the future.

Self-esteem and self-confidence are good and you are unusually attractive. Sexual experience should be plentiful and enjoyable – even if you don't know with whom it will happen. Flow with all the changes.

It's a very romantic year, but not a marriage year.

Those working towards a second or third marriage will have plenty of romantic flings, but not necessarily a marriage. Those working towards a fourth Marriage have good aspects.

The marriage of parents or parent figures is status quo. Children of marriageable age have improved aspects – their social life should improve – but marriage is doubtful. Grandchildren of marriageable age have a status quo year.

Your best romantic periods this year are January 20 to February 19, March 2 to March 27 and June 21 to August 22.

Finance and Career

Finances become important after August 27. They will be good all year, but especially after that period.

Lady Luck is with you all year. Earnings and earning opportunities should increase tremendously. There is luck in speculations and with creative projects. Many Leos are involved in entertainment industries and the creative arts and this should be a banner year for these fields.

What I like about these aspects is that they show 'happy money' – money that is earned while you're having fun. If you work for a living, you will enjoy your work more. But many earnings opportunities and windfalls will come when you're out on the town or at a party, the theatre or a sporting event.

In many cases it is the urge for leisure that is driving Leos' wealth urges these days. But the opposite is also true: leisure and leisure activities are actually catalysts for wealth. It's as if the state of joy itself produces the wealth necessary to sustain the joy. This year, 'earning your bread by the sweat of your brow' has no relevance for you. (Parents with Leo children should make note of this.)

Investors should look at the entertainment, sport, gaming, toys, resorts, utilities, gold and healthcare industries. Don't just rush in and buy blindly, but do your homework and watch prices. There are profit opportunities there for you.

One of the financial dangers this year, with Jupiter's influence so strong, is the danger of over-spending in unrealistic ways. Leos are big spenders even without a Jupiter influence. This year they are even more so. Try to keep a rational perspective. Don't spend what you don't have. Be generous with your abundance and not with the money you need for basic expenses.

Though fun, leisure and love affairs are the main headlines of the coming year, career shouldn't be ignored, either. The Moon's North Node will enter your Career House on April 14, showing that there is joy in that, too.

I can see many Leos changing jobs this year. Many of you want to work at something more meaningful both for yourself and for the world. Many of you will either work for charitable organizations – ministries, hospitals, large charities, etc. – or donate labour to these causes.

Mercury, your Financial Planet, usually retrogrades three times a year. This year, he retrogrades four times. This means that there will be more periods where your financial judgement will not be up to par. With your tendency to over-spend, these periods become even more significant. Nothing is going to stop your prosperity, but these retrogrades can throw glitches into it. We'll cover these in the month-by-month forecasts.

Self-improvement

The two main areas of self-improvement happening are in the realm of friendships and spirituality. The realm of friendships has needed work for the past two years. You've needed to re-define your meanings of friendship – the roles, duties and obligations that friends owe to each other. You've needed to be more careful of the friends you made and bad choices were pretty much instantly punished. Most of you have learned that in order to attract good friends you need to be a good friend. The rest is just mechanics. In Astrology, we have a most wonderful definition of a friend: a friend is someone who wishes for your own fondest hopes and is willing to help them come to pass. With this measurement in mind, you can easily separate the wheat from the chaff.

Many of you have also learned (in the past two years) that a few quality friends are worth more than hordes of lukewarm, undependable ones. The fact is, you don't need a lot of friends, just a few good ones.

There was also a need to learn forgiveness in the past two years. You needed to forgive your friends for disappointing you and to forgive yourself for mistaken choices.

Come June 4, there is a shift into spirituality. Saturn moves into your 12th House of Spirituality at that time. Uranus will be in your 8th House for a few months. And Mars (your Planet of Religion and Philosophy) makes a highly unusual six-month transit in your 8th House. All of this is pointing to a concern with the deeper things of life – with past lives, life and death, life after death, depth-psychology and your connection with spirit. Saturn in your 12th House suggests a methodical, scientific and disciplined spiritual regime. Something you do every day. Something you incorporate into your lifestyle. It shows a concern with your spiritual health as much as with your physical health. In truth, one goes with the other. Often when Saturn transits the 12th House, Leos experience either prophetic visions or ESP experiences that frighten them and they turn off for a while. Don't let this happen to you. Observe your visions objectively – like a journalist – write them down. And don't judge. These are not things to be frightened of, but gifts from a Higher Power. Saturn in the 12th House also suggests the need for verifying your intuitions, dreams and visions. Often the visions are correct, but the interpretation (of the lower mind) is incorrect and the message is something much different from what you thought at the time. The main ingredients for spiritual success now are steadiness and discipline.

Month-by-month Forecasts

January

Best Days Overall: 1st, 9th, 10th, 19th, 20th, 27th, 28th

Most Stressful Days Overall: 4th, 5th, 11th, 12th, 13th, 25th, 26th

Best Days for Love: 4th, 5th, 9th, 10th, 15th, 19th, 20th, 24th, 27th, 28th

Best Days for Money: 1st, 2nd, 3rd, 9th, 10th, 11th, 12th, 13th, 19th, 20th, 21st, 22nd, 27th, 28th, 29th, 30th

The year begins with 70% to 80% of the planets in the Western sector. Your 7th House of Love, Romance and Social Activities is very powerful – especially after the 20th. Thus you are in a strong social period – perhaps the strongest of your year. Let go of 'my way' and put other people first. Adapt, as best you can, to difficult situations and use diplomacy, tact and charm to get your way. Your good comes from the good graces of others and not from personal effort.

The lower half of your Horoscope is stronger than the upper half. Your 4th House of Home and Family is strong, while your 10th House of Career is empty (except for the Moon's visit on the 11th, 12th and 13th). Thus this is a more 'inner' month. A month for finding your emotional comfort zone – for dealing with family issues and establishing your home base on a more firm footing. This emphasis on moods, feelings and family will soon change, but for now this is how you feel.

Until the 17th, construction or beautification projects in the home go well. There are more family gatherings and entertainments from home.

A T-square in the fixed Signs shows the need to balance home, family, personal desires and social urges. The conflicts can be unusually dramatic this month – especially until the 17th.

Mercury, your Financial Planet, is retrograde from the 2nd to the 22nd. Thus be more careful with investments and major purchases during this period. Study these things, then act on them *after* the 22nd. Be especially careful of what seem like 'deals' – unusually good prices for things. Chances are that you will get the same item (or something even better) at a better price when Mercury goes forward. Money comes to you in the old-fashioned way this month – through work. Those seeking work should study job offers more carefully. Not only is Mercury retrograde, but Saturn (your Work Planet) is also retrograde. Health regimes and diets also need more study.

Finances will be status quo this month. Be patient with delays.

Your love and social life is blooming and booming. There are more social invitations and more romantic opportunities. You are the one who is reaching out to others. You go after what you want and are not waiting for your phone to ring. Personal popularity seems unusually strong now.

Though health is good overall, rest and relax more after the 20th.

An active dream life and unusual ESP experiences await you on the 30th and 31st.

February

Best Days Overall: 5th, 6th, 15th, 16th, 23rd, 24th

Most Stressful Days Overall: 1st, 2nd, 8th, 9th, 21st, 22nd, 28th

Best Days for Love: 1st, 2nd, 8th, 9th, 11th, 17th, 18th, 19th, 20th, 25th, 26th, 28th

Best Days for Money: 1st, 2nd, 5th, 6th, 10th, 11th, 15th, 16th, 17th, 18th, 21st, 23rd, 24th

70% to 80% of the planets are still in the west and your 7th House of Love and Romance is even stronger than last month. This is still a very strong and exciting social period. Like last month, work to attain your ends through compromise and consensus rather than self-will and self-assertion. Try as best as you can to adapt to difficult situations rather than change them forcefully. Practise being flexible now. The good news is that you are feeling very social and seem eager to please. You are putting other people first in a very natural way.

By the 13th, the planetary power shifts to the upper half of the Horoscope – but oh so slightly. Career and ambitions are getting more important, but you still need to think of feeling good and maintaining a feeling of emotional harmony.

90% of the planets are moving forward after the 22nd, showing that this is a month of forward progress and momentum towards your goals. You make progress, but it doesn't happen because of personal effort, but through the good graces of others.

Now that Mercury is moving forwards you can execute your financial plans in a more bold and confident way. Your financial judgement is strong now. As in other areas of life, financial good comes through social connections and perhaps your spouse or partner – especially after the 13th.

Before that it comes from work. After the 13th Mercury travels with Neptune, the most spiritual of all the planets. This is showing financial guidance through dreams, psychics and astrologers. Your financial intuition will be excellent. And intuition is always the short-cut to financial success. This period will also be good for paying off or refinancing debt, cutting expenses or finding investors for your projects. Job-seekers have an easier time after the 22nd as Saturn (your Work Planet) starts moving forwards again. Judgement in these matters is much improved.

On the 4th, your Career Planet (Venus) moves into your 6th House of Work. This shows that you advance your career in the old-fashioned way – through work and productivity.

Singles have many love opportunities this month. As in past years, the only issue is the stability of the love. In general there are more parties and invitations to go out. Around the 17th, there is a sudden and dramatic love opportunity that comes out of the blue. It looks very happy. After the 19th, love is physical and passionate. Libido soars.

Health is basically good, but rest and relax more until the 19th.

March

Best Days Overall: 5th, 6th, 14th, 15th, 23rd

Most Stressful Days Overall: 1st, 7th, 8th, 21st, 27th, 28th

Best Days for Love: 1st, 10th, 11th, 12th, 19th, 20th, 21st, 27th, 28th, 29th, 30th

Best Days for Money: 1st, 5th, 6th, 12th, 13th, 14th, 15th, 17th, 22nd, 23rd

After the 2nd, the power in the upper half of your Horoscope becomes decisively dominant. 80% to 90% of the planets are moving forward. This is a time to pursue career goals.

Good progress will be made. You can start de-emphasizing family and domestic responsibilities now. Doing right will lead to feeling right.

Like last month, 70% to 80% of the planets are in the West and your 7th House of Love and Romance is still strong (though not quite as strong as last month). Thus you still need the good graces of others to attain your goals. You still need to be flexible and adaptable and to seek consensus in all that you do.

Important love changes are happening for many of you this month – especially those of you born early in the Sign of Leo. Uranus, your Love Planet, makes a major move into Pisces and your 8th House. This brings idealism into your love life – a spiritual quality – a need for a spiritual connection with those you get involved with. Spiritual compatibility becomes as important as other kinds of compatibility – perhaps even more so. Also, your love life should become more stable. Those who are already married or involved in serious relationships find that your spouse or lover is becoming more involved in finance. Where they were interested in self, image and sensual pleasure up till now, their interest shifts to finance. You seem very involved in the financial life of your partner – taking an active role there. A business partnership could be brewing these days, too.

Venus moving through your 7th House from the 2nd to the 21st shows romantic opportunities for singles. High glamour comes into your social life.

Mercury, your Financial Planet, moves very speedily this month, showing even better financial confidence and judgement than last month. Money comes in a variety of ways and through a variety of situations. Until the 5th, it comes through social connections and your spouse or partner. After the 5th, it could come through borrowing or through cost-cutting – or perhaps seeing value where others can't see it. After the 21st, it can come from foreign lands or through foreigners. Speculations are favourable after the 21st as well.

Money can come as you're having fun – pursuing leisure activities. All in all, a prosperous month. You cover a lot of territory. Like last month, it is still good to divert excess cash to debt-reduction – especially from the 5th to the 21st. Important financial principles – which pertain to your particular situation – are revealed after the 21st.

Foreign lands and higher education call to you after the 21st. Opportunities for fulfilment here will come your way.

Health is much improved over last month. A powerful Grand Trine in Fire not only boosts your energy, but your spirits as well. All is right with you and with the world.

April

Best Days Overall: 1st, 2nd, 11th, 12th, 19th, 20th, 28th, 29th

Most Stressful Days Overall: 3rd, 4th, 5th, 17th, 18th, 23rd, 24th

Best Days for Love: 8th, 9th, 16th, 17th, 18th, 23rd, 24th, 25th, 26th, 28th, 29th

Best Days for Money: 1st, 2nd, 11th, 12th, 13th, 14th, 19th, 20th, 21st, 22nd, 28th, 29th

The power in the upper half of your Horoscope continues to grow. By the 21st, 70% to 80% of the planets will be in that sector. Moreover, your 10th House of Career starts to become powerful after the 20th, while your 4th House of Home and Family is empty (except for the Moon's visit on the 17th and 18th). The message is clear: focus on your career and your outer life and let family and domestic concerns go. This is a month for strong career progress and you can't pass up opportunities. Many family issues seem on hold anyway and will take time to sort out. Important domestic decisions should be postponed anyway, as Pluto is retrograde all month.

The planetary power is still overwhelmingly in the West. Thus, like last month, continue to seek consensus and avoid self-will and independence. As you put others first, your own good will come to you easily and effortlessly.

Mars moving into your 7th House of Love on the 21st is not only going to test a relationship but test your social grace and charm. You will be sorely tempted to enter into power struggles with your spouse, lover or with friends. Try to avoid this. Love opportunities come with foreigners or in foreign lands. Sexuality and sexual urges are much stronger now. Leo is always known for its strong libido – but now it is even stronger than usual. Those involved romantically with Leos should keep this in mind.

There will be a Grand Trine in Fire all month. A most fortunate aspect for you. It enhances health, boosts your energy levels and lifts your spirits. You feel that anything is possible for you now. Depression has no place in your mind or existence. With more energy, your earnings soar. Your perceptions increase so that you see financial opportunity where you didn't see it before. Also, with your increased energy, financial projects that seemed impossible now seem very possible.

The only problem with finance is Mercury's retrograde late in the month – on the 26th. Try to wrap up important deals, purchases and investments before then. With so much fire in the Horoscope, the temptation is to rush into things, which would not be wise after the 26th. But even Mercury's retrograde will not stop your prosperity. It will probably just cause some minor annoyances or delays. Be careful of over-spending on the 10th. Test and verify your intuition on the 13th.

Like last month, this is a travel and education period. Students should do well.

Your personal creativity and glamour are getting stronger day by day. Lady Luck is actually hunting you down. You couldn't escape her if you tried.

May

Best Days Overall: 8th, 9th, 16th, 17th, 25th, 26th, 27th

Most Stressful Days Overall: 1st, 2nd, 14th, 15th, 21st, 22nd, 28th, 29th

Best Days for Love: 5th, 6th, 8th, 9th, 13th, 14th, 18th, 21st, 22nd, 23rd, 28th, 29th

Best Days for Money: 1st, 2nd, 8th, 9th, 10th, 11th, 16th, 17th, 18th, 19th, 25th, 26th, 27th, 28th, 29th

Two eclipses this month ensure much excitement and tumult. Long-term change is happening personally and in the world. Definitely take a reduced schedule a few days before and about a day after each eclipse.

The Lunar eclipse of the 16th occurs in your 4th House of Home and Family, signalling major changes in this area. The family and domestic pattern will change. Flaws in present arrangements, whether on the physical or psychological level, are revealed so that constructive action can be taken. Often this indicates a move or renovation of the home. Sometimes it signals major repairs – things that have needed doing for a long time. During this eclipse period there will also be a tendency to emotional volatility. Try to keep it reduced, as it only makes matters worse.

Every Lunar eclipse affects your spiritual life. This one will be no different. Many will make changes to their meditation regimes or change teachers or techniques. Relations with charitable groups or ministries could undergo long-term change. But also you can expect much spiritual revelation. Your dream life is apt to be overly stimulated this period – it is wise not to give too much credence to it unless you get verification from other sources.

The Solar eclipse of the 31st occurs in your 11th House. Thus friendships and relations with organizations will get tested. Long-brewing issues will come up for cleansing and you will have to make important long-term decisions in this area.

Every Solar eclipse affects your Ruling Planet, the Sun. Thus there are always changes to your image, personal appearance and self-concept. You have a chance (every six months or so) to re-define, improve and fine-tune your personality. Impurities in the body can come up for cleansing and elimination – in most cases this does not indicate illness, though you can manifest symptoms. There is a 'housecleaning' of your body going on – it is best to co-operate with it.

Like last month, your career and 'outer' ambitions are highly stimulated. Good career progress is happening. Those on high are granting favours. Many of you will get pay rises and promotions. Mercury will be retrograde until the 20th, so it is vital that you communicate well with superiors or with anyone involved in your career. Like last month, Mercury's retrograde shows a need for caution in financial matters – study all details of every deal, project, purchase or investment more carefully than usual. Best to delay these things until after the 20th. In spite of Mercury's gyrations, this is a prosperous month.

Health is good, but rest and relax more until the 21st.

June

Best Days Overall: 4th, 5th, 13th, 14th, 22nd, 23rd

Most Stressful Days Overall: 11th, 12th, 17th, 18th, 24th, 25th

Best Days for Love: 1st, 2nd, 7th, 8th, 10th, 11th, 17th, 18th, 19th, 27th, 28th, 29th

Best Days for Money: 4th, 5th, 7th, 8th, 13th, 14th, 17th, 18th, 22nd, 23rd, 27th, 28th, 29th

Last month's eclipses have paved the way for a whole new environment, condition and circumstance. They were announcements of a new order. Many planets are changing Signs and Houses this month – some are long-term planets. Saturn will move into your 12th House of Spirituality on the 4th and stay there for the next two-and-a-half years. Mars will move into your 8th House for the next six months. In addition, the Sun, Venus and Mercury will also change Signs and Houses. Plans you made based on 'old circumstances' are no longer valid. Worries or fears you had turn out to be groundless, as they are now based on outdated scenarios.

As has been the case for the past few months, the planetary power is overwhelmingly in the upper half of your chart. So, continue to focus on your career and outer objectives. Family relations and the overall domestic situation is stormy this month, but there is little you can do about it except to minimize the negativity – practise damage control. Don't make things worse or inflame a difficult situation further. Time will cure things.

Last month the planets shifted to the Eastern sector of your chart. This is the case this month as well. Now you have greater independence, self-confidence and freedom to have things your way. The need for 'people-pleasing' is over (though you should never be rude or disrespectful). Now you have the power to change difficult situations rather than having to adapt to them. Your way is the best way. The world will adapt to you. Personal effort pays off. Take the bull by the horns – your happiness and success are up to you now.

Health is vastly improved over last month. Health can still be enhanced by paying attention to your spine, knees and teeth. But also mind your diet, emotional life, stomach and breasts.

The power struggle in love is still going on until the 17th. Your ever-strong sexuality gets even more powerful after the 17th. Love problems can be cured with some constructive experimentation. Make your relationship more like a love affair – the way it was when you first met. Try to inject some joy into the relationship. With your Love Planet going retrograde on the 7th, give your beloved more space as well. Singles have many sudden romantic opportunities after the 17th.

Finances are also vastly improved as Mercury moves speedily and confidently this month. You achieve financial goals rapidly. Your good reputation and professional status bring financial opportunities until the 13th. Good friends and knowing the right people are like money in the bank from the 13th to the 29th. But after the 29th, your intuition illuminates your path. There is an awesome financial genius in every person – the key to wealth is letting it have its way with you.

July

Best Days Overall: 2nd, 3rd, 10th, 11th, 19th, 20th, 29th, 30th

Most Stressful Days Overall: 8th, 9th, 14th, 15th, 21st, 22nd, 23rd

Best Days for Love: 7th, 8th, 9th, 14th, 15th, 16th, 17th, 18th, 26th, 28th, 29th

Best Days for Money: 2nd, 3rd, 4th, 5th, 8th, 9th, 10th, 11th, 19th, 20th, 29th, 30th, 31st

Most of the planets are in the East now and your 1st House of Self becomes very powerful after the 23rd. You have a golden opportunity to create conditions as you would like them to be – to design your life according to your personal specifications. Almost the entire Cosmos is supporting this. So long as you keep your desires constructive and not harmful to others, you can expect to see them manifest. Big things could take longer. Small things will happen straight away. Your personal effort matters now.

The planetary power is gradually shifting from the upper half of the Horoscope to the lower. The shift is not complete this month, but is happening as a process – gradually. Thus, career and outer ambitions are starting to become less important and home, family and emotional issues are becoming more important.

Health and vitality are getting better day by day. By the 23rd, you have the energy of 10 people. Your magnetism and personal charisma are super. Others sit up and take notice. But even more important, your increased energy levels make all kinds of things possible which weren't possible before. Just as a car with only a half a tank of petrol can go only so far, so it was with you when energy was low. But fill the tank up and your horizons increase tremendously.

Love is more complicated now, as your Love Planet is still retrograde. Important love decisions should be delayed now. On the other hand, there are many opportunities for romantic flings. There is also much sexual experimentation going on. Love is highly unstable and mood changes can be abrupt and extreme. Leos love a lot of drama and they are certainly getting it – enough and to spare – in their love life.

When Saturn moved into your 12th House last month, a new spiritual era began. The spiritual life took on a new importance for the long term. But this month, spirituality and idealism are even more magnified as 40% to 50% of the planets move through your 12th House. Thus many of you will be involved in 'other-worldly' phenomena – ESP, dreams, psychic experiences, prayer, meditation, charitable and volunteer-type activities. The reality of the invisible world is clearly evident to you these days. Of course, it would be wrong to jump to conclusions – as these phenomena need objective verification and testing.

All in all, this is a wonderful and happy month – especially after the 23rd. Seldom have you been so optimistic and creative. Sensual fantasies are manifest easily. Lady Luck is stalking you and happy surprises – both personal and financial – await you. A foreign trip could materialize out of nowhere. A creative project or idea could be sold. Prosperity is solid and comes easily, while you're having fun and/or pursuing leisure activities. Your child-like qualities give you peace and faith for the future. All is well with you.

August

Best Days Overall: 7th, 15th, 16th, 17th, 25th, 26th

Most Stressful Days Overall: 4th, 5th, 11th, 12th, 18th, 19th

Best Days for Love: 4th, 7th, 8th, 11th, 12th, 13th, 16th, 17th, 23rd, 27th, 28th

Best Days for Money: 1st, 7th, 8th, 9th, 10th, 16th, 17th, 18th, 19th, 26th, 27th, 28th

Most of the planets are still in the East and your 1st House is still very strong – especially until the 22nd. Thus, continue to build your life according to your personal specifications. But with 40% of the planets retrograde this month, be more patient about things. Progress is perhaps not as swift as you would like. Nevertheless, it is still happening.

The majority of planets are still below the horizon of your chart and your 10th House of Career is still empty (except for the Moon's visit on the 18th and 19th). Thus you can de-emphasize career and focus on getting into the 'right state' – cultivating your emotional well-being – now.

Two Houses are unusually powerful this month – your 1st House and your 2nd. Thus this is a month for fulfilling sensual desires, sprucing up your image and pampering yourself a bit. The power in your Money House after the 22nd ensures that you will have the resources to pay for this. This month is unusually prosperous. Jupiter, the planet of wealth and abundance, makes an important move into your Money

House on the 27th. The Sun will travel with Jupiter after the 22nd. These are all wealth messages – and happy wealth to boot. Speculations are favourable, creativity is strong and your financial judgement is sound (especially until the 28th). Assets you own – whether they be stocks, bonds, 'things' or intellectual property – will increase in value as the year goes on. Try to wrap up important purchases, deals, projects and investments before the 28th, when Mercury goes retrograde. Professional investors should look at health-care, vitamin companies and the health industry for profit opportunities. They will come. Job-seekers find opportunities close to home, through the family or family connections. They should also find success in non-profit-type organizations. There is much financial support from parents, elders, bosses and people in authority. Parents and elders prosper this month.

Though serious love is still volatile, confusing and subject to abrupt change, fun-and-games type of love is plentiful and happy. There is no reason not to enjoy yourself socially. This is definitely a month for going out and for enjoying leisure activities, parties and the like.

Health is wonderful now and your awareness of the spiritual aspects of health increases day by day.

September

Best Days Overall: 3rd, 4th, 12th, 13th, 22nd, 23rd, 30th

Most Stressful Days Overall: 1st, 2nd, 7th, 8th, 14th, 15th, 28th, 29th

Best Days for Love: 1st, 5th, 6th, 7th, 8th, 9th, 16th, 17th, 18th, 19th, 26th, 27th

Best Days for Money: 5th, 6th, 14th, 15th, 24th, 25th, 26th, 27th

Most planets are still in the East, and retrograde activity weakens. Thus you should make faster progress towards your goals this month. Again, work to build your life as you desire it to be. Your personal effort makes a huge difference. Seek to please number one without offending or hurting others.

Like last month, most of the planets are still below the horizon, so your emotional well-being takes priority over your career. Career opportunities and job changes (positive ones) could come, but you must always consider how these things will affect your emotional well-being.

Family issues are improving now (especially after the 23rd) as Pluto moves forwards after months of retrograde motion. The important thing is that clarity has been achieved and you know the direction in which you need to go. You are no longer wandering in the wilderness of chaos and confusion. Personal conflicts with family members should resolve after the 23rd. Financial issues seem a source of dispute for the long term, so compromise will be very important.

Prosperity is still strong in the coming month and not even Mercury's retrograde can stop it. But you can expect delays and minor glitches. Patience and good humour will see you through. These are not major problems, just minor inconveniences. Take time to communicate properly (take nothing for granted) with those involved in your financial life and in financial dealings in general. Unexpected family or home expenses could come, but you will have the resources to deal with them. Speculations are still favourable, but wait till after the 20th.

This is a great month for getting your financial house in order – for doing accounting, financial planning and research. It is also a wonderful period (after the 23rd) for pursuing intellectual interests, travelling locally and getting communications projects done.

Your Love Planet, Uranus, changes Signs this month. It moves back into Aquarius from Pisces. Thus there is the need for personal freedom in love. The lure of being a free spirit, beholden to no one, is strong. You still want love, but freedom is equally important. Love opportunities come in the neighbourhood or with neighbours after the 15th. Before that, they come as you pursue your financial goals.

Mars in your 8th House (now moving forward from the 27th onwards) indicates this as a good period for breaking addictions and bad character habits. Sexual desires are still intense, but the need to experiment is lessened.

October

Best Days Overall: 1st, 9th, 10th, 19th, 20th, 27th, 28th

Most Stressful Days Overall: 4th, 5th, 11th, 12th, 13th, 25th, 26th

Best Days for Love: 4th, 5th, 15th, 16th, 17th, 23rd, 24th, 25th, 26th

Best Days for Money: 2nd, 3rd, 11th, 12th, 13th, 14th, 15th, 21st, 22nd, 24th, 25th, 29th, 30th

Continue to give priority and attention to home, family and domestic concerns. Not only are most of the planets still below the horizon, but your 4th House of Home and Family is powerful after the 23rd, while your 10th House of Career is empty (except for the Moon's visit on the 11th, 12th and 13th). Being in right state inwardly is more important than a new deal here or there.

The planets are starting to shift from the Eastern sector to the Western sector. This shift happens by degrees and will be complete by the 23rd. Now, life will test your creations of the previous months. You will have to live with what you've created, good or bad. Your power to change conditions is lessening. Adaptability and flexibility are the key. The good news is that if you created well, you are enjoying life now. If you made mistakes, you will have opportunity to correct them in six months or so. Life is a continuous process of creating, perfecting and fine-tuning.

Prosperity and all the lucky breaks are still happening for you. Jupiter is in your Money House and Mercury (your Financial Planet) moves forwards speedily and confidently. Your financial judgement is sound these days. Your strongest financial period (in a strong financial month) seems from the 1st to the 7th. Unusual windfalls or opportunities should come your way. This is also a good time for shopping, as Mercury in the Sign of Virgo will be more careful and cost-conscious. From the 7th to the 29th, money comes from good marketing, PR and skilled use of the media. Getting the word out about your product or service seems important. After the 29th, money and financial opportunities come from family and family connections. Job-seekers need more patience and a lot more research. Job offers and conditions are not what they seem.

Love seems harmonious until the 23rd. Though marriage doesn't seem on the cards (and is probably not advisable), there is still much romance and happiness in this department. Marrieds enjoy more harmony within the marriage. For singles, romantic opportunities happen in the neighbourhood or with neighbours – also at parties and social gatherings.

This is an excellent period – from the 9th onwards – for family gatherings, entertaining from home or for beautifying the home. The New Moon of the 25th, which occurs in your 4th House, is going to bring clarity to all family and domestic issues.

Health is wonderful until the 23rd, but after that rest and relax more – pace yourself and focus on your real priorities.

November

Best Days Overall: 5th, 6th, 15th, 16th, 24th, 25th

Most Stressful Days Overall: 1st, 2nd, 8th, 9th, 22nd, 23rd, 28th, 29th

Best Days for Love: 1st, 2nd, 5th, 6th, 11th, 12th, 15th, 16th, 20th, 21st, 25th, 26th, 27th, 28th, 29th

Best Days for Money: 3rd, 4th, 8th, 9th, 15th, 16th, 18th, 19th, 24th, 25th, 26th, 27th

Rest and relax more until the 22nd. Avoid making hasty or radical changes to your diet or health regime as well. Research all these things more carefully.

The planetary power is now firmly in the Western sector. Your 1st House of Self is empty (with the exception of the Moon's visit on the 15th and 16th), while your 7th House of Love and Social Activities is strong. Thus, you are once again in a period where you need to put other people first and consider their needs and desires. Independence, self-will and personal effort are not what bring success – compromise, consensus, charm and grace are the qualities to be cultivated. With 90% of the planets forward, you ought to make rapid progress with less effort if you follow the above advice.

Most of the planets are still below the horizon, your 4th House (like last month) is still very strong (especially until the 22nd), while your 10th House of Career is basically empty. Thus, like last month, continue to give priority to the home, family and domestic responsibilities. You won't be able to avoid some focus on your career, however, as a Lunar eclipse occurs in your 10th House on the 9th. This is a powerful eclipse for you; it would be wise to take a reduced schedule for a few days before and about a day after. Avoid stressful, risk-taking activities during this period. This Lunar eclipse is bringing career changes for many Leos. Either you change companies or change your position within the same company. Changes and shake-ups are probably happening in the corporate hierarchy, which could affect your situation. Let the dust settle before making any decisions. There could be shake-ups and upheavals with parents or elders as well.

The Solar eclipse of the 23rd is more benign to you, but still, every Solar eclipse is significant in your chart. Thus you will again re-define your personality, image and self-concept. You will probably change the way you dress and present yourself. Long-term changes are happening with children and in your creative life – some of which could take the form of very natural, normal alterations. Speculations should be avoided during this eclipse period. Finances could be temporarily tricky, but over the long term, even the eclipse won't harm your prosperity. A love affair (not a marriage) could become unusually volatile.

Love is still stormy this month. You and your beloved seem very much out of synch – each wanting to do different things and having different positions on everything. But this should pass by the 23rd.

December

Best Days Overall: 2nd, 3rd, 4th, 12th, 13th, 14th, 21st, 22nd, 30th, 31st

Most Stressful Days Overall: 5th, 6th, 19th, 20th, 25th, 26th

Best Days for Love: 7th, 8th, 9th, 5th, 6th, 15th, 16th, 17th, 18th, 25th, 26th

Best Days for Money: 5th, 6th, 15th, 16th, 23rd, 24th

Now that the dust is settling from last month's eclipses, you can get round to the serious (and important) business of enjoying life. This is very much a party month – especially until the 22nd. There are parties, entertainments and much leisure activity – truly a Leo's paradise.

The planetary power mostly in the West still shows the need for charm, grace and consensus in attaining your ends. Adapting to situations will get you further than trying to change them. Your good comes effortlessly through the good graces of others.

Love is much improved over last month. Your Love Planet is moving forwards after many months of retrograde motion and receives much better aspects than last month. Love blooms.

Your 6th House of Health and Work is unusually powerful this month – especially after the 22nd. Thus, you are working harder than usual, being more productive and a bit more serious. Yes, you are enjoying life, but you're working hard, too.

Health is good and you seem more interested in it. You spend more on health items and health issues. Some of you might earn from this field, too – especially professional or serious investors. (Traders should exercise more caution from the 17th onwards, as Mercury is retrograde.)

Finances are unusually strong this month and this should be a very profitable holiday season for most of you. Try to do your holiday shopping before the 17th (I especially like the 5th and 6th, as there is a Grand Trine in Earth, making you a careful and astute shopper). Money comes from work or through co-workers this month. Employers could be having more difficulty with employees, but this is short-term.

Home and family issues still take priority over your career, but you can enhance your career through work (of course) and through social connections and mingling with the right people. Whom you know could be just as important careerwise as how hard you work (especially after the 21st).

You are mingling with people of power this month and on a romantic level seemed intrigued by these kinds of people. You like 'free spirits' the best, but power is alluring too.

On the 30th, Uranus, your Love Planet, makes his final move into Pisces. Thus you become more idealistic and spiritually inclined when it comes to love. Many of you want to explore the psychic depths with your beloved – but this is not for timid souls. In the coming years, love will not be just about 'good times' and excitement, but a journey into the unknown.

Virgo

♍

THE VIRGIN

Birthdays from

22nd August

to 22nd September

Personality Profile

VIRGO AT A GLANCE

Element – Earth

Ruling Planet – Mercury
Career Planet – Mercury
Love Planet – Neptune
Money Planet – Venus
Planet of Home and Family Life – Jupiter
Planet of Health and Work – Uranus
Planet of Pleasure – Saturn
Planet of Sexuality – Mars

Colours – earth tones, ochre, orange, yellow

Colour that promotes love, romance and social harmony – aqua blue

Colour that promotes earning power – jade green

Gems – agate, hyacinth

Metal – quicksilver

Scents – lavender, lilac, lily of the valley, storax

Quality – mutable (= flexibility)

Quality most needed for balance – a broader perspective

Strongest virtues – mental agility, analytical skills, ability to pay attention to detail, healing powers

Deepest needs – to be useful and productive

Characteristic to avoid – destructive criticism

Signs of greatest overall compatibility – Taurus, Capricorn

Signs of greatest overall incompatibility – Gemini, Sagittarius, Pisces

Sign most helpful to career – Gemini

Sign most helpful for emotional support – Sagittarius

Sign most helpful financially – Libra

Sign best for marriage and/or partnerships – Pisces

Sign most helpful for creative projects – Capricorn

Best Sign to have fun with – Capricorn

Signs most helpful in spiritual matters – Taurus, Leo

Best day of the week – Wednesday

Understanding a Virgo

The virgin is a particularly fitting symbol for those born under the Sign of Virgo. If you meditate on the image of the virgin you will get a good understanding of the essence of the Virgo type. The virgin is, of course, a symbol of purity and innocence – not naïve, but pure. A virginal object has not been touched. A virgin field is land that is true to itself, the way it has always been. The same is true of virgin forest: it is pristine, unaltered.

Apply the idea of purity to the thought processes, emotional life, physical body and activities and projects of the everyday world and you can see how Virgos approach life. Virgos desire the pure expression of the ideal in their mind, body and affairs. If they find impurities they will attempt to clear them away.

Impurities are the beginning of disorder, unhappiness and uneasiness. The job of the Virgo is to eject all impurities and keep only that which the body and mind can use and assimilate.

The secrets of good health are here revealed: 90 per cent of the art of staying well is maintaining a pure mind, a pure body and pure emotions. When you introduce more impurities than your mind and body can deal with, you will have what is known as 'dis-ease'. It is no wonder that Virgos make great doctors, nurses, healers and dietitians. They have an innate understanding of good health and they realize that good health is more than just physical. In all aspects of life, if you want a project to be successful, it must be kept as pure as possible. It must be protected against the adverse elements that will try to undermine it. This is the secret behind Virgo's awesome technical proficiency.

One could talk about Virgo's analytical powers – which are formidable. One could talk about their perfectionism and their almost superhuman attention to detail. But this would be to miss the point. All of these virtues are manifestations of a Virgo's desire for purity and perfection – a world without Virgos would have ruined itself long ago.

A vice is nothing more than a virtue turned inside out, misapplied or used in the wrong context. Virgos' apparent vices come from their inherent virtue. Their analytical powers, which should be used for healing, helping or perfecting a project in the world, sometimes get misapplied and turned against people. Their critical faculties, which should be used constructively to perfect a strategy or proposal, can sometimes be used destructively to harm or wound. Their desire for perfection can turn into worry and lack of confidence; their natural humility can become self-denial and self-abasement. When Virgos turn negative they are apt to turn their devastating criticism on themselves, sowing the seeds of self-destruction.

Finance

Virgos have all the attitudes that create wealth. They are hard-working, industrious, efficient, organized, thrifty, productive and eager to serve. A developed Virgo is every employer's dream. But until Virgos master some of the social graces of Libra, they will not even come close to fulfilling their financial potential. Purity and perfectionism, if not handled correctly or gracefully, can be very trying to others. Friction in human relationships can be devastating not only to your pet projects but – indirectly – to your wallet as well.

Virgos are quite interested in their financial security. Being hard-working, they know the true value of money. They do not like to take risks with their money, preferring to save for their retirement or for a rainy day. Virgos usually make prudent, calculated investments that involve a minimum of risk. These investments and savings usually work out well, helping Virgos to achieve the financial security they seek. The rich or even not-so-rich Virgo also likes to help his or her friends in need.

Career and Public Image

Virgos reach their full potential when they can communicate their knowledge in such a way that others can understand it. In order to get their ideas across better, Virgos need to develop greater verbal skills and less judgemental ways of expressing themselves. Virgos look up to teachers and communicators; they like their bosses to be good communicators. Virgos will probably not respect a superior who is not their intellectual equal – no matter how much money or power that superior has. Virgos themselves like to be perceived by others as being educated and intellectual.

The natural humility of Virgos often inhibits them from fulfilling their great ambitions, from acquiring name and fame. Virgos should indulge in a little more self-promotion if they are going to reach their career goals. They need to push themselves with the same ardour that they would use to foster others.

At work Virgos like to stay active. They are willing to learn any type of job as long as it serves their ultimate goal of financial security. Virgos may change occupations several times during their professional lives, until they find the one they really enjoy. Virgos work well with other people, are not afraid to work hard and always fulfil their responsibilities.

Love and Relationships

If you are an analyst or a critic you must, out of necessity, narrow your scope. You have to focus on a part and not the whole; this can create a temporary narrow-mindedness. Virgos do not like this kind of person. They like their partners to be broad-minded, with depth and vision. Virgos seek to get this broad-minded quality from their partners, since they sometimes lack it themselves.

Virgos are perfectionists in love just as they are in other areas of life. They need partners who are tolerant, open-minded and easy-going. If you are in love with a Virgo, do not waste time on impractical romantic gestures. Do practical and useful things for him or her – this is what will be appreciated and what will be done for you.

Virgos express their love through pragmatic and useful gestures, so do not be put off because your Virgo partner does not say 'I love you' day-in and day-out. Virgos are not that type. If they love you, they will demonstrate it in practical ways. They will always be there for you; they will show an interest in your health and finances; they will fix your sink or repair your video recorder. Virgos deem these actions to be superior to sending flowers, chocolates or Valentine's cards.

In love affairs Virgos are not particularly passionate or spontaneous. If you are in love with a Virgo, do not take this personally. It does not mean that you are not alluring enough or that your Virgo partner does not love or like you. It is just the way Virgos are. What they lack in passion they make up for in dedication and loyalty.

Home and Domestic Life

It goes without saying that the home of a Virgo will be spotless, sanitized and orderly. Everything will be in its proper place – and don't you dare move anything about! For Virgos to find domestic bliss they need to ease up a bit in the home, to allow their partner and kids more freedom and to be more generous and open-minded. Family members are not to be analysed under a microscope, they are individuals with their own virtues to express.

With these small difficulties resolved, Virgos like to stay in and entertain at home. They make good hosts and they like to keep their friends and families happy and entertained at family and social gatherings. Virgos love children, but they are strict with them – at times – since they want to make sure their children are brought up with the correct sense of family and values.

Horoscope for 2003

Major Trends

The past two years have been difficult on many levels, but things are starting to get easier this year. The past two years were about balancing domestic duties and your career; trying to advance your career through real achievement while maintaining some semblance of a home life. It has been a period of learning experiences to be sure, but by now you are a stronger and wiser person. By this year, career-testing should be about over. Career in general becomes less important. And the Cosmos has nice rewards for a job well done when Jupiter moves into your Sign on August 27.

Spirituality became important during the latter half of 2002 and continues to be important this year. Much spiritual growth and progress are taking place now.

Although the long-term planets are still stressing you out, many wonderful developments are taking place this year – the main ones being Jupiter's move into your own Sign on August 27 and Saturn leaving his stressful aspect on June 4.

Your love life, too, is becoming ever more exciting, but brace yourself for a lot of change. Uranus, the planet of sudden changes, is moving into your 7th House of Love. It will be there for only six months this year, but it is getting ready (by next year) to move in for seven years. This will be a year of preparation.

Your areas of greatest interest in the coming year will be: spirituality (until August 27); the body, image, personal pleasure and personal fulfilment (after August 27); home and family; health and work; love and romance; career (until June 4); friendships, group activities and organizations (after June 4).

Your paths to greatest fulfilment will be: career (until April 14); religion, philosophy, higher education, foreign travel (after April 14); spirituality (until August 27); personal pleasure and personal fulfilment (after August 27).

Health

No question about it, your health had to be watched over the past two years. If you got through OK, you'll get through almost anything. Though you should mind your health this year too, this should be slightly easier than it was last year.

On a positive note, Virgos are always interested in health and tend to stay on top of things. Add to this that your 6th House of Health is very strong and we see a 'passion for good health'. This is a great positive – you are unlikely to let problems get out of control.

Still, like last year, you need to watch your energy levels. You must focus only on the things that are important to you – and sometimes tough choices will have to be made – and let lesser things go. You just don't have the energy to be all things to all people all the time. Delegate responsibility wherever possible. Organize yourself so that more gets done with less effort. Let go of trivial thoughts, speech, actions and emotionality. In fact, it might be wise to let go of all the trivia in your life.

You can enhance your health by wearing the colours and gem stones of your Sign and by taking better care of your ankles and feet. Both should be massaged on a regular basis. Shoes should be comfortable and fit well. Avoid shoes that throw you off-balance or that pinch you, no matter how fashionable they are.

Fresh air and meditative breathing exercises will also enhance health. Water therapies – such as soaking in a hot tub, a spa or whirlpool – or even being near water – are also unusually helpful.

Your Health Planet (Uranus) makes a major, major move on March 10 – from Aquarius to Pisces. This only happens once every seven years. Now, this is not the full-blown transit – only a flirtation with Pisces. Uranus will move back into Aquarius on September 15. But it is an announcement – a harbinger – of the future.

First off, Uranus in your 7th House shows that good health means more to you than just the absence of disease – it means a healthy love and social life. It means healthy and nourishing relationships. (And you are right to think this.) It shows that love problems or dis-harmonies with friends can have an impact on your health. Thus you should always strive for harmony. If a health problem arises (especially from March 10 to September 15), check out what's happening in your love life and you'll likely find the cause. Clear the problem there first before running to a health professional. Chances are the condition will clear up on its own. (Even if the services of a professional are needed, because you've done the main work, the healing will be faster and easier.)

As mentioned, Jupiter is moving into your own Sign on August 27. While this is basically a happy period, a living of the good life, etc., be careful not to over-indulge. Enjoy, but don't over-do either food or sensual pleasures.

Ego, self-esteem and self-confidence are gradually improving this year – and this too is a positive health boon.

There is good news about the health of a spouse, partner or friend. The health of a parent or parent figure is also much improved after June 4. Health of siblings is status quo. Health of children is vastly improved after June 4. Health of grandchildren is status quo.

Home, Domestic and Family Issues

Your 4th House of Home and Family has been a House of Power for some years now. This trend continues in 2003. Pluto has been camping out in this house. His purpose is eventually to transform and renew your home, family relationships and entire emotional life. He keeps you focused on these issues so that you can see both the good and the negative. Then you can eliminate the negative.

For some years now, there's been a certain amount of emotional separation from the family. Perhaps it is not a 'physical separation' – i.e. you probably still attend family functions and gatherings – but it's not the same. You are not as emotionally involved with them as you have been in the past. Perhaps you have advanced spiritually and psychologically to a place where these things have no relevance for you. Or perhaps your goals in life are not congruent with theirs. Be careful, though, of trying to make them over into your image of perfection. This will not go well. Be there to help where possible and mind your own business. (This is not so easy for you, as you have a driving urge to 'purify' the family life.)

Some of you have had deaths in the family in recent years. Others have changed their whole domestic pattern. Long-term, deep-rooted change is taking place.

On a psychological level, great progress is happening. Your insights into the depths of feelings and moods have never been greater. You are able to diagnose a feeling or mood instantly – know where it comes from and what it is.

Pluto in the 4th House gives you great emotional and psychic power. Thus it must be used constructively. In classical astrology, this position is the signature of the magician or occultist – a person who can manifest what he or she wants whenever. Visualizing power is strong and so is concentration – manifestation (for good or ill) happens quickly.

Mind your temper at home and with family members. You have no idea how your word or gesture can devastate.

On a more mundane level, Pluto in the 4th House shows drastic make-overs of the residence – major renovations and repairs. It's as if you create a new house though you don't physically move. Many are installing new pipes, plumbing and sewer systems these days.

Until August 27, Jupiter makes beautiful aspects to Pluto. Thus, these renovations can be profitable and good investments. The sale or purchase of a home or move could also happen. Family relationships are basically happy in spite of the internal detachment that is going on. Family is supportive of you this year. And many Virgos are thinking of starting their own families. Family members will try to control you using the 'carrot' this year, but a part of you will feel very uneasy about it.

Love and Social Life

Though marriage wasn't that important to you in the past two years, you all had plenty of opportunities for that. Your love aspects were sensational. Now many of you are either thinking of marriage or thinking of dramatic changes in your whole social life.

Uranus in your 7th House is going to provide you with plenty of change and excitement. This position is not so good for committed relationships – often it denies them – because it gives urges to unconditional and absolute freedom.

When we see this position in an individual's natal Horoscope, one of two scenarios tend to occur. The person either never marries or marries many times.

Thus, existing relationships and marriages are soon to be tested. You will feel the initial stirring from March 10 to September 15. (People born early in the Sign of Virgo will feel it most.)

You are entering a period where love happens suddenly – like a lightning flash from on high. Virgos are not usually 'love at first sight' types of people, but now they are. Love can come suddenly and leave suddenly. The affections change rapidly. You can be in love one moment and out of love an hour later. When you are alone, with no prospects, and things look very bleak, love will suddenly appear – out of nowhere – as you are taking out the rubbish or browsing at the computer shop. Your whole social landscape, whether it be a desert or a garden, can change at any time. Thus your love life is in constant flux and you never know for sure where you stand at any given time.

Getting over insecurity is one of the lessons here. Learning to flow with change – and to enjoy it – is another lesson.

Astrologers, high-tech people, healers, health professionals and perhaps co-workers are all alluring these days. You gravitate towards people of high intelligence and unconventional ways. The more unconventional they are, the more attractive they are.

With Uranus in the 7th House, romance will often happen with people outside your religion and nationality.

With this position, there is a tendency to enter into relationships for their 'shock value' or to make social or political statements. This is not advisable. These kinds of relationships rarely last. Love and mutual attraction should be the sole basis.

There is an urge to learn about love and relationship through trial and error; to reject all the received wisdom of the ages and to start from square one; to break all humanly created social barriers. Those Virgos who have felt barriers to love in their personal lives will now start breaking these barriers – often by doing extreme things.

The highs of love will be very high, but the lows can be very low too. It's as if the Cosmos wants you to understand both sides of it.

How would we know bliss, if we didn't know loneliness and misery? How would we understand the rapture of love at first sight, if we didn't feel the pangs of rejection? How would we know a good relationship if we didn't have a few duds to compare it to?

Finance and Career

Though your 2nd House of Finance is not a House of Power this year and you are not that interested in money for money's sake, you will prosper in spite of yourself. It's as if you prosper *because* of your lack of interest. Since your attachment is not that strong, higher faculties come into play that show you the way to prosperity.

Career, professional status and your place in society are all much more important to you than mere money.

Your prosperity begins in earnest when Jupiter moves into your Sign of Virgo on August 27. This brings overall optimism, increased self-esteem and self-worth, the fulfilment of sensual fantasies, all the trappings of the good life – good food, wine, restaurants, travel, a new and more expensive wardrobe, accessories, etc.

The Cosmos wants you to have personal pleasure and fulfilment and will supply (one way or another) the means by which you shall have it. It's as if you are bursting out of a two-year log jam.

Career is still very important, but only until June 4. Those Virgos born later in the Sign will still feel career urges for months afterwards. But most of the lessons have been learned. You've had to work hard, keep a low profile, succeed through real merit and worthiness and not through political chicanery and public relations hype. Some of you have had very demanding bosses in the past two years. This too is about to change. You will either have a new, more relaxed boss or the old one becomes kinder and gentler. Those of you who worked hard and co-operated with the lessons of Saturn attained unprecedented career heights. By the latter part of 2003, you are ready to focus on other things – friendship, personal fulfilment, love, organizations.

Prosperity is coming through the family, family connections or people who are like family to you. Property and property investments and speculations seem profitable, too (though your individual chart cast for your specific time and place of birth could modify this). Professional investors should also look at the health industry.

Your most prosperous period this year would seem to be August 22 to October 23.

The finances of your spouse or partner are status quo – of course there will be ups and downs in the course of the year, but no major trends one way or the other. A parent or parent figure has to work harder for earnings and seems to be budgeting and cost-cutting. Finances of children seem unstable, but things could change at the drop of a hat. They need to strike out into the new and the unknown. Finances of siblings improve after June 4.

Self-improvement

In the past two years the main area of self-improvement was your career. You had to learn to take a long-term view of things, to do what was right regardless of whether you got recognition, to handle power and authority in very just and measured ways. You learned to rise through the ranks by virtue of quality work. This trend is continuing for the first half of 2003. After that, the lessons are coming in the area of friendship.

Saturn in your 11th House suggests a need for re-structuring your friendships in the next two years. Wheat must be separated from the chaff. Quality must take precedence over quantity. You will be exposed to some of the duties and responsibilities that friendship incurs and you will see why you need discernment. Real friends are like money in the bank. They enhance your energy and increase your power. False friends or lukewarm ones are energy vampires. Friends of low quality can drag you down to the depths. Rejoice when the Cosmos starts testing your friendships in the coming years – it is the prelude to a re-ordering.

Saturn in your 11th House is going to make you more active in organizations and clubs. The lesson is going to be how to work in a group or with groups – to work as part of a team. A lot of your perfectionist tendencies will have to be modified in group work. Not everyone is as perfection-orientated as you. Further, since the good of the group is the main priority, what seems like imperfection to you might be the best way when you look at the big picture.

Month-by-month Forecasts

January

Best Days Overall: 2nd, 3rd, 11th, 12th, 13th, 21st, 22nd, 29th, 30th

Most Stressful Days Overall: 1st, 6th, 7th, 8th, 14th, 15th, 27th, 28th

Best Days for Love: 4th, 5th, 6th, 7th, 8th, 9th, 10th, 14th, 15th, 19th, 20th, 23rd, 24th, 27th, 28th

Best Days for Money: 1st, 9th, 10th, 19th, 20th, 23rd, 24th, 27th, 28th

By the 17th, the planetary power will have shifted to the Western sector of your chart. 70% to 80% of them will be there. Thus, you are in a period where your flexibility, social grace and charm are the means for success and achieving your goals. Now is not the time for power struggles or excessive self-will. This is a time for putting other people first. As you do this, your own good will come to you naturally and normally by the law of karma.

70% to 80% of the planets are below the horizon of your chart. Thus, this is a period for cultivating emotional harmony, the right inner states, and stabilizing your home base. Career is definitely important, but you can shift more attention to these other matters. With both the Career Planets (Saturn and Mercury) retrograde for most of the month, there's not much to be done career-wise anyhow. Your career seems motivated by the love of children. You want to succeed because of them – to give them a better life. But you can give them a better life by being there for them now.

On the 17th, Mars will join Venus in your 4th House of Home and Family. Thus it is an excellent period for deep renovations and beautification of the home. Family relations seem bittersweet. There is love, but there is also much temper and volatility.

Basically, this is a month (especially until the 20th) of fun, joy and leisure-type activities. A cosmic holiday. Leisure restores your faculties so that you can be a more productive worker and person. Take advantage of these cosmic play periods. You will have plenty of time for work and serious things after the 20th.

Health is good this month and many of you will have super-natural healing experiences (either for yourself or others) after the 20th. The invisible, spiritual aspects of healing become very plain.

Finances seem status quo this month. There is no real financial problem, just lack of interest on your part. Until the 7th, money comes from sales, marketing and PR activities – also buying and selling. After the 7th, it comes from family and family connections. Be careful of compulsive spending on the 16th. A nice windfall or opportunity is likely on the 21st. Your financial judgement is particularly astute on the 25th, but be careful of a 'boom or bust' mentality. A sudden expense with children on the 29th is temporary and doesn't impact on finances in a long-term way.

Try to avoid speculations this month – even well-hedged ones.

Your love life starts to shine after the 20th as your Love Planet, Neptune, receives positive stimulation. The work place or doctor's surgery seems the scene of romance.

February

Best Days Overall: 8th, 9th, 17th, 18th, 25th, 26th

Most Stressful Days Overall: 3rd, 4th, 10th, 11th, 23rd, 24th

Best Days for Love: 1st, 2nd, 3rd, 4th, 8th, 9th, 10th, 11th, 17th, 18th, 19th, 20th, 25th, 26th, 28th

Best Days for Money: 5th, 6th, 8th, 9th, 15th, 16th, 17th, 18th, 19th, 20th, 23rd, 24th, 25th, 26th

The need for social grace, consensus and adaptability is even greater this month than last. 70% to 80% of the planets are still in the West and your 7th House of Love and Social Relationships becomes powerful after the 19th. In the meantime, your 1st House of Self is empty (except for the Moon's visit on the 17th and 18th). Now that Mercury is moving forwards you are feeling more confident, but this is not a time for power struggles or self-assertion. Personal effort will not ensure success now. Good comes from and through others.

Most of the planets are still below the horizon and your 4th House of Home and Family is still powerful. So, like last month, continue to give priority to the family, domestic responsibilities and your emotional life. Career is important and will prosper almost on its own. Your job is to stay happy and in harmony.

This is very much a work-orientated month and the pace at work quickens. Many will see job changes – within the same company or with a new company. This could happen suddenly and it looks very positive. Conditions at the work place are also subject to sudden change.

Health is delicate after the 19th. Do take a reduced schedule and focus only on what's important to you. You don't have energy to waste on frivolities. Respect your structure and capacity. When there is no petrol in the car, you've got to fill the tank. It is useless to *push* the car further.

This is a month for balancing career, children, domestic responsibilities and love and social obligations. All of these areas pull you in different directions. Your job is to make them co-operate.

Finances are reasonable. Until the 4th, money comes from family or family connections – perhaps from property investments. After the 4th, money comes from personal creativity or as you pursue leisure activities. Very important that you enjoy your means of livelihood this period, as this will enhance both your health and income.

This is one of the strongest social periods of your year. But you will need to exercise discretion. You can't attend every party or date every beau (or dance with every girl at the party). Focus on quality and not quantity. The spiritual connection in love – always important to you – seems even more so this month. Singles meet people they were fated to meet. Whether these connections lead to marriage is another story. Often what seems like a romance is really part of a whole other agenda on the spiritual level.

March

Best Days Overall: 7th, 8th, 17th, 25th, 26th

Most Stressful Days Overall: 2nd, 3rd, 10th, 11th, 23rd, 29th, 30th, 31st

Best Days for Love: 1st, 2nd, 3rd, 10th, 11th, 19th, 20th, 21st, 27th, 28th, 29th, 30th, 31st

Best Days for Money: 5th, 6th, 10th, 11th, 14th, 15th, 19th, 20th, 21st, 23rd, 29th, 30th

Health should be your number-one concern this month, Virgo. Happily, you don't need much convincing. Sure, there are many wonderful developments taking place, but you've got to take care of your health or you will never enjoy them. The temptations to over-socialize and over-work are tremendous now. Be aware of your capacity and act accordingly. Your ankles and feet need to be given more attention and should be massaged regularly.

Having said this, you are in one of the strongest social periods of your year. Romantic opportunities, parties and social gatherings are plentiful. With Uranus moving into your 7th House on the 10th, there is plenty of change and excitement too. Love becomes highly unstable, but a lot of fun. Anything can happen at any time, but you never know how long it will last. It's as if you get 'flashes of paradise', but have trouble living there. Again, love seems to come at the work place. The work place is your social milieu. Co-workers like to play Cupid as well. You are unusually popular and seem aggressive in social matters. You go after what you want, rather than waiting for the phone to ring.

Uranus' move into Pisces is signalling work and job changes for many of you.

Like last month, your good comes through others and by their grace. So avoid power struggles like the plague. 'Agree with thine adversary quickly' and conserve much-needed energy. Being right is not important now – conserving energy is.

Like last month, there is a T-square in the mutable Signs. Thus there are dramatic conflicts between love, career, family and personal obligations and desires. It is up to you to make them all co-operate with each other.

The planets are starting to make a shift to the upper half of your Horoscope. By the 21st, the majority of planets will be there. So, your attention is beginning to shift (little by little) towards your career and 'outer' ambitions. Still, balance is the key.

Finances seem strong this month, as Venus moves unusually quickly through three Signs and Houses of the Horoscope. (This is unusual for Venus.) Thus financial confidence is strong, decisions are made quickly and much ground is covered. Financial goals are attained quickly and through a variety of ways and means. Until the 2nd it comes through creativity and perhaps speculation. After the 2nd it comes through work. After the 21st, through social connections, your spouse or the partner. A business partnership could be brewing. Your financial intuition is unusually sharp on the 12th – a financial dream or vision should be given some weight. Your partner is unusually generous. A sudden windfall or opportunity (out of the blue) comes around the 28th.

April

Best Days Overall: 3rd, 4th, 5th, 13th, 14th, 21st, 22nd

Most Stressful Days Overall: 6th, 7th, 19th, 20th, 26th, 27th

Best Days for Love: 6th, 7th, 8th, 9th, 15th, 16th, 17th, 18th, 23rd, 24th, 26th, 27th, 28th, 29th

Best Days for Money: 1st, 2nd, 8th, 9th, 10th, 11th, 12th, 15th, 16th, 17th, 18th, 19th, 20th, 28th, 29th

Health is much improved this month, Virgo, but still needs to be watched. However, if you got through last month (a victory in itself), this month will be a breeze. Again, the challenge is to balance your home, career and social life in a right way.

This is still a very social period. Like last month, 70% to 80% of the planets are in the West and your 7th House of Social Activities is strong. Your 1st House of Self, by contrast, is empty – except for the Moon's visit on the 13th and 14th. So much of what was said last month still applies – use charm, grace, consensus and compromise to attain your ends. Win others over to your position. Adapt to difficult situations rather than trying to change them by force and, by all means, avoid power struggles with other people.

The planetary power is now pretty much established above the horizon of your chart. So, career and outer objectives are most important to you. But, as mentioned, you still have to balance home and career. This period, you might favour your career just a tad.

Love is still happy and exciting. Romance is blooming, but still unstable. Long-existing relationships are undergoing change and could be dissolved. This applies not only to romantic relationships but to friendships as well. Astrologers, scientists and high-tech types are coming into your social sphere. You love the unconventional in a partner. Old social patterns and attitudes are breaking up – this is Uranus' spiritual purpose. Sometimes you have to knock the house down in order to see the sky. Humdrum, conventional-type relationships are just not for you these days.

Romantic opportunities can come from the family or family connections after the 21st. Perhaps at a family gathering or party. An old love can come back into the picture and re-ignite old passions. And, as in past months, the work place is a source of romantic opportunity.

Finances are reasonable this month. Wealth comes from social connections, your spouse or partner and from a business partnership. A business partnership is brewing these days. After the 21st, channel spare cash towards debt repayment and work to reduce expenses and waste. In order to prosper, you need to put other people's financial interests ahead of your own – to see what you can do to help them prosper – to the degree that you are successful in this, you will prosper personally. Don't let a sudden expense or financial delay on the 17th get you down. It is temporary. A sudden windfall or opportunity comes around the 29th.

Until the 20th, you are in a great period for breaking addictions or transforming negative character traits. The deeper things of life call to you. Your libido will be unusually strong. This is normal. After the 20th, your interest shifts to religion, philosophy, higher education and foreign lands. Conflicts between religious teachings, your personal philosophy of life and your personal spiritual experience will lead you to higher ground if you accept the validity of each. In reality there are no contradictions.

May

Best Days Overall: 1st, 2nd, 10th, 11th, 18th, 19th, 28th, 29th

Most Stressful Days Overall: 3rd, 4th, 16th, 17th, 23rd, 24th, 30th, 31st

Best Days for Love: 3rd, 4th, 8th, 9th, 12th, 13th, 18th, 21st, 22nd, 23rd, 24th, 28th, 29th, 30th, 31st

Best Days for Money: 8th, 9th, 12th, 13th, 16th, 17th, 18th, 25th, 26th, 27th, 28th, 29th

Most of the planets are above the horizon of your chart, your 10th House of Career is powerful and there's a Solar eclipse in your 10th House on the 31st – all these point to dynamic career changes and a focus on these things. However, you need to take a reduced schedule from the 21st onwards and pay special attention to the Solar eclipse period of the 31st – for about two days before and a day after. Avoid stressful, risk-taking activities. In fact, you should avoid any activity that is not absolutely necessary. Best to rest, relax, read a book, stay close to home, meditate and pray. Only you know which activities are elective and which are necessary, so this calls for discernment on your part.

Stressful periods, crises and the like, always bring opportunity to those who can keep a cool head about them. Very often these stresses are actually answers to your prayers (spoken or unspoken), as these obstructions to your desires need to be cleared away. All of us, but especially you, Virgo, need to look deeper at stress and see the purpose behind it. It is usually wonderful. Yes, there is life after crisis. And crisis is often the short-cut to the true desire of your heart.

The Lunar eclipse on the 16th is much easier on you, but it won't hurt to take a reduced schedule anyway. This eclipse occurs in your 3rd House of Siblings, Neighbours and Communication. Students could make important educational changes during this period. Upheavals are likely at school – with the administration or teachers. Communication equipment and cars could use special checking, as long-hidden flaws are likely to be revealed. This might be the time to spring for that new computer, car or telephone. Since the Moon rules your 11th House of Friends, this eclipse can also test a friendship or cause upheavals in a social or professional organization that you're involved with.

Health is delicate after the 21st, so please keep in mind previous discussions in past reports. Continue to massage your ankles and feet regularly.

Finances are reasonable this month. Cost-cutting efforts and debt-repayment make you financially healthier. Thus when financial expansion starts happening from the 16th onwards, it will be healthier. After the 16th, the revelation of important financial principles helps you create your own good luck. The 'how to' of a given project or situation is revealed. Money and financial opportunities come from property, publishers, foreign lands or foreigners. Metaphysical practices such as prayer and meditation increase your wealth consciousness.

Love can suffer as you focus on your career after the 21st. Hopefully, your partner will understand.

June

Best Days Overall: 7th, 8th, 15th, 16th, 24th, 25th

Most Stressful Days Overall: 1st, 13th, 14th, 19th, 20th, 27th, 28th

Best Days for Love: 1st, 7th, 8th, 9th, 10th, 17th, 18th, 19th, 20th, 27th, 28th

Best Days for Money: 4th, 5th, 7th, 8th, 9th, 10th, 13th, 14th, 17th, 18th, 22nd, 23rd, 27th, 28th

Though Saturn leaving Gemini on the 4th is a positive boon, Mars moves into a stressful six-month alignment with you on the 17th. Health is still delicate and needs to be watched. Health can be much improved by avoiding power struggles with your beloved or with friends and pacing yourself at work. Overwork is probably the main health danger this period. Emotional volatility is also a health factor and you should strive, as much as possible, to cultivate equilibrium.

The planets are still mostly above the horizon, and your 10th House of Career is unusually active. You are ambitious these days. Nevertheless, your need to balance your ambitions with other aspects of life – social and domestic – is still very important. Try not to let ambitions outrun your basic energy. Keep your career goals few and modest for now – keep them in a range where they are achievable.

Last month the planets began an important shift from the Western sector to the Eastern sector. This month the shift is firmly established. The planetary power is now in the East for months to come. Thus you are more independent and more in charge of your destiny. You have more power to change difficult situations and conditions and to create new ones that suit you better. Though you might feel that going your own way will cause unpopularity, the truth is that it will not. Others will adapt to you.

The pace at work is hectic, as mentioned. There could be upheavals and tension at the work place. But Uranus' (your Work Planets') retrograde on the 7th counsels caution and the postponement of major decisions at work. Job-seekers, too, need to exercise more caution before accepting positions.

50% of the planets change Signs this month – an unusually high percentage – thus there is much change in your life and in the lives of others. Sit loose to things and cultivate a philosophical attitude. Change only causes discomfort when we are attached to things or situations. Loosen the attachments and the whole thing becomes enjoyable.

Finances are reasonable. In the short term there are ups and downs – sudden expense perhaps, but also sudden earnings or windfalls. Money comes from foreign lands, foreigners, publishing or educational institutions until the 10th. After that, it comes from elders, bosses, parents and those above you in status. They seem eager to support your financial goals. Many might receive pay rises during this period. The main positive financial signal now is that you pay more attention to finances. Venus is the most elevated planet in the chart for most of the month. Interest and focus lead to success. Good sales and marketing play an important role in earnings after the 10th.

Mars' move into your 7th House of Love increases the volatility of an already volatile love life. Love gets tested. Passions – both positive and negative – run high. Though you should avoid them, power struggles in love are tempting. Avoid making long-term love decisions now – though you will be sorely tempted. Neptune, your Love Planet, is retrograde and your judgement might not be realistic.

July

Best Days Overall: 4th, 5th, 12th, 13th, 21st, 22nd, 23rd, 31st

Most Stressful Days Overall: 10th, 11th, 17th, 18th, 24th, 25th

Best Days for Love: 6th, 7th, 8th, 9th, 14th, 15th, 17th, 18th, 24th, 25th, 28th, 29th

Best Days for Money: 2nd, 3rd, 8th, 9th, 10th, 11th, 19th, 20th, 29th, 30th

The pace of life seems to have slowed down as retrograde activity increases this month, but personally (except in love) you make fast progress. Mercury, your Ruling Planet, moves forward speedily. So does Venus, your Money Planet.

Health is improving, but still needs watching. Like last month, overwork, haste and impatience are the main dangers. Keep massaging your ankles and feet.

The planetary power is in the East and your personal confidence is strong. If you can manage to be independent without getting involved in power struggles (a neat trick this month), much can be accomplished. Be respectful of others, acknowledge their desires, but quietly go your own way and build your life as you desire it to be. You know what is best for you these days.

Most of the planets are still above the horizon, so continue to focus on your career and outer objectives. You won't be able to ignore family and social concerns, but you can de-emphasize them slightly.

Venus in your Career House until the 4th shows the favour of those above you in status – bosses, parents, government figures. They still support your financial goals and provide financial opportunity. Good career progress is made this month. You cover a lot of territory and seem very confident. Networking and joining professional organizations (or attending more of these types of meetings) fosters your career until the 13th. After that, charitable and volunteer-type activities boost your career. You make important contacts and your contributions look good on your CV. By the 30th, you are reaching career highs.

Money, too, comes from career activities, pay rises at work and the favour of superiors. After the 4th, it comes through friends and organizations to which you belong. Friends and organizations seem supportive of your financial goals. After the 29th, dreams and intuition guide your finances, though it is not always easy to discern the meaning of these things.

Love is volatile and exciting. Tempestuous. Like last month, passions are running high both positively and negatively. The temptation is to join the fray – but it would be wiser to duck and evade. Anything can happen in love this month – this is what makes things so confusing and exciting. Expect the unexpected.

August

Best Days Overall: 1st, 9th, 10th, 18th, 19th, 27th, 28th

Most Stressful Days Overall: 7th, 13th, 14th, 20th, 21st, 22nd

Best Days for Love: 2nd, 3rd, 7th, 8th, 11th, 12th, 13th, 14th, 16th, 17th, 20th, 21st, 22nd, 27th, 28th

Best Days for Money: 2nd, 3rd, 7th, 8th, 16th, 17th, 26th, 27th, 28th, 30th

Health is improving day by day, but still needs some watching. The appearance of many planets in your own Sign of Virgo after the 22nd enhances your energy, increases self-esteem and confidence and brings sensual delights. This is definitely a time for getting your way (whilst avoiding conflicts with others) and creating conditions as you like them.

This month begins a new era of luck and success. Jupiter makes a once-in-11-years move into your own Sign on the 27th. As mentioned in the yearly report, this brings travel, prosperity, new clothing, accessories and the good life. With Venus, the planet of beauty, in your own Sign after the 22nd, it is also an excellent period for buying clothing and accessories. Your aesthetic sense is unusually sharp. Probably these things are on their way to you.

The planets are making an important shift from the upper to the lower half of your Horoscope this month. By the 27th, 60% to 70% of the planets will be below the horizon and your interest will shift from career to family and emotional issues. Your job now will be to live in the 'right emotional state'. Everything else will proceed from there.

This is a prosperous month in a prosperous year. You spend on yourself – invest in yourself, dress for success, etc. You don the image of wealth. This is also a month where sensual fantasies come to pass. It is a month for good food, good wine and the pleasures of the body. You seem well pampered.

Intuition is still important in finance until the 22nd. You seem more charitable during this period as well. And, as you give, so do you receive. You might not always receive 'physical, tangible things' – often the law of karma brings you wealth ideas and connections instead.

Whenever a new cycle begins, it is always wise to review the past one and digest it – to see what you've achieved, what you did right and what you did wrong. It is a time for taking stock and planning the future. This is the case until the 22nd.

Though you are magnetic and look great, love is still very stormy. Mars and Uranus have been camping out in your 7th House of Love for some months. Relationships are being tested so that you can see what is what and who is who. Changes in your love life are the rule now rather than the exception. Some changes you can do nothing about, but where you have the choice – delay. The three planets involved in your love life are all retrograde – so things seem to be going backwards instead of forwards and your social judgement could be a lot better.

September

Best Days Overall: 5th, 6th, 14th, 15th, 24th, 25th

Most Stressful Days Overall: 3rd, 4th, 9th, 10th, 17th, 18th, 30th

Best Days for Love: 5th, 6th, 7th, 8th, 9th, 10th, 16th, 17th, 18th, 26th, 27th

Best Days for Money: 5th, 6th, 14th, 15th, 16th, 26th, 27th

Health is vastly improved this month as Uranus moves out of a stressful alignment with you and many planets in your own Sign strengthen you. Now only Mars and Pluto (not powers to be trifled with) are stressing you. It is still a situation, as we have seen in past months, of balancing home, family, love and personal desires and duties. I would give a bit more weight to your personal desires this period. Though you might meet with greater resistance to your personal desires and to your independence, it is still good to assert yourself now – in a non-confrontational way. Mercury's retrograde until the 20th suggests that you make haste slowly and carefully. Give more thought to your plans and projects – research them more carefully.

The planetary power below the horizon of your chart increases even further this month, as Uranus retrogrades back into Aquarius. Thus, like last month, focus on your emotional life and domestic stability and tranquillity. Feeling right becomes more important than 'doing right'. When you feel right you will do right very naturally. The psychological foundations for future success are being laid down now.

In spite of a few bumps in the road, this is a happy month. Two powerful beneficial Planets, Jupiter and Venus, are in your own Sign. These bring wealth, sensual pleasure, optimism, personal beauty and grace and enhanced self-esteem and self-worth. Honours and recognition come to you now. Family seems supportive – more supportive than they have been in a long time. They seem in your corner. These beneficial Planets also bring more parties and entertainments. Love opportunities come, but as in past months, love is unstable. Anything can happen at any time and it is difficult to make concrete plans. Love will be happy if you can accept spontaneity. Love should be easier after the 15th than before. Friendships seem much more stable than romantic affairs. (Those working towards a second marriage have a much easier time than those working towards a first. Significant opportunities are happening this month.)

Your financial life shines this period. Your Money House becomes very strong after the 23rd. Financial intuition is strong. You give personal attention to finance and thus you prosper. There are more dealings with bankers, brokers, money managers, financial planners, etc. The main financial danger is over-spending – spending what you don't have, based on over-optimism.

October

Best Days Overall: 2nd, 3rd, 11th, 12th, 13th, 21st, 22nd, 29th, 30th

Most Stressful Days Overall: 1st, 7th, 8th, 14th, 15th, 27th, 28th

Best Days for Love: 4th, 5th, 7th, 8th, 14th, 15th, 16th, 17th, 23rd, 24th, 25th, 26th

Best Days for Money: 2nd, 3rd, 4th, 5th, 11th, 12th, 13th, 16th, 17th, 21st, 22nd, 23rd, 24th, 25th, 26th, 29th, 30th

Health is reasonable this month, but Mars and Pluto are still in stressful alignment with you. Avoid power struggles and keep to a slow, deliberate pace – avoid haste and rush – and keep a lid on your temper. A month-long T-square (this has been in effect for many months now) shows the need to balance personal desires with domestic and social obligations. The conflicts between these areas are dramatic; it is up to you to bring them into harmony.

Most of the planets are still in the East, so you still have much free will and independence. Build your life, but don't rush about it. Every day certain things are possible and some are impossible – given your energy and circumstances. Do what is possible and enjoy your day.

Like last month, most of the planets are below the horizon of your chart. Your 4th House of Home and Family is strong (and will get even stronger), while your 10th House of Career is empty – except for the Moon's visit on the 14th and 15th. Career and outer objectives can be safely de-emphasized in favour of home and family duties. Like last month, staying in the right emotional state is more important than a deal here or there.

A power struggle with a friend or loved one should have no effect on other romantic opportunities coming your way. As in the past few months, avoid important love decisions (positive or negative) until after the 23rd, when your Love Planet starts moving forwards again. Love needs and attitudes are undergoing fundamental, rock-bottom change. Addictive types of love relationships are being broken up.

Like last month, this is a strong financial month. The year ahead is prosperous and this month is one of the more prosperous ones. True, there will be bumps on the road as different areas of life lay claims to your new prosperity – but these are easily dealt with using a sense of proportion. Allocate percentages of your income to each area of life. Like last month, your financial intuition is strong and this is the most important thing.

After the 9th, sales, marketing, buying, selling, trading and PR activities enhance your bottom line. With your Money Planet (Venus) in Scorpio, it is a good time to pay off debt or re-finance it more favourably. It is also good for seeing profit opportunities in turn-around situations – troubled companies or properties that can be brought back to profitability.

In general, you are in a period (after the 23rd) of intellectual expansion and development. Take those classes or read those books you've always wanted to read. Feed your mind now.

November

Best Days Overall: 8th, 9th, 18th, 19th, 26th, 27th

Most Stressful Days Overall: 3rd, 4th, 10th, 11th, 12th, 24th, 25th, 30th

Best Days for Love: 1st, 2nd, 3rd, 4th, 5th, 6th, 10th, 11th, 15th, 16th, 20th, 21st, 25th, 26th, 27th, 28th, 29th, 30th

Best Days for Money: 5th, 6th, 8th, 9th, 15th, 16th, 18th, 19th, 20th, 21st, 25th, 26th, 27th

The planets are making an important shift from the East to the West this month. This signals an important psychological shift for you. Now there will be less independence and personal power and a greater need for social power. Good will come through the good graces of others and not so much from personal effort. The need to adapt and to seek consensus in all things starts to become important. The shift happens gradually and will be complete by the 22nd.

Like last month, most of the planetary power is below the horizon, so continue to emphasize family and domestic duties over the career. Emotional well-being will eventually lead to career success.

Two eclipses this month make life more turbulent and exciting. Of the two, the Solar eclipse of the 23rd is the strongest on you. Do take a reduced schedule – for a few days before and about a day after. Actually, you should take a reduced schedule from the 22nd onwards, but definitely around the eclipse period. (Psychics and sensitives often experience an eclipse weeks before it happens, but for average people the orb lasts only a few days.) This eclipse occurs in your 4th House, showing long-term changes in your home and family situation. Moves often happen under these kinds of eclipses – and are likely now. Often major renovations happen. Hidden flaws in the home get revealed so that you can take corrective steps. Family and domestic patterns or relationships change – for the long term. Eclipses tend to bring upheaval, so let the dust settle before making important decisions. What you need to do will become very apparent once the brouhaha dies down.

The Lunar eclipse of the 9th occurs in your 9th House, signalling a testing of your personal philosophy of life and your view of the world. Everybody has a personal religion – a personal world view. With some it is conscious, with most it is unconscious. This world view has tremendous power over a person – in how he or she experiences life and interprets events. So, upheavals – crises of faith – are often good things. You can see where your beliefs and views have been wanting and can make changes. On a more mundane level, this eclipse brings important changes for students. In many cases these are normal – the student changes areas of study or university or graduates, etc. In some cases, there will be power shifts at the university or church you belong to.

Health is more delicate this month – especially after the 23rd – so keep in mind previous discussions about health. Keeping your ankles fit (by giving them more support and through massage) is an important way to enhance your overall health.

Finances are strong, but less important than they have been. Your interest has waned. Still, Venus' speedy motion (she covers three Signs and Houses this month) shows confidence and much forward progress.

Love is stressful.

December

Best Days Overall: 5th, 6th, 15th, 16th, 23rd, 24th

Most Stressful Days Overall: 1st, 7th, 8th, 9th, 21st, 22nd, 27th, 28th

Best Days for Love: 1st, 5th, 6th, 7th, 8th, 9th, 15th, 16th, 17th, 18th, 25th, 26th, 27th, 28th

Best Days for Money: 5th, 6th, 15th, 16th, 17th, 18th, 23rd, 24th, 25th, 26th

Health improves dramatically after the 16th as Mars moves away from a stressful six-month transit. Still, it won't hurt to pace yourself until the 22nd.

90% of the planets are moving forwards this month, so you will be making rapid progress towards your goals, though you might not feel it. The retrograde of Mercury, your Ruling Planet, makes you feel that you're not progressing even though you are.

The planets are still mostly in the West, so, as mentioned last month, this is a period for developing social skills, tact, charm and diplomacy. Your way is probably not the best way this period, as there are factors that you are not aware of. Let go of self-will and undue independence and allow your good to come to you.

The planetary power is still mostly in the lower half (below the horizon) of your chart. Again, like last month, cultivate harmonious emotional states and stabilize things at home. A strong home base will allow for career expansion later on.

Mars' move out of your 7th House of Love is a big plus on the romantic front. By now a serious relationship has either broken off or transformed itself into something more pleasing. But love is going to be volatile for many years to come, as Uranus moves into your 7th House (again) on the 30th. Uranus in the 7th is not really a marriage aspect. Often it denies marriage. Often it shows multiple – serial – marriages. Always it brings serial and unconventional relationships. Those working towards a second marriage, however, have wonderful opportunities until the 21st. Love awaits you at parties, social gatherings and as you pursue leisure activities.

After the 22nd, you are in a party period. A period for leisure and fun. A cosmic holiday. You deserve one. Finances seems strong and money is easily earned until the 21st. The money that comes is happy money. Speculations are favourable. After the 21st, money comes through work. A Grand Trine in your native element of Earth on the 15th and 16th not only enhances your health and energy, but brings financial windfalls, opportunities and big-ticket items for the home. After the 21st, Venus (your Money Planet), travels with Neptune, the planet of intuition and love (your Love Planet). This suggests money from your spouse or partner, profitable intuitive flashes and a possible business partnership or joint venture.

Libra

♎

THE SCALES

Birthdays from

23rd September

to 22nd October

Personality Profile

LIBRA AT A GLANCE

Element – Air

Ruling Planet – Venus
- *Career Planet* – Moon
- *Love Planet* – Mars
- *Money Planet* – Pluto
- *Planet of Communications* – Jupiter
- *Planet of Health and Work* – Neptune
- *Planet of Home and Family Life* – Saturn
- *Planet of Spirituality and Good Fortune* – Mercury

Colours – blue, jade green

Colours that promote love, romance and social harmony – carmine, red, scarlet

Colours that promote earning power – burgundy, red-violet, violet

Gems – carnelian, chrysolite, coral, emerald, jade, opal, quartz, white marble

Metal – copper

Scents – almond, rose, vanilla, violet

Quality – cardinal (= activity)

Qualities most needed for balance – a sense of self, self-reliance, independence

Strongest virtues – social grace, charm, tact, diplomacy

Deepest needs – love, romance, social harmony

Characteristic to avoid – violating what is right in order to be socially accepted

Signs of greatest overall compatibility – Gemini, Aquarius

Signs of greatest overall incompatibility – Aries, Cancer, Capricorn

Sign most helpful to career – Cancer

Sign most helpful for emotional support – Capricorn

Sign most helpful financially – Scorpio

Sign best for marriage and/or partnerships – Aries

Sign most helpful for creative projects – Aquarius

Best Sign to have fun with – Aquarius

Signs most helpful in spiritual matters – Gemini, Virgo

Best day of the week – Friday

Understanding a Libra

In the Sign of Libra, the universal mind – the soul – expresses its genius for relationships, that is, its power to harmonize diverse elements in a unified, organic way. Libra is the soul's power to express beauty in all of its forms. And where is beauty if not within relationships? Beauty does not exist in isolation. Beauty arises out of comparison – out of the just relationship between different parts. Without a fair and harmonious relationship, there is no beauty, whether it be in art, manners, ideas or the social or political forum.

There are two faculties humans have that exalt them above the animal kingdom: their rational faculty (expressed in the Signs of Gemini and Aquarius) and their aesthetic faculty, exemplified by Libra. Without an aesthetic sense, we would be little more than intelligent barbarians. Libra is the civilizing instinct or urge of the soul.

Beauty is the essence of what Librans are all about. They are here to beautify the world. One could discuss Librans' social grace, their sense of balance and fair play, their ability to see and love another person's point of view – but this would be to miss their central asset: their desire for beauty.

No one – no matter how alone he or she seems to be – exists in isolation. The universe is one vast collaboration of beings. Librans, more than most, understand this and understand the spiritual laws that make relationships bearable and enjoyable.

A Libra is always the unconscious (and in some cases conscious) civilizer, harmonizer and artist. This is a Libra's deepest urge and greatest genius. Librans love instinctively to bring people together and they are uniquely qualified to do so. They have a knack for seeing what unites people – the things that attract and bind rather than separate individuals.

Finance

In financial matters Librans can seem frivolous and illogical to others. This is because Librans appear to be more concerned with earning money for others than for themselves. But there is a logic to this financial attitude. Librans know that everything and everyone is connected and that it is impossible to help another to prosper without also prospering yourself. Since enhancing their partner's income and position tends to strengthen their relationship, Librans choose to do so. What could be more fun than building a relationship? You will rarely find a Libra enriching him- or herself at someone else's expense.

Scorpio is the Ruler of Libra's Solar 2nd House of Money, giving Libra unusual insight into financial matters – and the power to focus on these matters in a way that disguises a seeming indifference. In fact, many other Signs come to Librans for financial advice and guidance.

Given their social grace, Librans often spend great sums of money on entertaining and organizing social events. They also like to help others when they are in need. Librans would go out of their way to help a friend in dire straits, even if they have to borrow from others to do so. However, Librans are also very careful to pay back any debts they owe and like to make sure they never have to be reminded to do so.

Career and Public Image

Publicly, Librans like to appear as nurturers. Their friends and acquaintances are their family and they wield political power in parental ways. They also like bosses who are paternal or maternal.

The Sign of Cancer is on Libra's 10th House (of Career) cusp; the Moon is Libra's Career Planet. The Moon is by far the speediest, most changeable planet in the Horoscope. It alone among all the planets travels through the entire

Zodiac – all 12 Signs and Houses – every month. This is an important key to the way in which Librans approach their careers and also to what they need to do to maximize their career potential. The Moon is the Planet of Moods and Feelings – Librans need a career in which their emotions can have free expression. This is why so many Librans are involved in the creative arts. Libran's ambitions wax and wane with the Moon. They tend to wield power according to their mood.

The Moon 'rules' the masses – and that is why Libran's highest goal is to achieve a mass kind of acclaim and popularity. Librans who achieve fame cultivate the public as other people cultivate a lover or friend. Librans can be very flexible – and often fickle – in their career and ambitions. On the other hand, they can achieve their ends in a great variety of ways. They are not stuck in one attitude or with one way of doing things.

Love and Relationships

Librans express their true genius in love. In love, you could not find a partner more romantic, more seductive or more fair. If there is one thing that is sure to destroy a relationship – sure to block your love from flowing – it is injustice or imbalance between lover and beloved. If one party is giving too much or taking too much, resentment is sure to surface at some time or other. Librans are careful about this. If anything, Librans might err on the side of giving more, but never giving less.

If you are in love with a Libra, make sure you keep the aura of romance alive. Do all the little things – candle-lit dinners, travel to exotic places, flowers and small gifts. Give things that are beautiful, not necessarily expensive. Send cards. Ring regularly even if you have nothing in particular to say. The niceties are very important to a Libra. Your relationship is a work of art: make it beautiful and your

Libra lover will appreciate it. If you are creative about it, he or she will appreciate it even more; for this is how your Libra will behave towards you.

Librans like their partners to be aggressive and even a bit self-willed. They know that these are qualities they sometimes lack and so they like their partners to have them. In relationships, however, Librans can be very aggressive – but always in a subtle and charming way! Librans are determined in their efforts to charm the object of their desire – and this determination can be very pleasant if you are on the receiving end.

Home and Domestic Life

Since Librans are such social creatures, they do not particularly like mundane domestic duties. They like a well-organized home – clean and neat with everything they need – but housework is a chore and a burden, one of the unpleasant tasks in life that must be done, the quicker the better. If a Libra has enough money – and sometimes even if not – he or she will prefer to pay someone else to take care of the daily household chores. However, Librans like gardening; they love to have flowers and plants in the home.

A Libra's home is modern and furnished in excellent taste. You will find many paintings and sculptures there. Since Librans like to be with friends and family, they enjoy entertaining at home and they make great hosts.

Capricorn is on the cusp of Libra's 4th Solar House of Home and Family. Saturn, the Planet of Law, Order, Limits and Discipline, rules Libra's domestic affairs. If Librans want their home life to be supportive and happy they need to develop some of the virtues of Saturn – order, organization and discipline. Librans, being so creative and so intensely in need of harmony, can tend to be too lax in the home and too permissive with their children. Too much of this is not always good; children need freedom, but they also need limits.

Horoscope for 2003

Major Trends

Your aspects have been sensational for the past two years. Most of you prospered and enjoyed life to the fullest. Health should have been good. You moved forwards towards your goals rather easily. This year you will have to work a little harder to achieve your goals. The holiday isn't over, but it's more like a working holiday.

Job and career changes are in store which will entail taking on more responsibility. Your health, while still good, can't just be taken for granted.

This year is more of a career year than previous years. Spirituality becomes more important later in the year as well. Joy is not just sensual pleasure and you will see deeper aspects of it in the coming year. There is joy to be had in overcoming obstacles and transforming negatives into positives.

Saturn leaving the 9th House of Higher Education is a happy signal for university students. They don't have to work as hard as in previous years (especially after June 4).

Your most important areas of interest in the coming year are: communication and intellectual interests; fun, creativity, children and love affairs (not marriage); health and work (after March 10); religion, higher education, foreign travel (until June 4); career (after June 4); friendships, groups and group activities (until August 27); spirituality (after August 27).

Your paths of greatest fulfilment this year are: religion, metaphysics, higher education and foreign travel (until April 14); repayment of debt, helping others prosper; sex, personal transformation (after April 14); friendships, groups and group activities (until August 27; spirituality (after August 27).

Health

Your 6th House of Health hasn't been a House of Power for many years. So you've taken good health for granted – perhaps justifiably so. This year things are changing. Uranus is about ready to move into this House for a long time (the next seven years). This year he moves in for six months before retrograding back into your 5th House. Mars, which rarely stays in any one Sign for more than two months, will make a six-month transit in your 6th House from June 17 to December 16. Saturn, which has been making beautiful aspects to you for the past two years, moves into a stressful aspect on June 14. The message is clear – start focusing more on health and fitness.

These aspects are not showing sickness. On the contrary, most of the long-term planets are making nice aspects to you. They are only showing that it's time to pay more attention here. Health regimes and good health habits begun now will stand you in good stead later on.

The main health danger this year seems to come from over-ambition or over-work. Career becomes important and we see a lot of work burdens and responsibilities. You are carrying a lot of weight here and the tendency would be to over-work. Your sense of duty keeps your nose to the grindstone, but if over-done can lead to pessimism and depression. Thus you need to allow time for play and personal pleasure. Creative hobbies – things you do for the sheer joy of doing them – are also advisable.

Uranus in your 6th House (you're going to have this for many years to come) has many messages. It shows that you benefit from experimental and unorthodox therapies; that in general you are more experimental in health matters, willing to try new things; that the health of children is as important to you as your own personal health (you seem very involved in this area); that joy, rapture and just a good night out on the town is of itself a great healing for you (Uranus is the Lord of your 5th House); that many of you will benefit more from a night out on the town than a visit to a doctor's surgery; that your sense of playfulness is important for health; that your inner child needs to be found and given expression; that you would benefit from therapies involving sound, colour and drama. (Yes, drama was originally designed for healing purposes and in ancient times was under the control of the priesthood.)

Neptune is your Health Planet and he is still in your 5th House, reinforcing much of what was said above. Neptune as your Health Planet shows that you respond unusually well to foot reflexology and that the feet need better care – e.g. avoid ill-fitting shoes or shoes that throw you off-balance. Keep your feet warm in winter and soak and massage them regularly. (Uranus in Pisces is also reinforcing all this.)

Mars in your 6th House for the latter six months of the year is also showing many things. You respond well to vigorous exercise. Your notion of health means much more than just not being ill – it means physical fitness and athletic ability. Many of you will find an hour at the gym to be more effective than hosts of other therapies. Mars, being your Love Planet, shows that you desire a healthy love and social life as much as physical health – that health means a healthy love and social life – healthy relations. Librans always tend to think in these terms, but this year even more so.

In general, health problems are probably arising from these sources: pessimism or depression; the lack of play; marital or social dis-harmonies; lack of exercise; problems with the children. Thus, if you clear up these things at their root, if the services of a health professional are needed, things will go much more easily and quickly. In many cases you won't need the services of a health professional at all.

As mentioned, your health is basically good, the above are just ways to enhance it further.

Home, Domestic and Family Issues

Your 4th House of Home and Family is not a House of Power this year, Libra. Ordinarily, this would show a lack of interest and greater personal freedom in these issues. But your Family Planet, Saturn, will be on the Midheaven of your Solar Horoscope towards the latter part of the year – this shows great interest and priority.

Generally, when the Lord of the 4th House (your Family Planet) is in the 10th House, it indicates a desire to make your family your career or that you sublimate your personal career in favour of the career of the family members or for the status of the family as a whole. Often it indicates a desire to pursue a career from home, or with a family-orientated business. Since your Family Planet properly belongs in its own Sign and House – when it is in its opposite Sign and House (as is the case here), there is great ambivalence and confusion about both your domestic life and career. You are unsure whether to pursue a worldly career or a family life. When you pursue one or the other, there is a feeling that you are missing out on something. The idea here is to blend family and career in one seamless way. To get the best of both worlds – the pleasures of home and hearth together with outer achievement – the feeling of emotional comfort *and* career success. This is not about juggling family and career – as if they were two separate things. It's about blending both of them into one. I've seen cases under this aspect where the home itself becomes like an office – it's as if the person lives in an office rather than a home. Sometimes the home becomes a showcase to enhance the person's career and status. I've also seen cases where the office is made to resemble a home. Some will try to run their family life in a corporate, organized, cost-effective way. Others will try to inject some family feeling into their businesses. The distinctions between home and office get blurred.

Your Family Planet, Saturn, is a long-term, slow-moving planet. It stays in a Sign for two and a half years. Thus, when he changes Signs, it is a big deal. It shows that family attitudes and needs are changing. Domestic duties and responsibilities are changing. Often it shows a move or a change in the domestic pattern.

With Saturn on the Midheaven, there is much dealing with parents or parent figures. More so than in previous years. Relations with a parent or parent figure are more stressful than usual. You will need all your patience and social grace to deal with this. The important thing is to measure your energy and resources. Do what you can to help out and then let go. Don't let your personal health suffer over this.

Entertaining from home this year seems career-related. Redecorating projects and home entertaining go better from February 5 to March 27, from July 4 to July 29 and from October 9 to November 2.

Love and Social Life

Even though your 7th House of Love and Marriage is not a House of Power, being a Libra, this part of life will still be important to you. Not as important as in some past years, but still important. In love and marriage issues, I expect the status quo to prevail. Marrieds will tend to stay married, singles to stay single.

Your Love Planet, Mars, makes a highly unusual six-month transit in Pisces, your 6th Solar House. This is significant, as Mars rarely stays in a Sign for more than two months (and usually only a month and a half). This indicates many things. Love and love opportunities will tend to come at the work place – either with co-workers, employees or bosses. This is a classic indicator of office romance. The problem is that the relationship will get tested as Mars will go retrograde from July 29 to September 27. This will cool the passions considerably. If the relationship can survive this period, it could lead to something more serious.

Your Love Planet transiting the 6th House also shows an allure for doctors, nurses, healers and health professionals – people involved in your health. And what was mentioned above could also happen at the doctor's surgery or while you're getting a massage or spinal adjustment.

Your needs in love are service-orientated (especially from June 17 to December 16). You feel loved when someone is doing things for you – serving you in practical ways. This is also how you show love. Though you are usually the most romantic of all the Signs, this year you like some 'practical, down-to-earth' loving.

This is an excellent year for friendships, too. Perhaps you are enjoying friendships more than romance. New and significant friends are coming into the picture. Some are neighbours. Some are like brothers and sisters to you. Many of them are expanding your financial horizons or providing financial opportunities. They help make your financial dreams come true.

You will meet new friends in the neighbourhood, at schools, meetings or seminars. These are also people you can have a good time with.

Librans working towards a second marriage have better opportunities than last year – but the status quo will probably prevail. Those who are in their second marriage find more happiness within their marriage.

Wedding bells are ringing for those working towards a third marriage. Very strong aspects here. Again look in the neighbourhood, at meetings, classes and seminars.

Children of marriageable age are likely to marry or be involved in a serious relationship this year. In general, their social popularity and overall social activity increases.

Grandchildren of marriageable age need patience. Much social development is taking place to prepare the way for a serious relationship.

Finance and Career

Though your 2nd House of Finance is not a House of Power this year and you have little interest in these matters, there is going to be prosperity in spite of this.

Two beautiful, long-term financial trends are happening in 2003. Jupiter is making beautiful aspect to your Money Planet – especially until August 27. And Saturn is leaving a stressful two-and-a-half-year aspect by June 4. A lot of the strain and effort of earning is falling away. Financial goals are achieved easily. As mentioned, friends are going to be especially helpful and provide opportunities, knowledge or even actual funds. A good idea to get involved in clubs, organizations and group activities, as these will definitely enhance your bottom line.

Family expenses seem less of a burden after June 4.

Pluto, your Money Planet, has been in your Solar 3rd House for many years now – and he will be there for many years to come. Thus much of what was written last year still applies. Good communication, good use of the media, getting the word out about your product or service are major keys to earnings. In many cases, this position is showing that the communication industry itself is the path to earnings. Thus many Librans will excel in sales, marketing, public relations and the media in the year ahead and in coming years.

Writers and teachers will have a banner year.

Professional investors should look at the bond market and at telecommunication and transport industries for profit opportunities. Profit opportunities also come in property and with old-line, blue-chip companies. (Your individual Horoscope cast for your precise time and place of birth could modify this.)

The job situation seems volatile and highly unstable in the coming year. Uranus in your 6th House shows definite job changes – perhaps many of them. But though you feel insecure about this, have no fear – your overall prosperity is assured. Part of the instability is coming from a need for freedom at the job and from a need to enjoy one's work. There could be a lot of trial and error here. With Neptune (your Work Planet) and Uranus (your Joy Planet) occupying each other's Houses (this is called 'mutual reception' and is considered a very happy aspect, as it shows co-operation between the two planets) you will have eventual success in attaining work that you love. This mutual reception also suggests a creative type of job.

We discussed Saturn's entry into your 10th House of Career earlier, but we only discussed it as it pertained to family. In general, Saturn in the Career House shows a need for a long-term perspective in career matters. You advance gradually, by degrees, through earned effort and real achievement. In some cases, this shows a demanding and exacting boss – you've got to produce and, if you don't, the boss will be on your case. In other cases, it shows taking on more responsibility in the career – e.g. a promotion. Always it shows success through hard work. Saturn may be tough and demanding, but he is always fair. Hard work and real achievement are ALWAYS rewarded.

Self-improvement

With Pluto in your 3rd House of Communication for many years to come, it is definitely a good idea to work on improving your communication skills and your mind. These things are not only satisfying in their own right, but will make you a more valuable person and increase your earning power. Librans are generally good communicators naturally – but it won't hurt to hone these skills even further. A good idea to take classes in these things.

In the past two years, Saturn has been 'reality-testing' your religious beliefs, world view and personal philosophy of life. Many of these things didn't meet the test, had to be modified, clarified, put into context – and, in many cases, chucked overboard. Now, everybody has a personal 'metaphysics' – a personal religion they live by and certain axiomatic beliefs about the world and themselves. There is no exception to this. Even people who claim to be 'non-believers' or atheists are still expressing a metaphysical system – that of atheism. This re-ordering might not have been pleasant while it lasted, but it was very good and the consequences will be long term. For when you change your belief system and view of the world, you change your psychology (almost automatically) and your conditions and circumstances. Things become possible that were never possible before. This process is still going on until June and it is wise to co-operate with it rather than to fight it.

Saturn's move into your 10th House of Career (June 4) will initiate your next cycle of self-improvement. Saturn is not only going to make you insist on real achievement and merit, but also teach you the correct and responsible use of legitimate authority. For many of you will come into increased authority in the next two years.

Many people (especially when they are young and always taking orders) think 'How wonderful it would be to be in charge – to have all the power – and just have everyone do what I want.' I think everyone has this fantasy. They think of themselves as little czars making the world conform to their petty (and often erroneous) whims. Real power is never exercised on a 'whim' and never from selfish motives. These childhood fantasies about being empowered would be disastrous to the fantasizer if they were ever fulfilled the way he or she wanted. It would bring such karma on their heads that they would soon be wishing to be a plain ordinary person again. Over the next two years you will see why this is so. Every decision that affects others has immediate consequences. If one's judgement is warped by prejudice, immaturity, unfairness and lack of proportion the consequences will be unpleasant. But good judgement, fairness and a sense of proportion will be rewarded. Power is not something to be sought after, but 'grown into'.

Month-by-month Forecasts

January

Best Days Overall: 4th, 5th, 14th, 15th, 23rd, 24th

Most Stressful Days Overall: 2nd, 3rd, 9th, 10th, 16th, 17th, 29th, 30th

Best Days for Love: 9th, 10th, 19th, 20th, 27th, 28th

Best Days for Money: 1st, 9th, 10th, 19th, 20th, 25th, 26th, 27th, 28th

The planetary power is slightly westward this month, but the percentage will increase as time goes on. Thus you are in a position to exercise your genius – to cultivate the good graces of others and attain your ends through consensus, compromise, charm and grace. Though personal independence is lessened now, this is really Libra heaven.

70% to 80% of the planets are below the horizon of your chart this month, Libra, and your 4th House of Home and Family is unusually strong. Thus you are in a period where family and domestic issues take priority over your career. Cultivating emotional harmony and the right emotional states is more important than a new title or a new deal.

You have many interests this month; the danger is of dispersing your energies too frivolously and not achieving anything. While it is good to have many interests and a well-rounded development, give more attention to priorities.

Finances are important and successful all month. Interest in money matters wanes after the 17th and this is perhaps a weakness. Money comes from your spouse or partner and social connections and also from your personal effort. A nice windfall or opportunity happens around the 25th – perhaps through a neighbour, sibling or as a result of marketing activity. Beware of obsessive or impulsive spending during this period. Speculations become favourable after the 7th – but always speculate under the guidance of your intuition.

Love seems happy this month. You and your partner seem in synch until the 7th. Your partner is supportive financially and provides opportunities. Your partner (or love) shows his or her love through material gifts. After the 17th, good communication becomes important in love. You and your love are like 'brother and sister'. For singles, love is close to home, in the neighbourhood or as you pursue financial goals. The bank or brokerage house can be as much a romantic setting as the most lavish party or entertainment. The Cosmos can create romance in the most mundane places. Physical surroundings are never an issue for the Cosmos. You will see why romance is mostly a state of mind.

On an overall and long-term level, health is excellent, but it won't hurt to rest and relax more until the 20th.

Librans are generally creative people, but after the 20th, your creativity is even further enhanced. After the 20th, you are in a party period – a period for personal pleasure and leisure activities.

February

Best Days Overall: 1st, 2nd, 10th, 11th, 19th, 20th, 28th

Most Stressful Days Overall: 5th, 6th, 13th, 14th, 25th, 26th

Best Days for Love: 5th, 6th, 8th, 9th, 15th, 16th, 17th, 18th, 23rd, 24th, 25th, 26th

Best Days for Money: 5th, 6th, 15th, 16th, 21st, 22nd, 23rd, 24th

The party not only continues, but gets even stronger. It's as if you don't have a care in the world, but can live a life of joy. Some people might call you frivolous and irresponsible, but that's because they are not in on the great secret – joy creates wealth, health and positive circumstances. But you don't need to argue with these people – let your joy do the talking.

Like last month, creativity is strong. Artists and writers are very inspired and original now. Your ability to get on with children is enhanced, because you have found the child within and can relate to them almost on equal terms.

Much power in your native element of Air enhances your intellectual and communication powers. Students learn easily. Marketing efforts prosper.

The percentage of planets in the West increases over last month. So, your social genius will get plenty of exercise. With 90% of the planets moving forwards, your good should come to you easily, effortlessly and quickly.

Like last month, most of the planets are still below the horizon and Venus, your Ruling Planet, moves into your 4th House on the 4th. Focus on positive emotional states; everything else – career included – will fall into place. This is an excellent period for family gatherings and entertainments – also for beautifying the home.

Love is happy. Singles have options for either fun-and-games type love or more serious types. My guess is that singles will opt for fun. Good communication, financial support and harmony and material gifts are still important in love. This is how you show love and this is what makes you feel loved. Those in love with a Libra should pick up the phone more often.

Health is fabulous all month. You feel as light as a feather. You hardly touch ground. You seem more concerned with the health of friends than with personal health.

After the 19th, you get more serious. Work becomes more important.

Job-seekers meet with good success. Health regimes – especially group health regimes, like aerobics or yoga classes – go well and are appealing.

Finances are strong, though extra spending on the home or family members can create a sense of shortage (especially around the 20th). But this is only a temporary feeling. Money still comes from your spouse or partner or social connections. Sales, marketing, PR and media activities are still unusually vital to earnings.

March

Best Days Overall: 1st, 10th, 11th, 19th, 27th, 28th

Most Stressful Days Overall: 5th, 6th, 12th, 13th, 25th, 26th

Best Days for Love: 5th, 6th, 7th, 10th, 11th, 16th, 17th, 19th, 20th, 21st, 25th, 26th, 29th, 30th

Best Days for Money: 5th, 6th, 14th, 15th, 21st, 23rd

Though the party is far from over and you are still involved in creativity and leisure activities, now is the time to bring some of your joy into the work place and your daily chores. Of course, some employers won't like it if you giggle all day – but you can keep happy in a quiet way. For job-seekers, finding work that you love is a great priority. You should so love your job that you don't even feel that you're working – it's just an extension of the party.

Like last month, health is still good and health and workout regimes go well. You are more interested in health this month and stay on top of things. It won't hurt to rest and relax more after the 21st.

Most of the planets are still in the West and thus you are still in Libra heaven. Your good comes through your social grace and your ability to win others over to your side. Of course, this month you may have to do more compromising and go over to their side. I don't need to instruct a Libra on how to deal with others.

Most of the planets are still below the horizon of your chart, but this is soon to change. Little by little (you will feel the first inklings of a shift after the 21st), the planets will start energizing the upper half of your Horoscope. In the meantime, continue to build psychological and emotional foundations for career success. Shore up family relationships and cultivate positive emotional states. The time for focusing on your career is coming very shortly. This is still a wonderful period for family gatherings, entertaining from home and beautifying or redecorating the home.

Your love and social life shines after the 21st. There are more parties and gatherings – perhaps a wedding or two. You are in one of the most socially active periods of your year. A powerful Grand Trine in Fire from the 21st onwards brings social optimism and energy, enhances creativity and brings new and happy friendships into the picture – you can also expect financial windfalls and opportunities. A current love might not like all this socializing, but this disagreement is nothing you can't handle. Singles find love in the usual places this month – parties and gatherings – but also close to home. Family members like to play Cupid. Old flames could come back into your life. Nurturing and emotional support become important in love. Sharing feelings has become more important than other types of communication.

Your Money Planet (Pluto) goes retrograde on the 23rd, so give pending deals, investments and purchases (major ones) more study and thought. This retrograde doesn't affect your overall prosperity – which is unusually strong after the 21st. Just be patient with delays and minor annoyances.

April

Best Days Overall: 6th, 7th, 15th, 16th, 23rd, 24th

Most Stressful Days Overall: 1st, 2nd, 8th, 9th, 10th, 21st, 22nd, 28th, 29th

Best Days for Love: 1st, 2nd, 3rd, 4th, 5th, 8th, 9th, 13th, 14th, 17th, 18th, 23rd, 28th, 29th

Best Days for Money: 1st, 2nd, 11th, 12th, 17th, 18th, 19th, 20th, 28th, 29th

Though you could use more rest and relaxation until the 20th, this is a very happy and prosperous month. A month-long Grand Trine in Fire lifts your spirits, brings love and financial opportunities, and enhances your intellectual abilities.

Your Ruling Planet, Venus, spends a good part of the month in Pisces (until the 21st), her Sign of exaltation. Thus you are even more refined, idealistic and aesthetically inclined than usual. You are particularly sensitive to the nuances of feeling of those around you. ESP and psychic faculties are greatly magnified. But be careful of being overly sensitive. Psychic gifts can often be a curse rather than a blessing if they are not handled correctly. Be aware of the vibrations around you, but don't take them too personally. Aches and pains in your body are often not yours, but those of other people with whom you associate. Learn to discern these things.

Most of the planets are still in the West and your 7th House of Love and Social Activities is even stronger than last month. You are still very much in Libra heaven – getting your way through grace, charm and consensus. Your social skills, always strong, will get even stronger this month – especially after the 21st. You are still in one of the strongest social periods of your year. You seem to be mounting a charm offensive – going after what you want, letting those you are interested in know that you are available. You reach out to others and seem successful at it.

By the 21st, the planetary power shifts to the upper half of the Horoscope. This is an important shift – as it changes your attitudes for months to come. Now you become more interested in your 'outer' life – your career and worldly objectives. You know you came down to earth for a specific purpose – to serve the Most Holy Life Power in some specific way. Now is the time to get on with it. In most cases, this urge to serve Life manifests as one's career or life's work. The career is merely a disguise for one's 'Duty to Life'. So now you feel more ambitious and career-orientated. You can safely de-emphasize home, family and emotional issues, and focus instead on the world.

As mentioned, this is an unusually prosperous month. This in spite of the fact of Pluto's retrograde. The retrograde of your Money Planet suggests more caution and study of prospective deals, investments and purchases (and there will be plenty of these kinds of opportunities now). It can introduce minor delays or glitches into your financial life – for example, an expected payment comes late, the bank makes an error with your balance and you bounce a cheque, the credit card company has no record of your payment and now assesses a late fee, you find erroneous charges on your credit card bill, etc. But these annoyances (though time-consuming) don't affect your overall prosperity. You can expect many windfalls this month. There is luck in speculations. Friends and partners support your financial goals and provide opportunities. Sales and marketing projects go well.

May

Best Days Overall: 3rd, 4th, 12th, 13th, 21st, 22nd, 30th, 31st

Most Stressful Days Overall: 6th, 7th, 18th, 19th, 25th, 26th, 27th

Best Days for Love: 3rd, 4th, 8th, 9th, 12th, 13th, 18th, 21st, 22nd, 25th, 26th, 27th, 28th, 29th, 30th, 31st

Best Days for Money: 8th, 9th, 14th, 15th, 16th, 17th, 25th, 26th, 27th

Most of the planets are still above the horizon of your chart and though your 10th House is presently empty, it will become strong very shortly. Focus on career, worldly goals and the performance of your life's work – the work that you were born to do. Family seems to support your outer goals. Family duties and responsibilities could even be the factor behind your ambitiousness.

The planets, like last month, are still in the West, so you are still exercising your Libra genius – putting other people first, gaining their co-operation and support and obtaining consensus in everything. When you do this, you find that your own good comes almost automatically.

Two eclipses this month shake up the world around you and cause long-term change, but they seem very benign to you. In your case, they actually provide opportunity. Still it won't hurt to take a reduced schedule around these periods. You're OK, but others might not be up to par. Avoid risky types of activities – especially if they are elective.

The Lunar eclipse of the 9th announces long-term financial changes. In most cases, there is a revelation of flaws in thinking, financial plans or strategies. People change their investment plans under these aspects. Often they change banks, brokers or financial planners. Some people change the way they earn their living – not necessarily their job, but in the way they take compensation, etc. Unexpected tax or estate issues could arise and provoke these changes. Since the Moon is also your Career Planet, her eclipse is announcing career changes too. These are definitely in the works for many other reasons too. Some may change their whole career track. Others will be in different career circumstances because of shake-ups in the corporate hierarchy. Others could be offered jobs elsewhere or decide to work from home.

The Solar eclipse of the 31st occurs in your 9th House of Religion, Metaphysics, Philosophy and Higher Education. University students make long-term changes in their schooling – perhaps they change colleges, graduate or change areas of study. There could be temporary upheavals with university administrators. Non-students might decide to go back to school. But mostly, the eclipse will test (and eventually refine) your personal belief-system and view of life. Inadequacies (and these should be taken seriously) are revealed so that you can correct them.

In spite of financial upheavals, this will be a prosperous month. Since your Money Planet (Pluto) is still retrograde, don't be in too much of hurry to institute needed changes. Study things more carefully and let the dust settle from the eclipse.

Your social life still sparkles and your charm offensive is still on.

June

Best Days Overall: 1st, 9th, 10th, 17th, 18th, 27th, 28th

Most Stressful Days Overall: 2nd, 3rd, 15th, 16th, 22nd, 23rd, 30th

Best Days for Love: 1st, 7th, 8th, 9th, 10th, 17th, 18th, 19th, 22nd, 23rd, 27th, 28th, 29th, 30th

Best Days for Money: 4th, 5th, 11th, 12th, 13th, 14th, 22nd, 23rd

50% of the planets change Signs this month – some on a long-term basis. This is unusual. Much change is going on in your life and in the world. The important action is taking place in your job and career. Will you now opt to work from home? Will you make your family your career or go to work in the family business – perhaps establishing a family dynasty? Will you decide to promote the careers of family members rather than your own? Or will you enlist the support of family members to push forward your own agenda? All of these scenarios are possible now.

Ambitions are at their highest peak of the year. Not only are most of the planets above the horizon, but your 10th House of Career is one of the most powerful in the Horoscope. Yet, family and family status are also important. Whatever your outer goals are now, this is the time to push forwards. Saturn's move into your 10th House of Career on the 4th is going to teach you many things – it will show you the price tag of success: more work and more responsibility. It will (and this is a good thing) make you succeed because of real merit and achievement – you will have to perform and deliver the goods. Yet it will also give you 'stability and security' at the top. Your success will not be a 'flash in the pan' kind of thing, but something that endures.

Saturn's move into Cancer on the 4th is a stressful alignment for you. Health will need more watching in the coming years – but especially from the 21st onwards. Try to pace yourself better. Rest and relax more.

The planets are making an important shift from the Western (social) sector of your chart to the Eastern sector. This shift is still in flux this month and won't be truly established until next month. Right now you are in a 'cusp situation'. You are neither as dependent as you think, nor as independent. Sometimes you will get your way through charm and consensus, at other times through personal effort. In certain situations you will have to adapt and in others you will be able to make changes. You aren't decisively one way or the other.

Love is happy and exciting this month. A big party. Fun. You want to enjoy life with your lover and vice versa. Love is about going to parties, restaurants and entertainments.

The honeymoon aspect of romance appeal to you. And this month you get it. After the 17th, singles can find love suddenly, unexpectedly, out of the blue. Perhaps at the work place, with a co-worker or boss. Perhaps with someone in the health field or as you pursue health-related goals. This is very much a 'love at first sight' kind of period. When you meet that special someone you almost don't need words. The sparks fly and the electricity flows. Both you and your lover know that you are for each other.

July

Best Days Overall: 6th, 7th, 14th, 15th, 24th, 25th

Most Stressful Days Overall: 12th, 13th, 19th, 20th, 26th, 27th, 28th

Best Days for Love: 8th, 9th, 17th, 18th, 26th, 27th, 28th, 29th

Best Days for Money: 2nd, 3rd, 8th, 9th, 10th, 11th, 19th, 20th, 29th, 30th

By the 4th, the planetary shift to the East will be established. Thus, personal effort matters now. It's time to take the bull by the horns and create your own destiny and make your life what you want it to be. It's time to think of Number One. If you are well pleased, others will be well pleased. If you are fulfilled, then there is more fulfilment on the planet. You will not be socially ostracized for following personal fulfilment – provided you do it correctly. Keep your desires constructive and avoid being rude or arrogant to others.

Like last month, most of the planets are still above the horizon. Continue to push forward your career goals. Family and emotional harmony still matter, but these should be channelled towards the achievement of outer goals.

You are still in one of your yearly career peaks. Many of you are reaching the pinnacles of success and attainment now. Those with larger-than-life goals will see good progress towards them.

Many of the love trends that we wrote of last month are still in effect. Mars, your Love Planet, entered Pisces on June 16 and will stay there until December. You still want fun in love, but you also want to serve and be served. Love aspects are still very good. Mars, however, will go retrograde on the 24th. This could throw some complications into a present relationship. Give your lover space. Let love develop as it will. Avoid making long-term love decisions one way or the other. Enjoy your relationship for what it is at the present moment without projecting into the future. Now is always OK.

Your Love Planet in Pisces makes both you and your lover much more sensitive. On the one hand these sensitivities enhance romance as you can both experience subtle nuances of feeling that you ordinarily wouldn't. But the downside brings more pain when the 'vibrations' are not exactly up to par. Hand gestures, body language, voice tones, etc. have an unusual impact these days. It is very important to make sure that you are coming from love and not from pain. If the latter, you are endangering your relationship.

Three planets associated with work are retrograde this month, so job-seekers need to exercise a lot more caution. Job offers, pay and conditions at the work place are not what they seem. Get more facts.

Overall, finances are going to shine – especially after the 23rd. You couldn't ask for better financial aspects then. Even Pluto's retrograde will not affect your prosperity. Financial increase comes through networking, friends and organizations you belong to.

August

Best Days Overall: 2nd, 3rd, 11th, 12th, 20th, 21st, 22nd, 30th

Most Stressful Days Overall: 9th, 10th, 15th, 16th, 17th, 23rd, 24th

Best Days for Love: 4th, 5th, 7th, 8th, 13th, 14th, 15th, 16th, 17th, 23rd, 24th, 27th, 28th

Best Days for Money: 4th, 5th, 7th, 8th, 15th, 16th, 17th, 25th, 26th, 27th

Health is much improved this month, but continue to work smarter and not harder. Very important that you recognize your physical limits and stay within them. Health is enhanced through more attention to your feet, ankles and sexual organs. Sexuality should be kept in balance and not overdone one way or the other. Practise safe sex. Disharmony with friends or in a love relationship can unduly impact on your health. Do your best to keep the harmony.

The planetary power is still very much above the horizon, so continue to push your career projects. This situation is soon to change, so don't neglect opportunities. Both family and career activities are well aspected and seem happy.

Like last month, many planets in the East (and getting more intensely there) are giving you greater independence, confidence and energy. This is a time for building your life according to your own specifications. You need not compromise with others over things; your good is in your own hands. With 40% of the planets retrograde and with many planets in your 12th House of Spirituality, this is good month for clarifying your goals and objectives. It would be normal (especially from the 22nd onwards) to seek seclusion and spiritual guidance. You are entering an important spiritual-type year now and much change, progress and revelation are going to happen. Your dream life is now hyperactive and unusually significant. Keep a notebook handy and record them. Even your waking hours will be filled with many 'dream-like', intuitive and 'coincidental' types of events. These are all messages from your deeper self and are significant.

Until the 21st, you are very much interested in groups, organizations and group activities. But after that the emphasis changes to spirituality. Apart from more seclusion, many of you will be more involved with charities, causes, ministries and volunteer work.

Though overall your social life is happy, serious love is more complicated now as Mars, your Love Planet, is still retrograde. Spiritual interests could also conflict with romance, and perhaps spiritual insights change your love attitudes.

Finances are very strong until the 21st – in spite of minor annoyances and delays. But afterwards, you will have to work harder for earnings. It is good to be charitable but, as with anything else, keep a sense of proportion. Give only what you can afford.

September

Best Days Overall: 7th, 8th, 17th, 18th, 26th, 27th

Most Stressful Days Overall: 5th, 6th, 12th, 13th, 19th, 20th

Best Days for Love: 1st, 2nd, 5th, 6th, 9th, 10th, 12th, 13th, 16th, 17th, 19th, 20th, 26th, 27th, 28th, 29th

Best Days for Money: 1st, 2nd, 3rd, 4th, 5th, 6th, 12th, 13th, 14th, 15th, 22nd, 23rd, 26th, 27th, 28th, 29th, 30th

A very happy month, Libra. Enjoy.

Health is improving. Uranus' move back into Aquarius and much power in your own Sign are enhancing your energy and well-being. Self-confidence, self-esteem, personal magnetism and charisma are all unusually strong. Though you still need to research health regimes, diets and medications more carefully – you are in a very good shape.

Most of the planets are in the East, so continue to have things your way. If conditions or circumstances don't suit, change them to your liking or create new and better ones. There is more free will these days.

The planets will start to shift to the lower half of your Horoscope later in the month. Until the 15th, ambitions are still strong – so try to wrap up career goals by then. By the 23rd, the planetary power will be mostly below the horizon – this will be a time for cultivating the right emotional states and for dealing with family and domestic duties.

Your love life is also much improved this month. Venus, your Ruling Planet, will move into your Sign on the 15th. Thus you are more glamorous and stylish than usual. You look great. Your Love Planet, Mars, will start moving forwards on the 27th, resolving many issues in a current relationship and strengthening your social confidence and judgement. Love and romantic opportunity is still at the work place or as you pursue health-related goals.

Finances seem stressful (perhaps due to over-spending) until the 23rd. But afterwards money is earned much more easily. Pluto, moving forward, is also a help.

The spiritual life discussed earlier is still unusually strong – it will be strong for the entire year ahead, but especially until the 23rd. Watch your dream life and take notes. Attend spiritual meetings and seminars. Be alert for messages from the Higher Power. Get more involved in charities, ministries and causes that you believe in.

After the 23rd, you are in a period of personal pleasure and bodily fulfilment. It is always true – spiritual growth always leads to personal fulfilment. The within always becomes the without. This will be a very good period for buying personal accessories or clothing. Your always-good aesthetic sense gets even better.

Career gets a boost from your spouse or lover.

October

Best Days Overall: 4th, 5th, 14th, 15th, 23rd, 24th

Most Stressful Days Overall: 2nd, 3rd, 9th, 10th, 16th, 17th, 18th, 29th, 30th

Best Days for Love: 4th, 5th, 7th, 8th, 9th, 10th, 16th, 17th, 18th, 18th, 25th, 26th

Best Days for Money: 1st, 2nd, 3rd, 9th, 10th, 11th, 12th, 13th, 19th, 20th, 21st, 22nd, 25th, 26th, 27th, 28th, 29th, 30th

Another happy month. Basically a party. A month for personal fulfilment and for having things your way. A month to pamper yourself and enjoy the pleasures of the flesh. Until the 9th, it is still a good time for buying clothing and accessories.

Health is still wonderful. Your personal magnetism, charisma and sex appeal are still very strong. Personal freedom and independence are strong. You have all the tools. Your destiny is in your hands. Build your paradise on earth.

The planetary power below the horizon of your chart increases even further this month. By the 7th, 80% to 90% of the planets will be there – a huge percentage. Let career issues slide for a while and focus on building a solid and stable home base. Mend fences with family members. Cultivate the right inner states. Replenish your emotional resources. Feeling right will eventually lead to acting and achieving right.

Though you are not especially ambitious these days, finances are a priority – especially after the 9th. Your focus and interest, of themselves, lead to increase and success. This is a time to make financial plans for the future, to set investment strategies, to do accounting and tax planning, create budgets and the like. Money comes from personal effort, from your partner or spouse, friends and organizations you belong to and from your intuition – which is exceptionally sharp. After the 23rd, you have good aspects for reducing debt and waste.

Love is getting better and better. Existing relationships are more harmonious – especially after the 9th. A Grand Trine in Water makes love sweet, emotional and tender. This Grand Trine – a very fortunate aspect – is also bringing prosperity and financial opportunity. The work place is still the scene of romance. But romance could find you as you pursue health and financial goals as well. It's the kind of a month where you can meet Mr or Ms Right whilst waiting in the queue at the bank or broker's office or at the pharmacy.

Family relations could be better before the 9th, but there is much improvement afterwards. Relations with a parent or parent figure should also improve then. They seem to approve of the way you are taking charge of your financial life, reducing waste and debt. They seem supportive financially. Some family issues will need much more time to resolve and you should let them go. Saturn, your Family Planet, is retrograde. Also be cautious about expenditures or investments in the home. Best to research them now and act on them later.

November

Best Days Overall: 1st, 2nd, 10th, 11th, 12th, 20th, 21st, 28th, 29th

Most Stressful Days Overall: 5th, 6th, 13th, 14th, 26th, 27th

Best Days for Love: 3rd, 4th, 5th, 6th, 13th, 14th, 15th, 16th, 22nd, 23rd, 25th, 26th, 27th, 30th

Best Days for Money: 5th, 6th, 8th, 9th, 15th, 16th, 18th, 19th, 22nd, 23rd, 24th, 25th, 26th, 27th

The planets are still very much in the East; Venus, your Ruling Planet, moves forward speedily and 90% of the planets (after the 8th) are moving forwards. This is a month of fast and dynamic personal progress. Push forwards confidently towards your goals. This is not a time for waffling and fudging – move, act, succeed, make progress.

Health is still good this month.

Most of the planetary power is still below the horizon, so, like last month, focus on your family and emotional life. Career changes will happen in spite of what you do or don't do.

Two eclipses shake up the world around you and your environment this month, but you seem unscathed. In fact, the disruptions and dislocations are creating opportunities for you.

The Lunar eclipse of the 9th occurs in your 8th House, signalling long-term changes with debt, tax issues and sexual matters. Your spouse or partner is changing his or her financial strategy. If you have tax or property issues pending, the eclipse will mark a turning-point in these affairs. Every Lunar eclipse affects your career; this one is no different. Career changes or changes in your corporate hierarchy are happening now. Some of you will change jobs – either within the same company or by moving to a different one. Relations with a parent or boss could be temporarily turbulent.

The Solar eclipse of the 23rd occurs in your 3rd House and impacts on Pluto, your Money Planet. Thus, there are personal financial changes happening. Flaws in your financial planning or investments are revealed so that you can take corrective action.

Your car or communication equipment could behave erratically. Long-buried flaws in these things now need to be dealt with. Perhaps you will have to buy a new car. Neighbours and siblings could also behave erratically – but this again is coming from long-seething issues. Let the dust clear and you will see how to settle these things.

Every Solar eclipse tends to test your friendships. Real friendships will survive these things and get even better. But shaky ones or ones that are based on false motives, will probably go by the wayside.

In spite of the eclipse, finances look strong. Sales, marketing, communication, PR, teaching, etc. still seem to be the paths to profits.

Your love life moves forwards this month, but you need to do a lot of compromising from the 2nd to the 27th. You and your beloved seem out of synch – at odds. Your beloved wants to go to the movies, but you want to attend a lecture. Your beloved wants to work out, but you want to go shopping. These are all short-term issues.

December

Best Days Overall: 7th, 8th, 9th, 17th, 18th, 25th, 26th

Most Stressful Days Overall: 2nd, 3rd, 4th, 10th, 11th, 23rd, 24th, 30th, 31st

Best Days for Love: 1st, 2nd, 3rd, 4th, 5th, 6th, 10th, 11th, 15th, 16th, 21st, 22nd, 25th, 26th, 30th, 31st

Best Days for Money: 2nd, 3rd, 4th, 5th, 6th, 12th, 13th, 14th, 15th, 16th, 19th, 20th, 21st, 22nd, 23rd, 24th, 30th, 31st

Health gets much more delicate this month – especially after the 22nd. Remember your physical limits. Rest when tired. Every day, do what is possible and don't fret about the impossible. Home, career and social duties are all pulling you in different directions. You have to stand in the middle and give what you can to each department. You can't go too far in any direction.

Mars' move into your 7th House of Love (on the 16th) is a wonderful social aspect, as he is your Love Planet. You are in the mood for romance and so is your partner. But, as mentioned, career and family responsibilities are the main obstructions. You are invited to many more parties and gatherings than you can possibly attend. You will have to make tough choices. Singles could have more love opportunities than they can handle. Love is turbulent and stormy until the 21st, but gets more harmonious after that. You get more in synch with your partner. Part of the love problem is the non-acceptance of your beloved by family members. Love is at the work place until the 16th, then happens in the more conventional ways afterwards – at parties, gatherings and social events.

This being the holiday season, many of you will be travelling. But Mercury will be retrograde after the 17th, so exercise some caution. Allow more time for your journeys – avoid narrowly-timed connecting flights. Double-check travel arrangements and reservations.

Most of the planets are below the horizon and your 4th House of Home and Family is very powerful – so family is the major priority in the month ahead – family and your emotional life. But, you can't ignore your love life or career, either. It is normal to have more family parties, entertainments and gatherings this time of year, but this year they seem to go better than usual. It is also a good period for beautifying the home or buying objects of beauty for the home.

Finances seem good this month. Pluto is moving forward and receiving good aspects from the Sun (until the 22nd) and from Mars (after the 16th). This shows money from social connections – from friends and from your spouse or lover. They support your financial goals and bring you financial opportunities.

Sales and marketing projects have been important financially for some years now. They are important this month, too – only remember that Mercury is retrograde after the 17th. Get those mailings out before then.

Scorpio

♏

THE SCORPION

Birthdays from

23rd October

to 22nd November

Personality Profile

SCORPIO AT A GLANCE

Element – Water

Ruling Planet – Pluto
Co-ruling Planet – Mars
Career Planet – Sun
Love Planet – Venus
Money Planet – Jupiter
Planet of Health and Work – Mars
Planet of Home and Family Life – Uranus

Colour – red-violet

Colour that promotes love, romance and social harmony – green

Colour that promotes earning power – blue

SCORPIO

Gems – bloodstone, malachite, topaz

Metals – iron, radium, steel

Scents – cherry blossom, coconut, sandalwood, watermelon

Quality – fixed (= stability)

Quality most needed for balance – a wider view of things

Strongest virtues – loyalty, concentration, determination, courage, depth

Deepest needs – to penetrate and transform

Characteristics to avoid – jealousy, vindictiveness, fanaticism

Signs of greatest overall compatibility – Cancer, Pisces

Signs of greatest overall incompatibility – Taurus, Leo, Aquarius

Sign most helpful to career – Leo

Sign most helpful for emotional support – Aquarius

Sign most helpful financially – Sagittarius

Sign best for marriage and/or partnerships – Taurus

Sign most helpful for creative projects – Pisces

Best Sign to have fun with – Pisces

Signs most helpful in spiritual matters – Cancer, Libra

Best day of the week – Tuesday

Understanding a Scorpio

One symbol of the Sign of Scorpio is the phoenix. If you meditate upon the legend of the phoenix you will begin to understand the Scorpio character – his or her powers and abilities, interests and deepest urges.

The phoenix of mythology was a bird that could recreate and reproduce itself. It did so in a most intriguing way: it would seek a fire – usually in a religious temple – fly into it, consume itself in the flames and then emerge a new bird. If this is not the ultimate, most profound transformation, then what is?

Transformation is what Scorpios are all about – in their minds, bodies, affairs and relationships (Scorpios are also society's transformers). To change something in a natural, not an artificial, way involves a transformation from within. This type of change is a radical change as opposed to a mere cosmetic make-over. Some people think that change means altering just their appearance, but this is not the kind of change that interests a Scorpio. Scorpios seek deep, fundamental change. Since real change always proceeds from within, a Scorpio is very interested in – and usually accustomed to – the inner, intimate and philosophical side of life.

Scorpios are people of depth and intellect. If you want to interest them you must present them with more than just a superficial image. You and your interests, projects or business deals must have real substance to them in order to stimulate a Scorpio. If they haven't, he or she will find you out – and that will be the end of the story.

If we observe life – the processes of growth and decay – we see the transformational powers of Scorpio at work all the time. The caterpillar changes itself into a butterfly, the infant grows into a child and then an adult. To Scorpios, this definite and perpetual transformation is not something to be feared. They see it as a normal part of life. This acceptance of transformation gives Scorpios the key to understanding the true meaning of life.

Scorpios' understanding of life (including life's weaknesses) makes them powerful warriors – in all senses of the word. Add to this their depth, patience and endurance and you have a powerful personality. Scorpios have good, long memories and can at times be quite vindictive – they can wait years to get their revenge. As a friend, though, there is no one more loyal and true than a Scorpio. Few are willing to make the sacrifices that a Scorpio will make for a true friend.

The results of a transformation are quite obvious, although the process of transformation is invisible and secret. This is why Scorpios are considered secretive in nature. A seed will not grow properly if you keep digging it up and exposing it to the light of day. It must stay buried – invisible – until it starts to grow. In the same manner, Scorpios fear revealing too much about themselves or their hopes to other people. However, they will be more than happy to let you see the finished product – but only when it is completely wrapped up. On the other hand, Scorpios like knowing everyone else's secrets as much as they dislike anyone knowing theirs.

Finance

Love, birth and life as well as death are Nature's most potent transformations; Scorpios are interested in all of these. In our society, money is a transforming power, too, and a Scorpio is interested in money for that reason. To a Scorpio money is power, money causes change, money controls. It is the power of money that fascinates them. But Scorpios can be too materialistic if they are not careful. They can be overly awed by the power of money, to a point where they think that money rules the world.

Even the term plutocrat comes from Pluto, the Ruler of the Sign of Scorpio. Scorpios will – in one way or another –

achieve the financial status they strive for. When they do so, they are careful in the way they handle their wealth. Part of this financial carefulness is really a kind of honesty, for Scorpios are usually involved with other people's money – as accountants, lawyers, stockbrokers or corporate managers – and when you handle other people's money you have to be more cautious than when you handle your own.

In order to fulfil their financial goals, Scorpios have important lessons to learn. They need to develop qualities that do not come naturally to them, such as breadth of vision, optimism, faith, trust and, above all, generosity. They need to see the wealth in Nature and in life, as well as in its more obvious forms of money and power. When they develop generosity, their financial potential reaches great heights, for Jupiter, the Lord of Opulence and Good Fortune, is Scorpio's Money Planet.

Career and Public Image

Scorpio's greatest aspiration in life is to be considered by society as a source of light and life. They want to be leaders, to be stars. But they follow a very different road than do Leos, the other stars of the Zodiac. A Scorpio arrives at the goal secretly, without ostentation; a Leo pursues it openly. Scorpios seek the glamour and fun of the rich and famous in a restrained, discreet way.

Scorpios are by nature introverted and tend to avoid the limelight. But if they want to attain their highest career goals they need to open up a bit and to express themselves more. They need to stop hiding their light under a bushel and let it shine. Above all, they need to let go of any vindictiveness and small-mindedness. All their gifts and insights were given to them for one important reason – to serve life and to increase the joy of living for others.

Love and Relationships

Scorpio is another Zodiac Sign that likes committed, clearly defined, structured relationships. They are cautious about marriage, but when they do commit to a relationship they tend to be faithful – and heaven help the mate caught or even suspected of infidelity! The jealousy of the Scorpio is legendary. They can be so intense in their jealousy that even the thought or intention of infidelity will be detected and is likely to cause as much of a storm as if the deed had actually been done.

Scorpios tend to settle down with those who are wealthier than they are. They usually have enough intensity for two, so in their partners they seek someone pleasant, hard-working, amiable, stable and easy-going. They want someone they can lean on, someone loyal behind them as they fight the battles of life. To a Scorpio a partner, be it a lover or a friend, is a real partner – not an adversary. Most of all, a Scorpio is looking for an ally, not a competitor.

If you are in love with a Scorpio you will need a lot of patience. It takes a long time to get to know Scorpios, because they do not reveal themselves readily. But if you persist and your motives are honourable, you will gradually be allowed into a Scorpio's inner chambers of the mind and heart.

Home and Domestic Life

Uranus is Ruler of Scorpio's 4th Solar House of Home and Family. Uranus is the Planet of Science, Technology, Changes and Democracy. This tells us a lot about a Scorpio's conduct in the home and what he or she needs in order to have a happy, harmonious home life.

Scorpios can sometimes bring their passion, intensity and wilfulness into the home and family, which is not always the place for these qualities. These traits are good for the warrior and the transformer, but not so good for the nurturer and family member. Because of this (and also because of their need for change and transformation) the Scorpio may be prone to sudden changes of residence. If not carefully constrained, the sometimes inflexible Scorpio can produce turmoil and sudden upheavals within the family.

Scorpios need to develop some of the virtues of Aquarius in order to cope better with domestic matters. There is a need to build a team spirit at home, to treat family activities as truly group activities – family members should all have a say in what does and does not get done. For at times a Scorpio can be most dictatorial. When a Scorpio gets dictatorial, it is much worse than if a Leo or Capricorn (the two other power Signs in the Zodiac) does. For the dictatorship of a Scorpio is applied with more zeal, passion, intensity and concentration than is true of either a Leo or Capricorn. Obviously, this can be unbearable to family members – especially if they are sensitive types.

In order for a Scorpio to get the full benefit of the emotional support that a family can give, he or she needs to let go of conservatism and be a bit more experimental, to explore new techniques in child-rearing, be more democratic with family members and to try to manage things by consensus rather than by autocratic edict.

Horoscope for 2003

Major Trends

Coming through 1999, 2000 and 2001 with your health and sanity intact was no mean feat. That in itself was success. The stresses of those years will have strengthened your mental, emotional and spiritual muscles. It will have built character. This, combined with the easing of the planetary stress on you, should have made 2002 a successful year. 2003 is going to be even easier than 2002 on many, many levels. It should be more successful than 2002.

Three very important developments are taking place. Uranus, which has been in stressful aspect to you for seven years or so, is getting ready to move out of this position into a harmonious aspect. This year you will get a brief taste of this – for about six months. But by next year Uranus will be established in harmonious aspect to you.

Saturn was in a neutral aspect to you over the past two years. But by June 4 of this year, it will move into a long-term (two-and-a-half-year) harmonious aspect.

Jupiter, while helping your career, was in stressful aspect to you since late last year. By August 27, it will move into an harmonious aspect.

The wheels of the Cosmos are turning – and they are turning your way. By all means reach for your dreams fearlessly. Those desires you feel in your heart are the announcements of what is to be.

The major areas of interest in the coming year will be: finance; home and family issues; debt and repayment of debt, tax issues, helping others prosper, the deeper things of life and personal transformation (until June 4); religion, philosophy, higher education and foreign travel (after June 4); career (until August 27); friends, groups, group activities and organizations (after August 27).

Your paths to greatest fulfilment in the coming year are: debt, repayment of debt, helping others prosper, personal transformation (until April 14); love, romance and social activities (after April 14); career (until August 27); friendships, groups and group activities (after August 27).

Health

Health is vastly improved over last year. And you can look forward to ever-increasing energy and vigour in future years. As mentioned, the long-term planets (most of them) are, little by little, shifting in your favour.

With increased energy and life-force you have the wherewithal to resist most disease.

Your 6th House of Health is not a House of Power this year, which I read as a positive thing. You have little need to pay much attention to it.

Mars, your Health Planet, is a pretty fast-moving planet. He changes Signs every month and a half to two months. Thus your health attitudes and needs tend to fluctuate. Different kinds of therapies will work at different times.

This year, though, Mars makes an unusual six-month transit in Pisces, your 5th Solar House (from June 17 to December 16). This shows that you are involved in the health of children and probably more concerned about their health than your own. Since the 5th House rules the 'rapture of life', it shows that merely being happy and creative is a powerful healing tonic. A night out on the town, or playing a sport that you love, will do more for you than hosts of healing therapies. We all have a child within us. This child looks at the world with fresh eyes, with wonder, without preconceived notions or concepts, without a long memory of evil associated with things. This child is naturally joyous. It needs no excuse or outer condition to be happy. As long as you don't cause it pain, it is in eternal rapture. This child never worries about the future or the past. This child has faith that everything will be provided for it. It lives in the NOW moment. Contacting this child and giving it expression will do wonders for any health ailment that you have.

Your Health Planet in the 5th House would show that health problems would originate in dis-harmonies with children. Thus if a health problem arises, try to clear up the disharmony first, before running to a health professional. Chances are the condition will clear up on its own or, even if a health professional is needed, his or her job will be much easier.

The 5th House rules creativity. Thus, a creative hobby – something you do for the love of doing it – will do much to improve your health. Blocked creativity could also be the origin of a health problem.

In general, Mars rules sport, exercise and physical fitness. Thus, Scorpio views good health as being physically fit (just not being ill is not enough). Good health is measured in athletic prowess – how many laps you can swim or miles you can run. Thus the gym or track is as good a place for healing as any doctor's surgery. (The doctor will probably send you to the gym in many cases.)

The health of your spouse and children seems good. Children should take better care of their liver and thighs. Your spouse should take better care of his or her kidneys and hips. The health of grandchildren is improving. De-tox therapies help them. Recommendations for surgery require a second opinion.

Though health is good, in the coming year certain periods will tend to be more stressful. You should rest and relax more during these periods – from January 20 to February 19, from April 20 to May 21 and from July 23 to August 23.

Home, Domestic and Family Issues

This area of life has been important for some years now. Two powerful long-term planets have been camping out in your 4th House – Uranus and Neptune. This House is still strong in the year ahead, but gradually weakening in importance as Uranus prepares to move out permanently.

Uranus in your 4th House has caused many of you to move many times over the past seven years. If you haven't moved, then there have been multiple renovations of the residence. It produced a restlessness and unaccountable urges for change, upgrading and improvement. You were looking for the perfect home or domestic situation, on a trial-and-error basis. By now this has been achieved and these urges are abating. They aren't completely gone (especially for those of you born later in the Sign), but they are waning.

Uranus gave you the urge to instil a sense of 'teamwork' at home, to try to unite often conflicting family factions as members of a group, to instil a sense that the good of the family as a whole supersedes the good of any individual member. This was not an easy task, but by now you have got good at it.

With Uranus leaving your 4th House (this year only briefly, but next year permanently), there is an urge for permanency and stability in the home. You want to stop the 'wanderlust' and settle down. This will start to happen.

Neptune in your 4th House for many years now (and for years to come) is showing the urge for children. The home is a place for the kids and the kids are at the centre of it. Making the home fit for the children has been a major priority these past few years.

Neptune also gave you the urge to make the home a place of recreation as well as a home. You probably filled the place with toys (adults' and children's) and entertainment equipment. By the time Neptune is finished with you, you won't ever have to leave the house to have fun.

Most Scorpios have been emotionally volatile these past seven years. This too was caused by Uranus. This volatility could erupt at any time. Mood changes were swift and intense. Family members were also like this. Happily, these things are getting easier and more stable.

Aside from stocking the home with toys, I see much new electronic gadgetry in the home. This trend also continues in the year ahead.

Parents or parent figures are moving or expanding their residence in the year ahead. (They might have done this last year.) The domestic situation of siblings seems status quo (June could bring a sudden change or sudden renovation – but this is a short-term trend.)

Scorpios of childbearing age are unusually fertile.

Love and Social Life

Some years are more socially-orientated and some years are more finance and career-orientated. This is a year for the latter. Your 7th House of Love and Marriage is not a House of Power. Thus you seem satisfied with the status quo. Singles will tend to remain single and marrieds will tend to remain married.

Of course you will have a love life. And, if not, you should cultivate one, as it is a path of fulfilment this year. The only issue is the importance you place on it.

Certain times of the year will tend to be more socially active than others. Romantic opportunities increase during these periods. This year, May 20 to June 10 is such a period; October 9 to November 2 is another.

Though romance is not strongly aspected this year, friendships are. This will be a banner year for making new friends and acquaintances – and good ones to boot. These are people who help you financially, who support your financial goals and who are really on your side. You will start seeing this after August 27.

Venus is your Love Planet, Scorpio, and she is an excellent one to have as this is her natural domain. She is powerful on your behalf. But Venus is a fast-moving planet. During the year, she will move through all 12 Signs and Houses of your Horoscope. Thus romantic opportunities will come from many places and in a variety of ways in the year ahead. Also, your needs, tastes and preferences in love will change quickly – depending on Venus' position and aspects. We will cover these short-term trends in the month-by-month forecasts.

Up to now we have discussed serious romance, with marriage as a possibility. But those only looking for fun-and-games type relationships will have a good year. These are plentiful, especially from March 10 to September 15. Uranus' move into your 5th House of Love Affairs should provide plenty of excitement. None of these relationships seems stable. Any one of them can change at the drop of a hat and it is wise not to place too much importance on them or to get too attached. These relationships are about amusement and gaining experience.

Those in second marriages will see the marriage tested for the next two years. Real love will survive.

Those looking to get married for the second time need to exercise more caution. Opportunities will come, but don't rush into anything. Let love develop as it will. Let the circumstances of life test your love – you don't need to test it too much. An older person is coming into your life.

Those looking to marry for a third time have excellent aspects and opportunities, especially after August 27. A moneyed person is coming into your life. A marriage or quasi-marriage is very likely.

Children of marriageable age have an exciting year a head – many moves, perhaps. Love is in the air. Marriage or a serious relationship is probable.

Grandchildren of marriageable age need more patience. There is a need to build more self-esteem and confidence in the next two years before getting serious with anyone. Self-knowledge is the most important thing now.

The marriage of a sibling gets tested. The marriage of parents or parent figures is happier this year. If they are single, a marriage is likely. Their social life in general expands.

Finance and Career

Like last year, this is a strong money and career year. Both your 2nd House of Finance and 10th House of Career are Houses of Power. Jupiter, your Money Planet, is also the most elevated planet (on an overall basis) in your chart. This also points to the fact that finance is 'elevated' in your priorities.

Your career is blossoming and expanding. Pay rises, promotions and happy career opportunities are on their way.

Elders, bosses, superiors, authority figures and the government all seem favourably disposed to you – eager to grant their favours. Those of you who have issues with the government should get them sorted before August 27. Your overall social and professional status increase greatly. You are at the pinnacle of success and achievement.

Honours, too, are coming your way. Jupiter in the 10th House is a wonderful aspect for politicians or those running for office. The type of honours coming depend on your personal situation. I know of cases where someone has been invited to join a prestigious club – a club that was never open to him before; others were elected to community politics. People often win prizes or awards for achievement under this aspect. Students receive honour certificates. Honours could be coming from a group or organization you belong to as well.

Since you measure career success in financial terms, there is a lot more money coming to you. Part of it comes from your career, part from the good reputation you've established over the years.

Professional investors should look at recycling companies, health care, pharmaceuticals, gold, utilities, gaming, entertainment and resorts. Don't rush out blindly and buy these stocks – but do your homework and watch for opportunity. It will come.

There is much luck in speculations until August 27, but never indulge in this blindly or automatically – only under intuition and with no more than you can afford to lose. But your financial instincts are very sound and who am I to lecture you?

After August 27, your bottom line is enhanced through your friends and acquaintances and through your activities in clubs, groups and organizations. Professional investors should look at the technology sector around this time.

During the past two years debt could have been a burden on you. But with all this prosperity and with Saturn leaving your 8th House in June, debts should be easily paid.

Self-improvement

The past two years brought many lessons on the intricacies of debt, taxes, estates and the like. Many of you learned the correct way to use debt – for investment in things that go up in value. Many of you were heavily involved in debt, and learned these things the hard way. All of this is to the good and will help you in the future. These lessons are still going on for the first half of the year. Afterwards, the focus of self-improvement should be on your religious and metaphysical beliefs and your view of the world. Your belief systems – let's call it your personal religion – are getting tested for the next two years. It is getting 'reality checked'. Saturn is a genius at this sort of thing and knows exactly how to do it. Those beliefs that don't stand up to reality will either get modified, enlarged or discarded. It's uncomfortable when this happens. We tend to cling to our cherished beliefs with the zeal of the most radical fundamentalist. Sometimes it takes stern events to crack the shell. But really, the process is good. False beliefs are the cause of all our misery. The sooner they go by the wayside, the better off we are. These things are going to happen whether you like it or not, so things will go more easily if you co-operate with the process rather than resisting it. In fact, it might be wise to be pre-emptive about it. Look for opportunities to see if your beliefs match reality. Since many of these things are unconscious, bringing these things up to consciousness becomes an interesting meditation exercise. With pen and paper in hand, find some quiet and ask yourself what you really believe about different subjects – yourself, life, death, your financial abilities, how far you think you can go, why you are here, gender issues, relationship issues. As you proceed with this, many other subjects of interest will come up. From a calm state, examine what you've written. Are the beliefs true? Half-true? Sometimes true? Pure hogwash? Were they true at one time and no longer true now? Little by little, clarity will come. Your horizons will start to expand.

Month-by-month Forecasts

January

Best Days Overall: 6th, 7th, 8th, 16th, 17th, 25th, 26th

Most Stressful Days Overall: 4th, 5th, 11th, 12th, 13th, 19th, 20th

Best Days for Love: 9th, 10th, 11th, 12th, 13th, 19th, 20th, 27th, 28th

Best Days for Money: 1st, 9th, 10th, 19th, 20th, 27th, 28th

A powerful and dynamic T-square in the fixed Signs shows that you are working unusually hard to balance a booming career with heavy domestic responsibilities and intense personal urges and desires. Not an easy job and explosions often happen. As long as you're correct in principle, let the chips fall where they may. But keep working for the balance.

Health should be watched all month. Overwork, belligerence, haste and irritation are health dangers. Unnecessary conflicts and power struggles (and you seem prone to these this month) also drain your energy. The good news is that your Health Planet (Mars) is in your own Sign until the 17th, showing that overall health and health regimes are important to you. Thus you take care of problems *before* they get out of control.

The planetary power is shifting to the West later in the month. Get ready to exercise social skills to attain your ends. Personal independence and personal effort (even personal excellence) have less of an impact as the month progresses – it's your ability to charm and win others over that really counts.

Most of the planets are below the horizon this month. And though your 10th House of Career is strong (showing activity, interest and success), your 4th House of Home and

Family is even stronger. Thus you will have to shift some attention to family and emotional issues. Success is happening for you, but you really need the 'right kind' of success – success that happens without violating your feelings or emotional comfort. Lucrative business deals and perhaps job offers are coming to you – but you hesitate to take them because of their impact on family or your emotional comfort. This is wise. Many career opportunities will come to you in the coming months – you need to feel comfortable about them.

Finances will shine this month, but the retrograde of your Money Planet, Jupiter, suggests caution in financial dealings – especially when making important purchases, investments or financial commitments. Mars (your Work Planet) moves into Sagittarius on the 17th, indicating lucrative job offers. Employers will expand their work force. Money is earned through work. You are learning to overcome financial fear and take some calculated risks.

Love is fabulous all month, but especially after the 7th. Venus, your Love Planet, is in your own Sign until the 7th, bringing glamour and attractiveness to your image. Love pursues you. After the 7th, Venus starts to make sensational aspects to your Money Planet (Jupiter), which shows that romantic opportunities come as you pursue financial goals – or romance happens with people involved in your financial life. Singles make significant connections during this period. A business partnership could happen as well. Or, something that starts out as business partnership or business proposal ends up being something much more than that.

February

Best Days Overall: 3rd, 4th, 13th, 14th, 21st, 22nd

Most Stressful Days Overall: 1st, 2nd, 8th, 9th, 15th, 16th, 28th

Best Days for Love: 8th, 9th, 17th, 18th, 25th, 26th

Best Days for Money: 5th, 6th, 15th, 16th, 23rd, 24th

Most of the planets are still below the horizon and your 4th House of Home and Family is even stronger than last month. Though career is still happy and important, you have to shift some attention to the home. Like last month, you are beyond just being 'successful', you have to have success on your own terms – in comfortable ways.

The planets are shifting westward this month. The Western sector is still not dominant – that will happen later – but slightly stronger than the East. Little by little your grace, charm and social skills spell the difference between success and failure. Personal excellence is not enough now – people have to like you.

Health still needs to be watched. Pace yourself, focus on the important things – the essence of your desires – and avoid frivolous expenditures of energy. Rest and relax more. Don't let financial ups and downs – or delays – affect your health. Health is health and finance is finance. You are more than your bank account or financial statement. Mars travels with Pluto most of the month – a very dynamic aspect. Avoid haste, belligerence and impatience – especially from the 15th to the 18th. Financial drives are very intense during this period (also all month), but fanaticism and a boom-or-bust mentality can be dangerous.

With Mars and Pluto in your Money House, you are still learning financial fearlessness. But this should not mean doing foolhardy things. Calculated risks will pay off – but recklessness should be avoided. If you are taking risks, don't risk everything – risk a small portion of your wealth or assets. Also, with Jupiter retrograde, financial dealings need more scrutiny. Though you feel pressurized to move, make sure you have all the facts first and that there are no lingering doubts in your mind.

Love becomes more cautious this month. Your sense of security – your desire to avoid being hurt – seems strong. You want to know exactly where you stand before making important social moves or gestures. You tend to test romance this month. Love develops more slowly than your norm, but once in love you are loyal and unwavering.

After the 4th love is in the neighbourhood, with neighbours or at school or educational settings. An opportunity for a love affair (not a marriage) happens with a boss or someone involved in your career.

March

Best Days Overall: 2nd, 3rd, 12th, 13th, 21st, 29th, 30th, 31st

Most Stressful Days Overall: 1st, 7th, 8th, 14th, 15th, 27th, 28th

Best Days for Love: 7th, 8th, 10th, 11th, 19th, 20th, 21st, 29th, 30th

Best Days for Money: 5th, 6th, 14th, 15th, 23rd

Health and vitality are improving day by day. The planetary stresses and strains are easing up. Life is about to become much more enjoyable, carefree and happy this month. You certainly deserve it. The last two months were hard work.

The planetary power in the West increases even more this month. So the trends of the past month are continuing. You need to cultivate the good graces of others and adapt to difficult situations. Learning some adaptability is one of the great skills in life, so the opportunity to learn this should be welcomed.

Like last month, most of the power is below the horizon of your Horoscope – again, cultivate the right inner, emotional states. Try to feel good as you pursue career goals.

Give more time to family and domestic duties. Reinforce the stability of your home base. If you do this, you will be open to many new and happy career opportunities after the 21st. You will be in a position to take advantage of them.

Two major themes dominate the month: the joy of life and work. In reality they shouldn't contradict each other. Having work you enjoy is every person's right. Unfortunately, in most cases, there is a contradiction. So you will be both playing hard and working hard. But you should strive for work that you love – where going to the job is just as much fun as going to the cinema or theatre. Job-seekers (and employers) have wonderful opportunities for this right now.

Love is going to be very exciting in the coming month – especially after the 20th. Until then, love is about nurturing and giving and receiving emotional support. Until the 20th, you seem like a 'couch potato' in love – preferring quiet dinner dates at home. But afterwards, things liven up. Love is about fun, going out, excitement, experimentation, etc. Singles will have sudden and unexpected romantic opportunities after the 20th – but especially around the 28th. The highs of love are ultra-high, but the crashes can be ultra-low. A roller-coaster. Until the 21st, you find love close to home – perhaps through family members. Afterwards you find it in the usual places – at night clubs, discos, places of entertainment, parties, sporting events or as you pursue the life you love.

When Venus (your Love Planet) moves into Pisces on the 21st, you will experience nuances in love that you've rarely encountered before. Your ability to give and receive love is greatly enhanced. But you and your partner are more sensitive as well. So be more careful about thoughtless words, gestures and body language.

Uranus will make a major move into your 5th Solar House on the 10th. Thus your creative life is going to soar. You will discover an originality and genius that you never knew you had. Those who are already involved in creative efforts will see their skills increase even further. New technology makes more of the creative arts accessible to you.

Finances are less important this month and your Money Planet, Jupiter, is still retrograde. Continue to exercise caution in financial matters and dealings. Take nothing for granted. Check everything twice.

April

Best Days Overall: 8th, 9th, 10th, 17th, 18th, 26th, 27th

Most Stressful Days Overall: 3rd, 4th, 5th, 11th, 12th, 23rd, 24th

Best Days for Love: 3rd, 4th, 5th, 8th, 9th, 17th, 18th, 28th, 29th

Best Days for Money: 1st, 2nd, 11th, 12th, 19th, 20th, 28th, 29th

The planetary power in the West becomes overwhelmingly dominant after the 21st. More than last month. 70% to 80% of the planets are there. Again, continue to be adaptable, flexible and charming. Grace will succeed where personal effort and even excellence fail.

This month, after the 20th, there is a slight shift to the upper half of the Horoscope. The lower half still dominates, but not as much. Like last month, continue to cultivate the right emotional states and keep your home life solid and stable. Now that Uranus is out of your 4th House (especially for those of you born early in the Sign of Scorpio), things at home are calming down. Emotional volatility (a problem for many years now) is easing up. Mars will move into your 4th House on the 21st, making it an excellent period for renovation or construction projects in the home. Do-it-yourself projects also go well.

In spite of your lack of ambition, career is expanding and successful. Perhaps, when you were too intense – too anxious – you blocked things that should have happened. With a looser, more relaxed attitude, the good that should come can come much more easily. Finances, too, are excellent during this period. Your Money Planet, Jupiter, moves forwards on the 4th, restoring your confidence and enhancing your judgement. And, until the 20th, Jupiter receives wonderful aspects. Money comes from work, a new job, or from the favour of elders, parents and bosses. Your good reputation stands you in good stead financially.

All month there will be a wonderful Grand Trine in the Fire Signs. This Grand Trine consists of many planets important to you – the Lord of the Horoscope, your Money Planet, Health Planet, Work Planet and Love Planet. Thus you can expect financial windfalls, improved health, personal pleasure and happy romantic opportunities. Optimism runs high now – and this in itself cures many problems. The optimism reveals solutions that you couldn't see when you were feeling pessimistic. Optimism is like the headlamps of a car. The brighter they burn, the more of the road ahead you can see.

Like last month, love is happy, tender, romantic and fun-orientated. The love opportunities that come now are not marriage opportunities *per se,* but more about fun and games. Love happens in the normal places until the 21st – parties, places of entertainment or as you pursue leisure activities. After the 21st, the work place seems the source of romance – and a romantic fling with a co-worker, boss or employee is likely.

Health is much better these days, but rest and relax more after the 20th. Until the 21st, health is enhanced through paying more attention to your spine, knees and teeth. Afterwards, give your ankles and feet more attention.

May

Best Days Overall: 6th, 7th, 14th, 15th, 23rd, 24th

Most Stressful Days Overall: 1st, 2nd, 8th, 9th, 21st, 22nd, 28th, 29th

Best Days for Love: 1st, 2nd, 8th, 9th, 18th, 28th, 29th

Best Days for Money: 8th, 9th, 16th, 17th, 25th, 26th, 27th

By the 16th, the planetary power shifts to the upper half of the Horoscope. While home and family issues continue to be important, you are now becoming more ambitious and perhaps shifting some attention to your 'outer' goals.

Like last month, Mars is still in your 4th House, so it is still a good time for those renovation or DIY projects. Healthwise, you seem more concerned with the health of family members than with your own personal health. Emotional health seems a priority as well. Rest and relax more until the 21st and pay more attention to your ankles.

Two eclipses happen this month. One of them occurs in your own Sign of Scorpio. So this is a month of eventful and positive change.

The Lunar eclipse of the 16th occurs in your Sign. Do take a reduced schedule and avoid stressful, risk-taking activities around that period (for a few days before and a day after). Re-schedule these things for other times. This eclipse produces changes in your image, self-concept and the way you dress and present yourself. You have an opportunity now to fine-tune and upgrade your image. Since the eclipsed planet, the Moon, is your Religion Planet, your religious beliefs, philosophies and world view get tested. There could be a 'crisis of faith'. Flaws in these areas will come up so that you can make corrections. Your relation to a church or religious organization could change. The pastor or hierarchy could change there. Students could change universities or areas of study or make other long-term decisions about their education.

The Solar eclipse of the 31st occurs in your 8th House, which would affect the income of your spouse or partner. Perhaps he or she changes investment strategies, financial planners, bankers, brokers or accountants. Your spouse has a chance to fine-tune and upgrade his or her financial life. Those of you who have cases pending regarding property, royalties, insurance or taxes should see a turning-point now.

Since the Sun is your Career Planet, every Solar eclipse tends to produce career changes. This could manifest as a new job, a promotion, or changes in your corporate hierarchy. Long-term career decisions are being made. Flaws in career plans or in your present career situation surface so that corrections can be made.

Love is very active and happy this month, but you work hard to keep your social life, career and family in harmony. Love seems more serious these days, but the problem seems to be gaining family acceptance of your beloved. You are in one of the most active social periods of your year. Enjoy.

June

Best Days Overall: 2nd, 3rd, 11th, 12th, 19th, 20th, 30th

Most Stressful Days Overall: 4th, 5th, 17th, 18th, 24th, 25th

Best Days for Love: 7th, 8th, 17th, 18th, 24th, 25th, 27th, 28th

Best Days for Money: 4th, 5th, 13th, 14th, 22nd, 23rd

Health is improving day by day. Saturn's move into Cancer on the 4th (for the next two-and-a-half years) is a very positive long-term health signal. You will have more energy, more endurance and more support for your goals. Mars' move into Pisces on the 17th also fosters good health – you are more athletic and more into exercise regimes. Health regimes seem as much a good time as going to the cinema or theatre. Health can be enhanced through paying more attention to your feet – they should be massaged regularly.

The upper half of the Horoscope is still strongest this month. So, continue to pursue career goals. You won't be able to ignore home and family completely, but you can shift the emphasis a bit.

The planetary power continues to be mostly in the West, so avoid power struggles and undue self-assertion and cultivate charm, grace and your social skills. Adaptability and flexibility are potent assets now.

Love is still romantic and happy, but, after the 10th, could become unstable. Emotional volatility with your beloved – sudden changes of affection and mood – need to be guarded against. Real love will weather this storm. Like last month, there are some problems between your beloved and family members. Family could object to some of your friendships as well.

The 8th and the 9th Houses are unusually strong this month. Thus this is a good period for helping others prosper, paying off debt, cutting financial waste, studying the deeper things of life, personal reinvention and transformation, and the elimination of undesirable habits or character traits. A good time to take inventory of your possessions and get rid of what you don't need. Reduce the clutter in your life. Make room for the new good that wants to come in.

Later in the month is good for pursuing educational goals – especially higher education. This is a good period for getting a deeper understanding of scripture and your religious beliefs. Foreign cultures and foreign lands also call to you now and many of you will be travelling for business or career reasons. Others will be dealing more with foreigners.

Finances are strong this month. They become even stronger after the 17th. Money comes through your career, bosses, parents and elders. Continue to cultivate a good reputation in your field. It is money in the bank. Speculations seem favourable.

July

Best Days Overall: 8th, 9th, 17th, 18th, 26th, 27th, 28th

Most Stressful Days Overall: 2nd, 3rd, 14th, 15th, 21st, 22nd, 23rd, 29th, 30th

Best Days for Love: 8th, 9th, 17th, 18th, 21st, 22nd, 23rd, 28th, 29th

Best Days for Money: 2nd, 3rd, 10th, 11th, 19th, 20th, 29th, 30th

Most of the planets are above the horizon. Your 10th House of Career becomes unusually strong, while the planets involved in your home and family life are all retrograde. A very clear message: home and family issues need time to resolve themselves, while career opportunities are hot. You can safely downplay domestic issues in favour of your career.

Get ready for major career success this month – especially after the 23rd. You are entering a major career peak – not only for the year, but probably in your life thus far. Pay rises, promotions, honours and recognition are coming your way. Perhaps you get elected to a prestigious post at a club or community organization to which you belong. Professional politicians have wonderful aspects for advancement and could get elected to high office. (Much depends on their aspirations.) You socialize with the high, mighty and elevated this month. You have the favour of elders, bosses, parents and government officials. If you need favours from the government – or have issues pending with the government – this is a good time (after the 23rd) to pursue these things.

This month the planetary power is in the process of a major shift – from the West (where it has been for many months now) to the East. The shift is not complete this month – you are in a cusp situation, but you will find that you are already starting to have more independence and personal freedom than you've had. Little by little you are getting more control over your life. In the past few months, you've had a good taste of the areas that could be changed. Very soon now, you will be able to make those changes.

Finances are booming now – especially after the 23rd. Thus, you will have the financial independence to make the changes you want to make. Money comes (like last month, and most of the year) from the career, your professional status and your good reputation.

Love improves tremendously over last month – especially after the 4th. Love horizons expand. You are not as limited – socially – as you thought. Foreigners, highly educated people, teachers and mentor-types are unusually appealing. Those involved in a relationship can fan the flames of love by taking a trip to an exotic destination. Singles can find love in foreign lands as well.

Health is good, but rest and relax more after the 23rd. You are going to be very active, but you can save energy by delegating more and by focusing on essentials. Your Health Planet goes retrograde on the 29th, so avoid making drastic changes to your diet or health regime after then. Study dietary and medical claims very carefully.

August

Best Days Overall: 4th, 5th, 13th, 14th, 23rd, 24th

Most Stressful Days Overall: 11th, 12th, 18th, 19th, 25th, 26th

Best Days for Love: 7th, 8th, 16th, 17th, 18th, 19th, 27th, 28th

Best Days for Money: 7th, 8th, 16th, 17th, 26th, 27th

Like last month, the planets are mostly above the horizon, your 10th House is powerful and filled with beneficial planets (they're having a conference there, conspiring for your good and how best to advance your interests), while your 4th House of Home and Family is relatively weak. Like last month, the planets involved with home and family are still retrograde. So, seize the career moment and push forwards towards your goals. Big advancement is still happening. How far will you go? Much depends on the nature of your goals. If they are reasonable (within your sphere of availability), you will attain them. If they are very grand (and nothing wrong with that), you will see important progress towards them. This is still a wonderful period to seek favours from bosses, elders, parents or government officials.

Job-seekers should be more cautious about new job offers – as your Work Planet, Mars, is retrograde. Nail down all the details. Resolve any doubts. The same is true for new health regimes, medicines, miracle cures, diets, etc. Things are not what they seem – get more facts.

Try to rest and relax more until the 23rd. Pace yourself, focus on essentials and delegate more. After the 23rd, your health and vitality are greatly improved. Continue to enhance your health by paying more attention to the feet.

Most of the planets are now in the East – but the percentage is not dominating. It's really slightly tilted to the East, so you will attain your ends in two ways – by charm and grace when necessary and through personal effort at other times. The good news is that you are not so completely locked in by other people's desires and preferences. You have to take them into account, but you can change things.

Finances are still booming as the Sun and Venus are travelling with your Money Planet. Nice financial windfalls come your way. Big-ticket items are also coming. High-tech items – computers and gadgets – are also on their way.

Your Money Planet, Jupiter, makes a major move this month from Leo into Virgo. Thus, you might have to work harder for money now than you have in the past few months, but you will also be more careful with it. You'll be a better shopper and investor. You'll be more prudent and conservative. Friendships and networking play a bigger role in earnings these days. Your fondest financial (and career) hopes and wishes are coming to pass.

September

Best Days Overall: 1st, 2nd, 9th, 10th, 19th, 20th, 28th, 29th

Most Stressful Days Overall: 7th, 8th, 14th, 15th, 22nd, 23rd

Best Days for Love: 5th, 6th, 14th, 15th, 16th, 17th, 26th, 27th

Best Days for Money: 3rd, 4th, 5th, 6th, 14th, 15th, 26th, 27th, 30th

Jupiter's move into Virgo late last month has other implications than just financial ones. You are starting a new social cycle. New friends are coming into your life. You are getting involved with groups and organizations and are learning to be a part of a team. Money-making now has to do with team work, group effort. The better you function as part of a team, the better your finances will be. You will now have to think of the financial well-being of your group or team – your friends – as well as your own.

The Cosmos has wonderful ways of leading you into this new arena. The first and most obvious is finance. Your financial life depends on it. But love and romance are other lures. You will find that love and romantic opportunity await you at clubs, organizations and group activities.

The planets are still mostly in the East, so continue to change conditions that you dislike and build according to your specifications. Tailor your life around your needs. Social grace, consensus and compromise are still important, but focus on self-fulfilment. The Cosmos wants you to be a happy camper these days.

Most of the planets are still above the horizon, though your 10th House is weak this month. Thus ambitions, though strong, need to be tempered with emotional well-being and domestic tranquillity. Uranus will move back into your 4th House on the 15th, once again jazzing up your domestic sphere and emotions. Getting the family to work as a team and keeping emotional equilibrium once again become challenging.

Love can be complicated this month. Venus in the Sign of Virgo is not her best position. Thus perfectionism, hyper-criticism and nit-pickiness can plague romance. Also you seem out of synch with your beloved – having conflicting desires and interests. But all of this is short-term. By the 15th, love becomes more romantic – harmony is restored. You (and your beloved) relate more from the heart than from the head. Spiritual compatibility becomes important in love after the 15th. Singles can find romantic opportunity at prayer meetings, church functions, charities and as they pursue charitable activities.

Finances are strong, but you seem a little restless. They seem to interfere too much with what you personally want to do. The realities of finance force you to modify many of your financial preferences and attitudes. This is a long-term challenge. Balance is the key.

Health is good this month and Mars, your Health Ruler, moves forward on the 27th. Thus, you will soon be able to make the dietary and health changes you've been researching. Continue to enhance health by paying attention to your feet.

October

Best Days Overall: 7th, 8th, 16th, 17th, 18th, 25th, 26th

Most Stressful Days Overall: 4th, 5th, 11th, 12th, 13th, 19th, 20th

Best Days for Love: 4th, 5th, 11th, 12th, 13th, 16th, 17th, 25th, 26th

Best Days for Money: 1st, 2nd, 3rd, 11th, 12th, 13th, 21st, 22nd, 27th, 28th, 29th, 30th

Many of you are enjoying birthdays this month. Some will enjoy them next month. Your birthday, astrologically speaking, is the beginning of a new yearly cycle. It is the start of your Solar Return – the Sun returns to its original birth position. Before beginning a new cycle, it is always good to digest the past one. To review the past year – your successes and failures, hopes and dreams and the progress you've made (or haven't made). This review gives you an opportunity to correct mistakes and make better plans for the year ahead. In Astrology, your new year is not January 1 – it is your birthday.

This is a good time to do your review, because your 12th House of Spirituality is very strong until the 23rd. You will feel more reclusive and want your own space. Thus these kinds of activities are easier to accomplish. It is also good to attend spiritual classes, read spiritual books or scripture or get involved in charitable or volunteer-type activities. This is a way of laying down the karma of the past year and beginning the New Year afresh – with a fresh slate.

Your personal independence is growing every day and, by the 23rd, will be unusually strong. Thus, build your life as you desire it to be. If you can enlist the aid of other people, all well and good, but if not, you should go it alone. Change undesirable conditions or create new ones that are more desirable.

Love is starting to pursue you these days. Right now it is behind the scenes – perhaps you don't know about it. But come the 9th it will appear. Nothing much you need to do, either. It will find you. In general, you look great and your health is excellent. Your personal magnetism and charisma are unusually strong. Your love or partner goes out of his or her way to please you. Your sense of style is unusually good after the 9th, so it is a good time for buying clothing, jewellery or fashion accessories – a great period to beautify the body.

Though the planets are starting to shift below the horizon, career is still important. Pay rises and promotions could still happen. But the importance of career will wane in the coming months. You probably seem more ambitious than you are. You are dressing for success, presenting an image of status, even though your real interests are elsewhere.

Finances are mixed this month and you still need to balance your personal desires (the desire for sensual pleasure and personal fulfilment) with the need to earn a living. You can't go too far in either direction.

November

Best Days Overall: 3rd, 4th, 13th, 14th, 22nd, 23rd, 30th

Most Stressful Days Overall: 1st, 2nd, 8th, 9th, 15th, 16th, 28th, 29th

Best Days for Love: 5th, 6th, 8th, 9th, 15th, 16th, 25th, 26th, 27th

Best Days for Money: 8th, 9th, 18th, 19th, 24th, 25th, 26th, 27th

The financial tension you've been feeling recently seems like it will resolve itself as a Lunar eclipse in your Money House brings up all the relevant issues. Long-term changes will have to be made. Financial disagreements with friends or with organizations will surface and corrective action will be taken. This is all to the good. A good blow-out every now and then can be healthy and lead to constructive change.

Health is good this period and, like last month, you've never looked better. Others sit up and take notice. Love continues to pursue you. Later in the month, singles find love as they pursue their normal financial goals. Love is more materialistic these days. Material gifts are romantic turn-ons. Love is shown in material ways – through financial support or through helping others prosper. Friends and partners are financially supportive. Social connections aid your bottom line.

The planetary power is now decisively below the horizon and your 4th House of Home and Family is once again powerful. Further, the planets connected to the 4th House are now moving forwards – so things at home are getting clearer and forward progress is being made. Pay more attention to your emotional and family life and less to your career. Career goals now revolve around personal desires – finding self-fulfilment – and finance. Success is measured in these terms.

Two eclipses shake up the world this month. There is a Lunar eclipse on the 9th (which is strong on you, so take a reduced schedule) and a Solar eclipse on the 23rd.

The Lunar eclipse occurs in your 7th House of Love and will test a romantic relationship, marriage or friendship. Flaws in these areas or long-seething issues will surface – sometimes explosively – so that corrective actions can be taken. Sometimes an eclipse signals the end of a relationship, sometimes the taking of a relationship to the next level and sometimes a change in marital status.

The Solar eclipse of the 23rd occurs in your Money House, as discussed. Also it brings career changes.

December

Best Days Overall: 1st, 10th, 11th, 19th, 20th, 27th, 28th

Most Stressful Days Overall: 5th, 6th, 12th, 13th, 14th, 25th, 26th

Best Days for Love: 5th, 6th, 15th, 16th, 25th, 26th

Best Days for Money: 5th, 6th, 15th, 16th, 21st, 22nd, 23rd, 24th

The planetary power is still below the horizon and your 4th House of Home and Family is still very powerful. Continue to cultivate emotional harmony and the right inner state and let your career slide for a while. Like last month, career success seems measured by financial success and not by honour or prestige. Finances are high on the agenda. Elders, bosses and parents seem supportive. A pay rise, bonus or promotion is likely.

The Eastern and Western sectors of your Horoscope are more or less balanced this month – especially after the 21st. You are neither as dependent nor as independent as you think. In certain matters you will have to adapt and cultivate the support of others; in others you will have more personal freedom. This will change by next month, as the Western sector gains power.

You seem to have a lot of freedom and independence in career and financial issues, but not in creative projects, domestic affairs or day-to-day work. In these areas you must compromise and seek consensus.

Finances are still strong and will get stronger after the 22nd. Holiday booty should be larger than usual, as the aspects to your Money Planet are sensational. Probably you will spend more as well. Sales, marketing and PR activities are important financially. As we have seen for many months, networking and friendships are also important.

Money-making is still a team effort, but you have more personal leeway here.

Love continues to be practical – down to earth and materialistic. You want a love that will last. You are more cautious in love. You want to test it too much. But these tendencies will pass by the 21st. Then love is about nurturing, the sharing of feelings and emotional support. Love is in the neighbourhood this month and close to home. Home is the scene of romantic encounters and dates. Someone very spiritual or artistic is coming into your life after the 21st.

Health is good this month. Mars, your Health Planet, makes an important move out of Pisces (where he's been for six months) into Aries, his own Sign and House. This shows many things. Health is now enhanced by paying attention to your head. Health regimes are more active and competitive. You like active sports now. Athletes perform much better than of late.

In many cases, Mars' move is indicating job changes and different attitudes to work. You like work that is more physical these days. You work harder and earn more. You are more productive. Competition at work could heat up, but you seem to thrive on it.

Sagittarius

♐

THE ARCHER

Birthdays from
23rd November
to 20th December

Personality Profile

SAGITTARIUS AT A GLANCE

Element – Fire

Ruling Planet – Jupiter
Career Planet – Mercury
Love Planet – Mercury
Money Planet – Saturn
Planet of Health and Work – Venus
Planet of Home and Family Life – Neptune
Planet of Spirituality – Pluto

Colours – blue, dark blue

Colours that promote love, romance and social harmony – yellow, yellow-orange

Colours that promote earning power – black, indigo

Gems – carbuncle, turquoise

Metal – tin

Scents – carnation, jasmine, myrrh

Quality – mutable (= flexibility)

Qualities most needed for balance – attention to detail, administrative and organizational skills

Strongest virtues – generosity, honesty, broad-mindedness, tremendous vision

Deepest need – to expand mentally

Characteristics to avoid – over-optimism, exaggeration, being too generous with other people's money

Signs of greatest overall compatibility – Aries, Leo

Signs of greatest overall incompatibility – Gemini, Virgo, Pisces

Sign most helpful to career – Virgo

Sign most helpful for emotional support – Pisces

Sign most helpful financially – Capricorn

Sign best for marriage and/or partnerships – Gemini

Sign most helpful for creative projects – Aries

Best Sign to have fun with – Aries

Signs most helpful in spiritual matters – Leo, Scorpio

Best day of the week – Thursday

Understanding a Sagittarius

If you look at the symbol of the archer you will gain a good, intuitive understanding of a person born under this astrological Sign. The development of archery was humanity's first refinement of the power to hunt and wage war. The ability to shoot an arrow far beyond the ordinary range of a spear extended humanity's horizons, wealth, personal will and power.

Today, instead of using bows and arrows we project our power with fuels and mighty engines, but the essential reason for using these new powers remains the same. These powers represent our ability to extend our personal sphere of influence – and this is what Sagittarius is all about. Sagittarians are always seeking to expand their horizons, to cover more territory and increase their range and scope. This applies to all aspects of their lives: economic, social and intellectual.

Sagittarians are noted for the development of the mind – the higher intellect – which understands philosophical, metaphysical and spiritual concepts. This mind represents the higher part of the psychic nature and is motivated not by self-centred considerations but by the light and grace of a Higher Power. Thus, Sagittarians love higher education of all kinds. They might be bored with formal schooling but they love to study on their own and in their own way. A love of foreign travel and interest in places far away from home are also noteworthy characteristics of the Sagittarian type.

If you give some thought to all these Sagittarian attributes you will see that they spring from the inner Sagittarian desire to develop. To travel more is to know more, to know more is to be more, to cultivate the higher mind is to grow and to reach more. All these traits tend to broaden the intellectual – and indirectly, the economic and material – horizons of the Sagittarian.

The generosity of the Sagittarian is legendary. There are many reasons for this. One is that Sagittarians seem to have an inborn consciousness of wealth. They feel that they are rich, that they are lucky, that they can attain any financial goal – and so they feel that they can afford to be generous. Sagittarians do not carry the burdens of want and limitation – which stop most other people from giving generously. Another reason for their generosity is their religious and philosophical idealism, derived from the higher mind. This higher mind is by nature generous because it is unaffected by material circumstances. Still another reason is that the act of giving tends to enhance their emotional nature. Every act of giving seems to be enriching and this is reward enough for the Sagittarian.

Finance

Sagittarians generally entice wealth. They either attract it or create it. They have the ideas, energy and talent to make their vision of paradise on Earth a reality. However, mere wealth is not enough. Sagittarians want luxury – earning a comfortable living seems small and insignificant to them.

In order for Sagittarians to attain their true earning potential they must develop better managerial and organizational skills. They must learn to set limits, to arrive at their goals through a series of attainable sub-goals or objectives. It is very rare that a person goes from rags to riches overnight. But a long, drawn-out process is difficult for Sagittarians. Like Leos, they want to achieve wealth and success quickly and impressively. They must be aware, however, that this over-optimism can lead to unrealistic financial ventures and disappointing losses. Of course, no Zodiac Sign can bounce back as quickly as Sagittarius, but only needless heartache will be caused by this attitude. Sagittarians need to maintain their vision – never letting it go – but must also work towards it in practical and efficient ways.

Career and Public Image

Sagittarians are big thinkers. They want it all: money, fame, glamour, prestige, public acclaim and a place in history. They often go after all these goals. Some attain them, some do not – much depends on each individual's personal horoscope. But if Sagittarians want to attain public and professional status, they must understand that these things are not conferred to enhance one's ego but as rewards for the amount of service that one does for the whole of humanity. If and when they figure out ways to serve more, Sagittarians can rise to the top.

The ego of the Sagittarian is gigantic – and perhaps rightly so. They have much to be proud of. If they want public acclaim, however, they will have to learn to tone down the ego a bit, to become more humble and self-effacing, without falling into the trap of self-denial and self-abasement. They must also learn to master the details of life, which can sometimes elude them.

At their jobs Sagittarians are hard workers who like to please their bosses and co-workers. They are dependable, trustworthy and enjoy a challenge. Sagittarians are friendly to work with and helpful to their colleagues. They usually contribute intelligent ideas or new methods that improve the work environment for everyone. Sagittarians always look for challenging positions and careers that develop their intellect, even if they have to work very hard in order to succeed. They also work well under the supervision of others, although by nature they would rather be the supervisors and increase their sphere of influence. Sagittarians excel at professions that allow them to be in contact with many different people and to travel to new and exciting locations.

Love and Relationships

Sagittarians love freedom for themselves and will readily grant it to their partners. They like their relationships to be fluid and ever-changing. Sagittarians tend to be fickle in love and to change their minds about their partners quite frequently.

Sagittarians feel threatened by a clearly defined, well-structured relationship, as they feel this limits their freedom. The Sagittarian tends to marry more than once in life.

Sagittarians in love are passionate, generous, open, benevolent and very active. They demonstrate their affections very openly. However, just like an Aries, they tend to be egocentric in the way they relate to their partners. Sagittarians should develop the ability to see others' points of view, not just their own. They need to develop some objectivity and cool intellectual clarity in their relationships so that they can develop better two-way communication with their partners. Sagittarians tend to be overly idealistic about their partners and about love in general. A cool and rational attitude will help them to perceive reality more clearly and enable them to avoid disappointment.

Home and Domestic Life

Sagittarians tend to grant a lot of freedom to their family. They like big homes and many children and are one of the most fertile Signs of the Zodiac. However, when it comes to their children Sagittarians generally err on the side of allowing them too much freedom. Sometimes their children get the idea that there are no limits. However, allowing freedom in the home is basically a positive thing – so long as some measure of balance is maintained – for it enables all family members to develop as they should.

Horoscope for 2003

Major Trends

Last year could only be characterized as bittersweet. But more sweet than bitter. This so-so state of affairs continues this year. The Cosmos pushes you towards your goals and growth with both the carrot and the stick. Perhaps in future years you will see how ingenious this marvellous alternation was.

On the one hand, in 2002 Saturn opposed you. He tested your relationships and forced you to watch your energy and be aware of personal limitations. He forced you to test your spiritual ideals in the world – in the practical affairs of life. Jupiter, in the meantime, was being Santa Claus, giving you optimism for the battle, enlarged horizons, spurts of luck and philosophical clarity. Between these two forces, great spiritual progress was made.

The year 2002 was a year for succeeding through hard work. Luck didn't just come spontaneously, but your earned effort created good luck for you.

These trends are continuing for the first half of 2003. Health and energy levels still need to be watched. Work and discipline will produce good luck. Success comes through real merit and work. The good news is that work pays off – it WILL produce success – especially after August.

Moves and career changes are the main headlines of 2003. Benevolent Jupiter moves into your 10th House of Career on August 27, bringing promotions, pay rises, honours and more public and professional recognition. Uranus makes a once-in-seven-years move from your 3rd House into your 4th House (for six months), showing important changes in the domestic patterns. More on this later.

Saturn moves away from a two-year stressful aspect on June 4. This should improve your self-esteem and relationships.

Your important areas of interest in 2003 are: the body, image, personal appearance and sensual pleasures; intellectual interests and communication; home and family (from March 10 to September 15); love, romance and social activities (until June 4); debt, repayment of debt, helping others prosper, taxes, sex, personal transformation (after June 4); religion, philosophy, metaphysics, higher education, foreign travel (until August 27); career and public status (after August 27).

Your paths to greatest fulfilment in 2003 are: love, romance and social activities (until April 14); health and work (after April 14); religion, philosophy, metaphysics, higher education, foreign travel (until August 27); career and public status (after August 27).

Health

Health is more or less the same as it was last year. While Saturn does move away from a stressful aspect to you, Uranus moves into one. So the net effect is the same. Although this doesn't mean sickness, it does mean a need to watch your energy and vitality, to pace yourself better, organize yourself so that you can achieve more with less effort, focus on real priorities and let go of trivialities.

Pluto has been camping out in your 1st Solar House for many years now. So many of the trends written of in previous reports are still in effect. There is a great interest and focus on personal transformation, giving birth to your ideal self; on purifying the body and ridding of it effete materials; on transforming your concept of yourself into something nobler and finer; on the right diet and nutrition, and weight loss; on refining the body and making it more of a spiritual instrument.

This position has enhanced your glamour and sex appeal. Many of you are able to manifest any 'image' or 'look' that you desire. Your body has become more sensitive to psychic vibrations and you now must be more careful of the company you keep and the food you eat.

Many aches and pains that 'feel like' disease are in reality vibrations you are picking up from other people or the environment as a whole. When you go to the doctor to have your 'symptoms' checked out, they find nothing.

Discerning what symptoms are and are not yours is one of the long-term health lessons for Sagittarius.

Uranus' move into your 4th House for six months this year is only a harbinger of things to come. It will move into your 4th on a long-term basis (for seven years) next year. Though this transit brings much excitement and change in the home, there is a downside. It also brings greater emotional volatility and sudden mood changes. These mood changes can often be extreme. Thus there is a need to cultivate emotional equilibrium and balance. To sort of live in a place that is 'above' the emotions. To feel but not be identified with the feeling. This practice will enhance your overall health tremendously and save much energy. It will also make you more successful in other areas of life as well.

Venus is your Health Planet. Thus, the kidneys and hips generally need more attention. The hips can be massaged regularly. The kidneys can be strengthened by hosts of natural and drugless therapies, such as foot and hand reflexology, kinesiology, reiki, acupuncture and acupressure, shiatsu and herbology. (This list is by no means complete – but it gives you an idea.)

Venus is a fast-moving planet. In the course of the year, she will move through all the Signs and Houses of your Horoscope. Thus health needs and effective remedies can fluctuate month to month. Something that was effective one month might be less effective another, because Venus has changed her position. We will cover these short-term trends in the month-by-month forecasts.

The North Node of the Moon (considered a happiness indicator) will move into your 6th House after April 14.

Thus, you will find fulfilment and happiness by following health regimes and learning more about this subject.

Home, Domestic and Family Issues

Your 4th House of Home and Family has not been a House of Power for many years. Thus there has been a status-quo effect for years. You had little need to make major changes nor much interest in doing so. This is about to change – and how!

Dynamic Uranus moves into this House on March 10 and stays there until September 15. Next year, he will move into this House for seven years.

This indicates not merely a move, but perhaps a series of moves over the years. There is a restlessness in the home. There is a search for the ideal home – the 'perfect residence'. No sooner do you think that you have found one than another appears that is even better. Often this position points to many – serial – renovations of the home. It's as if you are constantly upgrading it. Your home (in your mind) gets obsolete as fast as computer equipment does. Often, this aspect shows a nomadic type of existence – living in different places for a certain time and then moving on.

Along with this, there is a need for freedom in the home. You will feel this, but family members could also be feeling it. There is a need for breaking the domestic routine (the rut), the domestic patterns and stifling family relationships. Many of you have felt stifled for many years, but never did anything about it. Now, you will. Though there is undoubtedly great love between you and many family members, you will attempt to change the relationship into something more liberating.

For older Sagittarians, this aspect is probably showing more freedom in the home due to very natural causes – the kids are growing up, going off to school or getting their own apartments and now you have the house to yourself. You are free – relieved of many responsibilities.

Those of you with children will be more experimental in child-rearing. Probably you will toy with all the latest and trendiest methods. But basically, you will take a trial-and-error approach. Many of you will find that the most ancient methods are the most effective.

On a more mundane level, technology is being brought into the home. Over the next seven years or so you are buying all the latest gadgets for the home. It is getting a technological upgrade.

A parent or parent figure is moving and also being nomadic. He or she is changing the image and self-concept – perhaps many times. The domestic life of siblings seems status quo.

Love and Social Life

Saturn leaving your 7th House of Love, Romance and Marriage is very good news for singles or those married for the first time. Singles have had limited romantic opportunities for the past two years and were forced to focus on quality rather than quantity of relationships. There was much fear and caution in love. The head was over-ruling the heart. A romantic mood was harder to attain, as practical issues kept creeping in. Marrieds had their relationships tested. The honeymoon was over and there were day-to-day realities to be dealt with – duties and obligations that come with a marriage.

I think these testings are a great thing, though not always pleasant to go through. When things are all wonderful and everything is a big honeymoon, you don't really know whether you are in love or just in a pleasant circumstance. But when things start to get tough – when the rough spots hit – and still you feel love for the other – then you know it's real love. Real love has to be able to withstand the bumps and potholes on the road. And this is what the Cosmos was doing over the past two years. It was test-driving your marriage over rough terrain. Those of you whose marriages survived the past two years have something wonderful. You will most likely survive the next six months. After that, the testing will be over – especially for those of you born early in the Sign.

When Saturn leaves your 7th House, singles should start dating more. Though we don't necessarily see a marriage, there is more romantic opportunity and you seem more open to it.

The movements of and aspects to Mercury (your Love Planet) will determine the short-term fluctuations of love and social affairs. When Mercury is positioned correctly or has favourable aspects, romance will tend to go well. When Mercury is being stressfully aspected, romance will feel challenged.

Mercury is a very fast-moving planet. In a year, he will move through all the Signs and Houses of your Horoscope. Thus love and romantic opportunity will come from many different areas and ways. Your needs and attitudes to love will also vary greatly through the year. We will cover these short-term trends in the month-by-month forecasts.

Those in a second marriage are not experiencing too many of these love testings (perhaps this is happening with friends) and the marriage looks very happy. Those who are looking to marry for a second time still have wonderful aspects most of the year. A marriage or quasi-marriage is very likely.

Those working towards or involved in a third marriage have a status-quo year. The married will tend to stay married and singles will tend to stay single.

Those in a fourth marriage have undergone a severe testing these past two years. Things are getting a little easier, though. Those looking to marry for a fourth time have good aspects, but they need to change many of their love attitudes.

A parent or parent figure could marry this year (if he or she is single). If he or she is married, there is more romance and happiness within the marriage. In general, the social life expands. Single siblings have wonderful aspects for marriage or a quasi-marriage.

Children of marriageable age have a status-quo year. Singles will tend to stay single and marrieds will tend to stay married. Grandchildren of marriageable age have wonderful aspects for marriage or a serious relationship this year. Up until now the aspects were too unstable. But with Uranus moving away from their Love House, there is a greater probability for something long lasting.

Finance and Career

Ambitions are very much heightened in the year ahead as Jupiter crosses the Midheaven of the chart and occupies your 10th House after August 27. This position shows that you are reaching the pinnacle of success and attainment – each according to your level and ability. (The file clerk is not going to suddenly become the president of the company – but he or she will be recognized for the good work that is being done and will likely get a promotion or pay rise or both.) Career horizons are expanding. Some of you will be elected to public office. Others will be elected to office in a group, club or organization you belong to. New and better job offers are coming – some with your present company and some with different companies. Your public and professional status are very much enhanced. Those of you who have very large career aspirations (and which Sagittarian hasn't?) will see much forward progress towards these things. Big goals often take more time and development.

Though your 2nd House of Finance is not a House of Power, you will earn more by virtue of the above. Money will be one of the side-effects of increased career success, and not an end in itself. This year, if you had to choose between a prestigious job that paid less and a less prestigious one that paid more – you would choose the former.

Finances were reasonable last year and they are reasonable this year. But important changes are happening. Your Money Planet moves from your 7th House to your 8th House after June 4. This shows important and long-term changes in your financial life. For the past two years, earnings depended on social connections, business partnerships, networking and, in many cases, your marriage. Though these areas are still important on a financial level, the emphasis is shifting to debt and the repayment or refinancing of it. You are entering a two-year period where debts will be repaid rather easily and you should take advantage of it.

Your Money Planet in the 8th House also shows a need to help others prosper and to put the financial interests of others ahead of your own. As you do this, you inevitably prosper on a personal level.

Professional investors should look at bonds and property for profit opportunities.

Self-improvement

Saturn in your 7th House for the past two years forced most of you to re-organize and re-structure your social life. (This is aside from the testing of your marriage.) You had to become more discerning in both the friendships you made and in the social occasions you attended. You couldn't attend every single function. So, you had to think about the friendships that really mattered. This caused a weeding-out process in your friendships. In many cases, disappointments with friends caused you to re-think and re-order this department. The Cosmos wasn't looking to punish you, only to make your social life more stable and healthy. You kept your quality friendships and let go of the rest. Learning the art of forgiveness also became important in the past two years. Hopefully, you arrived at forgiveness not as a platitude but from a place of understanding. When you understood the other party and why they had to do what they did or be what they were, forgiveness became natural. This trend continues for the first half of this year.

Saturn in your 8th House (after June 4) favours a disciplined, organized approach to debt-reduction. Set up a plan. Budget *X* amount of resources towards debt-reduction. Pay off the higher-interest loans first and the lower-interest ones later. Where possible (and many opportunities will come in 2003), refinance the higher-interest debt at more favourable rates. Spare cash that would go to savings or frivolous activities should be allocated to debt-reduction. Most importantly, stick to your plan. In two years, you will be amazed at your progress. It is the day-by-day discipline over the long haul that makes the magic.

Astrology also has some help for those who want to reduce debt. Try to make your payments on a waning moon. This will be in line with the cosmic energy of 'reduction' and your debts should be paid off faster and more easily.

Month-by-month Forecasts

January

Best Days Overall: 1st, 9th, 10th, 19th, 20th, 27th, 28th

Most Stressful Days Overall: 6th, 7th, 8th, 14th, 15th, 21st, 22nd

Best Days for Love: 2nd, 3rd, 9th, 10th, 11th, 12th, 13th, 19th, 20th, 21st, 22nd, 27th, 28th, 29th, 30th

Best Days for Money: 1st, 2nd, 3rd, 4th, 5th, 9th, 10th, 14th, 15th, 19th, 20th, 23rd, 24th, 27th, 28th

Most of the planets are in the East now and your 1st House of Self is very powerful after the 7th. Thus, you are in a cycle where you can have things your own way (not in everything, though) and can change undesirable conditions and create new ones if necessary. You should focus on building the life of your dreams.

Mars in your own Sign after the 17th gives you extra energy, personal magnetism and sex appeal, and enhances your athletic ability. But when he teams up with Pluto (already in your Sign for many years), the mixture can be combustive. Hurry, temper tantrums, belligerence, impatience and rashness are some of the dangers to be careful about. Try to channel this extra energy into creative or athletic pursuits.

Love is a bit difficult this month, though this has nothing to do with you *per se*. You look great, have exceptional style and taste – yet, love is complicated. Your Love Planet, Mercury, is retrograde from the 2nd to the 22nd and Saturn is still camped out in your House of Love. All of this is suggesting caution and a go-slow attitude in love. But with your hormones roaring these days (Mars, Pluto and Venus in your own Sign), going slow is difficult. Your lover or spouse almost can't help feeling a sense of coercion, even if you don't mean it. You don't realize your power and intensity these days.

A big part of you wants to party, but financial issues seem a problem. Probably your idea of a party exceeds your budget. If you scale things down a bit you can have plenty of fun this month. Finances are not as bad as you think and much progress is happening behind the scenes, but the retrograde of your Money Planet (Saturn) suggests caution and a wait-and-see attitude in finance. Foreigners and foreign lands play a big role in finance now. Professional investors should look at publishing, long-distance carriers, gold and utilities. Happily, the New Moon of the 2nd is going to clear up a lot of financial confusion.

By the 17th, the dominance of planetary power will be below the horizon – 70% to 80% of the planets will be there. With your Career Planet, Mercury, retrograde you can safely de-emphasize career and 'outer' goals and focus on the home, family and emotional issues.

Health is reasonable. The main danger comes from risk-taking activities. Your lust for danger and adventure is unusually strong – try to give it a safe outlet. Health can be enhanced by paying more attention to your thighs and kidneys. For you, this month, good health is about looking good. When you feel well, your appearance automatically shines – and vice versa. A trip to the gym or beauty salon can be as much of a healing as vitamins and visits to the doctor's surgery.

February

Best Days Overall: 5th, 6th, 15th, 16th, 23rd, 24th

Most Stressful Days Overall: 3rd, 4th, 10th, 11th, 17th, 18th

Best Days for Love: 8th, 9th, 10th, 11th, 17th, 18th, 19th, 20th, 25th, 26th, 28th

Best Days for Money: 1st, 2nd, 5th, 6th, 10th, 11th, 15th, 16th, 19th, 20th, 23rd, 24th, 25th, 26th, 28th

Like last month, the planets are mostly in the East. So, build your life according to your personal specifications. Your way (except in finance) is the best way for you now. You have enough energy and independence to go your own way even if others don't go along with you.

Again, like last month, the planets are mostly below the horizon. This is a period for preparing the psychological foundations for future success – for getting family support for your goals and for cultivating the right inner states.

Career success is happening – and in a big way – this year, but it needs some preparation.

Mars and Pluto are still in your Sign, so keep in mind our discussion about last month. This dynamic duo (not powers to be taken lightly) are giving you energy, drive and one-pointed focus. They enhance athletic ability and increase libido. They give courage and independence – but they also can cause impatience, irritability, anger and haste. Your appetite for risk-taking – always strong – is even stronger than usual. So these drives can complicate love and your relationships with others. You are so sure of your own position that you have trouble seeing the others' perspective. You tend to push your way too hard on others. Use your energy for constructive purposes – creatively or athletically. Those involved with Sagittarians don't want to get into a power struggle with them now. Definitely not advisable.

Finances are vastly improved over last month. Much financial confusion is ending as your Financial Planet, Saturn, starts moving forwards again on the 22nd. Sound financial judgement returns. Money comes from work (or perhaps from the health field), social connections and the good grace of your spouse or partner. Like last month, your urge to party could bust your budget. But if you scale things down you can still have a very good time. A little creativity is needed, that's all.

Love is improving, but financial disagreements (or differences in philosophy) with your spouse or partner are complicating things – creating some tension. Singles find love as they pursue their normal financial goals until the 13th. After that, they find it in educational settings – classes, school functions, seminars, etc. Love is close to home in the neighbourhood.

Your 3rd House of Communication and Intellectual Interests is very strong this month. Many of you will be travelling (domestically) this month. Many of you will be pursuing your intellectual interests – reading more, studying more, taking courses, etc. Students will do well in school this period. Those of you involved in sales and marketing should launch those projects this month.

Rest and relax more after the 19th.

March

Best Days Overall: 5th, 6th, 14th, 15th, 23rd

Most Stressful Days Overall: 2nd, 3rd, 10th, 11th, 17th, 29th, 30th, 31st

Best Days for Love: 1st, 10th, 11th, 12th, 13th, 19th, 20th, 21st, 22nd, 23rd, 29th, 30th

Best Days for Money: 1st, 5th, 6th, 10th, 11th, 14th, 15th, 19th, 23rd, 25th, 26th, 27th, 28th

Health is the major priority this month, Sagittarius. But telling someone to rest and relax more when Mars and Pluto are in their Sign is like telling a gazelle not to run. The gazelle will say 'I can't help it.' So, instead, we will advise focusing on the important things in life and avoiding wasting energy on frivolities. Even a gazelle will rest when tired and so should you. Avoid burning the candle at both ends. Happily, Mars moves out of your Sign on the 4th, lessening your lust for action. Health can be enhanced in various ways this month. Until the 2nd, pay attention to your spine, knees and teeth. After the 2nd, pay attention to your ankles. After the 21st, pay attention to your feet and your emotional health. Different types of therapies will work at different times this month, as Venus, your Health Planet, moves through three different Signs and Houses of your Horoscope.

This is a month where there is dramatic conflict between personal desires and urges, home and family responsibilities and your love and social life. Each pulls you in a different direction. Each vies for your complete attention – yet you can't give yourself over to any of these areas in a complete way. So, usually, no matter what you do, someone somewhere is displeased. Your job is to create as much harmony as you can, to give to each what is due, to make these areas co-operate rather than conflict. Ultimately you have to guide yourself by your Highest Concept of Right and then let the chips fall where they may. If you're going to take flak, at least let it be out of principle – then the flak will eventually honour you.

Aside from all this, an important planetary shift takes place by the 21st. (This is a gradual process that happens little by little.) The planetary power shifts from the East to the West, causing an important psychological shift for you. Personal independence is lessened. You need the grace of other people to attain your ends. You are less able to change conditions and must be more adaptable and flexible with what is. You become more 'other-orientated' than 'me-orientated'. So, whereas you've been thinking of Number One for the past few months, now you must put other people first. By the karmic law, your own good will eventually come.

Like last month, most of the planets are below the horizon. But this month your 4th House of Home and Family becomes unusually powerful. A lot of action, change and ferment is going on at home. Emotions can run high (as change always causes emotional volatility) and you will have to work hard to cultivate equilibrium. Moves could happen this month. You are working to build a team spirit in the family and at home. You can safely de-emphasize career and focus on the family. If you can keep some stability at home, your career will take care of itself.

Finances are more stressful this period. But earnings will happen. You just need to work harder and be willing to go the extra mile.

April

Best Days Overall: 1st, 2nd, 11th, 12th, 19th, 20th, 28th, 29th

Most Stressful Days Overall: 6th, 7th, 13th, 14th, 26th, 27th

Best Days for Love: 1st, 2nd, 6th, 7th, 8th, 9th, 13th, 14th, 17th, 18th, 21st, 22nd, 28th, 29th

Best Days for Money: 1st, 2nd, 6th, 7th, 11th, 12th, 15th, 16th, 19th, 20th, 21st, 22nd, 23rd, 24th, 28th, 29th

Health improves dramatically this month, but still needs to be watched. A Grand Trine in Fire all month lifts your spirits. Spiritual changes are bringing up impurities in the body, which might feel uncomfortable. This is not necessarily disease. Don't let financial stresses get you down, either. Much of this is short term. Emotional health is unusually important – and probably more difficult to attain. Your emotions and moods are like a roller-coaster – both the highs and lows are extreme. You can tame this bucking bronco by staying centred and above it all. Just be aware in the here/now moment. Your awareness puts you on another level. Discharge undesirable feelings by writing them out on paper and then throwing the paper away. Don't repress, but express harmlessly. Health is enhanced through foot massage and through paying extra attention to your head.

Like last month, most of the planets are below the horizon, so career takes a back seat to emotional and family issues. Finding your emotional comfort zone (and living there) should be your main priority.

Like last month, the planets are mostly in the West. Continue to cultivate your social graces and attain your ends through consensus and compromise. Charm will succeed where self-will and self-assertion fail. (You'll get more with the carrot than the stick.)

With your 5th House very powerful, this is very much a party month – a month for pursuing personal pleasure and leisure activities. Finances are much improved, too. As you relax and enjoy life, many hidden blockages are removed. The clogged financial channels get unclogged. Andrew Carnegie once quipped that 'in leisure, there is luck' – he knew what he was talking about. Unlike in past months, you have the resources to enjoy yourself.

Job-seekers have two prerequisites this month. They need a job where they are treated as family and not as 'a number' or 'profit centre' – a nurturing work environment. But they also need a job that they enjoy. This can be approached by degrees. The ideal is to have work where you don't *feel* like you're working. Where going to the job is as much fun as going to the theatre. While it may be impossible to attain the ideal this period, you can shoot for something that comes close. A good job this month will also enhance your love life. Romantic opportunities come at work or as you pursue your health goals.

May

Best Days Overall: 8th, 9th, 16th, 17th, 25th, 26th, 27th

Most Stressful Days Overall: 3rd, 4th, 10th, 11th, 23rd, 24th, 30th, 31st

Best Days for Love: 1st, 2nd, 3rd, 4th, 8th, 9th, 10th, 11th, 18th, 19th, 28th, 29th, 30th, 31st

Best Days for Money: 3rd, 4th, 8th, 9th, 12th, 13th, 16th, 17th, 18th, 19th, 21st, 22nd, 25th, 26th, 27th, 30th, 31st

You still need to make health a priority this month – especially after the 21st. Where possible, take a reduced schedule and focus only on the things that are important to you. Delegate jobs where possible. Don't let erratic emotional swings distract you from your purposes – observe them, stay above them and, where possible, discharge them harmlessly. Health can be enhanced by enjoying life and cultivating a sense of joy. Give your head, neck and throat more attention. Sunshine is healthy until the 16th (if you have allergies, protect yourself as you sunbathe). Heat treatments, saunas and the like also seem good. After the 16th, mountainous places or mineral baths seem good.

Most of the planets are still below the horizon (though this is soon to change), so continue to pay attention to your emotional life and family responsibilities. You can safely de-emphasize career.

The planets, this month, are approaching their maximum westward power. Your 7th House of Love and Romance becomes very powerful after the 21st – more powerful than your 1st House of Self. So continue to practise social skills and de-emphasize personal will, self-assertion and personal power struggles.

You are entering one of your strongest, most active and happiest social periods of your year. A Solar eclipse on the 31st is going to shake up your love and social life and change the patterns for the better. Relationships get tested. Marital status could change (i.e. singles could take the plunge, while marrieds could divorce or separate). Since the Sun is the Lord of your 9th House, this eclipse tests your religious, philosophical and metaphysical beliefs. Flaws in these get tested (perhaps by a crisis of faith) so that you can make improvements. University students change areas of study or schools – or perhaps make other long-term changes in their educational plans. In most cases, this indicates graduation. Do take a reduced schedule during this eclipse period, as it is strong on you.

A Lunar eclipse on the 16th occurs in your 12th House of Spirituality. Thus, important spiritual changes are happening now. Important revelation comes to you which changes attitudes long-term. Many will embark on a spiritual discipline now. Others might change their methods, techniques or teachers. Upheavals occur in a charity or cause you're involved with.

Finances will be strong this month. Your spouse or partner seems generous. Financial horizons are expanding. Social connections help your bottom line. Financial aims are still attained by compromise and consensus. Job-seekers meet with good success this month too. A New Moon on the 1st clarifies job offers and your work situation in general.

June

Best Days Overall: 4th, 5th, 13th, 14th, 22nd, 23rd

Most Stressful Days Overall: 1st, 7th, 8th, 19th, 20th, 27th, 28th

Best Days for Love: 1st, 7th, 8th, 17th, 18th, 27th, 28th, 29th

Best Days for Money: 1st, 4th, 5th, 10th, 11th, 13th, 14th, 15th, 16th, 18th, 19th, 22nd, 23rd, 29th

Give health priority now. Rest and relax more whenever possible. Avoid power struggles and risky, stressful activities. Try to maintain emotional equilibrium (it will be difficult) and 'agree with thine adversary quickly.' The management of your energy is your key to getting through this month. You can strengthen yourself by paying extra attention to your neck, throat, shoulders and lungs. Keep speech to a minimum and keep it constructive and positive. Say nice things to your body and praise your organs for serving you so wonderfully. You respond well to mineral baths and crystal therapy until the 10th. After the 10th, fresh air therapy seems good.

There is an important planetary shift this month from the lower to the upper half of your Horoscope. Thus, 'outer' ambitions are becoming ever more important. You won't be able to ignore your home or family – not with dynamic Mars and Uranus in your 4th House – but you can shift some focus to your outer goals. Moves and renovations of the home seem likely this month. Perhaps new high-tech equipment is being installed there. New toys (adults' and/or children's) are coming to the home. You are working to make the home more enjoyable – more of a place of entertainment. Many of you are building play rooms or play areas, or rooms for children. Emotional volatility is most intense until the 21st, but calms down somewhat afterwards.

Most of the planets are still in the West and your 7th House of Love and Romance is still very strong. Thus you are in a social period, where social skills and charm count. Your ability to get on with others is more important than your personal excellence. Now that Saturn is leaving your 7th House of Love, your love and social life is going to become much happier. It's as if you leave many of your past fears and insecurities behind. New social confidence is happening. Love has more of an opportunity to bloom, as many of your inhibitions about it are removed. Singles find love at the work place, parties and social gatherings (perhaps at weddings) and as they work to help others prosper.

Your Money Planet, Saturn, makes a once-in-two-and-a-half-years move from Gemini into Cancer on the 4th. Thus, your job is to make money for other people. Your success will be judged on this – how well you enrich others. You are entering a long-term period where you will be able to reduce (or eliminate) debt, expenses and financial waste. Speculations seem more favourable after the 17th and money seems to come in unexpected ways.

Libido needs to be managed better in the coming years.

July

Best Days Overall: 2nd, 3rd, 10th, 11th, 19th, 20th, 29th, 30th

Most Stressful Days Overall: 4th, 5th, 17th, 18th, 24th, 25th, 31st

Best Days for Love: 8th, 9th, 17th, 18th, 19th, 20th, 24th, 25th, 28th, 29th, 30th

Best Days for Money: 2nd, 3rd, 7th, 8th, 10th, 11th, 12th, 13th, 16th, 17th, 19th, 20th, 26th, 27th, 29th, 30th

Health is much improved after the 4th as the planetary stresses on you weaken. Much power in your native element of Fire is also helping matters. This lifts your spirits, banishes depression and brings personal pleasure, sensual fulfilment and many travel opportunities. A month where travel is accentuated could only be Sagittarian heaven. Still, with two powerful planets in stressful alignment, pay more attention to your health. Enhance health by paying more attention to your arms, shoulders, lungs, stomach, breasts and heart this month. Emotional health is unusually important for physical health as well.

The planetary power is still mostly above the horizon and your 10th House of Career gets activated late in the month. Like last month, turn your attention to outer matters. Happily, your domestic life seems calmer this month. Not completely calm by any means, but less volatile than it has been the last few months.

Like last month, the planetary power is still mostly in the West. Continue to cultivate the social graces. Your goals are attained 'not by might nor by power but by my spirit'. In other words, by grace.

Your 8th House is unusually powerful until the 23rd. Thus, this is a period to pay off debt, reduce financial waste, work to help others prosper and get rid of some of the excess in your life – possessions, undesirable character traits, physical weight and the like. It is a good period to break addictions of any nature – whether they be to substances, compulsive spending or emotional-mental patterns. It is a month for personal reinvention and transformation. When the 8th House is powerful, people are often confronted with their fears about death. Events happen that trigger these fears and it is a good time to come to grips and get a deeper understanding of them. When we understand death correctly, we will also understand life.

Your 9th House of Religion, Metaphysics, Higher Education and Foreign Travel has been strong for some months now, but it gets very powerful after the 23rd. 40-50% of the planets will either be there or moving through there. Thus your natural love for education and philosophy is even further stimulated. Educational opportunities will come and you should take them. It is a good time for attaining religious and philosophical clarity. The study of scripture and other religious writings goes well and seems interesting.

Love seems happy this month – tender and romantic. With your Love Planet moving speedily (through three Signs and Houses of the chart), your social confidence is strong. Singles do a lot of dating, perhaps with various people. Your needs in love change rapidly, which is perhaps why a marriage should be avoided. Libido is unusually strong this month; love is expressed in that way until the 13th. After that, you are attracted to mentor-type people. And after that (by the 30th), you are allured by people of high social, political and economic status. You mix with the high and mighty.

Finances are excellent. A Grand Trine in Water on the 8th and 9th brings windfalls and opportunity. After the 4th, a new and happy job opportunity could come.

August

Best Days Overall: 7th, 15th, 16th, 17th, 25th, 26th

Most Stressful Days Overall: 1st, 13th, 14th, 20th, 21st, 22nd, 27th, 28th

Best Days for Love: 1st, 7th, 8th, 9th, 10th, 16th, 17th, 18th, 19th, 20th, 21st, 22nd, 27th, 28th

Best Days for Money: 4th, 5th, 7th, 8th, 9th, 10th, 13th, 14th, 16th, 17th, 23rd, 24th, 26th, 27th

Though overall this is a happy and unusually successful month, you must give priority to your health. If you stay healthy, you'll be able to enjoy all these blessings. Definitely pace yourself after the 22nd. Family life and emotional passions get stormy again and you have to cultivate equilibrium. Career success – pay rises, promotions, honours, etc. – could de-stabilize the home environment. In many cases, career advancement is causing a move – this could be the cause for a lot of the stress. Focus on your career, but don't over-focus. Much good fortune will happen this month and in the year ahead.

By the 27th, there is an important shift of planetary power from the West to the East. By that time, 60% to 70% of the planets will be in the East. Thus, gradually, as the month progresses, you are gaining more and more personal control over your life and destiny. Suddenly you discover that you are not as dependent on others as you thought and options open up for ways to change uncomfortable situations and conditions. You are entering a period where being 'Mr or Ms Nice Guy' won't bring success. Personal effort and personal excellence will do it. In financial matters you will still need to do things by consensus and through the co-operation of others. But in most other areas of life, you can go it alone if necessary.

Finances are strong, but not as interesting to you as other areas of life. Earnings will come easily, but you don't seem financially driven. Status, prestige and your place in the hierarchy are much more important than mere money these days.

Love is happy – though, on the 28th, your Love Planet, Mercury, goes retrograde. Until then, though, you have many love opportunities. Perhaps you are overly perfectionist in love these days – but that's OK, so long as you don't get hyper-critical about it. Like last month, you are socializing with the high and mighty – people of status and power. A love opportunity with a boss or someone of high status is likely – a work place romance.

You are reaching the pinnacle of career success this month (and over the year ahead) – you're in one of the strongest career periods of your life. But, as with all success, there is a price tag. You lack time to play and have fun. Leisure activities suffer. Spiritual interests could also suffer. But never mind, you must seize the opportunities as they come. You will be able to give more attention to these other areas in future months.

September

Best Days Overall: 3rd, 4th, 12th, 13th, 22nd, 23rd, 30th

Most Stressful Days Overall: 9th, 10th, 17th, 18th, 24th, 25th

Best Days for Love: 5th, 6th, 14th, 15th, 16th, 17th, 18th, 24th, 25th, 26th, 27th

Best Days for Money: 1st, 2nd, 5th, 6th, 9th, 10th, 14th, 15th, 19th, 20th, 26th, 27th, 28th, 29th

Most of the planets are still above the horizon and your 10th House is filled with beneficial and loving powers. It's as if the most benevolent powers in the universe are having a conference – conspiring – as to how best advance your career and bring you maximum success. These aspects are also fortunate for dealing with the government or authority figures. If you need favours from those above or have pending issues with them, this is the time to get them sorted – before the 15th, if possible.

Health still needs to be watched until the 23rd. Emotional volatility at home should ease up after the 15th as Uranus moves out of your 4th House and back into the 3rd (on the 15th). Health can be enhanced through the right diet and more attention on your kidneys, hips, buttocks and intestines.

Though career is still very important, there is still a need to balance your personal desires and inclinations with the career and the home. The conflicts between these areas are more dramatic these days and it is difficult to please everyone all the time. Thus, you must give to each its due and ultimately stand on principle. When the attacks or displays of displeasure come, you will be in a stronger position to handle them.

With most of the planets still in the East, this is a time for action, independence and taking the bull by the horns. Work to design your life as you desire it to be. Negative conditions can be changed now – you can do it.

Finances are strong – especially until the 23rd – and your financial judgement is sound. After the 23rd, you work harder for earnings, but they will come. Speculations are favourable after the 27th. It's still a good time to pay off debt and cut wasteful expenditures. Parents or parent figures are prospering greatly now.

Love is stormy until the 20th. Romance is still at the work place or with people involved in your career. You are still mingling and socializing with socially prominent people – people above you in status. But love needs time to develop, as your Love Planet is retrograde until the 20th. Social confidence could be better. After the 20th, you'll more or less know where a current relationship is going. Getting family to accept your current love seems difficult. Children are also not thrilled with your current love. But these are short-term trends – by next month, these issues will straighten out. Friendships and group activities are going better this month – especially after the 15th. Job-seekers get good leads from friends or from organizations they belong to. New and significant friends come into the picture now.

October

Best Days Overall: 1st, 9th, 10th, 19th, 20th, 27th, 28th

Most Stressful Days Overall: 7th, 8th, 14th, 15th, 21st, 22nd

Best Days for Love: 2nd, 3rd, 4th, 5th, 14th, 15th, 16th, 17th, 24th, 25th, 26th

Best Days for Money: 2nd, 3rd, 7th, 8th, 11th, 12th, 13th, 16th, 17th, 21st, 22nd, 25th, 26th, 29th, 30th

Health is much improved, but still can't be taken for granted. Enhance health by paying attention to your kidneys, hips, buttocks and sexual organs. De-tox regimes are effective after the 9th. Don't let relations with friends deteriorate, as social issues play a big factor in your overall health.

Most of the planets are still in the East and you can have life on your terms during this period (except for finance). This is the time to custom-design your life as you would like it to be. Personal effort makes a big difference. Your destiny is in your hands.

The upper half of the Horoscope is stronger than the lower half. So, as in recent months, continue to focus on your career and outer goals. Doing right will help you to feel right and, ultimately, help the family and domestic situation. Let family members know that you care about them and that it's precisely because you care that you are pursuing your outer goals. This could assuage passions.

Finances are a bit stressful until the 23rd. Your Financial Planet, Saturn, goes retrograde on the 25th. You need to work a little harder for earnings – go the extra mile, compromise, etc. and be much more cautious with major purchases, investments and commitments. After the 23rd, in spite of the retrograde, the financial aspects improve. There could be minor delays and annoyances, but there is still prosperity. Your financial intuition becomes very strong after the 9th.

A beautiful Grand Trine in Water from the 9th onwards not only brings prosperity, financial windfalls and opportunity, but luck in speculations, a happy job offer and enhanced creativity. There will be more opportunities to have fun and enjoy leisure activities as well.

Friendship and spirituality are the two most important areas of life this month. There is more involvement with organizations, groups and group activities. Astrology and science become more important. Many of your fondest hopes and wishes will come to pass and, as they do, you begin formulating a new set of 'fondest hopes and wishes'. Spirituality becomes important after the 23rd. This is a period for more seclusion, prayer and meditation. It is a time for involvement in charitable or volunteer-type activities. A time for spiritual study and progress. Your dream life will become very active, and these dreams have many revelations for you. ESP and prophetic abilities increase. You will probably be witness to spiritual healings and the like. Unemployed people can enhance future work prospects by volunteering their services to hospitals, causes they believe in or ministries.

Love is much happier after the 7th. Love opportunities also come from the pursuit of spiritual goals and group activities. Friends like playing Cupid this month. Friendship seems just as important as romance.

Like last month, health is reasonable but precautions are still needed. Enhance health by paying extra attention to your sexual organs, thighs and liver this month. De-tox regimes seem effective until the 2nd.

Like last month, most of the planets are in the East and your 1st House of Self becomes a major House of Power after the 22nd – 40% to 50% of the planets are there or move through there. This is a high percentage. So, continue to build your life according to your personal specifications. Personal effort pays off. Your way is the best way this month (except perhaps in finance). Give respect to others, but follow your own path.

November

Best Days Overall: 5th, 6th, 15th, 16th, 24th, 25th

Most Stressful Days Overall: 3rd, 4th, 10th, 11th, 12th, 18th, 19th, 30th

Best Days for Love: 3rd, 4th, 5th, 6th, 10th, 11th, 12th, 15th, 16th, 24th, 25th, 26th, 27th

Best Days for Money: 3rd, 4th, 8th, 9th, 13th, 14th, 18th, 19th, 22nd, 23rd, 26th, 27th

This month, the planetary power shifts once again, from the upper half to the lower half of your Horoscope. This represents an important psychological shift for you. By the 22nd (when this shift is complete), you will be less interested in career and more interested in 'feeling good' and having the right inner state. By now you are accustomed to success and are perhaps a bit sated with it. Another deal here or another opportunity there is of little moment. You want to feel good as you succeed. Career opportunities (and there will be many) will be judged on this basis.

There are two eclipses this month. The Lunar eclipse of the 9th occurs in your 6th House, signalling job changes and perhaps some long-term changes in your health regime. Conditions at work are undergoing long-term – and dramatic – change. There could be upheavals with uncles or aunts. Long-brewing flaws in these areas are surfacing for cleansing.

Though this Lunar eclipse is benign to you, it won't hurt to take a reduced schedule and to avoid risky activities.

The Solar eclipse of the 23rd is a much stronger one. Thus, here it is advisable to take a reduced schedule – a few days before and about a day after. This eclipse occurs in your own Sign of Sagittarius and signals changes in the image, body and self-concept. You get an opportunity to re-define and fine-tune your personality. Many of you will change your image and the way you dress. Others will present a new and improved sense of self to the world. As you already know, every Solar eclipse tests your religious and philosophical beliefs. This one is no different. So, flaws or discrepancies are opportunities to make corrections.

Love is happy this month and is pursuing you. By the 12th it will find you. It is inescapable.

Finances are strong, though your Money Planet is still retrograde. Earnings are coming, but you need to exercise more caution with major purchases and investments.

December

Best Days Overall: 2nd, 3rd, 4th, 12th, 13th, 14th, 21st, 22nd, 30th, 31st

Most Stressful Days Overall: 1st, 7th, 8th, 9th, 15th, 16th, 27th, 28th

Best Days for Love: 5th, 6th, 7th, 8th, 9th, 15th, 16th, 23rd, 24th, 25th, 26th

Best Days for Money: 1st, 5th, 6th, 10th, 11th, 15th, 16th, 19th, 20th, 23rd, 24th

Continue to design your life as you desire it to be. It's all up to you now. It doesn't matter whom you know or how many friends you have, success is up to you and comes by personal merit and effort. You have to please yourself. If you are pleased, the world will be pleased.

Overall this is a happy and optimistic month. There are travel opportunities, sensual delights and all the joys of the good life. Personal horizons are expanding. Self-esteem and self-confidence are strong. Your ideas and goals are larger than life. Efforts at reinvention and personal transformation make excellent progress this month.

Having most of the planets below the horizon shows, like last month, a need for 'emotionally comfortable success'. Continue to cultivate the right inner states and to stabilize (as best you can) the domestic situation. The domestic situation is about to turn volatile again as Uranus now moves into your 4th House for good (on the 30th). As always, cultivate equilibrium.

Prosperity is even stronger than last month. You are more interested in finance and thus are more willing to overcome obstacles to succeed. Your interest creates success. Finances are complicated by two factors – your Money Planet, Saturn, is still retrograde and this month receives stressful aspects. Thus there is difficulty in balancing your personal financial interest with those of others. Financial judgement could be better and more caution should be taken with holiday shopping. (Mercury is also going retrograde on the 17th.) Be more careful about how you communicate about financial matters and to people involved in your finances. Mis-communication can be expensive and time-consuming.

Also, impulsive, rash spending (especially after the 17th) can crimp your bottom line. Try to keep your spending proportional – that is the key. Be prepared to work harder for earnings.

Health is reasonable, but still needs watching. Give extra attention to your spine, knees, teeth and ankles.

Love is still basically happy; your beloved is going way out of his or her way to please you. But your Love Planet, Mercury, goes retrograde on the 17th, so give your lover space and don't try to rush love. Love is expressed in material ways this month – through money or material gifts.

Capricorn

♑

THE GOAT

Birthdays from

21st December

to 19th January

Personality Profile

CAPRICORN AT A GLANCE

Element – Earth

Ruling Planet – Saturn
Career Planet – Venus
Love Planet – Moon
Money Planet – Uranus
Planet of Communications – Neptune
Planet of Health and Work – Mercury
Planet of Home and Family Life – Mars
Planet of Spirituality – Jupiter

Colours – black, indigo

Colours that promote love, romance and social harmony – puce, silver

Colour that promotes earning power – ultramarine blue

Gem – black onyx

Metal – lead

Scents – magnolia, pine, sweet pea, wintergreen

Quality – cardinal (= activity)

Qualities most needed for balance – warmth, spontaneity, a sense of fun

Strongest virtues – sense of duty, organization, perseverance, patience, ability to take the long-term view

Deepest needs – to manage, take charge and administrate

Characteristics to avoid – pessimism, depression, undue materialism and undue conservatism

Signs of greatest overall compatibility – Taurus, Virgo

Signs of greatest overall incompatibility – Aries, Cancer, Libra

Sign most helpful to career – Libra

Sign most helpful for emotional support – Aries

Sign most helpful financially – Aquarius

Sign best for marriage and/or partnerships – Cancer

Sign most helpful for creative projects – Taurus

Best Sign to have fun with – Taurus

Signs most helpful in spiritual matters – Virgo, Sagittarius

Best day of the week – Saturday

Understanding a Capricorn

The virtues of Capricorns are such that there will always be people for and against them. Many admire them, many dislike them. Why? It seems to be because of Capricorn's power urges. A well-developed Capricorn has his or her eyes set on the heights of power, prestige and authority. In the Sign of Capricorn, ambition is not a fatal flaw, but rather the highest virtue.

Capricorns are not frightened by the resentment their authority may sometimes breed. In Capricorn's cool, calculated, organized mind all the dangers are already factored into the equation – the unpopularity, the animosity, the misunderstandings, even the outright slander – and a plan is always in place for dealing with these things in the most efficient way. To the Capricorn, situations that would terrify an ordinary mind are merely problems to be managed, bumps on the road to ever-growing power, effectiveness and prestige.

Some people attribute pessimism to the Capricorn Sign, but this is a bit deceptive. It is true that Capricorns like to take into account the negative side of things. It is also true that they love to imagine the worst possible scenario in every undertaking. Other people might find such analyses depressing, but Capricorns only do these things so that they can formulate a way out – an escape route.

Capricorns will argue with success. They will show you that you are not doing as well as you think you are. Capricorns do this to themselves as well as to others. They do not mean to discourage you but rather to root out any impediments to your greater success. A Capricorn boss or supervisor feels that, no matter how good the performance, there is always room for improvement. This explains why Capricorn supervisors are difficult to handle and even infuriating at times. Their actions are, however, quite often effective – they can get their subordinates to improve and become better at their jobs.

Capricorn is a born manager and administrator. Leo is better at being king or queen, but Capricorn is better at being prime minister – the person actually wielding power.

Capricorn is interested in the virtues that last, in the things that will stand the test of time and trials of circumstance. Temporary fads and fashions mean little to a Capricorn – except as things to be used for profit or power. Capricorns apply this attitude to business, love, to their thinking and even to their philosophy and religion.

Finance

Capricorns generally attain wealth and they usually earn it. They are willing to work long and hard for what they want. They are quite amenable to foregoing a short-term gain in favour of long-term benefits. Financially, they come into their own later in life.

However, if Capricorns are to attain their financial goals, they must shed some of their strong conservatism. Perhaps this is the least desirable trait of the Capricorn. They can resist anything new merely because it is new and untried. They are afraid of experimentation. Capricorns need to be willing to take a few risks. They should be more eager to market new products or explore different managerial techniques. Otherwise, progress will leave them behind. If necessary, Capricorns must be ready to change with the times, to discard old methods that no longer work.

Very often this experimentation will mean that Capricorns have to break with existing authority. They might even consider changing their present position or starting their own ventures. If so, they should be willing to accept all the risks and just get on with it. Only then will a Capricorn be on the road to highest financial gain.

Career and Public Image

A Capricorn's ambition and quest for power are evident. It is perhaps the most ambitious Sign of the Zodiac – and usually the most successful in a worldly sense. However, there are lessons Capricorns need to learn in order to fulfil their highest aspirations.

Intelligence, hard work, cool efficiency and organization will take them a certain distance, but will not carry them to the very top. Capricorns need to cultivate their social graces, to develop a social style, along with charm and an ability to get along with people. They need to bring beauty into their lives and to cultivate the right social contacts. They must learn to wield power gracefully, so that people love them for it – a very delicate art. They also need to learn how to bring people together in order to fulfil certain objectives. In short, Capricorns require some of the gifts – the social grace – of the Libra to get to the top.

Once they have learned this, Capricorns will be successful in their careers. They are ambitious, hard workers who are not afraid of putting in the required time and effort. Capricorns take their time in getting the job done – in order to do it well – and they like moving up the corporate ladder slowly but surely. Being so driven by success, Capricorns are generally liked by their bosses, who respect and trust them.

Love and Relationships

Like Scorpio and Pisces, Capricorn is a difficult Sign to get to know. They are deep, introverted and like to keep their own counsel. Capricorns do not like to reveal their innermost thoughts. If you are in love with a Capricorn, be patient and take your time. Little by little you will get to understand him or her.

Capricorns have a deep romantic nature, but they do not show it straight away. They are cool, matter of fact and not especially emotional. They will often show their love in practical ways.

It takes time for a Capricorn – male or female – to fall in love. They are not the love-at-first-sight kind. If a Capricorn is involved with a Leo or Aries, these Fire types will be totally mystified – to them the Capricorn will seem cold, unfeeling, unaffectionate and not very spontaneous. Of course none of this is true, it is just that Capricorn likes to take things slowly. They like to be sure of their ground before making any demonstrations of love or commitment.

Even in love affairs Capricorns are deliberate. They need more time to make decisions than is true of the other Signs of the Zodiac, but given this time they become just as passionate. Capricorns like a relationship to be structured, committed, well regulated, well defined, predictable and even routine. They prefer partners who are nurturers and they in turn like to nurture their partners. This is their basic psychology. Whether such a relationship is good for them is another issue altogether. Capricorns have enough routine in their lives as it is. They might be better off in relationships that are a bit more stimulating, changeable and fluctuating.

Home and Domestic Life

The home of a Capricorn – as with a Virgo – is going to be tidy and well organized. Capricorns tend to manage their families in the same way they manage their businesses. Capricorns are often so career-driven that they find little time for the home and family. They should try to get more actively involved in their family and domestic life. Capricorns do, however, take their children very seriously and are very proud parents, particularly if their children should grow up to become respected members of society.

Horoscope for 2003

Major Trends

2002 should have been a healthy and successful year, Capricorn. 2003 looks even better – especially the latter half. Almost all the long-term planets are either leaving you alone or are in harmonious aspect.

2002 was a work and financial year. Being efficient, productive and achieving work goals were your main objectives. This trend will continue for a while (until June 4), and then your love and social life become much more important. 2003 will be a very strong social year.

Jupiter will move into a beautiful aspect beginning August 27. This brings optimism, joy, travel, luck in speculations, honours, recognition and financial success. Perhaps most importantly, he brings religious and philosophical revelation and happy educational opportunities.

We see a greater interest in education in other ways too, as Uranus begins a once-in-seven-years move into your 3rd House of Intellectual Interests. Students – both university and secondary school – should have a successful year.

The most important areas of interest in 2003 are: finance; communication and intellectual interests (from March 10 to September 15); health and work (until June 4); love, romance and social activities (after June 4); sex, debt and the repayment of debt, taxes, helping others prosper, personal transformation (until August 27); religion, philosophy, higher education, foreign travel (after August 27); spirituality.

Your paths to greatest fulfilment in the coming year are: health and work (until April 14); children, creativity and leisure activities (after April 14); debt and the repayment of debt, taxes, helping others prosper, sex, personal transformation (until August 27); religion, philosophy, higher education, foreign travel (after August 27).

Health

Health was good last year and should get even better this year – especially in the latter half of the year.

Your 6th House of Health was important last year and will continue to be important (a House of Power) until June 4. Since health and vitality look superb, I read this as a love for health regimes for their own sake and not to cure any disease. You are into keeping fit and looking good. Always disciplined and organized, you apply these traits to your health regimes. You are methodical and scientific about it.

With Saturn in your 6th House, you can enhance your already good health by paying more attention to your spine, knees and teeth. (As a Capricorn, these organs are important on their own – but now they are even more important than usual.) Regular visits to a chiropractor or osteopath will keep your spine aligned and well adjusted. The knees should be massaged regularly and given more support – especially when indulging in strenuous exercise.

Mercury is your Health Ruler. Mercury rules the brain, nervous system, lungs, arms, shoulders and intestines. Thus, as a general rule, these parts of the body need more attention than others. Keeping them fit acts as a powerful preventative to disease. There are many natural, drugless ways to do this – herbology, gemology, chiropractice, kinesiology, homoeopathy, foot and hand reflexology, acupressure and acupuncture, reiki and massage. (There are many more therapies not mentioned, but these give you something to start off with.)

Mercury is a fast-moving planet. He will move through all the Signs and Houses of your Horoscope in any given year. Thus your needs in health will fluctuate. Healings can come to you in a variety of ways and from a variety of sources. Therapies that might work well one month might not work that well another month, as by then Mercury has changed position. Thus a good intuition is a big help in health maintenance – that or a personal astrologer. We will cover these short-term trends in the month-by-month forecasts.

Mercury rules communication and the mind. Thus, the message here is that mental health is as important to you as physical health – and this is as it should be. The mind needs a healthy diet, just as the physical body needs one. The mind needs healthy ideas, truth and wisdom to keep it nourished. Thus these things are important not only for your mental health but for your physical health as well.

Health problems can often originate in blockages in communication or self-expression. Thus, it is important either to have good friends you can exchange ideas with or to keep a diary and express yourself that way.

Mercury as your Health Ruler shows that your words and thoughts have a dramatic impact on your health. Now, this is so for everyone in some degree, but for you it is very dramatic. Thus, always say nice things about your body and organs. Praise them regularly. Think nice thoughts about them. Hold nice images of them. If you do this regularly, you will be amazed at how your body responds.

You should hear some good news about the health of a sibling. The health of your spouse or partner is improving after June 4. Joy is a great healer for your spouse – he or she should avoid depression like the plague.

The health of children seems status quo. Health of grandchildren is good, but will get even better after August 27. Grandchildren respond well to foot reflexology.

Home, Domestic and Family Issues

Your 4th House of Home and Family has not been a House of Power for years, so I expect the status quo will prevail in the year ahead. The Cosmos doesn't push you one way or the other here. Thus you have much freedom to shape this area as you will. This freedom often goes unused due to lack of interest on your part.

Mars, your Family Planet, does make an unusual transit this year. It will spend six months in the Sign of Pisces, your 3rd House – from June 17 to December 16. This would show that good communication becomes important (more so than usual) in dealing with family members. Perhaps you are installing new communication equipment in the home. The problem is that Mars will go retrograde from July 29 to September 26 – making good communication harder to achieve. You will just need to work harder and take nothing for granted.

This transit shows more involvement with neighbours. Perhaps more socializing with them, etc.

If you're doing renovations and heavy construction in the home, I like March 9 to April 21 and December 16 onwards. For beautifying, redecorating and buying objects of beauty for the home, I like April 21 to May 16 (also good for entertaining from home).

Your 5th House of Children is not a House of Power either. Yet, with the North Node of the Moon entering there from April 14 onwards, this is an area that should be cultivated as it brings joy and fulfilment. Spend more time with your children (if you have them) or with children in general. More importantly, spend more time with your inner child and give him or her adequate expression. Adults have much to learn from children.

The domestic situation of a parent or parent figure seems cramped, but a move is not in order at this time. Better to make more efficient use of the space they have. Children are moving to larger quarters and have beautiful aspects for the fortunate purchase or sale of a home.

Love and Social Life

Many a single Capricorn is going to walk down the aisle in coming years. Many will enter serious relationships that are like marriage, but perhaps not legally sealed. A new and very powerful social trend begins on June 4 when Saturn, your Ruling Planet, enters your 7th House of Love and Marriage.

Though Saturn is considered a difficult planet, in your case he is beneficial. He is the Lord of your chart and the Lord of one's Horoscope is ALWAYS beneficial and helpful.

This move into your 7th House signals social interest. That is, your love and romantic urges become much more intense than usual. The inevitable consequence is that love is more likely to come to you. Add to this the fact that Saturn is well aspected in his transit through your House of Marriage and you have the recipe for a serious relationship.

Now it is usually wrong to apply the word 'aggressive' to a Capricorn. With a Capricorn, even their aggressiveness is tempered with patience, planning and organization – they move slowly and very methodically towards their goals. Yet we see more social aggressiveness on your part this year and in coming years. Now, you are unlikely to employ cave-man tactics, but you will be reaching out more to others, going after what you want, working on your social skills, developing the social graces, etc. You are not going to sit idly by waiting for the phone to ring. You will take the bull by the horns.

Capricorns, in general, are not love-at-first-sight types of people. They are deeply romantic, but beneath a cool exterior. They don't display their affections outwardly. Usually (though your individual horoscope cast for your precise time and place of birth could modify this), they are not the 'touchy-feely' types. This will be even more true in coming years. But we get a sense of someone 'building' a social life, the way a person builds a house – brick by brick, piece by piece. The end result will be a 'well-crafted' product. A glittering and desirable social life – friends in the right places, friends who can be relied upon, friends who can help you achieve your goals, friends you really enjoy being around.

If anyone is capable of choosing the right mate in the coming years, it is a Capricorn. Of course, love will be a major factor. But a Capricorn will take into account many, many other issues. The Capricorn will test love in various ways. And, nobody needs to tell a Capricorn about the merits of 'caution'.

Those looking to marry for a second time also have amazing aspects this year – especially after August 27. This person will be a mentor-type – very educated, very spiritual – you will feel a strong spiritual connection to this person. You will know him or her when you meet them.

Those already in a second marriage have a more romantic relationship within the marriage. The marriage looks happy.

Those looking to marry for a third time also have wonderful aspects until August 27. This person, too, is spiritual – more like a friend than a lover.

A single sibling has beautiful aspects for marriage or a serious relationship after August 27. Children of marriageable age also have wonderful love aspects – up to August 27. Grandchildren of marriageable age shouldn't marry for a while, though they will have opportunities. Their social life is much too unstable and they seem very unsettled in their social desires.

Jupiter in your 8th House shows enhanced libido and much increased sexual activity in the year ahead.

Finance and Career

Though you are always ambitious, your 10th House of Career is not a House of Power. Thus you have more freedom to shape this area as you will. But you are less ambitious this year than you usually are. I expect a status-quo situation in the year ahead.

Finances are, however, unusually important – and they've been important for some years now. Both your 2nd House (personal earnings) and 8th House (other people's money) are strong this year.

For some years now communication, sales, marketing and good PR have been major factors in earnings. This was true whether you were in your own business or worked for someone else. Good communication was not enough, you needed to communicate your message in very original and unique ways – in ways that drew attention to yourself, your product or your service. Many of you got mileage out of shock value types of PR or by using the Internet or other electronic media in very creative ways. The important thing was to be original.

This trend continues in 2003 and, if anything, is even stronger. Your Money Planet, Uranus, will start moving into your 3rd House of Communication. This year, he will be there for six months, but next year he will move in for seven years.

The good news is that there is much success in these marketing, sales and PR ventures. Looks like you've finally got the feel for it. (Your Communication Planet, Neptune, and your Money Planet, Uranus, are in mutual reception – showing a beautiful co-operation between these two areas of life.)

These aspects are unusually good for those of you who are writers, teachers or lecturers – you are in a period of long-term prosperity.

Professional investors should look for opportunities in telecommunications, oil, natural gas, energy, high-tech industries and transport. Don't rush out and just buy these stocks blindly, but follow the prices and do your homework. Many opportunities will come to you and you will have a good natural instinct for them.

Benevolent Jupiter is in your 8th House until August 27. This shows greater access to outside capital. Your line of credit increases. You easily attract investors to your ideas. Your ability to help others prosper increases. Debts are easily paid – but also more easily incurred. Many of you can be out of debt in one fell swoop in the year ahead. Tax, property and insurance issues go favourably. Some of you inherit large sums this year – but no one has to die.

Self-improvement

For the past two years, you've been working on health and fitness. Many of you wisely adopted a disciplined, daily (and relentless) health regime. You were more careful of dietary issues. You studied health more. You were involved in preventative types of therapies. You worked to build a healthy image. These trends continue for the first half of 2003. Now that this has been achieved, you will have more confidence to pursue your social aspirations.

It's as if you didn't feel confident about social issues until you got your body and image in shape. (By the way, you needn't have worried, as your true friends and true mate would have come anyway – but still, being healthy and fit is a good thing.)

The latter half of the year will be devoted to improving your social life. Not just your love life, but friendships and the social agenda as a whole. We mentioned earlier that you will take a methodical, scientific approach to this. Basically, it is good. But still, the tendency to let 'practical' issues take priority can be an obstruction to romance and friendship. By all means keep your Capricorn cool and your head on your shoulders. But allow the mood of romance to happen. Romance is 95% magic and 5% logic. You've got to know when to leave the logic alone and let the magic happen. Nothing is more sure to kill a romantic feeling than fear, worry and science – or the attempt to test love too much. Romance is more than just 'marketing yourself' the way you market a product in business. Often the very attempts to 'market' interfere with the natural flow that should happen. There is a time to think, plan and organize and there is a time to let go and let the love forces flow. Discerning the difference here will do much to improve your love life.

Spirituality has been important for some years now. This year it becomes even more important as Jupiter moves into your 9th House of Religion. Jupiter brings good luck, as mentioned, but more importantly he reveals the principle that brings good luck, which is a different thing. When you understand the principle you can create good luck when you will. Enjoy the toys and the happy experiences that Jupiter brings, but don't let them divert you from the main gift – the revelation.

Religious and philosophical studies will be very enjoyable in the year ahead and you should pay them more attention.

Month-by-month Forecasts

January

Best Days Overall: 2nd, 3rd, 11th, 12th, 13th, 21st, 22nd, 29th, 30th

Most Stressful Days Overall: 9th, 10th, 16th, 17th, 23rd, 24th

Best Days for Love: 2nd, 3rd, 9th, 10th, 11th, 12th, 13th, 16th, 17th, 19th, 20th, 23rd, 24th, 27th, 28th

Best Days for Money: 1st, 4th, 5th, 9th, 10th, 15th, 19th, 20th, 24th, 27th, 28th

The year begins with most of the planets in the East and your own Sign of Capricorn very strong. Thus you are in a cycle of independence. You can have your way in life. You can change conditions that are unpleasant and need not adapt to them. Though you should give due respect to others, ultimately you must follow your own path of happiness. The only problem now is that you might not be sure what this path is – it is well worth thinking about and clarifying these issues.

The bottom half of the Horoscope is slightly stronger than the top half. Thus 'outer' ambitions are less important than home, family and emotional issues. Of course, since the percentage is only slight, you will still be dealing with outer goals, but you tilt slightly towards home and family and the need to feel good.

This is very much a month of sensual pleasure and fulfilment. It's about leading the good life – eating good food, drinking fine wine, pampering yourself and fulfilling sensual fantasies. Happily, being a Capricorn you are not likely to overdo things – and weight-loss programmes should go well.

Finances have been an important area of life for many years. They are unusually important this month as well. Prosperity is unusually strong. Earnings are high. Money is earned easily. And, after the 20th, you will have opportunities (and probably the inclination) to get financially healthier by cutting waste, paying off debt and focusing on core strengths and goals. A good period to deal with tax issues as well.

Love seems status quo this month. You look great. Your personal magnetism and charisma are strong. You are attractive – but the problem seems one of lack of interest rather than lack of opportunity. Social affairs should be stronger (you have more enthusiasm for them) from the 2nd to the 18th – the Moon's waxing period – than afterwards. Libido is unusually strong until the 20th.

Health is good all month. It can be enhanced by paying extra attention to your spine, knees and teeth. The retrograde of your Health Planet, Mercury, from the 2nd to the 22nd suggests caution about major changes in diet, health regime or medication. Study these things more carefully during the retrograde period and execute them (if they pass your research standards) afterwards.

Health and good looks go together this month. When you are healthy, you look good and vice versa. Much of your health interests (and you are more interested this month) could stem from image issues rather than actual health issues.

February

Best Days Overall: 8th, 9th, 17th, 18th, 25th, 26th

Most Stressful Days Overall: 5th, 6th, 13th, 14th, 19th, 20th

Best Days for Love: 1st, 2nd, 8th, 9th, 10th, 11th, 13th, 14th, 17th, 18th, 21st, 25th, 26th

Best Days for Money: 1st, 2nd, 5th, 6th, 11th, 15th, 16th, 20th, 23rd, 24th, 28th

Again, like last month, most of the planets are in the East and your 1st House of Self is powerful. Continue to take the bull by the horns and create conditions as you desire them to be. Personal effort counts for much now. Your personal happiness – though it might seem selfish – is actually in the best interests of the entire Cosmos. It makes the world a happier place.

Though you give off an air of ambition this month (and other people see you that way), with most of the planets below the horizon (and the percentage keeps getting higher). you are really interested in feeling good and personal fulfilment. Home and family issues are more accentuated now. You are in the process of creating a solid psychological foundation for future success.

Venus is in your own Sign after the 4th, thus your personal appearance, personal glamour, attractiveness, etc. are vastly increased. A great month for buying personal accessories – clothing, jewellery, etc. – as your sense of style is very sharp. Like last month, though, love is status quo in spite of your personal attractiveness and charm. Love affairs are very likely after the 4th – and these kinds of relationships are pursuing you – but serious romance? There seems to be (like last month) a lack of interest. Your social life will be active all month, but mostly from the 1st to the 16th – when the Moon waxes. Serious romantic opportunity is more likely during this period than afterwards.

Health is fabulous now and health regimes go well. You can enhance health even further by paying more attention to your spine, knees and teeth (like last month) and to your ankles and feet (after the 13th).

Your Ruling Plant, Saturn, starts moving forwards on the 22nd. This will improve self-confidence and clarify your personal desires and urges.

Prosperity is still very strong and can come in a variety of ways and through a variety of situations. With so many planets in your Money House this month (40% to 50% of the planets move through there), you have a lot of irons in the fire. It looks like you alternate between ways of making money.

You are dressing expensively these days – in ways that will improve your status and prestige. Dressing for success. Only a Capricorn will feel as comfortable in a three-piece suit as in jeans or a T-shirt.

March

Best Days Overall: 7th, 8th, 17th, 25th, 26th

Most Stressful Days Overall: 5th, 6th, 12th, 13th, 19th

Best Days for Love: 2nd, 3rd, 10th, 11th, 12th, 13th, 19th, 20th, 21st, 22nd, 23rd, 29th, 30th

Best Days for Money: 1st, 5th, 6th, 11th, 12th, 14th, 15th, 20th, 23rd, 27th, 28th, 29th

Though some of the planets are shifting from the East to the West later in the month, your personal independence continues to be strong. Mars' move into your own Sign on the 4th is the major reason. It gives you energy, dynamism and a hard-charging attitude. You get things done in a hurry, with little of the muss, fuss or bother that most people go through. When an idea or plan is clear in your mind, execution happens very easily. The problem now could come from haste, bad temper and impatience. Temper tantrums need to be avoided. Use Mars' energy to get constructive projects done and to increase your athletic excellence.

The planetary power below the horizon increases even further this month. By the 4th, 70% to 80% of them will be there. Thus, continue to cultivate the right inner state. Give home and domestic responsibilities the attention they deserve. Stabilize things at home so that your future success will happen more easily.

Happily, with Mars (your Family Planet) now in your own Sign and with your 4th House becoming powerful after the 21st, this family focus will be easy to achieve. All your decisions and actions will be filtered though the lens of 'how will this affect my family and home?' After the 21st, a good spring-cleaning at home seems called for. Get rid of unnecessary furnishings or clutter. Make room for the new good that wants to come in.

Important financial changes are happening now as well. Your Money Planet, Uranus, makes a major move into Pisces, your 3rd House. Thus communication, sales, marketing, PR and intellectual activities are the road to riches now. Also, you will see that though you have a good product or service, this must somehow be delivered – transported – to the customer promptly and in good order. So, this aspect of finance – delivering the goods – becomes unusually important and you will make improvements here. The need for intuition in finance has been important for many years – and this need continues. One momentary flash of real intuition is worth years and years of hard labour. Yet, finances are still strong. Speculations (well-hedged ones) are favourable. Personal creativity aids your bottom line. Like last month, there are many planets in your Money House – this shows you've got a lot of irons in the fire. Multiple ways and means by which prosperity can come. You go from one to the other.

Love, like last month, is still status quo. It will probably be strongest and most happy from the 3rd to the 18th, as the Moon waxes.

Health continues to be good, but rest and relax more after the 21st. Enhance health by paying extra attention to your feet and ankles (have them massaged regularly and try to wear shoes that fit and are comfortable) and to your head.

April

Best Days Overall: 3rd, 4th, 5th, 13th, 14th, 21st, 22nd

Most Stressful Days Overall: 1st, 2nd, 8th, 9th, 10th, 15th, 16th, 28th, 29th

Best Days for Love: 1st, 2nd, 8th, 9th, 10th, 17th, 18th, 21st, 28th, 29th

Best Days for Money: 1st, 2nd, 8th, 11th, 12th, 16th, 17th, 19th, 20th, 23rd, 24th, 25th, 26th, 28th, 29th

Important planetary shifts are happening this month, Capricorn. First, the planetary power shifts to the West after the 21st. And, on that day, Mars (the planet of self-will and independence) will leave your Sign. So right now you are in a borderline situation. Personal independence and self-will are strong until the 21st, but afterwards the social graces become important. Until the 21st, personal effort brings success; afterwards it comes through consensus, compromise and winning others over to your position. You still have an opportunity to create conditions as you like them; very shortly you will have to live with your own created conditions – so build wisely.

Not only is the planetary power below the horizon, but your 4th House of Home and Family is unusually powerful. This is a month for letting go of outer concerns and for dealing with family obligations and responsibilities. Like last month, it is still a good period for reducing clutter in the home. It is also good for renovation, remodelling and overall home beautification. Those involved in psychological therapy should make important breakthroughs this month. The groundwork for future career plans should be strategized and planned now.

Health is good and will improve further after the 20th. In the meantime, rest and relax more. Your Health Planet, Mercury, goes retrograde at the end of the month (on the 26th), so important changes to your health regime or diet (changing doctors, etc.) should be done before then. Health can be enhanced by focusing on good psychological health, maintaining harmony with family members and children and healthy creative expression. Give extra attention to your head, neck and throat this month. Mineral baths, mud baths and the like seem very effective after the 5th.

After the 20th, you are in a party period where leisure activities are highlighted. Experiencing the joy of life is not only pleasurable in its own right, but also a great health tonic.

Finances are mixed this month. Prosperity is still there, but you have to work harder for it – especially after the 20th. Mars' move into your Money House shows a more risk-taking attitude to finance. Just making money with regularity, like clockwork, is a humdrum routine and is getting a little boring. You want to inject some adventure and risk into it. With most Signs I'd have to caution them to go easy on the risk-taking, but you, Capricorn, will do this naturally. It is a period for overcoming financial fear and inertia, for making things happen rather than just letting them happen. Be careful about speculations after the 20th – though you will be sorely tempted.

Serious love continues to be status quo. Love affairs seem plentiful after the 20th. Your social magnetism will be strongest from the 1st to the 16th – as the Moon waxes. You can schedule important social functions accordingly.

May

Best Days Overall: 1st, 2nd, 10th, 11th, 18th, 19th, 28th, 29th

Most Stressful Days Overall: 6th, 7th, 12th, 13th, 25th, 26th, 27th

Best Days for Love: 1st, 2nd, 6th, 7th, 8th, 9th, 10th, 11th, 18th, 19th, 20th, 21st, 28th, 29th, 30th, 31st

Best Days for Money: 5th, 6th, 8th, 9th, 13th, 14th, 16th, 17th, 21st, 22nd, 23rd, 25th, 26th, 27th, 31st

A very happy month ahead, Capricorn. Enjoy. It is a month for personal pleasure and for exploring the joys of life.

The planetary power is firmly in the West. Independence, self-will and undue self-assertion don't bring success. Compromise, consensus, charm, grace and putting other people first will.

Like last month, most of the planetary power is still below the horizon, so continue to cultivate the right inner state, plan your career and focus on family and domestic issues. A focus on children, especially, is called for this period.

Two eclipses occur this period, but they seem benign to you. Though they shake up the world and your environment, they will probably clear away obstructions to your good.

The Lunar eclipse of the 16th occurs in your 11th House, testing friendships and your relations with professional or other organizations. Since the Moon is also your Love Planet, a love relationship or marriage will be tested. Long-seething issues will finally come to the surface so that they can be dealt with and cleared up. No more hiding things under the rug. For singles this could mean a change in marital status – or a desire to change the marital status. Good relationships and good marriages will survive and thrive.

The Solar eclipse of the 31st occurs in the your 6th House of Health and Work. Thus job changes or important changes in working conditions or the work place are happening. Health regimes, diets and doctors could change as well. Since the Sun is the Lord of your 8th House, every Solar eclipse brings changes in your sexual attitudes and the income of your spouse. Your spouse will make important long-term changes in finance now, as flaws in his or her present situation are highlighted and no longer tenable.

Health is good this month and getting better. Enhance health even further by paying extra attention to your neck and throat and by enjoying life. A night out on the town is as much a tonic as any standard medication.

Your social life meets certain tests brought on by the eclipses, but still it seems mostly orientated towards 'fun and games' type relationships rather than serious romance. Your social magnetism is strongest from the 1st to the 16 – as the Moon waxes.

Financial trends are pretty much the same as last month. You have to work harder for earnings, but overall prosperity is still there. Earnings will come more easily after the 21st than before.

June

Best Days Overall: 7th, 8th, 15th, 16th, 24th, 25th

Most Stressful Days Overall: 2nd, 3rd, 9th, 10th, 22nd, 23rd, 30th

Best Days for Love: 1st, 2nd, 3rd, 7th, 8th, 9th, 10th, 17th, 18th, 27th, 28th, 29th, 30th

Best Days for Money: 1st, 2nd, 4th, 5th, 10th, 11th, 13th, 14th, 17th, 18th, 19th, 22nd, 23rd, 29th

The planets are now in their maximum Western position. Not only are most of them in the West, but your 7th House of Love – long-empty and dormant – becomes an important House of Power. Thus, being popular, being liked, being able to cultivate the good graces of others are much more important to you than personal effort or personal excellence. Happily, with your Ruling Planet (Saturn) moving into your 7th House on the 4th, you seem inclined to pursue this path. You are now in one of the most important and active social periods of your year. Enjoy.

Another important shift is occurring now. The planetary power is moving from the lower half of the Horoscope to the upper half. The shift is not yet complete, but happens little by little as the month progresses. Thus, this is an important 'turning-point' month for you. Not only do social affairs take on a new importance, but career and outer goals are also becoming ever more important. Presumably, by now you have found your point of emotional harmony. Now you want to take that and translate it into career success and positive achievement.

Health is good, but rest and relax more after the 21st. Enhance health through more attention to your neck, throat, arms, shoulders, lungs, stomach and breasts. The right diet seems more of a health factor this month as well.

Now that your 7th House is prominent for years to come, many a Capricorn will tie the knot. Social opportunities come as you pursue personal transformation, the study of past lives, depth-psychology and health goals. The work place is also the likely scene of romance. For singles, love complications could come from too many opportunities rather than too few. But you are the aggressor in love. You are not waiting for the phone to ring, but taking the bull by the horns. If you like someone, that person will certainly know it. By all means accept social invitations (and they seem plentiful) and extend them. A good period for being host or hostess of parties and entertainments.

Finances are still excellent. Some of your risk-taking attitudes are reduced as the Mars leaves your Money House on the 17th. Money could come from a property investment or speculation. A family member turns unexpectedly generous. You seem to be spending more on the home as well.

July

Best Days Overall: 4th, 5th, 12th, 13th, 21st, 22nd, 23rd, 31st

Most Stressful Days Overall: 6th, 7th, 19th, 20th, 26th, 27th, 28th

Best Days for Love: 8th, 9th, 17th, 18th, 26th, 27th, 28th, 29th, 30th

Best Days for Money: 2nd, 3rd, 7th, 8th, 10th, 11th, 14th, 15th, 16th, 17th, 19th, 20th, 26th, 29th, 30th

The social whirl heats up even more this month, as romantic Venus moves into your 7th House of Love on the 4th. Serious romance is in the air. There are more parties and social gatherings. You are both attending and hosting more of these. You put other people first these days and are enjoying unprecedented popularity. Thus, your good comes to you easily and effortlessly, as a matter of course. Progress might be a little slower this month, as 30% to 40% of the planets are retrograde – but it does happen. A lot of it is 'behind the scenes', so you don't recognize it.

By the 4th, the dominance of the upper half of your Horoscope becomes even stronger than last month. With your Family Planet retrograde and your 4th House more or less empty (only the Moon will visit there on the 19th and

20th), you can safely put family and domestic issues on hold and focus on your career and outer objectives.

Two important interests dominate the month. The first is your social life, which is becoming very happy and exciting. This is a time to achieve social and romantic goals, to reach out to people and make new friends. The other important interest is the 8th House, which becomes very powerful after the 23rd. This will increase libido and sexual activity. It will give you both the interest and ability to pay off or refinance debt, to attract investors to your plans and projects and to deal with tax and estate issues. It is also a period for exploring the deeper things in life – death and rebirth, past lives, the occult, depth-psychology and personal transformation. It is a period where you have more power to break addictions, whether they be to substances or to thinking or feeling patterns. It is, in short, a period of getting rid of the excess in your life.

The two planets most involved in your financial life (Uranus, your Financial Planet, and Neptune, occupying your Money House) are both retrograde. Thus there could be delays, glitches and minor annoyances in finance. Overall prosperity is still very strong – especially until the 23rd. But many new deals or new directions in finances seem pending – they need more thought and study. Not much you can do at the moment. You are better off channelling spare cash to pay off debt or to eliminate waste – to become financially healthier. Also, it might be a good time to let go of your personal financial interest and see what you can do to help others prosper – especially your spouse or partner. This is a valid road to earnings this month. And, though superficially it might seem that you don't 'get anything out of it', the truth is otherwise. You create good karma for yourself which will eventually bear fruit.

Health is good, but rest and relax more until the 23rd. Enhance health by taking better care of your stomach, breasts, heart and intestines. Like last month, the right diet is particularly important for good health.

August

Best Days Overall: 1st, 9th, 10th, 18th, 19th, 27th, 28th

Most Stressful Days Overall: 2nd, 3rd, 15th, 16th, 17th, 23rd, 24th, 30th

Best Days for Love: 6th, 7th, 8th, 16th, 17th, 23rd, 24th, 27th, 28th

Best Days for Money: 4th, 7th, 8th, 11th, 12th, 13th, 16th, 17th, 23rd, 26th, 27th

Like last month, the upper half of the Horoscope dominates in terms of power and importance. Your 4th House of Home and Family is still empty (except for the Moon's visit on the 15th, 16th and 17th) and your Family Planet, Mars, is still retrograde. So continue to de-emphasize home and domestic issues and focus on your career, life work and outer goals. Not much can be done at home these days and time is needed to clarify things. But you can improve things by watching how you communicate with family members. Take extra time and effort to ensure that they understand (with all the nuances) what you say and what you mean. Take nothing for granted. Better to be accused of being pedantic and repetitive than to mis-communicate. For you will pay a price for this later on. Also make sure that you hear and understand what they are saying to you. (Your Family Planet is retrograde in your 3rd House of Communication.)

Most of the planets are still in the West. Your 7th House, though not as strong as last month, is still stronger than your 1st House of Self. Your Ruling Planet, Saturn, is at the maximum Western position in the Horoscope. Thus this is not a time for independence or going it alone. This is a time for teamwork and for winning others over to your position. And if persuasion fails, you must adapt and compromise. Personal effort is less important now, other people's good will is more so.

Like last month, the planets involved in finance are retrograde. So proceed slowly and cautiously in the financial realm. There is no real rush. This is a time for improving and perfecting financial projects – for fine-tuning them – and not for executing them. It is a good time to review and re-evaluate your financial strategies and tactics – also your assumptions. Important deals are pending – growing and developing behind the scenes. Like a seed planted in the ground, all you can do is water it and let nature take its course.

Your love life has slowed down a bit, but is still prominent and important. You get personal fulfilment from social activities these days. Like any good Capricorn, you are focusing on quality and not quantity. Though things have slowed down, your popularity has not abated. Your social magnetism will be strongest from the 1st to the 12th and from the 27th to the 31st – as the Moon waxes.

Health is excellent this month – especially after the 23rd. Enhance health through the right diet and by paying more attention to your intestines.

September

Best Days Overall: 5th, 6th, 14th, 15th, 24th, 25th

Most Stressful Days Overall: 12th, 13th, 19th, 20th, 26th, 27th

Best Days for Love: 5th, 6th, 14th, 15th, 16th, 17th, 19th, 20th, 26th, 27th

Best Days for Money: 5th, 6th, 7th, 8th, 9th, 14th, 15th, 18th, 26th, 27th

An important planetary shift occurs this month. The dominance of power will shift from the West to the East after the 23rd. Thus you are starting to become more independent and personally wilful. You are less dependent on others. You can go your own way. With your Ruling Planet in the 7th House of Love and Social Activities you are still cultivating the good graces of others, but where popularity or loss of friendship are not issues, you are going your own way. The need to adapt to difficult situations is passing. You can create new ones more harmonious to you.

The planetary power is still mostly above the horizon, and your 10th House of Career is becoming increasingly important. Your 4th House is still mostly empty and your 4th House Ruler, Mars, is still retrograde most of the month. Thus you have opportunities for important career progress this month. Blockages to goals are coming down. You have the favour of elders, bosses and authority figures. If you need favours from the government, this is a good time to seek them. If you have issues pending in the courts, you have great aspects for a favourable solution – best-case scenarios should happen.

Communication with family members (see last month) still needs watching. This will pass by the 27th, as Mars starts moving forwards again.

Your 9th House of Religion, Higher Education, Philosophy, Metaphysics and Foreign Travel is unusually powerful this month. Powerful and filled with beneficial planets. There is a conspiracy of love and benevolence afoot – to expand your horizons, to 'enlarge the borders of your tents', to reveal important principles to you, to help you look at life in a more constructive way. Students should hear good news on educational issues. Happy educational and travel opportunities come – perhaps as a delayed reaction. The scriptures of your religion become an open book and yield their secret message. Health is enhanced. There is an overall feeling of optimism. All is right with you and the world.

Be patient with finances this month (see last month). Many of the trends of last month are still in effect now. It might seem to you that you are moving backwards financially, but this is not the case. You are re-tracing certain steps, correcting errors and laying the groundwork for the future. Enjoy the moment. Regardless of fears or worries, right now you have enough for what you really need to do. And when another need comes, you will have enough for that.

Love is status quo. Career focus could create short-term stresses either in your social plans or in a relationship. But these things will pass. Your social magnetism will be strongest from the 1st to the 10th and from the 26th to the 30th. Those working towards a second marriage could hear wedding bells now.

October

Best Days Overall: 2nd, 3rd, 11th, 12th, 13th, 21st, 22nd, 29th, 30th

Most Stressful Days Overall: 9th, 10th, 16th, 17th, 18th, 23rd, 24th

Best Days for Love: 4th, 5th, 14th, 15th, 16th, 17th, 18th, 25th, 26th

Best Days for Money: 2nd, 3rd, 4th, 5th, 6th, 11th, 12th, 13th, 15th, 21st, 22nd, 24th, 29th, 30th

By the 7th, the planetary shift to the Eastern sector is overwhelming. 70% to 80% of the planets are now there. Thus, like last month, work to build your life as you desire it to be. You can have things (more or less) your way. You can go it alone if you need to. Personal effort pays off.

Like last month, the planetary power is still above the horizon and your 10th House of Career is very strong – not only strong, but filled with beneficial planets. Thus, push forwards towards your career goals. Much career progress is made now. Pay rises, promotions and more public and professional esteem happen now. You still have the favour of elders, bosses and parents. The family situation seems much calmer and probably doesn't need much attention. Things are straightening out of their own accord.

Health will improve after the 23rd, but in the meantime, rest and relax more. Pace yourself and focus on priorities. Enhance health by paying more attention to your intestines, kidneys, hips and sexual organs.

Though you are more independent these days, the retrograde of your Ruling Planet, Saturn, shows that you might not be sure of what you want to build – or where personal fulfilment lies. Not a bad idea to give this area more thought and attention.

Personal popularity is still strong, though, like last month, career focus detracts somewhat from it. Career focus could also complicate a current relationship. But this should resolve after the 23rd. Those working towards a second marriage still have beautiful opportunities now. Love opportunities will come in a variety of ways and through a variety of situations. In other words, it can happen anywhere – much depends on where the Moon is on a given day. But your social magnetism will be strongest from the 1st to the 10th and from the 25th onwards.

Financial directions for the future are clarifying somewhat this month, as Neptune (the occupant of your Money House) starts moving forwards on the 23rd. Still, patience is necessary, as your Money Planet is still retrograde. Overall – day-to-day – prosperity is strong all month. Your career success and increased professional prestige are big factors now. Job-seekers have luck this month and the 'good word' of elders or bosses plays a big role.

November

Best Days Overall: 8th, 9th, 18th, 19th, 26th, 27th

Most Stressful Days Overall: 5th, 6th, 13th, 14th, 20th, 21st

Best Days for Love: 3rd, 4th, 5th, 6th, 13th, 14th, 15th, 16th, 22nd, 23rd, 25th, 26th, 27th, 30th

Best Days for Money: 1st, 2nd, 8th, 9th, 11th, 12th, 18th, 19th, 21st, 26th, 27th, 28th, 29th

Like last month, 70% to 80% of the planets are in the East. Towards the end of the month, your 1st House of Self becomes strong. Thus, continue to take the bull by the horns and create conditions as you desire them to be. Give some extra thought as to what you want to build. Take more time to clarify these things and then launch into action. Mistakes will be quickly rectified. Be polite and graceful to others, but go your own way and follow your own star.

Career is still important as most of the planets are still above the horizon. But your 10th House is not as strong as it was last month. Presumably many of your outer objectives have been attained and now you want to focus on some of the fruits of your labours – good friendships, good connections, involvement with professional organizations.

Two eclipses shake up the environment this month, but both seem benign to you. The Lunar eclipse of the 9th occurs in your 5th House, testing a love affair, a marriage or serious relationship, bringing long-term changes to your creative life and in your relations with children. Flaws in these areas will surface so that you can correct them. In fact, the eclipse usually leaves you with little choice. You MUST correct these things. Your lover or children can be unusually temperamental during this period too.

The Solar eclipse of the 23rd occurs in your 12th House of Spirituality. Thus you can expect that your dream life will be hyper-active and restless during this period (perhaps even all month). None of the images you see should be taken too seriously (some can appear to be very negative). Much of this is flotsam and jetsam stirred up by the eclipse. For many this is bringing a new spirituality and the beginning of a spiritual discipline. For others it means spiritual revelation that changes their techniques, paths or teachers. For others it shows upheavals in charities, ministries or causes they believe in. Since the Sun rules your 8th House, every Solar eclipse brings changes in your partner's earnings and financial strategy. In some cases events happen to help you pay off debt. In other cases new debts are incurred. Sexuality and libido go through some upheaval. Many of you will have to deal with your fears of death and understand them in a deeper way.

Finances are finally starting to clarify. Uranus, your Money Planet, starts moving forwards on the 8th. Many stalled deals or projects are now starting to move forwards. You work harder for earnings until the 22nd, but afterwards prosperity just flows.

Love is pursuing you this month and by the 27th will find you. Venus moving into your own Sign then will give you a sense of style and great personal glamour. Whatever your age, you will start looking younger and more glamorous. The spirit of the child is upon you.

December

Best Days Overall: 5th, 6th, 15th, 16th, 23rd, 24th

Most Stressful Days Overall: 2nd, 3rd, 4th, 10th, 11th, 17th, 18th, 30th, 31st

Best Days for Love: 2nd, 3rd, 4th, 5th, 6th, 10th, 11th, 12th, 13th, 14th, 15th, 16th, 23rd, 24th, 25th, 26th

Best Days for Money: 5th, 6th, 9th, 15th, 16th, 18th, 23rd, 24th, 25th, 26th

The planets are now in their maximum Eastern position. Your personal independence and power soar. Your way is the best way during this period. Push forwards towards your dreams. Uncomfortable situations can be changed or re-created now. Personal effort pays off.

The planets shift to the lower half of the Horoscope after the 22nd. Thus your career is becoming less important and emotional fulfilment is becoming more important. Around this time (on the 16th), Mars, your Family Planet, moves into his own Sign and House – your 4th House of Home and Family. Thus you are in a period where the simple pleasures of home and hearth call to you. This is an excellent period (after the 16th) to renovate or remodel the home. Once again we are back we were started at the beginning of the year. The wheel of life has made a revolution. Again it is time to cultivate the right emotional state and firm up the foundations of future career success.

Many planets in your 1st House shows enhanced personal magnetism and charisma. You look great. Your sense of style is still wonderful. A great period for getting your body and image in order. Weight-loss programmes go well. It is a month for sensual pleasure and fulfilment – and, being a Capricorn, you are unlikely to overdo it.

Finances should be exceptionally strong this month. Both of the planets involved with your finances are moving forwards and receive good aspects. Venus moves into your Money House on the 21st, bringing luck in speculations, happy money – money that is earned in happy ways, as you pursue leisure activities. Young women, high-tech types, spiritual people and astrologers all seem helpful and supportive in your financial life. A touch of glamour could aid your business these days.

Your love life should be happy this month, as you look great and are very attractive. Romantic opportunities should be plentiful. But you seem undecided about a certain someone you've been seeing. Only time will resolve these doubts.

Those working towards a second marriage have really fabulous opportunities now – especially after the 21st.

Health is good and can be enhanced through paying more attention to your spine, knees and teeth.

Aquarius

♒

THE WATER-BEARER

Birthdays from

20th January

to 18th February

Personality Profile

AQUARIUS AT A GLANCE

Element – Air

Ruling Planet – Uranus
Career Planet – Pluto
Love Planet – Venus
Money Planet – Neptune
Planet of Health and Work – Moon
Planet of Home and Family Life – Venus

Colours – electric blue, grey, ultramarine blue

Colours that promote love, romance and social harmony – gold, orange

Colour that promotes earning power – aqua

Gems – black pearl, obsidian, opal, sapphire

Metal – lead

Scents – azalea, gardenia

Quality – fixed (= stability)

Qualities most needed for balance – warmth, feeling and emotion

Strongest virtues – great intellectual power, the ability to communicate and to form and understand abstract concepts, love for the new and avant-garde

Deepest needs – to know and to bring in the new

Characteristics to avoid – coldness, rebelliousness for its own sake, fixed ideas

Signs of greatest overall compatibility – Gemini, Libra

Signs of greatest overall incompatibility – Taurus, Leo, Scorpio

Sign most helpful to career – Scorpio

Sign most helpful for emotional support – Taurus

Sign most helpful financially – Pisces

Sign best for marriage and/or partnerships – Leo

Sign most helpful for creative projects – Gemini

Best Sign to have fun with – Gemini

Signs most helpful in spiritual matters – Libra, Capricorn

Best day of the week – Saturday

Understanding an Aquarius

Among Aquarians, intellectual faculties are perhaps the most highly developed of any Sign in the Zodiac. Aquarians are clear, scientific thinkers. They have the ability to think abstractly and to formulate laws, theories and clear concepts from masses of observed facts. Geminis might be very good at gathering information, but Aquarians take this a step further, excelling at interpreting the information gathered.

Practical people – men and women of the world – mistakenly consider abstract thinking as impractical. It is true that the realm of abstract thought takes us out of the physical world, but the discoveries made in this realm generally end up having tremendous practical consequences. All real scientific inventions and breakthroughs come from this abstract realm.

Aquarians, more so than most, are ideally suited to explore these abstract dimensions. Those who have explored these regions know that there is little feeling or emotion there. In fact, emotions are a hindrance to functioning in these dimensions; thus Aquarians seem – at times – cold and emotionless to others. It is not that Aquarians haven't got feelings and deep emotions, it is just that too much feeling clouds their ability to think and invent. The concept of 'too much feeling' cannot be tolerated or even understood by some of the other Signs. Nevertheless, this Aquarian objectivity is ideal for science, communication and friendship.

Aquarians are very friendly people, but they do not make a big show about it. They do the right thing by their friends, even if sometimes they do it without passion or excitement.

Aquarians have a deep passion for clear thinking. Second in importance, but related, is their passion for breaking with the establishment and traditional authority. Aquarians delight in this, because for them rebellion is like a great game or challenge. Very often they will rebel strictly for the fun of rebelling, regardless of whether the authority they defy is right or wrong. Right or wrong has little to do with the rebellious actions of an Aquarian, because, to a true Aquarian, authority and power must be challenged as a matter of principle.

Where Capricorn or Taurus will err on the side of tradition and the status quo, an Aquarian will err on the side of the new. Without this virtue it is doubtful whether any progress would be made in the world. The conservative-minded would obstruct progress. Originality and invention imply an ability to break barriers; every new discovery represents the toppling of an impediment to thought. Aquarians are very interested in breaking barriers and making walls tumble – scientifically, socially and politically. Other Zodiac Signs, such as Capricorn, also have scientific talents. But Aquarians are particularly excellent in the social sciences and humanities.

Finance

In financial matters Aquarians tend to be idealistic and humanitarian – to the point of self-sacrifice. They are usually generous contributors to social and political causes. When they contribute it differs from when a Capricorn or Taurus contributes. A Capricorn or Taurus may expect some favour or return for a gift; an Aquarian contributes selflessly.

Aquarians tend to be as cool and rational about money as they are about most things in life. Money is something they need and they set about acquiring it scientifically. No need for fuss; they get on with it in the most rational and scientific ways available.

Money to the Aquarian is especially nice for what it can do, not for the status it may bring (as is the case for other Signs). Aquarians are neither big spenders nor penny-pinchers and use their finances in practical ways; for example to facilitate progress for themselves, their families or even strangers.

However, if Aquarians want to reach their fullest financial potential they will have to explore their intuitive nature. If they follow only their financial theories – or what they believe to be theoretically correct – they may suffer some losses and disappointments. Instead, Aquarians should call on their intuition, which knows without thinking. For Aquarians, intuition is the short-cut to financial success.

Career and Public Image

Aquarians like to be perceived not only as the breakers of barriers, but also as the transformers of society and the world. They long to be seen in this light and to play this role. They also look up to and respect other people in this position and even expect their superiors to act this way.

Aquarians prefer jobs that have a bit of idealism attached to them – careers with a philosophical basis. Aquarians need to be creative at work, to have access to new techniques and methods. They like to keep busy and enjoy getting down to business straight away, without wasting any time. They are often the quickest workers and usually have suggestions for improvements that will benefit their employers. Aquarians are also very helpful with their co-workers and welcome responsibility, preferring this to having to take orders from others.

If Aquarians want to reach their highest career goals, they have to develop more emotional sensitivity, depth of feeling and passion. They need to learn to narrow their focus on the essentials and concentrate more on the job in hand. Aquarians need 'a fire in the belly' – a consuming passion and desire – in order to rise to the very top. Once this passion exists, they will succeed easily in whatever they attempt.

Love and Relationships

Aquarians are good at friendships, but a bit weak when it comes to love. Of course they fall in love, but their lovers always get the impression that they are more best friends than paramours.

Like Capricorns, they are cool customers. They are not prone to displays of passion nor to outward demonstrations of their affections. In fact, they feel uncomfortable when their mate hugs and touches them too much. This does not mean that they do not love their partners. They do, only they show it in other ways. Curiously enough, in relationships they tend to attract the very things that they feel uncomfortable with. They seem to attract hot, passionate, romantic, demonstrative people. Perhaps they know instinctively that these people have qualities they lack and so seek them out. In any event, these relationships do seem to work, Aquarius' coolness calming the more passionate partner while the fires of passion warm the cold-blooded Aquarius.

The qualities Aquarians need to develop in their love life are warmth, generosity, passion and fun. Aquarians love relationships of the mind. Here they excel. If the intellectual factor is missing in a relationship an Aquarian will soon become bored or feel unfulfilled.

Home and Domestic Life

In family and domestic matters, Aquarians can have a tendency to be too non-conformist, changeable and unstable. They are as willing to break the barriers of family constraints as they are those of other areas of life.

Even so, Aquarians are very sociable people. They like to have a nice home where they can entertain family and friends. Their house is usually decorated modernly and full of state-of-the-art appliances and gadgets – an environment Aquarians find absolutely necessary.

If their home life is to be healthy and fulfilling Aquarians need to inject it with a quality of stability – yes, even some conservatism. They need at least one area of life to be enduring and steady; this area is usually their home and family life.

Venus, the Planet of Love, rules the Aquarian's 4th Solar House of Home and Family as well, which means that when it comes to the family and child-rearing, theories, cool thinking and intellect are not always enough. Aquarians need to bring love into the equation in order to have a great domestic life.

Horoscope for 2003

Major Trends

Since the year 2000, every year has got progressively easier and more harmonious. It was a step-by-step, gradual process. This trend continues in the year ahead.

Uranus, your Ruling Planet, makes a very important move from your own Sign to the Sign of Pisces. This year he will be in Pisces for only six months, but by next year he will settle in for the next seven years. This is showing major changes in your life, attitudes and interests. Most importantly, it is bringing some long-needed stability into your life. Many of you have been restless vagabonds for the past seven years. Nomads. Many of you have been tinkering and tinkering with your image and personality. Many of you have been living a life of 'absolute freedom' (or trying to). These urges are getting modified now. Your life is taking on more permanence.

Last year was an unusually good social year and this trend continues. Perhaps the meeting of a significant other or of some good-quality friends is contributing to your new-found stability.

Neptune, the most spiritual of all the planets, has been in your Sign for some years now and he will be there for all of 2003. The spiritual revolution taking place in your mind and affairs is continuing. Higher spiritual influences continue to pour in on you, radically changing your perspective on many things. Psychic abilities continue to increase. You don't need to go to the movies for entertainment, all you need to do is close your eyes or take a nap, to watch the most fantastic full-colour images and scenes.

Saturn, your personal Spiritual Planet, is making a major move from your 5th House (Children and Creativity) to your 6th House of Health. Thus the thrust of your spiritual life is shifting from creativity to healing.

Your most important areas of interest in the coming year are: the body, the image, the appearance, the self-concept; finance (especially from March 10 to September 15); children, creativity, leisure activities (until June 4); health and work (after June 4); love and romance (until August 27); sex, debt and the repayment of debt, personal transformation, taxes, helping others prosper (after August 27); friends, groups, group activities, organizations.

Your paths to greatest fulfilment in the coming year are: children, creativity and leisure activities (though you have to work harder at them – until April 14); home, family and domestic interests (after April 14); love and romance (until August 27); helping others prosper, paying off debt, personal transformation and sex (after August 27).

Health

Health is good this year and your 6th House of Health gets powerful after June 4. The power in your 6th is most likely showing your interest in preventative medicine, spiritual healing and in disciplined and sustained health regimes.

Saturn, the planet of discipline and order, is moving into your House of Health on June 4. Thus you will be much more inclined to go on that diet and to take on a serious regime. It won't feel like that much of an effort because the desire will be there.

Saturn rules the spine, knees, teeth and skeletal structure. Thus, his position in your House of Health is showing a need to pay extra attention to these organs. The knees should be regularly massaged and given more support. The spine and skeleton can be kept in shape through regular visits to the chiropractor or osteopath; the teeth through regular check-ups with the dentist.

Saturn also happens to be your Spiritual Planet. So, his position in the 6th House has other messages. It shows spiritual healing for the self and others, as mentioned, you get good results from metaphysical, meditational types of therapies, being rightly aligned with the Higher Power is of itself the greatest therapy and this year your intuition is being trained in health matters. Intuition, when it is 'on' and interpreted correctly, is the short-cut to good health.

The Moon is your Health Planet. Thus, you Aquarians already know that emotional health is as important as physical health, that one impacts on the other very dramatically. Thus, good health is enhanced by maintaining good emotional health, by cultivating positive moods and positive states of mind and by avoiding depression and emotional instability. The Moon also rules the stomach and breasts. So these parts of the body always need more attention.

The Moon, being a fast-moving planet – the fastest of them all – will move through all the Signs and Houses of your Horoscope in any given month. Thus health needs and health attitudes change almost daily. Therapies that worked last week might not work this week and vice versa. Hence the need to cultivate a good intuition about the body. This is happening in the year ahead.

In general you will feel better and more energetic when the Moon is waxing than when she is waning.

The gems, herbs, colours, aromas and scents of your Sign are all natural health tonics. The scents, gems, colours and herbs of the Moon are also very powerful for you. Silver is both a healing colour and a nice metal to wear. Pearl is a nice gem. White Lily is a nice plant (and can be taken as a tea, flower essence or herbal concoction). Cucumbers and green peppers are good foods for you.

The health of your spouse or partner seems OK, but he or she is also getting more interested in health regimes.

Health of children is vastly improved – especially after June 4. Health of grandchildren can be enhanced by experimental or unorthodox therapies. Health of parents or parent figures is status quo.

Home, Domestic and Family Issues

Your 4th House of Home and Family is not a House of Power and thus you have much freedom in this area. However, I expect there will be a lot less moving around, wandering and remodellings going on than there have been the past few years. As mentioned, there is a craving for some permanency and stability in your life.

Further, with the North Node of the Moon moving into your 4th House after April 14, family and family life are unusually fulfilling. This will be a surprise to most Aquarians, who tend to be free spirits and hate any kind of binding ties.

The simple virtues of home and hearth, the daily domestic routine and chores, the ability to be who you are and accepted for who you are, the comfort of having a 'home base' and the pleasures of children – all have lessons for you.

Venus is your Family Planet. She is a fast-moving planet and will move through all the Signs and Houses of your Horoscope in a given year. Thus family interests and relationships will fluctuate month to month. We will cover these in the month-by-month forecasts.

If you are redecorating or entertaining from home (or buying objects of beauty for the home), I like April 20 to June 10.

Though we don't see moves *per se,* career changes could prompt one.

A Lunar eclipse on November 9 could temporarily shake things up at home. If there are hidden flaws in your residence, these are sure to be revealed so that you can take corrective action. Temporary upheavals in the domestic pattern – in family relationships – are also likely, but these will clear the air.

Relations with parents or parent figures are status quo. Parents or parent figures are likely either to move, remodel or buy an additional home. Relations with children will improve as you will take a greater interest in them. Relations with an 'in-law' could be improved.

A sibling wants to move, but now is not the time. Children look like they're moving to bigger homes, changing roommates, etc.

Love and Social Life

Though marriage hasn't been advisable for single Aquarians for some years now, this year it is. For sure you were attractive and had many romantic opportunities, but you were too personally unsettled to stick with any one person for too long. (Your individual chart cast for your precise time and place of birth could have modified this.)

But now the restlessness and mood changes are abating. Stability, little by little, is coming into your life and a marriage could work.

With Jupiter in your 7th House, there is a serious relationship in the picture. Perhaps it is a friend who has become more than that. Perhaps it is someone you met at a club or professional organization. Singles are likely to marry. Marrieds should have more romance and joy within their relationship. Your circle of friends is also expanding. There is more social activity – more going out, more parties, etc. All very happy and fulfilling.

After August 27, Jupiter will move into your 8th House, enhancing your libido and increasing sexual activity. So this is a happy social year.

Those working towards a second marriage will see an improved social life in general but the status quo should prevail. Marrieds will stay married and singles with probably stay single.

Those into a third marriage have seen their marriages severely tested these past two years. Most of the stress is over. If you can last the first six months of 2003, you can survive almost anything. Those working towards a third marriage are likely to be successful. A special someone is there – you might have already met him or her.

Those working on a fourth marriage also have good aspects. There is a very wealthy (also very spiritual) person in your life. Perhaps he or she is involved in your financial life in some way – a broker, an accountant, financial planner, etc. Perhaps you meet (or met) this person as you pursue your financial goals. You had good aspects for marriage (or quasi-marriage), last year and you have them this year too.

Your social life will be active most of the year, but January 20 to February 19, March 2 to March 27 and July 23 to August 23 seem especially active.

Friendships are also going well this year. This is especially gratifying for you, as this is your forte and love. Hard to tell the difference between your platonic friends and your friends of the heart. Your group activities and involvement with clubs and organizations are also very happy.

The main threat to serious romance is your personal instability and the desire for 'absolute freedom'. Happily, this is abating.

The marriage of parents or parent figures is status quo. The love life of siblings likewise. The marriage of a child will get easier after June 4. Self-esteem issues were at the core of the problem. Grandchildren of marriageable age have a status quo year – singles will tend to be single and marrieds married.

Finance and Career

2003 is shaping up to be a strong financial as well as social year. Finances have been important for some years now and the trend is continuing – perhaps getting even stronger. Great interest in something will produce better results than just good aspects would. For the drive, the fire in the belly, is what gives a person energy to overcome all obstacles. To have wealth, one must desire it. This is what we see here.

Two important developments are taking place this year. Uranus, your Ruling Planet, is making a once-in-seven-years move into your 2nd House of Finance. This year, he will only be there for six months, but next year he will move in permanently. After August 27, beneficial Jupiter will move into your 8th House of Other People's Money. So finance is unquestionably one of the main interests in the year ahead.

The first trend (and this has been going on for a while) is your personal involvement in your financial life. You are not delegating these tasks to others, but taking personal responsibility for both earnings and financial management. Second, you see yourself – your body, image, abilities, personal appearance and well-being – as your best investment (and this is very wise). Many of you are in jobs or industries where the body and personal appearance and demeanour are the means for earning – athletes, models, marketing people, etc. As in past years, you are dressing for success – dressing expensively – donning the image of wealth, as it were. There is much metaphysical magic to this strategy, for as you don the image of wealth, you move into the subtle vibrations of wealth and all kinds of things start happening. Opportunities come that you wouldn't have had in normal circumstances. There is great success with this strategy. There is also great prosperity this year, as your Money Planet (Neptune) and your Ruling Planet (Uranus) are in mutual reception – they occupy each other's Houses and are thus co-operating with each other.

Professional investors should look at high-tech industries, computers, cutting-edge inventions, oil, natural gas, energy and water companies. Don't rush in blindly and just buy the stocks, but do your homework, check prices and follow these industries. Profit opportunities will certainly come. Aquarians who are not professional investors might find that they are working for these kinds of companies or attracting clients from these industries. Thus they contribute to your wealth in that way.

Neptune is the planet of intuition. Thus, as in past years, you are developing an intuitive sense about wealth, earnings and investing. One second of real intuition is worth 20 years of hard labour. You Aquarians understand this these days and are certainly applying it.

Another positive financial trend is Jupiter's entry into your 8th House on August 27. This shows that you will have good fortune in reducing your debts. In many cases you will refinance at better rates. In other cases, earnings will be so strong that you can pay them off without refinancing. Tax and property issues go favourably for you and those who have cases pending should delay them until after August when the aspects are in your favour.

Jupiter in the 8th House shows the prosperity of your spouse or partner and his or her generosity towards you. Those of you who have good ideas can easily attract investors to your projects. There is unusually good access to outside capital.

After August 27, professional investors should look at bonds and the bond market for profit opportunities.

Self-improvement

In the past two years, the main areas of self-improvement – where you needed to work consciously at it – were creativity and children. Those of you involved in the creative or performing arts learned that creativity is 5% inspiration and

95% perspiration. The inspiration comes in a flash of rapture, but working out the inspiration, bringing it down to the material world, is often hard work. There was a need to make your powerful inspirations practical in the everyday world or for others. Little details, organization and structure, which seem unimportant when we are in the 'inspiration' phase, become big deals when we develop our ideas. The perspiration part of creativity is often neglected by creators. This was the lesson you've learned in the past two years. This trend continues until June 4.

Disciplining and managing children was another area of self-improvement for many of you. You were faced with the classic problem of the ages: How to discipline the child (who definitely needs it) while fostering the child's development, self-esteem and creativity? Learning to set intelligent limits was a challenge and a delicate balancing act. How to be the 'authoritarian' and yet still be loving was another. How to be the 'authoritarian' and yet still foster independent thought in the child was another. These lessons were particularly difficult for you, as by nature Aquarians are freedom-loving – and personally abhor hierarchy or authority. By now many of you have seen that hierarchy is not only a principle in nature, but essential in maintaining order.

After June 4, the process of self-improvement moves on to the health field. This will initiate a serious and scientific study of health, fitness and diet. By nature, you are unorthodox, but now you will see that you can't blandly dismiss something merely because it is 'orthodox and traditional'. It is only by gaining personal knowledge that you can discern when it's right (and safe) to dispense with orthodoxy, and when it should be followed.

Month-by-month Forecasts

January

Best Days Overall: 4th, 5th, 14th, 15th, 23rd, 24th

Most Stressful Days Overall: 11th, 12th, 13th, 19th, 20th, 25th, 26th

Best Days for Love: 2nd, 3rd, 9th, 10th, 11th, 12th, 13th, 19th, 20th, 23rd, 24th, 27th, 28th

Best Days for Money: 1st, 4th, 5th, 6th, 7th, 8th, 9th, 10th, 14th, 15th, 19th, 20th, 23rd, 24th, 27th, 28th

Looks like a happy and healthy month ahead, Aquarius. Enjoy. Strong power in your native element of Air, many planets in your own Sign – especially after the 20th – and two planets (Mars and Venus) moving out of a stressful alignment all portend to the good. Intellectual and communication abilities – always strong – are even stronger. Health and vitality soar. You're very much at ease and at home in this kind of astrological climate.

Most of the planets are in the Eastern sector of the chart this month – 70% to 80% of them. Thus the month ahead is about asserting independence, about changing undesirable conditions and about pursuing personal fulfilment. The universe assents to your personal happiness and will support it. Your way is the best way. Personal effort counts now.

The planets are more or less evenly distributed between the upper and lower halves of the Horoscope – this will soon change, but for now this is how it is. Thus you need to balance home, family and emotional issues with career and outer objectives. Career is important – your 10th House is very strong until the 17th – but you need your emotional comfort zone as well. This need to pursue career with emotional comfort is further reinforced by the fact that Venus (your Family Planet) is in the House of Career until the 7th.

It also shows that the family as a whole is raised in status. And that family members support your career objectives and you support their careers.

Though career demands are strong this month – very competitive – you will do well. You have the favour of bosses and elders. This is a good time to ask for a well-deserved pay rise or promotion. It is also good for asking for other types of favours as well. If you need favours from the government – or have issues pending with the government – try to achieve these things before the 7th.

All this power in Air (including a Grand Trine in Air on the 23rd and 24th) is ensuring overall prosperity. Your financial intuition is sharp. Your financial ideas find favour. Sales, marketing, communication, writing, teaching – your natural fortes – are all important financially and go well. A financial windfall or opportunity comes on the 30th or 31st – possibly from your lover, partner or a friend.

Love is happy this month as well. Nothing much you need to do to find it, as it is looking for you. Your spouse, partner or lover is going out of his or her way to please you. After the 20th, you look exceptionally good – magnetic and attractive – and others sit up and take notice. Until the 20th, love opportunities happen at charities, volunteer activities, church or religious functions. You are in a powerful social period in an exceptionally good social year.

February

Best Days Overall: 1st, 2nd, 10th, 11th, 19th, 20th, 28th

Most Stressful Days Overall: 8th, 9th, 15th, 16th, 21st, 22nd

Best Days for Love: 1st, 2nd, 8th, 9th, 10th, 11th, 15th, 16th, 17th, 18th, 21st, 25th, 26th

Best Days for Money: 1st, 2nd, 3rd, 4th, 5th, 6th, 10th, 11th, 15th, 16th, 19th, 20th, 23rd, 24th, 28th

Like last month, the planets are mostly in the East. But your 1st House of Self is even stronger than last month. Thus personal independence is stronger than usual. You can and will have things your way – life on your terms. Don't try to adapt to difficult situations, but use your energy to create new and better ones. Be respectful and polite to others, but go your own way.

Like last month, there is a lot of power in your native element of Air – so your intellectual and communication faculties are firing on all cylinders. Students learn easily and should do well in their studies. Teachers, writers and marketing people are prospering. Health continues to be good.

After the 13th, the planetary power shifts to the lower half of the Horoscope. Career is less important now; family, domestic and emotional issues take priority. Your main job now is to find your emotional comfort zone and function from there. Career success will happen as a natural side-effect – later on.

With many planets in your own Sign, this is a month for personal pleasure, sprucing up your image and enjoying the good life. The Cosmos wants to pamper you. Expensive personal accessories come to you. Invitations to good restaurants, spas and the like come to you.

Love continues to pursue you. Like last month, you get your way in love and your spouse, partner or lover is going out of his or her way to please. Your lover seems firmly in your corner – firmly committed to you and to your interests. After the 19th, he or she will be involved in your financial life and supportive of your financial goals. Love is interesting, experimental but volatile on the 17th. Singles could meet someone special that day – out of the blue and close to home. Until the 19th, love is physical and must be expressed physically. After the 19th, practical issues become important. Love is expressed through material gifts and financial support. Singles find love opportunities with those involved in their finances or as they pursue their financial goals.

Love and money are unusually interconnected.

Prosperity looks strong all month. Avoid speculations after the 19th. Be careful of over-spending on frivolous, fun things. This doesn't mean that you shouldn't have fun – only that you should keep a sense of proportion. Children may not need as much as you think they do. They really need love, attention and someone to admire their splendour. Given that, they'll be happy with any other trifles they receive.

March

Best Days Overall: 1st, 10th, 11th, 19th, 27th, 28th

Most Stressful Days Overall: 7th, 8th, 14th, 15th, 21st

Best Days for Love: 2nd, 3rd, 10th, 11th, 12th, 13th, 14th, 15th, 19th, 20th, 21st, 22nd, 23rd, 29th, 30th

Best Days for Money: 1st, 2nd, 3rd, 5th, 6th, 10th, 11th, 14th, 15th, 19th, 23rd, 27th, 28th, 29th, 30th, 31st

Like last month, the planetary power is mostly in the East and your 1st House is still very strong. Continue to build your life as you desire it to be. Don't compromise. Accept nothing less than perfect happiness and fulfilment – and, of course, exert effort towards it.

The planetary power below the horizon of your chart keeps getting stronger. So, continue to cultivate positive emotional states and function from your emotional comfort zone. Career can be safely de-emphasized.

Uranus, your Ruling Planet, makes a major move into Pisces on the 10th. This kind of move only happens once in seven years or so – so it is a headline for the month. Your spiritual and creative tendencies, strong for some years now, become even stronger. You are under very powerful and intense spiritual energies now – so there is great interest in psychic phenomena, astrology, past lives, healing, the occult and the like.

There is also a great interest in finance and you seem very focused on it. Intuition will guide you here. Also astrologers, psychics, gurus and ministers have important information to impart. Professional investors should look at oil, natural gas, water utilities, footwear and shipping for profit opportunities. Non-professional investors might find that they have important clients in these fields or get jobs in these kinds of industries.

Venus in your own Sign from the 2nd to the 21st brings unusual glamour to your image and the appearance – supernatural glamour – not of this world, for she is travelling with Neptune in your own Sign. You've rarely looked better. Your personal sense of style is truly inspired. Others take notice. This is a good period for buying clothing or personal accessories as well. You seem very practical in love these days. You are allured by wealth, by people who can help you attain financial goals. Material gifts and financial support are both the ways you show love and the way you feel loved. Happily, your spouse, partner or lover seems eager to supply these things. After the 21st, you want good communication in love – an ability to share ideas with someone as you would with a brother or sister. There is a tendency to rashness in love after the 21st – to jump into new relationships prematurely. You are in a 'love-at-first-sight' period. Many marriage or serious love opportunities come after the 21st for singles.

Your image and demeanour are very important factors in earnings this month – it's been this way for some time, but especially now. Prosperity is strong this month and money comes through social connections, family members, family connections and creative projects.

April

Best Days Overall: 6th, 7th, 15th, 16th, 23rd, 24th

Most Stressful Days Overall: 3rd, 4th, 5th, 11th, 12th, 17th, 18th

Best Days for Love: 1st, 2nd, 8th, 9th, 11th, 12th, 17th, 18th, 21st, 28th, 29th

Best Days for Money: 1st, 2nd, 6th, 7th, 11th, 12th, 15th, 16th, 19th, 20th, 23rd, 24th, 26th, 27th, 28th, 29th

Most of the planets are still in the East and, on the 21st, dynamic Mars will move into your own Sign – personal independence and self-will are even stronger than last month. You have more than enough energy to attain to every righteous goal now. Be respectful of others, but have things your way.

Mars in your own Sign enhances athletic performance, overall energy and sex appeal. On the other hand, it can make you impatient and irritable when things don't move fast enough for you. Try to be more patient with others who don't have Mars in their own Sign.

Like last month, most of the planets are still below the horizon and Pluto, your Career Planet, is still retrograde. So, you can de-emphasize career and build the psychological and emotional foundation for future career success. In spite of Pluto's retrograde and your lack of interest, this is a good career month and progress happens almost on its own – but the important thing is to maintain your emotional and family harmony. Careers that fit in with that are advisable. If not, pass on them.

Finances still look strong. Personal effort plus the support of family members boost the bottom line. Property seems like a source of profit as well. There could be sudden moves or sudden 're-arrangements' of the domestic situation this month. Family seems eager to please you. A parent or parent figure is very supportive. Professional investors should continue to look at oil, natural gas, water utilities, ships and shipping and the beauty industry.

Love seems stormy after the 20th. You have to divide your time between friendships and organizational activities, intellectual interests and the needs of your partner. It's difficult to please everyone. However, this condition is not forever and will pass by next month.

Love seems much more harmonious before the 20th. Communication and the exchange of ideas still seem important. After the 20th, you want emotional nurturing and support – as does your partner or lover.

Jupiter starts moving forwards in your House of Love on the 4th. He has been retrograde for many months now. A friendship is starting to move forwards again. This friendship can easily develop into something much more serious. Those working towards a second marriage find opportunities as they pursue normal financial goals or in educational-type settings. Love is in the neighbourhood.

Overall health is good, but rest and relax more after the 20th.

May

Best Days Overall: 3rd, 4th, 12th, 13th, 21st, 22nd, 30th, 31st

Most Stressful Days Overall: 1st, 2nd, 8th, 9th, 14th, 15th, 28th, 29th

Best Days for Love: 1st, 2nd, 8th, 9th, 10th, 11th, 18th, 19th, 20th, 21st, 28th, 29th, 30th, 31st

Best Days for Money: 3rd, 4th, 8th, 9th, 12th, 13th, 16th, 17th, 21st, 22nd, 23rd, 24th, 25th, 26th, 27th, 30th, 31st

You're in a curious situation now, Aquarius. Mars in your own Sign spurs your independence and makes you want to go it alone. You want things done yesterday. But this month the planets shift from the East to the West and this kind of attitude could be counter-productive. You are in a period where social grace counts, where the favour of other people brings you where you want to go, where things are done by consensus and consultation with others and not by yourself. Yes, consensus and consultation take longer, but somehow you have to muster the patience to handle it. (In financial matters, independence counts – you seem to have things your way. But in most other areas, you need to compromise and adapt.)

Like last month, the planets are mostly below the horizon and Pluto, your Career Planet, is still retrograde. Further, your 4th House of Home and Family is unusually strong, while your 10th House of Career is empty (except for the Moon's visit on the 14th and 15th). So, continue to deal with family and domestic issues and let go of career issues for a while. With a Lunar eclipse (on the 16th) happening in your 10th House of Career, making career plans now could be unrealistic. You need to wait for the dust to settle to see where you stand.

This eclipse of the 16th is a strong one on you, so do take a reduced schedule. Elective activities – especially if they are stressful – should be rescheduled. Aside from bringing career and work changes, this eclipse also brings long-term changes to your health regime and diet. Flaws are revealed so that you can make corrections.

The Solar eclipse of the 31st is more benign to you, but it won't hurt to take a reduced schedule. This eclipse tests a serious relationship or love affair. Short-term upheavals reveal long-seething problems which should be dealt with. True love becomes even stronger as the air is cleared. Children are making long-term, serious decisions these days. Your relationship with them will change in a deep way.

Those involved in the creative arts take a new turn in their creativity.

Though overall prosperity is strong, this month (especially until the 21st) you have to work harder for earnings. Earnings come, but you need to go that extra mile.

With both the Sun and Venus in your 4th House of Home and Family (at varying times), this is a good month for family gatherings, entertaining from home and beautifying the home.

Though the eclipse will shake things up temporarily, love is greatly improved after the 21st – especially for singles. Those working towards a second marriage should look close to home for opportunities.

June

Best Days Overall: 1st, 9th, 10th, 17th, 18th, 27th, 28th

Most Stressful Days Overall: 4th, 5th, 11th, 12th, 24th, 25th

Best Days for Love: 1st, 4th, 5th, 7th, 8th, 9th, 10th, 17th, 18th, 27th, 28th, 29th, 30th

Best Days for Money: 1st, 4th, 5th, 9th, 10th, 13th, 14th, 17th, 18th, 19th, 20th, 22nd, 23rd, 27th, 28th

Last month's two eclipses signalled important and long-term changes. This month the changes continue, as 50% of the planets change Signs – highly unusual. It's as if you are in a whole new psychological and physical environment. Plans you made based on the old environment are no longer relevant. You (and many, many other people) have to go back to the drawing board and see what to do.

Like last month, most of the planets are now in the West. And, though Mars is still pushing you to be 'activist' and independent, you really need to be cultivating social skills. Patience and forbearance are important virtues now.

Most of the planets are still below the horizon and your 4th House (though getting weaker) is still stronger than your 10th House of Career. Thus, like last month, continue to downplay the career in favour of domestic and family duties. Continue to focus on the right inner states.

Health is much improved over last month. Mars in your own Sign gives you energy and magnetism and enhances your athletic performance. Much power in your 6th House of Health shows that you are interested in health issues this month and are not apt to let problems slide. Health and exercise regimes should go well. With the Lord of your 12th House, Saturn, now in your House of Health, you should combine spiritual and meditative techniques with your regular regime. 'Inner workouts' can be just as potent as 'physical' ones.

Love is improving day by day. Most of the tension between you and your beloved seems dissipated. This month, love is about fun and service. You show love by giving your lover a 'good time' and also by serving his or her practical needs. This is also how you feel loved. For singles, love opportunities await in the normal places – parties, sporting events, concerts, entertainments and the like. After the 21st, love opportunities come as you pursue your normal health goals – it could happen at the gym, doctor's surgery or yoga studio. Friendships are happy these days as well. And new friends are definitely in the picture.

Finances become more active and aggressive after the 17th as Mars moves into your Money House. You are into 'making' prosperity happen rather than allowing it to happen. Still, you have great energy to pursue and attain your financial goals. As we have seen for many months now, sales, marketing, PR and communication are all important for the bottom line. Cars, computers and communication equipment need checking after the 17th. Avoid wild, speculative financial risk-taking. Calculated risks will pay off.

July

Best Days Overall: 6th, 7th, 14th, 15th, 24th, 25th

Most Stressful Days Overall: 2nd, 3rd, 8th, 9th, 21st, 22nd, 23rd, 29th, 30th

Best Days for Love: 2nd, 3rd, 8th, 9th, 17th, 18th, 28th, 29th, 30th

Best Days for Money: 2nd, 3rd, 6th, 7th, 10th, 11th, 14th, 15th, 17th, 18th, 19th, 20th, 24th, 25th, 29th, 30th

Tone down self-will and self-assertion. Smile. Be gracious. You are in one of the best social periods of your year (and perhaps your life). 40% to 50% of the planets will move through your 7th House of Love this month – all of them beneficial. Whether you are working towards your first or second marriage, the aspects couldn't be better. Many an Aquarian is either walking down the aisle or drinking toasts at an engagement party. This is a month for serious love and serious love opportunity. This is a month to put other people first and to let your good come to you naturally and effortlessly – by the karmic law.

Another important change happens this month. The planetary power starts shifting to the upper half of the Horoscope. This doesn't happen all at once, but by degrees. By the 27th, the shift will be established. Hopefully, in the past few months you've made the psychological progress that you needed to make. You are comfortable in your own skin and your domestic situation is stable. Now you can focus on your career and outer objectives. Though your Career Planet, Pluto, is retrograde it receives so many benevolent aspects that good things must happen – opportunities are coming – albeit as a delayed reaction. Of course you will have to weigh each of these propositions carefully, as things might not be as they seem. But important career progress is happening now.

With so much happening socially, it is understandable that finances are taking a back seat. Yes, they are important, but the three planets involved with them are all retrograde. So, many a deal or project is either on hold or awaiting more study or the approval of others. Prosperity seems stronger before the 23rd than afterwards. But don't despair, the retrogrades are showing that important subjective, behind-the-scenes growth and development are taking place. After the 24th, it is a good time to review your finances, your projects and services and see where you can make improvements. It is a time for planning and perfecting financial strategies and projects, but not so great for executing them.

Overall, your health is still good. Your interest in health and health issues is also strong. But rest and relax more after the 23rd. Much power in the element of Fire could induce you to burn the candle at both ends – to be overly optimistic about your energy – and this would be a mistake. There is much partying happening this month, but try to keep it in moderation.

August

Best Days Overall: 2nd, 3rd, 11th, 12th, 20th, 21st, 22nd, 30th

Most Stressful Days Overall: 4th, 5th, 18th, 19th, 25th, 26th

Best Days for Love: 6th, 7th, 8th, 16th, 17th, 25th, 26th, 27th, 28th

Best Days for Money: 2nd, 3rd, 7th, 8th, 11th, 12th, 13th, 14th, 16th, 17th, 20th, 21st, 22nd, 26th, 27th, 30th

With your Ruling Planet, Uranus, still retrograde and the power in your 7th House of Love still very awesome, much of what we have written about last month is still in effect.

You are in an incredible social and romantic period. Three powerful beneficial influences are conspiring to bring love to you – playing Cupid on your behalf. Hard to see how you could avoid a marriage, partnership or serious relationship. Even if you were to hide out in a cave or desert island, these influences would manage to find you. Like last month, tone down self-will and self-assertion. Avoid power struggles. Adapt to situations. The truth is, other people know what's best at the moment. Your way could foul things up.

60% to 70% of the planets are now above the horizon of the chart. So, career is becoming increasingly important. Though Pluto, your Career Planet, is still retrograde (until the 29th), career aspects are still beautiful until the 21st. Pay rises, promotions or important (and prestigious) assignments are in the works now – these could happen as a delayed reaction, but they are probably being discussed or planned. After the 21st, your career faces more resistance. You have to work harder, go the extra mile to achieve goals – but it's worth doing.

Health is still good, but continue to rest and relax more until the 21st. After that, health and vitality are much improved.

With dynamic Mars still in your Money House, it will be hard to be patient in financial matters – yet this is what is needed. Many things will need time (and nothing else) to sort out. If it takes two hours to bake a cake, you must allow the two hours – your impatience will only make matters worse. This month your personal earning power is not that strong, but money or financial opportunity comes from your spouse or partner. You prosper as you help others prosper. After the 21st, channel spare cash towards debt repayment and think about cutting expenses or waste. Debts are easily made and easily paid. Jupiter's move into your 8th House on the 27th signals good fortune for those looking for outside investors or who have tax issues with the government. Writers and artists can expect increased royalty payments.

With much power in your 8th House after the 21st, libido will soar. Love is expressed in sexual ways. It is also a good period for weight loss, de-tox projects, reinventing yourself, breaking addictions and eliminating bad habits or character traits. Also good for eliminating excess possessions that you no longer need. Make room for the new and the better that wants to come in.

September

Best Days Overall: 7th, 8th, 17th, 18th, 26th, 27th

Most Stressful Days Overall: 1st, 2nd, 14th, 15th, 22nd, 23rd, 28th, 29th

Best Days for Love: 5th, 6th, 14th, 15th, 16th, 17th, 22nd, 23rd, 26th, 27th

Best Days for Money: 5th, 6th, 7th, 8th, 9th, 10th, 14th, 15th, 17th, 18th, 26th, 27th

Though your social life is not as frenetic as it has been the past two months, most of the planets are still in the West. Thus, continue to practise your social skills, avoid self-will and undue self-assertion, compromise wherever possible and adapt to situations. This is not a time for independence or too much personal effort. Your ability to be liked and to win others over are what bring success.

Like last month, the planets are mostly above the horizon. Continue to focus on your career and de-emphasize the domestic sphere. Doing right will lead to feeling right. Career success will lead to happier domestic and family circumstances. With your Career Planet, Pluto, now moving forward (and for many months to come), there is clarity in career matters now. You know where you have to move and what you need to do. Career still requires more work until the 23rd; after that you get a lot of help and progress more easily.

Health is good and will get even better after the 23rd. Health regimes will go better from the 1st to the 10th and from the 26th onwards – the Moon's waxing periods. Weight loss and de-tox types of regimes will go better from the 10th to the 26th as the Moon wanes.

With all the planets involved in your financial life still retrograde, you need patience in financial matters (like last month). Financial judgement and confidence are not as strong as they should be (and will be). Like last month, money comes from your spouse or partner, as you help others prosper and from insurance, royalties or estates. Though your personal earning power could be better, you have unusually good access to outside capital. Thus if you are seeking outside investors or credit, there is success now.

Love is still happy and your hormones are racing. Purity in love and in friendships seems important now. You want to make sure that only the purest feelings and purest motives exist between you and your beloved. Hyper-criticism – nit-pickiness – is the main danger to love these days. Keep criticism constructive. After the 23rd, love becomes more educational. There is a need for philosophical harmony between you and your beloved. There is a desire to teach and to learn. Singles will find love opportunities in foreign lands or with foreigners. Singles will want someone who is highly educated and refined – someone they can look up to. Those working towards a second marriage have wonderful aspects after the 23rd.

This is still a good period for breaking addictions, eliminating the effete and needless from your life – whether it be physical possessions or character traits – and for self-reinvention.

After the 23rd, it is a good time to pursue educational opportunities and travel and to deepen your religious understanding.

October

Best Days Overall: 4th, 5th, 14th, 15th, 23rd, 24th

Most Stressful Days Overall: 11th, 12th, 13th, 19th, 20th, 25th, 26th

Best Days for Love: 4th, 5th, 14th, 15th, 16th, 17th, 19th, 20th, 25th, 26th

Best Days for Money: 2nd, 3rd, 4th, 5th, 7th, 8th, 11th, 12th, 13th, 14th, 15th, 21st, 22nd, 23rd, 24th, 29th, 30th

Though you should rest and relax more after the 23rd, the month ahead is basically happy and harmonious. Much power in your native element of Air enhances your already strong mind and communication skills. Students, teachers, writers and marketers should have an outstanding month.

Like last month, most of the planets are above the horizon. But this month – beginning the 9th – your 10th House of Career becomes very powerful. So, this is an ambitious month and much 'outer' and professional progress is happening. Career is enhanced through social skills, the support of your spouse, lover or partner and through the favour of those above you. Career seems like fun in the month ahead. Even your family supports your career goals. And, as we have mentioned, attainment of professional objectives will probably help – not hinder – your family situation.

This month, the planets are making an important shift from the Western sector, where they have been for many months, to the Eastern sector. This shift will be complete by the 24th. So, your days of people-pleasing and dependency are about over. A new vigour, drive and spirit of independence will come in. You will be able to change or create conditions as you would like them to be. Your personal effort will make an important difference to your happiness.

Love seems happy this month. You are still attracted by highly educated and 'teacher-type' people. Through love you learn about subjects that have always interested you – foreign cultures or foreign languages, philosophy, religion and the like. Later in the month, you are socializing with people of high status. A romantic opportunity with a boss could happen. Perhaps the boss plays Cupid in your life. People who can help your career exert a romantic allure.

Stuck financial deals and projects are now becoming unstuck. Mars is now moving forwards in your Money House and Neptune, your Financial Planet, moves forwards on the 23rd. Your financial confidence and sound judgement are returning. You are back to 'making' prosperity happen through direct action. You thrive on competition and could be a bit of a risk-taker. Prosperity gets stronger and stronger as the month progresses.

After the 9th, there is a Grand Trine in the Water element, which boosts both finances and creativity. Women of childbearing age are more fertile than usual. Financial intuition soars.

November

Best Days Overall: 1st, 2nd, 10th, 11th, 12th, 20th, 21st, 28th, 29th

Most Stressful Days Overall: 8th, 9th, 15th, 16th, 22nd, 23rd

Best Days for Love: 3rd, 4th, 5th, 6th, 13th, 14th, 15th, 16th, 23rd, 24th, 25th, 26th, 27th

Best Days for Money: 1st, 2nd, 3rd, 4th, 8th, 9th, 10th, 11th, 18th, 19th, 20th, 21st, 26th, 27th, 28th, 29th, 30th

Health is basically good, but you need to rest and relax more until the 23rd. Your career demands much of your energy and you have little to spare for trivial or irrelevant things. Two eclipses this month also suggest a reduced schedule – although, of the two, only one is strong on you.

Like last month, your 10th House of Career is still powerful and very well aspected. The planetary power is above the horizon. Push forwards boldly to the pinnacle of success. This is a good month to ask the boss for a pay rise – or to ask favours of those in authority. It's also good if you have issues pending with the government or government regulators.

The planetary power is now mostly in the East and on the 8th, Uranus (your Ruling Planet) will start moving forwards again. Personal confidence, self-reliance and independence are getting stronger day by day. Be nice and polite to others, but go your own way. Your way is the best way (for you) now. Aim your life towards personal fulfilment and happiness.

Last month's Grand Trine in Water is still in effect until the 22nd. So, prosperity is still strong. This Grand Trine also boosts your career and love life.

The Lunar eclipse of the 9th is strong on you, so do take a reduced schedule – a few days before and for about a day after. This eclipse occurs in your 4th House, which suggests either a move, renovation or repair of the home. Family patterns are changing. Emotions could be highly charged during this eclipse period, so do your best to stay calm. Since the eclipsed planet, the Moon, is your Health Planet, the eclipse brings changes in doctors, therapies, diet or your overall health regime. Flaws will be revealed so that you can take corrective action.

The Solar eclipse of the 23rd is easier on you. It occurs in your 11th House of Friends and the eclipsed planet, the Sun, is your Love Planet. Thus this eclipse is announcing social changes – in a current love affair, marriage or friendship. For singles this eclipse can signal a marriage – a step forward in the relationship. For marrieds, it can show a testing and purification of the relationship. Long-brewing issues surface – perhaps explosively – so that you can correct them. These upheavals can happen with friendships, too. The good relationships will survive and eventually get even better. But the seriously flawed ones can end.

December

Best Days Overall: 7th, 8th, 9th, 17th, 18th, 25th, 26th

Most Stressful Days Overall: 5th, 6th, 12th, 13th, 14th, 19th, 20th

Best Days for Love: 2nd, 3rd, 4th, 5th, 6th, 12th, 13th, 14th, 15th, 16th, 23rd, 24th, 25th, 26th

Best Days for Money: 1st, 5th, 6th, 7th, 8th, 9th, 15th, 16th, 17th, 18th, 23rd, 24th, 25th, 26th, 27th, 28th

Most of the planets are still above the horizon and your career is still active and happy. But soon (by the 21st) your ambition will weaken and you'll become more interested in home, family and emotional issues. Your spouse, partner or friends are boosting your career goals now. You find favour with those above you in status. Social connections are a definite plus, careerwise. Attending the right parties (or hosting them) will also aid your career.

Like last month, the planetary power is mostly in the East, so continue to have life on your terms. Don't be rude to others, but don't compromise. Nothing less than total fulfilment will do. Insist on it for yourself and work towards it. Personal effort and excellence count now. Who you are and what you can do matters more than whom you know.

You are still financially aggressive. You want to make things happen. You want to create prosperity and are working hard towards it. Financial goals are achieved quickly. Rush and impatience are dangers. Undue risk-taking is also dangerous. But you are like an arrow winging to its mark – once you are clear on what needs to be done, you do it quickly and efficiently. With your Ruling Planet, Uranus, moving into your Money House (for good this time) on the 30th, finances are a major focus for years to come. As has been true for most of the year, money comes from sales, marketing, communication and PR activities. Your personal appearance and deportment are unusually important. You need to project a certain type of image for success to happen. After the 21st, money comes from family members, property or foreigners. Some big-ticket items for the home and personal accessories are coming too.

Venus will be in your own Sign after the 21st. This enhances your personal glamour and beauty. Others will take notice. Your needs in love will change this month. Until the 21st, you want friendship more than passion and attachment. After the 21st, you want a spiritual connection and spiritual compatibility. Love is behind the scenes now for singles. It is stalking you (in a good way) and presently will find you. Look for love at group activities, charitable or religious functions. You are more likely to find love at church than at a nightclub.

Health is wonderful. Health and fitness regimes will go better from the 1st to the 16th and from the 23rd onwards – as the Moon waxes. Diets and de-tox regimes will go better from the 16th to the 23rd – as the Moon wanes.

Relations with children can be complicated from the 17th onwards. It is very important that you take the time to communicate properly with them. Mis-communication is at the root of the problem.

Pisces

♓

THE FISH

Birthdays from

19th February

to 20th March

Personality Profile

PISCES AT A GLANCE

Element – Water

Ruling Planet – Neptune
Career Planet – Pluto
Love Planet – Mercury
Money Planet – Mars
Planet of Health and Work – Sun
Planet of Home and Family Life – Mercury
Planet of Love Affairs, Creativity and Children – Moon

Colours – aqua, blue-green

Colours that promote love, romance and social harmony – earth tones, yellow, yellow-orange

Colours that promote earning power – red, scarlet

Gem – white diamond

Metal – tin

Scent – lotus

Quality – mutable (= flexibility)

Qualities most needed for balance – structure and the ability to handle form

Strongest virtues – psychic power, sensitivity, self-sacrifice, altruism

Deepest needs – spiritual illumination, liberation

Characteristics to avoid – escapism, keeping bad company, negative moods

Signs of greatest overall compatibility – Cancer, Scorpio

Signs of greatest overall incompatibility – Gemini, Virgo, Sagittarius

Sign most helpful to career – Sagittarius

Sign most helpful for emotional support – Gemini

Sign most helpful financially – Aries

Sign best for marriage and/or partnerships – Virgo

Sign most helpful for creative projects – Cancer

Best Sign to have fun with – Cancer

Signs most helpful in spiritual matters – Scorpio, Aquarius

Best day of the week – Thursday

Understanding a Pisces

If Pisceans have one outstanding quality it is their belief in the invisible, spiritual and psychic side of things. This side of things is as real to them as the hard earth beneath their feet – so real, in fact, that they will often ignore the visible, tangible aspects of reality in order to focus on the invisible and so-called intangible ones.

Of all the Signs of the Zodiac, the intuitive and emotional faculties of the Pisces are the most highly developed. They are committed to living by their intuition and this can at times be infuriating to other people – especially those who are materially-, scientifically- or technically-orientated. If you think that money or status or worldly success are the only goals in life, then you will never understand a Pisces.

Pisceans have intellect, but to them intellect is only a means by which they can rationalize what they know intuitively. To an Aquarius or a Gemini, the intellect is a tool with which to gain knowledge. To a well-developed Pisces, it is a tool by which to express knowledge.

Pisceans feel like fish in an infinite ocean of thought and feeling. This ocean has many depths, currents and subcurrents. They long for purer waters where the denizens are good, true and beautiful, but they are sometimes pulled to the lower, murkier depths. Pisceans know that they do not generate thoughts but only tune in to thoughts that already exist; this is why they seek the purer waters. This ability to tune in to higher thoughts inspires them artistically and musically.

Since Pisces is so spiritually-orientated – though many Pisceans in the corporate world may hide this fact – we will deal with this aspect in greater detail, for otherwise it is difficult to understand the true Pisces personality.

There are four basic attitudes of the spirit. One is outright scepticism – the attitude of secular humanists. The second is an intellectual or emotional belief, where one worships a far-distant God figure – the attitude of most modern church-going people. The third is not only belief, but direct personal spiritual experience – this is the attitude of some 'born-again' religious people. The fourth is actual unity with the divinity, an intermingling with the spiritual world – this is the attitude of yoga. This fourth attitude is the deepest urge of a Pisces and a Pisces is uniquely qualified to pursue and perform this work.

Consciously or unconsciously, Pisceans seek this union with the spiritual world. The belief in a greater reality makes Pisceans very tolerant and understanding of others – perhaps even too tolerant. There are instances in their lives when they should say 'enough is enough' and be ready to defend their position and put up a fight. However, because of their qualities, it takes a good deal of doing to get them into that frame of mind.

Pisceans basically want and aspire to be 'saints'. They do so in their own way and according to their own rules. Others should not try to impose their concept of saintliness on a Pisces, because he or she always tries to find it for him- or herself.

Finance

Money is generally not that important to Pisces. Of course, they need it as much as anyone else and many of them attain great wealth. But money is not generally a primary objective. Doing good, feeling good about oneself, peace of mind, the relief of pain and suffering – these are the things that matter most to a Pisces.

Pisceans earn money intuitively and instinctively. They follow their hunches rather than their logic. They tend to be generous and perhaps overly charitable. Almost any kind of misfortune is enough to move a Pisces to give. Although this is one of their greatest virtues, Pisceans should be more careful with their finances. They should try to be more choosy about the people to whom they lend money, so that they are not being taken advantage of. If they give money to charities, they should follow it up to see that their contributions are put to good use. Even when Pisceans are not rich, they still like to spend money on helping others. In this case, they should really be careful, however: they must learn to say no sometimes and help themselves first.

Perhaps the biggest financial stumbling block for the Pisces is general passivity – a *laissez faire* attitude. In general Pisceans like to go with the flow of events. When it comes to financial matters especially, they need to be more aggressive. They need to make things happen, to create their own wealth. A passive attitude will only cause loss and missed opportunity. Worrying about financial security will not provide that security. Pisceans need to go after what they want tenaciously.

Career and Public Image

Pisceans like to be perceived by the public as people of spiritual or material wealth, of generosity and philanthropy. They look up to big-hearted, philanthropic types. They admire people engaged in large-scale undertakings and eventually would like to head up these big enterprises themselves. In short, they like to be connected with big organizations that are doing things in a big way.

If Pisceans are to realize their full career and professional potential, they need to travel more, educate themselves more and learn more about the actual world. In other words, they need some of the unflagging optimism of the Sagittarius in order to reach the top.

Because of all their caring and generous characteristics, Pisceans often choose professions through which they can help and touch the lives of other people. That is why many Pisceans become doctors, nurses, social workers or teachers. Sometimes it takes a while before Pisceans realize what they really want to do in their professional lives, but once they find a career that lets them manifest their interests and virtues they will excel at it.

Love and Relationships

It is not surprising that someone as 'other-worldly' as the Pisces would like a partner who is practical and down to earth. Pisceans prefer a partner who is on top of all the details of life, because they dislike details. Pisceans seek this quality in both their romantic and professional partners. More than anything else, this gives Pisces a feeling of being grounded, of being in touch with reality.

As expected, these kinds of relationships – though necessary – are sure to have many ups and downs. Misunderstandings will take place because the two attitudes are poles apart. If you are in love with a Pisces you will experience these fluctuations and will need a lot of patience to see things stabilize. Pisceans are moody, intuitive, affectionate and difficult to get to know. Only time and the right attitude will yield Pisceans' deepest secrets. However, when in love with a Pisces you will find that riding the waves is worth it because they are good, sensitive people who need and like to give love and affection.

When in love, Pisceans like to fantasize. For them fantasy is 90 per cent of the fun of a relationship. They tend to idealize their partner, which can be good and bad at the same time. It is bad in that it is difficult for anyone to live up to the high ideals their Piscean lover sets.

Home and Domestic Life

In their family and domestic life Pisceans have to resist the tendency to relate only by feelings and moods. It is unrealistic to expect that your partner and other family members will be as intuitive as you are. There is a need for more verbal communication between a Pisces and his or her family. A cool, unemotional exchange of ideas and opinions will benefit everyone.

Some Pisceans tend to like mobility and moving around. For them too much stability feels like a restriction on their freedom. They hate to be locked in one location for ever.

The Sign of Gemini sits on Pisces' 4th Solar House (of Home and Family) cusp. This shows that the Pisces likes and needs a home environment that promotes intellectual and mental interests. They tend to treat their neighbours as family – or extended family. Some Pisceans can have a dual attitude towards the home and family – on the one hand, they like the emotional support of the family, but on the other, they dislike the obligations, restrictions and duties involved with it. For Pisces, finding a balance is the key to a happy family life.

Horoscope for 2003

Major Trends

The past two years were testing times, Pisces. They were about attaining success through hard work and conscious effort, about overcoming obstacles, transforming negatives into positives and getting more organized. Health and vitality were not up to their usual standards and had to be monitored. Family and career vied with each other for importance, leaving you in the middle. Many of you felt 'locked into' an untenable situation. Happily, this testing period is about over. You've got another six months of it, but by now you have learned the lessons and you're ready to move on. Saturn, which has been the tester, is now going to reward you for your efforts – exactly in proportion to what you have mastered. He moves away from his stressful aspect on June 4 and begins to make harmonious aspects to you. Healthwise, you will feel almost immediately uplifted.

Uranus, your Spiritual Planet, has been in your 12th House for the past seven years, enhancing spirituality, causing many changes in your inner life, bringing revelation, breaking spiritual barriers and helping you to find your own very unique path to the Higher Power. Now he is moving into your own Sign of Pisces from March 10 to September 15. By next year, he will be in your Sign for the next seven years. This transit is announcing major changes in your life – in your appearance, image, body; in your personal lifestyle and probably in your residence. The previous two-and-half-year period of restriction is now changing into a period of enhanced personal freedom. More on this later.

Your social life, too, is getting ready to shine. Come August 27, Jupiter will move into your 7th House of Love and Marriage, bringing new friends, expanding your social circle and in many cases bringing marriage or a serious relationship.

Your important areas of interest are: spirituality; the body, image, personal appearance and sensual pleasure (from March 10 to September 15); home and family (until June 4); children, creativity and leisure activities (after June 4); health and work (until August 27); love and romance (after August 27); career. Please note, Pisces, that you have a lot of areas of interest. The danger here is the dispersion of your energy and lack of focus.

Your paths to greatest fulfilment are: home and family (until April 14); communication and intellectual interests (after April 14); health and work (until August 27); love and romance (after August 27).

Health

Though health is improving day by day, you still need to be more careful here – especially for the first half of the year.

The good news is that your 6th House of Health and Work is a House of Power – good health is important to you and you give it the attention it deserves.

Like last year, you've got to rest when tired, avoid depression, cultivate positive states and positive moods, organize yourself so that you can do more with less effort and work rhythmically.

Much of what we wrote of last year still applies now. You need to drop trivialities from your life and focus on essentials. Talk less and listen more. Think less, but be more aware. Do less, but let the quality of your actions be better.

Jupiter in your 6th House until August 27 is showing the importance of the thighs and liver. The thighs should be regularly massaged. The liver can be strengthened by hosts of natural therapies – foot and hand reflexology, shiatsu, massage, acupuncture and acupressure, kinesiology, herbology, etc.

Jupiter is your Career Planet. Thus, this position is showing that good health for you includes a healthy and meaningful career. Career ups and downs can impact on health as well – though you shouldn't allow them to.

Generically, Jupiter is the planet of Higher Knowledge – of religion, philosophy and metaphysics. Thus, understanding the philosophy of health and disease – in a true way – is unusually important for health. Bad health concepts or false beliefs will be very costly. Good ones are better than health insurance. Lately, there has been much progress in exploring the mind-body connection of health and disease. But little has been written about the impact of one's world view and philosophy on health and disease. This is an area to explore in the coming year.

The Sun is your Health Planet (he rules your 6th House). Thus the heart always needs special attention. Keeping the heart fit will be a powerful preventative to other problems. The Sun, generically, rules children, creativity and leisure activities – the joy of life. So, just being happy is a powerful tonic for you. If you feel under the weather, have a night out on the town. Creative hobbies will enhance your health. Blockages to your natural creativity can cause health problems. Relations with children should be kept as harmonious as possible. Many a health problem has its origin here as well.

Uranus moving into your own Sign and Solar 1st House is showing much change and excitement coming into your life. There will be much experimenting with the body – as if you were testing its limits. This is fine, but keep the experiments constructive and do your homework beforehand.

Diet is now becoming a major issue in your life as the Lord of the 12th House of Spirituality enters your 1st House. This transit refines the body and makes it ultra-sensitive. Thus dietary habits that were OK last year or a few years ago – things that never bothered you – might start bothering you. You need a purer, more refined diet.

Home, Domestic and Family Issues

Your 4th House of Home and Family has been a House of Power for two years now and it is still powerful for the first half of 2003.

Home and family life has been bittersweet. On the one hand, Saturn forced you to re-organize and re-structure this area – both physically and emotionally. On the physical level, you had to take on more responsibility in the home. There were duties and obligations (often burdensome) to family members that couldn't be avoided. There was a need to manage daily domestic affairs more efficiently. Though you felt cramped in your present home, you couldn't move but had to make better use of the space you had – often this entailed much re-arranging and re-designing, etc. There was a need for order and discipline in the home.

On an emotional level, there was a need to manage your moods and feelings. It wasn't safe to express what you really felt and many of you repressed these things. Others took a more correct approach and expressed the feelings in harmless ways, by writing them out or talking them out on a tape or to a therapist.

Further complicating your domestic life were career demands, which have been intense for many years now. But you couldn't progress careerwise until you established order at home. And establishing order at home distracted you from your career. It was a vicious circle. By now you have learned to balance these two areas – which you still need to do for the first half of 2003.

Yet, when you shoulder the responsibility and do what needs to be done, there is great happiness and fulfilment.

With Uranus moving into your own Sign from March 10 to September 15, you will feel much more restless than in the past. Often this shows many moves – serial moves. Often it shows living in various places for extended periods of time – a few months here and few months there. A nomadic existence. Where for two years you've been taking on responsibility and being dutiful at home, now you want to go to the opposite extreme and claim absolute personal freedom.

You won't feel the full impact of this (only stirrings) this year, but by next year you will.

A Solar eclipse on May 31 seems to be the catalyst for the domestic changes and changes in the family relationships we've been describing. Perhaps it brings on a temporary crisis ('God's opportunity') that forces the changes. You should rejoice in this crisis as it is announcing the lifting of many onerous domestic and family burdens. It is announcing your new era of freedom.

Love and Social Life

In general, this is a very happy social year – especially after August 27. Jupiter will move into your 7th House of Love and Marriage. For singles, this means a significant relationship and marriage opportunities. For marrieds this brings more happiness and romance within the marriage and greater social activity – more going out, more parties, etc.

For all of you, it brings the enlargement of your social circle – new friends (and significant ones) come into the picture. Since Jupiter is the Lord of your 10th House, it shows that you are mingling with the high and mighty, with people of power, prestige and position, with people above you in social status. It shows that a significant relationship or marriage will likely be with someone above you in status – with someone prominent and powerful. Often this position shows the marriage of an employee with a boss. Equally often it shows a desire to make one's marriage (or social life) one's career – one's main life work. You gravitate to people who can help your career or raise your social status.

But here's the challenge with marriage. Yes, Jupiter is going to bring the opportunity – the desired relationships. But Uranus in your 1st House will start to test this relationship. This will happen for a bit this year and more seriously next year. As mentioned, Uranus gives the urge for absolute freedom. It makes you constantly tinker and experiment with your image and self-concept – as if you were trying to figure out who you are. Can you have absolute freedom and yet have a committed relationship? Further, as you change, you can become a mystery to your lover, who thought he or she was in love with one person and now discovers he or she is with 'someone else'. Those in love with Pisceans in the coming year should be aware of these facts. Give Pisces as much freedom as possible and try to enjoy the different changes and experiments – things will go more easily for you if you do.

The ideal relationship in the year ahead is with someone who can provide freedom, change and variety within the relationship, with someone who considers it charming that you've dyed your hair a different colour every month and have changed your personality on a weekly basis, with someone who enjoys new and unpredictable behaviour, who is devoted but allows you personal freedom. A tall order.

Many people don't realize that when they change their self-concept, change their identity, they inevitably change their relationships. This is in the natural order of things.

Those looking to marry for a second time also have wonderful aspects – especially until August 27. This lover is found at work or in the pursuit of career objectives. This relationship will also get tested after August 27, as career demands can stress it out.

Those looking to marry for a third time will have a love affair, but marriage is questionable. This person is close to home and is almost like a family member.

Your most active (and perhaps complicated) social period will be from August 23 to September 15. It is complicated because your Love Planet is retrograde for much of the time. Thus there is much uncertainty and confusion going on.

Singles find love opportunities at the work place or the doctor's surgery – perhaps whilst visiting a friend in hospital. Health professionals and people of status are particularly alluring. After August 27, romantic opportunity comes in the normal places – at social gatherings, parties, weddings, etc.

Children of marriageable age will have a status quo year. There is a need to get their body and image in order and come to terms with who they are before they enter a serious relationship. Grandchildren of marriageable age seem happy overall, but marriage is status quo. Those who are married will tend to stay married, those who are single will tend to stay single.

The marriage of a parent or parent figure is bittersweet. If single, a marriage opportunity could come, but there is a testing of the relationship.

Finance and Career

Though your 2nd House of Finance is not a House of Power, this is still going to be a prosperous year. Mars, your Financial Planet, spends an unusual six-month spell in your Sign – from June 17 to December 16. Your Financial Planet in your own Sign makes finances important even though your 2nd House is empty.

Career has been important for many years and this trend continues in 2003. There is much career expansion going on – especially until August 27. Benevolent Jupiter is making sensational aspects to Pluto in your House of Career. This brings pay rises, promotions, the enlargement of your career perspective, job offers and new career opportunities. Many of you will have career opportunities in foreign lands or expand your present business into foreign lands. The problem with your career (as mentioned) is that you haven't been able to devote your full energy to it – your domestic situation and family responsibilities were major distractions. On the other hand, this did provide some balance in your life.

Job-seekers have sensational aspects this year – especially until August 27. A dream job is likely to manifest. Those who employ others are still expanding the work force. Job-seekers can find work through social connections or even by working for a friend or spouse.

Your Financial Planet in your own Sign shows that you spend on yourself; that you consider yourself a worthy investment. So, many of you are spending on wardrobes, accessories and on sensual pleasures. This also shows dressing expensively and taking on and projecting an 'image of wealth'. They call this dressing for success. Many of you will wear expensive clothing or jewellery more for the 'vibrational' value than for anything else. When you wear good and expensive things, it makes you feel more prosperous. And you tend to attract more prosperity for that reason.

Others will dress expensively to further their career and impress others. Also, many will have jobs where personal appearance is a major factor in success.

Your Financial Planet in your own Sign shows that you are taking a personal interest in finance and investing and not delegating these matters to others. You feel that your prosperity is up to you and you alone. You've got to 'take the bull by the horns'. In financial matters, you feel that 'your way is the best way' and will tend to ignore the advice of others.

This Mars transit in your own Sign will make many of you more aggressive in financial matters – more risk-taking, more inclined to 'make things happen' rather than let things happen. While this is a good thing in most cases, beware of the Mars retrograde from July 29 to September 27. This is a period for more caution and not aggressiveness. Be aggressively cautious. Do more homework. When in doubt about a given investment or expenditure, do nothing until your doubts are resolved. When you are sure of a course of action, wealth goals will manifest very quickly.

Self-improvement

Uranus' move into your own Sign means much more than just 'busting loose' of all restraints – though this will happen. This transit, for the next seven years or so, has a very definite spiritual purpose. It represents your next stage in growth. There is a need now to break free of all attachments – whether to your body image, your personal ego, your dietary preferences, the place where you live, your career, etc. Most of these attachments have been holding you back. When you break free of them, you discover a whole new world and a new vista of opportunity. Remember that Uranus is your Spiritual Planet and he is not working haphazardly, though it might seem that way. Eventually you will have only one attachment – to the Higher Power within you. Rest assured that Uranus will know which attachments to break and which to leave alone. All attachments will not be broken at once, but as a gradual process. When you break the attachment to specific home or neighbourhood, you find that you are happy living anywhere. When you break your food attachments, you get exposed to new and undreamed-of delicacies. When you break your attachment to your ego, you discover a much vaster Ego and discover that your previous attachment was actually short-changing you. When you break your attachment to 'things', you discover the power behind all things and you discover that you haven't lost anything but have gained everything.

A child is clinging so hard to the penny in his hand that when Mum wants to put a pound there, she can't. The child can't accept it as he holds the penny so tightly. Along comes Uranus, who sends another child to take the penny or perhaps the child falls and is forced to let go. Now Mum can dust him off and give him the pound.

Another child is sitting in a mansion surrounded by antiques, art objects and a fully-stocked larder. But he holds a penny in his hand and his attention is fixated on that. He is so fixated on the penny that he doesn't realize he is surrounded by so much wealth. He goes to the sweet shop to buy something with his penny and he is denied. He goes back to his mansion depressed. So along comes Uranus and knocks the penny from his hand, so that he can see the reality of his condition.

This is about the best way to describe the coming period.

Month-by-month Forecasts

January

Best Days Overall: 6th, 7th, 8th, 16th, 17th, 25th, 26th

Most Stressful Days Overall: 1st, 14th, 15th, 21st, 22nd, 27th, 28th

Best Days for Love: 2nd, 3rd, 9th, 10th, 11th, 12th, 13th, 19th, 20th, 21st, 22nd, 27th, 28th, 29th, 30th

Best Days for Money: 1st, 9th, 10th, 19th, 20th, 27th, 28th

70% to 80% of the planets are above the horizon. Your 10th House of Career is unusually powerful. The planets involved in home and family issues (Mercury and Saturn) are retrograde. The message couldn't be more clear: Let go of domestic concerns and focus on your career. Domestic problems will need time to sort out – not much you can do right now anyway. So you may as well channel your energy towards 'outer' goals.

Three planets associated with transformation – death and renewal – are in your House of Career. The Lord of your 8th House (Venus) enters there on the 7th and Pluto, generic Lord of these things, has been there for many years. Mars (by classical astrology, the natural Lord of the 8th House) enters on the 17th. Thus, you are 'reinventing' your career – giving birth to something new and wonderful, to the career you've always dreamed of. Your public image is also being reinvented and redefined – this is all very positive. You will have to let go of many long-held concepts and beliefs. Aside from this, Venus in your 10th brings the favour of elders, bosses and parents. Also the government.

Career is very competitive now and you are working hard in that area. You have to succeed by being the best.

By the 17th, the planetary power will shift to the Eastern sector of your Horoscope – 70% to 80% of the planets will now be in the East. Thus you are in a period of independence and activism. You have the power and the desire to create conditions as you like them to be – to have your way in life. You are not in the mood for compromising – nor should you be. Build the life your dreams. Take positive steps. Personal effort counts. If others don't support you, go it alone.

Finances look strong this month. Your Money Planet, Mars, in the beneficial 9th House until the 17th, suggests expanded income and enlarged financial horizons. Money and financial opportunities come from foreign lands or from foreigners. Your understanding of financial principles is enlarged and thus there is more prosperity. After the 17th, money comes from your career and good reputation. There can be pay rises or bonuses.

Love is complicated by two factors: one, the retrograde of your Love Planet (Mercury) from the 2nd to the 22nd, and two, lack of interest – your 7th House is empty (except for the Moon's visit on the 21st and 22nd). So be patient in a current relationship and try not to make important long-range love decisions while Mercury is retrograde. After the 22nd, you will be more clear on things. Singles find love opportunities at group functions or organizations. You want friendship more than a romance. You want personal freedom and a non-committed attitude.

Health needs more attention – especially after the 17th. Yes you are busy and probably won't be able to slow down, but you can keep your focus on priorities and let trivialities go. Enhance health by paying more attention to your spine, knees, teeth and skeletal alignment – also your ankles.

February

Best Days Overall: 3rd, 4th, 13th, 14th, 21st, 22nd

Most Stressful Days Overall: 10th, 11th, 17th, 18th, 23rd, 24th

Best Days for Love: 8th, 9th, 17th, 18th, 19th, 20th, 25th, 26th, 28th

Best Days for Money: 5th, 6th, 15th, 16th, 23rd, 24th

Like last month, health needs more attention. Career is demanding and taking up much of your energy, but see if you can work more rhythmically. Delegate wherever possible. Enhance health by paying more attention to your heart, ankles and feet. Inner, spiritual workouts are as powerful as physical workouts after the 19th. The good news is that health becomes important to you after the 19th and you are unlikely to ignore it or let problems fester. Vanity, if nothing else, spurs you on.

The planetary shift to the East is even stronger than last month. By the 19th, your 1st House of Self becomes an important house of Power, while your 7th House of Others is empty (except for the Moon's visit on the 17th and 18th). So this is a time for having things your way – having life on your terms – and for insisting on complete fulfilment. Whether others support you or not is irrelevant now. Happiness is up to you and the personal actions you take. A little 'brattiness' now (without being disrespectful of others) will stand you in good stead.

Like last month, most of the planetary power is above the horizon and your 10th House of Career is still very strong. So, continue to de-emphasize home and domestic duties and focus on your career. The home and family situation should be improved this month – almost by itself – as your Family Planet is now moving forwards. But still, time is the answer to most family problems.

The transformation of your career and public image continues apace. Perhaps there are power struggles at the job or in your corporate hierarchy. The result of these struggles will produce important change and lead you closer to your heart's true desire. You still have a need to redefine your public image – to fine-tune it and gain more clarity here.

After the 13th, dreams will clarify many of your family and love relationships. A moment of spiritual insight will do more for you than years of normal effort. The light gets turned on and you see what to do and why you have to do it.

Love is much improved this month, especially after the 13th. Singles are meeting significant people – perhaps at a religious, spiritual or charitable function – perhaps through the introduction of family members. A flame from the past could come back into the picture. Love is very idealistic these days. A spiritual connection and spiritual harmony seems most important. For love to be interesting you want the 'stamp of approval' of a Higher Power.

March

Best Days Overall: 2nd, 3rd, 12th, 13th, 21st, 29th, 30th, 31st

Most Stressful Days Overall: 10th, 11th, 17th, 23rd

Best Days for Love: 1st, 10th, 11th, 12th, 13th, 17th, 19th, 20th, 21st, 22nd, 23rd, 29th, 30th

Best Days for Money: 5th, 6th, 7th, 14th, 15th, 16th, 17th, 23rd, 25th, 26th

Health is much improved this month, Pisces. Energy and vitality are back to high levels. You can enhance health further by paying more attention your feet, heart and head. (Regular scalp and face massage will be potent after the 21st.) You spend more on health this month and also have the opportunity to earn from this field or from people involved in this field. Don't allow financial issues to affect your health. Finance is finance and it has its normal ups and downs and health is health – keep them distinct in your mind.

The planets are now in their maximum Eastern position, so personal independence and self-will are very strong. This is as it should be. So long as you don't trample others, have your way in life. If others don't support you, you will find support in unexpected ways and through unexpected means. Build your paradise on earth now. Take positive steps. Be bold.

Your 10th House of Career is becoming less important as Mars moves out of there on the 4th. Also, the planetary power is shifting to the lower half of the Horoscope. By the 23rd, the majority of planets will be there. So, you are beginning a phase where how you feel is more important than what you do or what you achieve. Feeling right brings more satisfaction than career success. With your family planets now moving forwards (Saturn began moving forwards late last month), you have clarity on domestic issues and can take positive steps. You are entering a period where you are building the psychological foundations of future (and greater) career success.

Love is very happy this month. Your two love planets (Venus on a generic level and Mercury on an actual level) are in your own Sign. You look great. Personal glamour soars. Love pursues you – you only need to show up. You have your way in love just as you do in most areas of life now.

Uranus makes a once-in-88-years move into your own Sign on the 10th. This is a major headline for the month. It shows major personal changes coming up in your life – moves, a need for personal freedom, perhaps a more nomadic existence, a desire to break old patterns and barriers. An exciting period. In the next few months you will understand the scripture, 'unless the Lord buildeth the house, they labour in vain who build.' Yes, the best-laid plans of mice and men can all come to naught as Uranus comes into the picture and shows a higher (and better) plan. Uranus is a genius at this sort of thing and he knows what he's doing.

Prosperity is strong this month – especially after the 21st. Money comes from work, the favour of elders, your good professional reputation, social contacts, friends and your spouse, lover or partner.

April

Best Days Overall: 8th, 9th, 10th, 17th, 18th, 26th, 27th

Most Stressful Days Overall: 6th, 7th, 13th, 14th, 19th, 20th

Best Days for Love: 1st, 2nd, 8th, 9th, 13th, 14th, 17th, 18th, 21st, 22nd, 28th, 29th

Best Days for Money: 1st, 2nd, 3rd, 4th, 5th, 11th, 12th, 13th, 14th, 19th, 20th, 23rd, 28th, 29th

Like last month, most of the planets are below the horizon of the chart, so continue to emphasize home, family and emotional issues and let your career go for a while – that is, do what you have to do, but channel more attention and energy to domestic issues.

Also like last month, the planetary power is mostly in the East, so continue to create conditions as you desire them to be. Personal fulfilment is more important than social popularity. The curious thing is, as you are fulfilled, you find you don't lose any popularity. In fact you might start meeting people who are more in harmony with your sense of personal fulfilment.

Venus in your own Sign enhances glamour and personal beauty. Your image shines. Your gestures and movements are rhythmic and beautiful. If there are love problems, they're certainly not your fault. This is a good month to buy clothing and personal accessories, as your sense of style is very sharp. Love can be unstable this month as Venus travels near Uranus – but it is also more exciting. The highs of love are ultra-high – and your ability to express and receive love is unusually strong. Problems can come from hypersensitivity. Until the 5th, love is expressed through material gifts and support. This is how you show love; this is what you expect when in love. But after the 5th, good communication and a 'brotherly-sisterly' feeling is alluring. Singles find love opportunities as they pursue their normal financial and intellectual goals. There are opportunities with people involved in these things as well.

The social component is strong in your financial life as well. Money and financial opportunity come through friends, organizations and your spouse, lover or social contacts. After the 21st, your financial intuition becomes important. In many cases you will have to transcend logic and reason to achieve your goals. Sales, marketing and PR activities also become important.

Health is still good this month. You can enhance it further by paying more attention to your head, neck and throat. Be careful to speak only words of good health after the 20th. Your word becomes an important factor in good health then.

Your Love Planet, Mercury, will go retrograde towards the end of the month – on the 26th. So avoid making important, long-range love decisions until next month. If a relationship seems like it's going backwards, don't panic. Allow space to your lover. The relationship is under review – and a good thing too.

May

Best Days Overall: 6th, 7th, 14th, 15th, 23rd, 24th

Most Stressful Days Overall: 3rd, 4th, 10th, 11th, 16th, 17th, 30th, 31st

Best Days for Love: 1st, 2nd, 8th, 9th, 10th, 11th, 18th, 19th, 28th, 29th

Best Days for Money: 3rd, 4th, 8th, 9th, 12th, 13th, 16th, 17th, 21st, 22nd, 25th, 26th, 27th, 30th, 31st

Like last month, the planetary power is still mostly in the East, so continue to take the bull by the horns. Assert yourself, take positive action towards your personal goals, change conditions that disturb you and create new conditions according to your specifications. Seize the moment now, as the planets are getting ready to shift westward. We see this beginning this month; by next month the shift will be established.

Like last month, the planetary power is mostly below the horizon, so continue to cultivate the right emotional state and build a solid, stable home life. Home and family issues are important this month for other reasons as well. Your 4th House is very strong and there is a Solar eclipse there on the 31st.

There are two eclipses this month, one of which is basically benign – the Lunar eclipse of the 16th – and another one, the Solar eclipse of the 31st, which seems stronger on you. Do take a reduced schedule around the 31st – and even a day later.

Health is a priority after the 21st. By all means pace yourself, avoid power struggles and let go of trivialities. Enhance health by paying extra attention to your neck, throat, lungs, intestines and nervous system.

The Lunar eclipse of the 16th occurs in your 9th House of Religion, Metaphysics and Higher Education. This is the House that governs your belief systems and world view.

Thus you can expect that these things will get tested. Flaws there will be revealed so that you can redefine and fine-tune these things. A good thing too. A crisis of faith will lead to higher knowledge eventually. For students, this eclipse signals changes in their educational status. Perhaps they change schools, graduate, have an upheaval or two with administrators or change areas of study. Flaws in their educational plans or strategies are revealed and corrective actions have to be taken.

The Solar eclipse of the 31st could bring long-term changes to your health regime or diet or with people involved in your health. Job changes could also happen. Since this eclipse occurs in your 4th House, there could be repairs or renovations of the home – even a move. Long-standing problems in the home or with family members are forced to the surface, sometimes explosively, and you are forced to make corrections. Over the long haul, you will see this as a good thing, but while it's happening it can feel very disruptive.

Love is still 'brotherly-sisterly' this month. Romantic opportunities happen in educational settings, as you pursue intellectual interests or in the neighbourhood. Mercury's forward motion on the 20th should clarify an existing love relationship – one way or another, you'll see clearly what needs to be done.

Prosperity is still strong, but lack of interest is probably the main problem after the 16th.

June

Best Days Overall: 2nd, 3rd, 11th, 12th, 19th, 20th, 30th

Most Stressful Days Overall: 1st, 7th, 8th, 13th, 14th, 27th, 28th

Best Days for Love: 7th, 8th, 17th, 18th, 27th, 28th, 29th

Best Days for Money: 1st, 4th, 5th, 9th, 10th, 13th, 14th, 19th, 22nd, 23rd, 29th, 30th

Continue to give priority to your health, Pisces. Overwork, hyperactivity, rush, haste and impatience are the main dangers. You've got a lot on your plate, but be intelligent about it. Plan and organize your day better. Practise 'the art of the possible' and let what seems 'impossible' go. Tomorrow or the next day the 'impossible' will become possible and you can achieve it. Refuse to worry about a future that hasn't arrived yet. 'Sufficient unto the day is the evil thereof.' Now is always OK.

Enhance health by paying more attention to your heart, lungs, intestines, nervous system, stomach and breasts. Emotional health – balanced and loving feelings – are unusually important for your overall health after the 21st. If you follow these rules, health should improve dramatically after the 21st.

Like last month, the planetary power is mostly below the horizon and your 4th House of Home and Family is very powerful. So continue to build a stable and happy home situation. Happily, this is about to get much easier as Saturn is leaving your 4th House on the 4th – not to return for another 28 to 30 years. Big family or emotional burdens are leaving you.

Dynamic Mars moves into your own Sign on the 17th. He will stay there for the next six months or so. Though this will enhance your energy and personal magnetism, help you excel athletically and increase your libido, the danger, as mentioned, is rush, haste, impatience and excessive self-will. Be patient with the foibles of others. Strive to understand their perspective and position on things. This need is especially strong now as the planets are shifting Westward and social grace and the co-operation of others are becoming more important to you. This shift is not complete this month, but will be complete next month.

Mars also happens to be your Financial Planet. So, his move into your own Sign has financial implications – and good ones. You are investing in yourself, dressing for success, cultivating an image of wealth. You are taking personal charge of finances and not delegating these things to others. You are more aggressive in financial matters and are into making prosperity happen. Mars travelling with Uranus after the 17th suggests 'sudden wealth' or sudden financial opportunity. Be aware of flashes of financial intuition during this period – they could be significant. There is an urge to break out of an existing financial mould. You seem willing to strike out in new and untried directions – basically a good thing. You never know if something works until you try (just use common sense). Prosperity is strong this month – especially after the 21st.

Love is much improved this month – though a conflict over finances could complicate things. Singles find love at educational settings, in the neighbourhood, close to home or through family members. After the 29th, you find it at parties, entertainments and as you pursue leisure-type activities.

July

Best Days Overall: 8th, 9th, 17th, 18th, 26th, 27th, 28th

Most Stressful Days Overall: 4th, 5th, 10th, 11th, 24th, 25th, 31st

Best Days for Love: 4th, 5th, 8th, 9th, 17th, 18th, 19th, 20th, 28th, 29th, 30th, 31st

Best Days for Money: 2nd, 3rd, 8th, 9th, 10th, 11th, 17th, 18th, 19th, 20th, 26th, 27th, 28th, 29th, 30th

Health is much improved this month, Pisces. Getting through last month with your health and sanity intact should be considered a major achievement. You can enhance health further through creative activities and through the sheer joy of life. Avoid depression like the plague. Give extra attention to your stomach, breasts and heart this month. Also, with your 6th House of Health very strong now, you are on top of things – aware of every little ache, pain or twinge. You'll take care of problems promptly. Health and diet regimes should also go better this period.

You deserve a little break and the Cosmos supplies. You are in a party holiday period until the 23rd. Enjoying life – gosh, there's so much to enjoy! – will rejuvenate your faculties, reveal solutions to problems that you didn't know existed and enhance your creative abilities.

The planetary power is now mostly in the West. So, you need to drop your sense of independence and self-will (which won't be easy) and cultivate the good graces of others. Mind your temper. Let others have their way if it is not destructive to you. Though you are eager for action, this won't bring success (except in finances). The good graces of others will.

Like last month, the planetary power is still mostly below the horizon. Continue to downplay your career and cultivate the right emotional states. Though much career opportunity is happening for you after the 23rd, demand it in ways that are emotionally comfortable to you. Definitely not a time to sell your soul for outer success.

Finances are still wonderful – especially until the 23rd. In this realm, personal and direct action pay off. Financial goals are up to you. Money comes through creative efforts and as you pursue leisure activities. Your lover or spouse seems unusually supportive until the 13th. Job-seekers have good fortune all month, but especially after the 23rd. Towards the end of the month – on the 29th – your Financial Planet goes retrograde. Thus you will need to study potential deals and investments much more carefully. Things are not what they seem and your financial judgement is not as sound as it usually is.

Love is happy this month. It's about having fun and pleasure. The honeymoon aspects of love are what appeal now. After the 13th, love is expressed through mutual service. Singles find love as they pursue leisure activities or at the job. Whether you are working towards a first or second marriage, there are wonderful aspects this month. For those working towards a second marriage, the aspects are better from the 13th to the 29th. For those working towards their first, the aspects are better after the 29th.

August

Best Days Overall: 4th, 5th, 13th, 14th, 23rd, 24th

Most Stressful Days Overall: 1st, 7th, 20th, 21st, 22nd, 27th, 28th

Best Days for Love: 1st, 7th, 8th, 9th, 10th, 16th, 17th, 18th, 19th, 27th, 28th

Best Days for Money: 4th, 5th, 7th, 8th, 13th, 14th, 15th, 16th, 17th, 23rd, 24th, 26th, 27th

An important, significant 'turning-point' kind of month ahead, Pisces. There are challenges to be sure, but handling them properly can lead to the pinnacle of happiness and success. It's as if you stand before the gates of a magnificent palace where all manner of delights await you, but the gatekeeper has questions that you must answer correctly. Should you not answer correctly, you will still get some good – he might refer you to a lesser palace – but not the true good. If you answer correctly, you will be let inside.

Can you be strong in yourself, respect yourself, yet put other people first? Can you be personally strong and yet operate by consensus? Can you sublimate temporary financial good in order to attain a larger social good? Can you exhibit patience under duress? Can you balance your outer objectives with personal desires and with your social needs? If so, the world is your oyster now – the cattle on a thousand hills are yours.

Much is happening this month. Jupiter makes a once-in-11-years move into your 7th House of Love towards the end of the month. A new and important social cycle is beginning. Not only is Jupiter in your House of Love now, but 40% to 50% of the planets move through there – all of them beneficial. Love and romance are definitely in the air these days. Many a Pisces will be dancing at their wedding or toasting a new and lucrative business partnership.

But before this happens, the Cosmic helpers (Jupiter, the Sun and Venus) are going to land you a dream job and boost your career. Once this happens you will be in a position to accept the new social rapture that awaits you. It's as if you need to be put into some kind of 'right status' and 'right livelihood' first before you can meet Mr or Ms Right. The planetary genii are nothing if not thorough. Employers are expanding their work force – and in a quality way. Now that your service to the world is established, love can find you.

These same helpers landing you that dream job and boosting your career are also conspiring, in very clever ways, to bring love and romance to you. Although there is always free will on your part – you can always say no – they are clever enough to know how to make you say yes.

Health should be watched after the 23rd. Health is enhanced through paying more attention to your heart, intestines and kidneys.

Be patient in finances, as the Money Planet, Mars, is retrograde all month. Study all important purchases, investments or deals more thoroughly. This is a month for perfecting and improving your financial plans, products or services.

September

Best Days Overall: 1st, 2nd, 9th, 10th, 19th, 20th, 28th, 29th

Most Stressful Days Overall: 3rd, 4th, 17th, 18th, 24th, 25th, 30th

Best Days for Love: 5th, 6th, 14th, 15th, 16th, 17th, 24th, 25th, 26th, 27th

Best Days for Money: 1st, 2nd, 5th, 6th, 9th, 10th, 12th, 13th, 14th, 15th, 19th, 20th, 26th, 27th, 28th, 29th

Late last month the planets made an important shift from the lower half of your Horoscope to the upper half. The balance of power towards the top half is even stronger this month. So, where in past months you were striving to feel good and to build a stable home base, now you are focusing on the outer world and your career objectives. You can safely de-empathize home and family issues and focus on your career now. The main career challenge (like last month) is balancing it with your very active (and happy) social life. The temptation to lose yourself in the social whirl is great. But ignoring your career would be a mistake. Give it its due.

The planets are still very much in the West. Your 7th House of Love is ultra-powerful. Though you have much self-confidence and know what you want, you have to sublimate much of your self-will to placate others. Like last month, this is the challenge. You've got to mind your temper and beware of irritation and impatience. Even your voice tones (though you say nothing that is out of order) will be picked up by others and could cause complications that you don't need. Cultivate the social graces now. Fill your mind with love and loving thoughts and feelings of anger will dissipate. Speak softly. Give in on issues that don't affect your principles or major purposes in life.

Finances are still not what they should be and this is because a lot of internal and subjective development has to happen in your financial life. Seeds need time to germinate in the ground before they can sprout. This is the situation you are in. But after the 23rd, you should start seeing some improvement and more improvement after the 27th, when your Financial Planet starts moving forwards again. Continue to study all major purchases and investments more thoroughly until the 27th. In fact, if you can delay important financial decisions until then – all the better. (Of course, Mars' retrograde shouldn't stop you from shopping for groceries – only big-ticket items.)

Love is still amazingly good. All the important beneficial planets are still camped out in your 7th House of Love until the 15th. Great and loving geniuses are meticulously mapping out social happiness for you – it's difficult to see how you could avoid it. Love makes the world go round this month. Even the retrograde of your Love Planet until the 20th will not stop love from happening. This one factor is simply outgunned by all the good.

Health needs more attention until the 23rd. Try to rest and relax more where possible. Enhance health by paying more attention to your intestines, kidneys and hips.

October

Best Days Overall: 7th, 8th, 16th, 17th, 18th, 25th, 26th

Most Stressful Days Overall: 1st, 14th, 15th, 21st, 22nd, 27th, 28th

Best Days for Love: 2nd, 3rd, 4th, 5th, 14th, 15th, 16th, 17th, 21st, 22nd, 24th, 25th, 26th

Best Days for Money: 2nd, 3rd, 7th, 8th, 9th, 10th, 11th, 12th, 13th, 16th, 17th, 21st, 22nd, 25th, 26th, 29th, 30th

Like last month, the planets are mostly above the horizon. Continue to focus on your career and outer life. Doing right, achieving right will lead to 'feeling right'.

Most of the planets are still in the West, so this is still a very social month where other people come first and where success comes because of the good graces of others.

As has been the case for the past few months, the main challenge is balancing your career, social urges, personal desires and personal financial interests. High-status career options are opening up for you, but in the short term you might have to sacrifice (or tone down) your financial goals. You have to ask yourself, do I want status and prestige now and let wealth follow as a matter of course? Or do I want wealth now and not be concerned about status? The answer is somewhere in the middle.

Finances are much improved this month. A beautiful Grand Trine in Water (your native element) is boosting not only your health, but your finances as well. Your financial patience these past few months starts to pay off. By the 23rd, there is strong prosperity as your Financial Planet receives beautiful aspects. Speculations are favourable. Money can come from creative projects, foreigners or foreign companies and through the revelation of important financial principles. Until the 23rd, channel spare cash towards debt repayment and the elimination of financial waste. This will be a good period to refinance debt more favourably or to attract outside capital to your projects.

Love is still very happy. You are mixing with people of high status and prestige. People of power. Your social confidence is strong. Elders, bosses, authority figures rejoice in playing Cupid. The saying that 'power is the ultimate aphrodisiac' certainly applies to you these days. You gravitate towards those who can help your career. And, social means – cultivating the right friends, attending the right parties, hosting parties – will tend to boost your career.

Your 9th House becomes very strong after the 23rd. Thus foreign lands and cultures call to you. Travel opportunities come – some related to business – but there is pleasure involved as well. Educational opportunities will also come.

Health and well-being are wonderful now – especially after the 9th. The Grand Trine in Water is very comfortable for you, as your innate qualities of sensitivity and compassion are 'in' now – they are appreciated. Your already strong psychic abilities become even stronger. You know who will call before they call. You sense things about people – their character and circumstances. You dream prophetic dreams. Health can be enhanced even further by paying more attention to your kidneys, hips and sexual organs. After the 23rd, de-tox therapies seem unusually potent.

November

Best Days Overall: 3rd, 4th, 13th, 14th, 22nd, 23rd, 30th

Most Stressful Days Overall: 10th, 11th, 12th, 18th, 19th, 24th, 25th

Best Days for Love: 3rd, 4th, 5th, 6th, 15th, 16th, 18th, 19th, 24th, 25th, 26th, 27th

Best Days for Money: 3rd, 4th, 5th, 6th, 8th, 9th, 13th, 14th, 18th, 19th, 22nd, 23rd, 26th, 27th, 30th

Most of the planets are still above the horizon, but this month your 10th House of Career becomes a House of Power. This is a powerful career month. You can expect much success and progress – pay rises, promotions, overall prestige, etc. But you will work for them. It's not a free ride. You still have to balance your career with your happy social life and with your personal desires and financial interests. Much of the same challenges that we wrote of earlier still apply – do you go for the bottom line or for status?

For many months now the planets were in the Western sector of your chart – forcing you (and sometimes in uncomfortable ways) to sublimate your own self-interest in favour of others. To put others first, to compromise and give in. But this is about to change towards the end of the month. The balance of power will start shifting to the East and you will find yourself more independent and more in control of your life.

We have two eclipses this month – cosmic announcements of long-term change. The Lunar eclipse of the 9th is basically benign to you. It occurs in your 3rd House of Communication. It signals new communication equipment coming to you – perhaps as a result of flaws in the old equipment. It won't hurt to have your car checked out, too. Relations with siblings or neighbours will get purified as the eclipse brings up long-seething issues and forces you to take corrective measures – one way or the other.

The Solar eclipse of the 23rd is the more powerful one for you. It occurs near the Midheaven of your chart – enhancing its prominence. This is showing long-term and important career changes. There could be shake-ups in your company, industry or corporate hierarchy that change the 'balance of power' for the long term. New and better job offers could come – either within your company or with another one. There could be important long-term changes in your diet and health regime. Changes of doctors also happen during these kinds of eclipses. Relations with a parent or parent figure could change. Definitely take a reduced schedule here – a few days before and about a day after. Do only what is necessary. Elective activities – especially if they are risky – should be rescheduled.

Health becomes a priority after the 23rd. Rest and relax more where possible. Strive to maintain high energy levels by working smarter and not harder, delegating where possible and letting go of trivia. Keep your energy for the things that are important to you. De-tox therapies are unusually good until the 23rd. Enhance health by paying more attention to your sexual organs, thighs and liver.

Be more patient in love and financial matters after the 23rd. Earnings will come, but you will have to work harder for them. Social success also comes through increased effort.

December

Best Days Overall: 1st, 10th, 11th, 19th, 20th, 27th, 28th

Most Stressful Days Overall: 7th, 8th, 9th, 15th, 16th, 21st, 22nd

Best Days for Love: 5th, 6th, 15th, 16th, 23rd, 24th, 25th, 26th

Best Days for Money: 1st, 2nd, 3rd, 4th, 5th, 6th, 10th, 11th, 15th, 16th, 21st, 22nd, 23rd, 24th, 30th, 31st

Continue to give priority to your health until the 22nd. Review what we wrote last month. Enhance health by paying more attention to your liver, thighs, spine, knees and skeletal alignment. You seem as much concerned with the health of your career as you are with your physical health. You also seem concerned about the health of a parent, parent figure and friends. Personal health improves dramatically after the 22nd.

Most of the planets are still above the horizon and your 10th House of Career is still very strong. Much career success is happening now, but through the old-fashioned way – work and effort. There is some travel related to work and career this month. Perhaps you are taking work-related courses or seminars as well. All of this is good as it makes you more valuable. Home and family issues can be safely de-emphasized.

70% to 80% of the planets are now in the East. Uranus is moving back into your Sign at the end of the month. This is the time to make positive personal changes – to take control of your own life and affairs and to create things the way you want them to be. Your social popularity is still strong and if you aren't rude or arrogant to others, your efforts won't detract from your popularity. They might even enhance it.

Finances are still tricky this month. On the one hand, you have a lot of financial drive and desire. But perhaps your haste and zeal are bringing about opposition in others. Perhaps they threaten the status quo. Make haste slowly. Earnings will come, but you will have to work harder for them. Mars' move into your Money House on the 16th enhances prosperity and helps you develop fearlessness in finance. Better to make a few mistakes and overcome fear than to stay paralysed by fear and do nothing. This is a period for financial activism – only do it slowly and carefully.

Love is still happy, but Uranus' move into your own Sign poses important philosophical questions for you. Do you want a committed relationship or do you want personal independence? You can't have both, as they are mutually exclusive. Perhaps you can have a little of each. Perhaps you can alternate between periods of serious love and periods of personal freedom. But this is the conundrum you are facing these days, Pisces. Sometimes the limitation of personal freedom leads to other kinds of freedom – the freedom from worrying who your date will be on New Year's Eve, the freedom to pursue other interests without worrying about love, the freedom to pursue the family dimension. So you need to give thought to your freedom urges. The retrograde of your Love Planet from the 17th onwards will give you time to clarify your thinking.